For Steve and Judy,
in remembrance of a very pleasant
dinner together
and in friendship
Michael

JUDAISM
within
Modernity

JUDAISM

within
Modernity

Essays on
Jewish History and Religion

MICHAEL A. MEYER

WAYNE STATE UNIVERSITY PRESS   DETROIT

Library of Congress Cataloging-in-Publication Data

Meyer, Michael A.
   Judaism within modernity : essays on Jewish history and religion /
Michael A. Meyer.
        p.   cm.
Includes bibliographical references (p.   ) and index.
   ISBN 0-8143-2874-1 (cloth : alk. paper)
   1. Judaism—Historiography.   2. Jews—Historiography.   3.
Judaism—History—Modern period, 1750–   .   4.
Judaism—Germany—History—20th century.   I. Title.
   BM190 .M49 2001
   296'.09'03—dc21   00-012161

Contents

Acknowledgments

Grateful acknowledgment is made to the following for permission to reprint previously published material:

American Jewish Congress: "Where Does the Modern Period of Jewish History Begin?" Originally published in *Judaism: A Quarterly Journal of Jewish Life and Thought,* Summer 1975, pp. 329–38. Copyright © American Jewish Congress.

University Press of New England: "Reflections on Jewish Modernization," originally published in Elisheva Carlebach et al., eds., *Jewish History and Jewish Memory: Essays in Honor of Yosef Hayim Yerushalmi,* 1998, pp. 369–77; "Liberal Judaism and Zionism in Germany," originally published in Shmuel Almog et al., eds., *Zionism and Religion,* 1998, pp. 93–106. Reprinted by permission.

Blackwell Publishers: "The Emergence of Modern Jewish Historiography: Motives and Motifs," originally published in *History and Theory* 27:4 (1989): pp. 160–75. Reprinted by permission.

Modern Judaism: "Heinrich Graetz and Heinrich von Treitschke: A Comparison of Their Historical Images of the Modern Jew," originally published in *Modern Judaism* 6 (1986): pp. 1–11. Reprinted by permission.

Leo Baeck Institute (London): "Jews as Jews versus Jews as Germans: Two Historical Perspectives," originally published as the introduction to Arnold Paucker, ed., *Leo Baeck Institute Year Book* 36 (1991): xv–xxii; " 'How Awesome is This Place!' The Reconceptualization of the Synagogue in Nineteenth-Century Germany," originally published in J. A. S. Grenville, ed., *Leo Baeck Institute Year Book* 41 (1996): pp. 51–63; "Jewish Religious Reform in Germany and Britain," originally published in Michael Brenner et al., eds., *Two Nations: British and German Jews in Comparative Perspective* (Schriftenreihe wissenschaftlicher Abhandlungen des Leo Baeck Instituts 60). Tübingen: J. C. B. Mohr (Paul Siebeck), 1999, pp. 67–83. Reprinted by permission.

Institute of the World Jewish Congress: "The Question of Continuity in Jewish History," originally published in Hebrew in *Gesher: Journal of*

8 ■ ACKNOWLEDGMENTS

Jewish Affairs, Spring–Summer, 1979, pp. 14–21. Reprinted in translation by permission.

New York University Press: "The German Jews: Some Perspectives on their History," published in Alan S. Berger, ed., *Judaism in the Modern World,* 1994, pp. 73–86. Reprinted by permission.

Verlag Herder: " 'Scripture or Spirit?'—The Revelation Question in German-Jewish Thought of the Nineteenth Century," originally published in German in J. J. Petuchowski and Walter Strolz, eds., *Offenbarung im jüdischen und christlichen Glaubensverständnis,* 1981, pp. 162–79. Reprinted in translation by permission.

Oxford University Press: "Jewish Scholarship and Jewish Identity: Their Historical Relationship in Modern Germany," originally published in Peter Y. Medding, ed., *Studies in Contemporary Jewry* 8 (1992): pp. 181–93. Copyright © Oxford University Press. Reprinted by permission.

Leo Baeck Institute (New York): "German Political Pressure and Jewish Religious Response in the Nineteenth Century" (The Leo Baeck Memorial Lecture #25), 1981. Reprinted by permission.

Hebrew Union College Press: "Should and Can an 'Antiquated' Religion Become Modern? The Jewish Reform Movement in Germany as Seen by Jews and Christians," English version originally published in Wolfgang Beck, ed., *The Jews in European History: Seven Lectures,* 1994, pp. 57–72.

Indiana University Press: "*Gemeinschaft* within *Gemeinde:* Religious Ferment in Weimar Liberal Judaism," originally published in Michael Brenner and Derek J. Penslar, eds., *In Search of Jewish Community: Jewish Identities in Germany and Austria, 1918–1933,* 1998, pp. 15–35. Reprinted by permission.

The Center for Jewish Studies of Harvard University: "The German Model of Religious Reform and Russian Jewry," originally published in Isadore Twersky, ed., *Danzig Between East and West: Aspects of Modern Jewish History,* 1985, pp. 67–91. Reprinted by permission.

Transaction Publishers: "German-Jewish Identity in Nineteenth-Century America," originally published in Jacob Katz, ed., *Toward Mo-*

dernity: The European Jewish Model pp. 247–67. Copyright © Transaction Publishers, 1987.

KTAV Publishing House: "The Refugee Scholars Project of the Hebrew Union College," originally published in Bertram W. Korn, ed., *A Bicentennial Festschrift for Jacob Rader Marcus,* 1976, pp. 359–75. Reprinted by permission.

Frank Cass Publishers: "American Reform Judaism and Zionism: Early Efforts at Ideological Rapprochement," originally published in *Studies in Zionism* 7 (Spring 1983): pp. 49–64; "Abba Hillel Silver as Zionist within the Camp of Reform Judaism," originally published in *The Journal of Israeli History* 17:1 (1996): pp. 9–31. Reprinted by permission.

Colloquium Verlag: " 'Wholly According to the Established Custom'? The Spiritual Life of Berlin Jewry Following the Edict of 1823," originally published in Marianne Awerbuch and Stefi Jersch-Wenzel, eds., *Bild und Selbstbild der Juden Berlins zwischen Aufklärung und Romantik,* 1992, pp. 229–43. It was not possible to contact the Colloquium Verlag, which is not listed in the most recent guide to publishers.

"Jewish Political Leadership in Nazi Germany" was delivered as a lecture at a conference sponsored by Bar-Ilan University and the Center for Jewish Studies of Harvard University and held at Bar-Ilan in January 1999. It appears here for the first time.

Introduction

Nearly forty years ago, when I began thinking of subjects for my doctoral dissertation, I rapidly came to the conclusion that a study of the initial effects of modernization on Jewish self-understanding would help to clarify how Jews in the present differed from their ancient and medieval forebears and how their reconceptualization of Judaism had been a response to their new situation. Ever since, I have been fascinated by the complex impact of modernity on Jewish religion and culture. In the essays collected here, written as early as 1975 and as recently as 1998, I have endeavored to probe this impact in different areas of Jewish life, especially religion, but also Jewish scholarship, Jewish historiography, and the integration into Jewish consciousness of a Jewish nationalist identity. My focus has been on Germany, but I have made forays into other European lands and into the United States. My close professional and personal attachment to Reform Judaism has no doubt contributed to the attention I have paid to the history of the Reform movement in Europe and America. However, my intent in all of the essays included here has been to approach their subjects with the ethos of the historian who seeks to understand, not to advocate. All but one of the essays ("Jewish Political Leadership in Nazi Germany") have appeared in periodicals or collective volumes, but two of these not yet in English. Taken together, they illustrate the complex grappling with modernity that has shaped contemporary Jewry.

One of the ways in which modern Jews distinguished themselves from their medieval ancestors was by the attention they began to give their own history. Their turn to historiography thereupon necessitated a scheme of periodization that would meaningfully divide one age from another. No boundary was as important—and as controversial—as the one delineating the beginning of their own times. Where a particular historian placed the break and what he saw as creating it reveals much not only about his approach to history but also his Jewish self-understanding. The first essay in this volume, "Where Does the Modern Period of Jewish History Begin?" illustrates the divergence. Ultimately, however, it concludes that the project of setting a single starting point for all Jewry is misconceived: there is no one year or generation of beginning, only a process of modernization that expands outward to embrace an ever

11

larger circle of Jews within it. The second essay, "Reflections on Jewish Modernization," moves from the temporal issue to the substantive one. It acknowledges that to a high degree Jewish modernization was no more than an integration into non-Jewish economies, societies, and cultures, themselves in the process of modifying or breaking with venerable traditions. But it concludes that Jewish modernization is also set apart in that viewpoints and sensibilities gained from the environment were applied to Jewish thought and practice, transforming them to fit modern paradigms but not divesting them of their particularity. The result has been a parallel modernization with character and content of its own.

Secularly educated Jews began to turn to their own history for many reasons. These included apologetics and didactics, unearthing precedents for religious reform, and deepening historical knowledge. Interestingly, they also included the contradictory desires to gain liberation from the heavy hand of the past and to discover strands of continuity with it. "The Emergence of Modern Jewish Historiography: Motives and Motifs" looks critically at the justifications that the first modern Jewish historians gave for their endeavors. Among these historians none was more influential than Heinrich Graetz, whose historical intent was to enable Jews in nineteenth-century Germany to strengthen their identity as Jews by enabling them to identify with their past. Thus he made figures prominent in medieval Jewish history more acceptable to modern proclivities and anchored Jewish figures acclaimed in modern general history (like Spinoza and Heine) within Jewish tradition. Graetz's evaluations of nineteenth-century German-Jewish writers and politicians and his judgments of gentile figures by how they treated Jews grated severely on his contemporary in general German history, Heinrich von Treitschke, whose perception of these figures sharply differed from that of Graetz. "Heinrich Graetz and Heinrich von Treitschke: A Comparison of Their Historical Images of the Modern Jew" contrasts the radically differing views of these two historians, who in their passionate and judgmental approach to the past were, ironically, very similar.

In dealing with German Jewry, Graetz and Treitschke could differ as they did because the boundaries between Jewish and German identity were so porous and were continually shifting to allow more room for the latter. Increasingly, German Jews came to differ from Jews elsewhere and become more like other Germans. The implications of this process of integration for the writing of German-Jewish history is the subject of "Jews as Jews versus Jews as Germans: Two Historical Perspectives." It calls attention to the intertwined but incongruous frameworks and the different emphases created for the study of German Jewry by seeing German Jews as a part of world Jewry or within German society and culture and it suggests four ways in which Jews are relevant for modern German history.

The final essay in the first section is more programmatic. "The Question of Continuity in Jewish History" looks at the attempts Jewish historians have made to find the "scarlet thread" that they believed ran through all of Jewish history, linking one age and one center of Jewish life to all others. I argue that these attempts to define the Jewish historical entity either in religious or in national terms are futile, and suggest, instead, a paradigm that provides the required sense of continuity.

The second section is devoted to the Jews of Germany with regard to issues other than religious reform. It opens with an overview, entitled "The German Jews: Some Perspectives on Their History," that focuses on the legacy of German Jewry. This piece, which originated as a popular lecture, seeks to correct distortions and stereotypes, dwells upon particular ironies of German-Jewish history, and compares the historical experience of the German Jews with American Jewish history. Finally, it turns to the question of German Jewry's influence on Jews elsewhere and concludes with an attempt to characterize its peculiar spirit.

The essays that follow deal with three aspects of German-Jewish history: religion, scholarship, and communal leadership. For Jewish theologians in Germany, as " 'Scripture or Spirit?': The Revelation Question in German-Jewish Thought of the Nineteenth Century" indicates, the source of divine authority was crucial. Like their Christian counterparts, they were divided on the influence they attributed to sacred texts as opposed to personal religious experience—their commitment to theonomy versus spiritual autonomy. Using a comparative approach, the essay focuses on the neo-Orthodox Samson Raphael Hirsch, the philosopher Samuel Hirsch, and the Reformer Abraham Geiger.

Central to the legacy of German Jewry is Wissenschaft des Judentums, the scientific study of Judaism. Not only did it produce an abundant and largely still valuable literature, it represented a new way to approach Jewish tradition that both distanced the past and provided fresh access to it. For some of the scholars themselves it became their way of being Jewish. "Jewish Scholarship and Jewish Identity: Their Historical Relationship in Modern Germany" looks at the ambiguous consequences of the turn to critical scholarship, both strengthening and weakening the identification with Judaism.

It compares the attitudes of Jewish traditionalists to historical criticism with those of modernists and recounts the arduous and mostly futile struggle to gain a place for objective Jewish scholarship in the German academic world. It also traces the changing values and priorities of Jewish scholarship from its beginnings early in the nineteenth century to the reassessment that arose in the twentieth.

Jewish religion and modern scholarship in Germany were both modulated by political circumstances that were neither as negative as in Eastern Europe nor as positive as in post-Revolutionary France. German states held out hope of emancipation but insisted that Jews first prove themselves worthy. These prerequisites have led some scholars to speak of a "price" that Jews were required to pay for emancipation, which included not only occupational redistribution and cultural reeducation but also religious reform. They suggest that it was a price German Jews were quite ready to pay. "German Political Pressure and Jewish Religious Response in the Nineteenth Century" rejects that point of view. It argues that the leadership of German Jewry, across the religious spectrum, refused to pay the price if that meant compromising their own principles. Political pressure for Jewish educational, cultural, and religious reform was not without its effect. But the religious and political leaders of German Jewry insisted that they alone could determine what reforms were desirable by the standards of intrinsic merit. Often they responded to pressure with moral outrage. Even political liberalism in Germany, they increasingly realized, was a dubious ally because it lacked genuine appreciation for diversity.

What was true for German liberals was the more true for ruling conservative circles that preferred to keep Jews separate and clearly distinguishable. When the Prussian government turned to reaction in the years following the defeat of Napoleon, it instituted measures determined to divest Judaism of any signs of life and certainly of any influence on non-Jews. The second and third decades of the nineteenth century represented a distinct decline for Berlin Jewry from the heady days of Moses Mendelssohn and the Jewish Enlightenment. Yet the stagnation was by no means complete. " 'Wholly According to Established Custom'? The Spiritual Life of Berlin Jewry Following the Edict of 1823" looks especially at the struggles over Jewish education within the community and with the government and shows how community schools, both traditional and religiously liberal, soon became centers of religious innovation.

The last essay in this section, "Jewish Political Leadership in Nazi Germany," extends beyond the usual temporal boundaries of my research. Here, however, was the extreme example of political pressure, and I wanted to examine how Jews responded to it. The story is a complex and still disputed one. My intent was to describe its contours, understand how Nazi policies and Jewish responses moved from phase to phase, and relate Jewish tactics and objectives to Nazi ones. Originally, I had intended to focus only on Rabbi Leo Baeck, on whom the mantle of highest leadership had fallen. But I soon realized that his work could not be understood apart from the broader picture of the external and internal struggles of Jewish leadership on the brink of the Holocaust.

With only one exception—the study of Jewish religious innovation in Russia—the essays gathered in the third section, devoted to the Reform movement in Europe, were all written after the appearance of my book, *Response to Modernity: A History of the Reform Movement in Judaism,* in 1988. The first presents a new perspective on the subject—the way in which the movement was viewed by those not a part of it, especially by non-Jews. Entitled "Should and Can an 'Antiquated' Religion Become Modern? The Jewish Reform Movement in Germany as Seen by Jews and Christians," it documents the prevalent view, held even by friends of the Jews, that their religion was incapable of renewal. Invariably, Christians concluded that Judaism and modernity were inherently incompatible and that Judaism was therefore destined to slow extinction. Antisemites went further, stressing how pernicious it was to make Judaism appear similar to Christianity. Others, more favorably inclined, saw it as a bridge leading to conversion. Liberal Christian theologians of the nineteenth century were unable or unwilling to perceive that the liberalization of Judaism might be an endeavor parallel to their own.

The narrowing of formal Jewish identity to its religious component in Germany during the nineteenth century transformed the synagogue into a sanctuary on the model of the church. " 'How Awesome is this Place!' The Reconceptualization of the Synagogue in Nineteenth-Century Germany" examines thirty-two sermons delivered at the dedication of new synagogues in order to determine how the traditional conception of the synagogue as meeting place for prayer and study was transformed into an awe-inspiring sacred space more like the ancient temple in Jerusalem—and the Christian cathedral—than the typical diaspora *bet keneset.* The synagogue building was now seen as itself constituting a source of inspiration and contributing to the subjective religious experience of worship. Following the German theologian Friedrich Schleiermacher, some of the preachers stressed that the purpose of public prayer was not to change God's will but to edify the worshipper.

The following two essays deal with religious reform in Germany during a period that has received very little attention in this regard, the Weimar Republic. They significantly modify two prevalent notions regarding Jewish religious life during the 1920s: that Liberal Judaism was unmitigatedly opposed to Zionism and that it was religiously stagnant. "Liberal Judaism and Zionism in Germany" looks initially at Liberal Jews' theological critique of Zionism, based on the latter's giving centrality to nationhood over religion. And it documents the deep enmity that Zionist leaders harbored toward Liberal Judaism. However, in the 1920s the Zionists began to woo the Liberals by finding room for Liberal Judaism within the Zionist worldview, and Liberal rabbis, for their part, increasingly opened up to Zionism. In a second essay, the conventional portrait of Jewish religious life becomes the subject of revision. It is well-known that German Jewry during the Weimar years experienced a religious and cultural revival associated with names like Franz Rosenzweig and Martin Buber. However, it had been thought that Liberal Judaism— with its cavernous and usually empty synagogues where worshippers were no more than an audience that listened to organ music, sermons, and choir—stood outside this revival. In *"Gemeinschaft* within *Gemeinde:* Religious Ferment in Weimar Liberal Judaism" I was able to show that this was only part of the story. Within Liberal Judaism a small movement developed to bring Buber's idea of religious community into the framework of regular religious services. A circle composed of educators and average members of the Liberal faction in Berlin inaugurated participatory worship, where men and women sat and sang together, where leadership tasks were shared, and where a sense of religious intimacy replaced the customary anomie.

A comparative approach underlies the final two essays in this section. The Reform movement, which transformed the great majority of German Jews into adherents of Liberal Judaism by the end of the nineteenth century, had only the most limited and short-lived success in Russia. "The German Model of Religious Reform and Russian Jewry" not only adduces reasons for that practical failure, flowing from the very different situation of Russian Jewry, but also examines the religious debates that took place, differentiating the issues that absorbed Russian Jews from those that occupied the attention of their coreligionists in Germany. In Great Britain religious reform was statistically more successful than in Russia, but less than in Germany. Split into two movements by the second decade of the twentieth century, a more traditional Reform and a more radical Liberal Judaism, both had connections with the German Reform movement. Yet the differing political, religious, and intellectual milieus resulted in differences on such issues as whether Judaism was inherently progressive, whether the Bible was directly the word of God, and what was the role of social justice in Judaism. When German-Jewish refugees fled to Great Britain in the 1930s, they often felt more comfortable in synagogues that reproduced the ambiance of their former homeland than in their English counterparts.

The German Jews who came to the United States in the nineteenth century were no less determined than those who later came to Britain to hold on to the traditions of their youth. They created a "German-Jewish Identity in Nineteenth-Century America" that proved remarkably resistant to Americanization for the immigrant generation and, to some extent, also for their children. They clung to the German language and literature and tried to pass it on to the next generation, born in the United States. Often they looked down upon what they believed to be an inferior American culture. They oriented their religious life to the variegated German model. Yet, as American Reform Judaism became more radical than the dominant German Liberal Judaism, as Germany proved itself unable to overcome antisemitism, and as American Judaism matured religiously and culturally, the acceptance of German-Jewish hegemony declined. Nonetheless, personal ties remained, as did appreciation for German-Jewish scholarship. "The Refugee Scholars Project of the Hebrew Union College" examines the frustrations experienced by HUC president Julian Morgenstern in his attempt to gain American non-quota visas for endangered scholars working in Jewish studies. Ultimately successful in eleven instances, he failed in others. The chicaneries of the State Department to prevent the scholars' immigration represent yet another example of official prejudice and xenophobia.

The last two essays in the volume look at the relationship between Reform Judaism and Zionism in the United States. The first, "American Reform Judaism and Zionism: Early Efforts at Ideological Rapprochement," demonstrates that even in the early years of American Zionism, before 1920, there were prominent Reform rabbis who came out in favor of Zionism. It also analyzes the arguments they used to refute the prevalent notion that Reform and Zionism were incompatible. Although Reform Judaism remained officially opposed to Zionism until the mid-1930s, by that time the increasing number of Zionists in its ranks had worked out a mediating ideology that could easily encompass it. Among Reform leaders none played a more significant role in both the Reform movement and American Zionism than the rabbi of "The Temple" in Cleveland. "Abba Hillel Silver as Zionist Within the Camp of Reform Judaism" analyzes Silver's two identifications, traces the manifestations of his Zionism within Reform circles and concludes that his Reform congregation was no mere base for his Zionist work, that he remained a firm adherent of the Classical Reform Judaism he had adopted as a rabbinical student in every respect but its official attitude to Zionism.

I have entitled this volume *Judaism within Modernity* in order to call attention to the fact that Judaism, initially responding to a modernity that affected it from the outside, came increasingly to dwell within it, even as modernity, to varying degrees, was absorbed by Judaism. By modernity I mean the world that developed gradually and differentially in the West over the last three centuries, characterized especially by unifying theories and technological advance, cultural innovation, and reliance upon human reason. Although it has become popular in some circles to speak of a fragmentizing "postmodernism," I am convinced that the essential elements of modernity remain dominant at the beginning of the twenty-first century and that Judaism's quest for survival will continue to take place within a modernity that, even as it threatens to swallow up the faith of a diminishing minority, also offers the possibility for differentiation, development, and renewal.

PART I

Reflections on Jewish Historiography

CHAPTER 1

Where Does the Modern Period
of Jewish History Begin?

The endeavor to divide history into distinct and meaningful periods
has met with so little success that contemporary historians have
treated the subject with utmost caution. Grand theoretical specula-
tions, such as the bold efforts of Hegel to assert clearly defined
stages in the development of the human spirit, or of Marx to locate
similar stages in the various forms of production, have all come to
grief at the hands of empirical inquiry. Few historians today still
believe that world history allows of any simple, precise division, let
alone that any suggested plan is rooted in the very nature of reality.
All-embracing schemes of periodization, nearly everyone now acknowledges, rest more on stipulation than on inference. Though a
division of some kind is still considered necessary as an instrument
for understanding turning points and transitions in history, each
proposal is generally recognized as merely provisional, subject to
correction not only by new evidence but also by the lengthened perspective gained in the passage of time.[1]

For Jewish history, periodization is fraught with all of the
methodological difficulties that attend the division of world history.
Scattered among the nations, the Jews have participated to varying
degrees in simultaneous and successive foreign civilizations while
at the same time carrying on their own heritage. The very diversity
and uniqueness of their Diaspora experience have militated against
any agreement on its division. Though the major Jewish historians
have all had to utilize some system of periodization to organize their
material, they have differed vastly in the schemes which they employed. In part, methodological considerations have determined this

divergence of systems, but, to no small degree, religious and ideological motivations have played a role as well. Nowhere is the operation of both factors more apparent and instructive than with regard to the problem of setting the threshold of the modern period in Jewish history. In fact, tracing the various theories regarding the onset of Jewish modernity reflects with amazing clarity both the course of Jewish historical thinking and the shifting conceptions of Jewish existence that have characterized the last hundred and fifty years.

The first Jewish scholar since Josephus to undertake a comprehensive history of the Jews was Isaac Marcus Jost, a German Jew who wrote a nine-volume *History of the Israelites* that was published from 1820 to 1828. Jost grew up in the period when German Jewry was given its first measure of civil equality. Responding to this new situation, a considerable segment of the community had come to see in the changed political attitude a sharp break with the past or even to perceive the messianic prospect of full Jewish participation in the political and cultural life of Europe. Although by the time Jost began to write his history the post-Napoleonic reaction had cast serious doubts on the realization of that hope, he remained of the opinion that an unalterable process had been set in motion, and, as a loyal Prussian, he chose to see its origins in Prussia. Jost, therefore, designated 1740 as the beginning of modern Jewish history, since, in that year, Frederick the Great ascended the Prussian throne. He realized, of course, that Frederick's policy had, if anything, been more restrictive toward the Jews than were the regulations of the monarchs who had preceded him. But, even as late as 1846, Jost still claimed that the enlightened despot had awakened a spirit "which strides over the ghetto walls and glances into the dismal apartments of the Jewish streets . . . ; it declares liberty to the oppressed, and this one word, even before its content is grasped and appreciated, arouses the soul to glad hope and the yearning for a better life."[2]

Since Jost was writing for German gentiles as well as for Jews, he doubtless wanted to link the turning point of the modern age in Jewish history with the monarch who had brought Prussia to a position of power in Europe. At the same time, he tried to make his Jewish readers appreciative of what they owed to the Prussian state. It was, he thought, in response to this new enlightened spirit emanating from Frederick that the fundamental transformations in the Jewish community which generated modernity came about: the decline of unquestioned rabbinic authority, the shift from a corporate entity to a religious denomination, and the increasing participation by Jews in German culture and political life. With the origin of these changes in Prussia, Jost saw the beginning of a new epoch for all Jewry, one which he termed "the age of spiritual liberation."

Jewish writers contemporary with Jost shared his sense of living in a new and hopeful time for both Europe and for the Jews. That was certainly true of the young Leopold Zunz and his circle when they laid the foundations of the scientific study of Judaism, declaring that the time had come to render account of a past that was now closed and determining to use their scholarly tools to further the process of political and cultural integration. When Nahman Krochmal, the profound Galician Jewish philosopher and historian, divided Jewish history into successive cycles of growth, blossoming and decay, he chose to conclude the most recent period of decline with the Cossack persecutions of the mid-seventeenth century. His own age, by implication, represented a new period of germination, the first stage of a fresh cycle.[3]

The best known of the nineteenth-century Jewish historians, Heinrich Graetz, did not, however, fully share the earlier messianic enthusiasm. A severe moral critic of modern European culture,[4] he set the Redemption far into the future. But, like Jost, he, too, thought that the most significant break in recent Jewish history had occurred in the preceding century. Because of his predilection for the internal intellectual history of the Jews, and his ascription of the dominant role in historical change to prominent individuals, Graetz assigned the beginning of the modern period of Jewish history to the appearance of Moses Mendelssohn. In the biography of this first significant figure to link Judaism with modern European culture, Graetz found what he called "a model for the history of the Jews in modern times, for their upward striving from lowliness and contempt to greatness and self-consciousness."[5]

Graetz's selection of Moses Mendelssohn as the turning point met severe challenge a generation later at the hands of Eastern Europe's most significant Jewish historian, Simon Dubnow. For him, Graetz's selection was questionable on three grounds. First it was—no less than Jost's view—distinctly Germano-centric. Beginning with Mendelssohn, Graetz had gone on to devote two-thirds of his last volume to tracing developments in Germany—supposedly set in motion by Mendelssohn—while paying scant attention to the vastly larger Jewish settlement in Eastern Europe. Second, Graetz's emphasis on the role of individuals and of intellectual processes in history was out of keeping with the positivist approach that had meanwhile come to dominate European historiography and had influenced Dubnow. Finally, Dubnow simply could not see in Mendelssohn a model for the modern period. The Jewish philosopher's cherished goal of acculturation ran directly counter to Dubnow's autonomist ideology which advocated separate, highly indepen- dent, communal entities within the frameworks of non-Jewish states. Dubnow favored political integration within the larger soci- ety but, at the same time, argued for cultural separatism. It is, there- fore, not surprising that in his own writing he should have linked Jewish modernity to political, rather than cultural, transformation. In his *World History of the Jewish People,* which appeared in the 1920s, it is the French Revolution, the period when the Jews first gained citizenship, and not the beginning of the Haskalah, the Jewish en- lightenment, which serves as the watershed.[6] And it is the process of political emancipation which began here—including the setbacks which it suffered—that serves him as the dominant motif of the modern age.

More recently, the majority of Jewish historians have preferred to fix the boundary line about a century or more before the French Revolution. They have chosen the earlier threshold for a variety of reasons. The most blatantly ideological justification for such an ear- lier terminus a quo is that which was given by Ben Zion Dinur, who died in 1973 after a productive and influential career as professor of Jewish history at the Hebrew University in Jerusalem. As an ardent Zionist, Dinur could not resist selecting the first evidence for a movement of return to the Land as the beginning of the modern period of Jewish history. What acculturation had been for Graetz and emancipation for Dubnow, Zionism became for Dinur. One might have expected him, therefore, to select a very late date, per- haps the appearance of the first Zionist classic, Moses Hess's *Rome and Jerusalem,* in 1862, or the formation of the Hibat Zion movement and the agricultural settlement which it fostered in the 1880s, or even the publication of Herzl's *The Jewish State* in 1896. Instead, how- ever, Dinur chose the year 1700, for in that year Rabbi Judah the Pious led some one thousand Jews to Palestine. For Dinur, this sym- bolic event (the immigration was actually a failure) was portentous for the future. It represented the beginnings of a rebellion against the *galut* (exile) and the endeavor to seek Israel's national salvation in its own land.[7]

Dinur's theory effectively eliminates Diaspora Jewish moder- nity from the basic structure of Jewish history. Its commonly ac- cepted characteristics are not determinative of an age. Although Dinur does recognize the relative significance of Jewish emancipa- tion and acculturation, these are essentially conceived as forces making for Jewish national dissolution and as foils—albeit neces- sary—for the primary process, which is the rebuilding of the Jewish nation in Palestine. Unlike Diaspora Jewish historians, Dinur placed a definite final terminus on this modern period. It concluded in November 1947 with the United Nations resolution to establish a Jewish state and with the declaration of its coming into existence the following spring. The modern era, thus, lasted almost exactly 250 years, and the birth of the State of Israel brought it to an end. With 1948 this final stage of Diaspora Jewish history has definitely reached its climax. For the last generation, Jewish history has been essentially postmodern, the history of the people in its land with that portion which remains on the Diaspora periphery playing, at best, a secondary role.

Gershom Scholem's revisionism has been much less obviously ideological, but he, too, has had a specific purpose in view. He devoted most of his life to establishing the central significance of the kabbalah, not merely as a byroad of Jewish history, as Graetz insisted, but as a main highway. Scholem was able to show that the kabbalistically influenced, Sabbatian, pseudo-messianic movement of the seventeenth century had an enormous influence in its time, and he tried to raise its significance even further by arguing that it made possible Jewish modernity. The unorthodox theses of the radical Sabbatians, their ideological doctrines, as well as their attitude toward practice, Scholem argued, shattered the world of traditional Judaism beyond repair. Once these messianists ceased to be "believers," they could no longer return to contemporary rabbinic Judaism. Instead, "when the flame of their faith finally flickered out, they soon reappeared as leaders of Reform Judaism, secular intellectuals, or simply complete and indifferent skeptics."[8] Scholem thus not only regarded the Jewish history of the late sixteenth and seventeenth centuries as dominated by kabbalism and pseudo-messianism, but made even the anti-mystical Judaism of nineteenth-century Western Europe ironically, embarrassingly—and unconvincingly—an outgrowth of it.

Other Jewish historians have shared Scholem's preference for the seventeenth century but have argued for the determinative significance of factors other than mysticism and messianism. Shmuel Ettinger, for many years professor of modern Jewish history at the Hebrew University, developed the theory that the emergence of the centralized absolutistic state was the most crucial factor in initiating the changes that differentiated modern Jewish existence from previous forms. The new state was no longer willing to tolerate separate corporate entities with their own structures of law and authority. The resulting deprivation of Jewish communal autonomy spurred the integration of the Jews into European society and resulted in the intellectual response of the Haskalah.[9] But, for Ettinger, the process of cultural and political integration, set in motion by the development of the centralized state, was characteristic of modern Jewish history only during the first of two stages. Beginning with the resurgence of antisemitism in the 1880s, a reversal took place which resulted in the success of Jewish nationalism and the creation of the Jewish state. For Ettinger, as for Dinur, the establishment of the state constitutes the climax of modern Jewish history.[10]

Finally, we may consider the view of Salo Baron, until his death in 1989 the dean of Jewish historians in America. It, too, focuses on the seventeenth century, except that for Baron no single factor is determinative:

> The Jewish Emancipation era has often been dated from the formal pronunciamentos of Jewish equality of rights by the French Revolution, or somewhat more obliquely, by the American Constitution. However, departing from this purely legalistic approach, I have long felt that the underlying more decisive socioeconomic and cultural transformations accompanying the rise of modern capitalism, the rapid growth of Western populations, the international migrations, the after-effects of Humanism, the Reformation, and the progress of modern science, long antedated these formal constitutional fiats. While such developments can never be so precisely dated as legal enactments, treaties, wars, or biographies of leading personalities, the mid-seventeenth century may indeed be considered a major turning point in both world and Jewish history.[11]

Baron's enumeration of such a variety of causes leaves little room for criticizing the selection of a particular feature to the exclusion or relative diminution of others. But his direct linkage of Jewish modernity with phenomena of world history which had only limited, indirect, or delayed effect upon the Jews raises serious doubts; the general transformations which he lists here—important as they were for general history—had little modernizing influence on any considerable segment of the Jews in Europe in the seventeenth century. No less subject to dispute is his willingness to set a single watershed at a distinct point in time—and even to declare in the title of the later volumes of his *A Social and Religious History of the Jews* that the "Late Middle Ages" of the Jews stretches specifically from 1200 to 1650.

Of course, neither Baron nor any Jewish historian, from Jost down to the present, has regarded the exact line of demarcation which he chose as more than symbolic. All were far too aware of the gradual passing of one age into another to assume that such precise boundaries could be anything other than instrumental or suggestive. Yet, the fact that they selected a particular year or, at least, a limited period of time during which, they argue, the chief characteristics of modern Jewish history made their appearance, itself raises a number of questions which have yet to be resolved.

Perhaps the most basic question concerns the principal causes and characteristics of modernity. It seems most unlikely that agreement here will be achieved, not only because of the continued effect of ideology but also because economic, social, and intellectual influences will continue to be weighted as variously by Jewish historians as they are by their colleagues in general history. Jewish scholars have spanned the entire gamut—from Marxist economic determinism to an idealism which largely ignores the relevance of societal change. In particular, it is by no means resolved whether the Jewish Enlightenment and Emancipation were primarily a response to the rise of capitalist modes of production, to the need for more efficient government, or to a more favorable social attitude emanating from a growing class of liberal intellectuals. Nor is there agreement whether what is basic for Jewish history is demography (and, hence, the change in the migration pattern from west-to-east to east-to-west in the seventeenth century would loom as a decisive event), or community structure and cohesion, or the intellectual and emotional world of the individual Jew.

But even if there could be agreement on the characteristics determinative of the modern period, difference of opinion would remain as to when they emerged. Even if economic, political, and cultural integration be taken together as representative of Jewish modernity, the question as to when they became constitutive must still be settled. The proponents of a boundary line in the seventeenth or early eighteenth centuries have pointed to widespread evidence of the decline of rabbinic authority, the pursuit of secular education, and the disregard of traditional Jewish norms in Central Europe decades or more before the appearance of Moses Mendelssohn.[12] Their critics have held that such manifestations of dissolution, taken in historical context, really do not indicate a break at all. They are simply aberrant phenomena in a society which is still basically intact. Even where Jewish laws were violated, the violation was not yet justified by an appeal to values drawn from outside the Jewish community.[13] But in admitting a seedtime for Jewish modernity which precedes its initial boundary, the critics, in turn, are forced to assume the difficult task of determining at which point the heretofore exceptional or deviant instances become normative.

The issue is further complicated by the differentiation that must be made, even by non-Marxists, between the various classes within the Jewish communities. Jacob Toury, for many years at Tel Aviv University, argued that the integration of the Jews into German society proceeded much more rapidly among the wealthiest and the poorest classes of Jews, while the lower middle classes remained impervious to outside influences for a relatively much longer period.[14] While, increasingly, during the eighteenth century, both economically successful Jewish merchants and destitute Jewish vagrants mingled freely with their gentile counterparts and adopted some of their values, the bulk of the German Jews still retained their traditional norms.

Even more significant than the qualification by social class is the one necessitated by geographical differentiation. During the eighteenth century, Eastern and Western (including Central) European Jewries came to differ enormously. Although the sociologist and historian Jacob Katz attempted to argue the simultaneous emergence of modernity among Ashkenazic Jews through Hasidism in the East and through Haskalah in the West, he was forced to admit that Hasidism did no more than "distort" the framework of the traditional Jewish society while the Haskalah actually shattered it.[15] However much Hasidism challenged some of the norms of rabbinic Judaism, it surely did not create the characteristics of Jewish modernity. On the contrary, it soon became the most vociferous opponent of Jewish enlightenment.

If integration, on various levels, into non-Jewish society be taken as the basic criterion of the modern period, then the determination of a watershed for Eastern Europe in either the seventeenth or the eighteenth century is very hard to justify. A much better argument could be made for a turning point in the mid-nineteenth century during the relatively liberal reign of Alexander II or even as late as the Bolshevik Revolution. As for the Jewish communities of the Orient and North Africa, with the exception of a small upper class, there seems to have been relatively little interruption of their mode of Jewish existence until they were exposed to their Ashkenazi brethren in the State of Israel. These Eastern communities have been the stepchildren of Jewish historiography, virtually ignored in textbooks and lecture courses until their aliyah in the 1950s. As their descendants now gradually make their way into Jewish scholarship, especially in Israel, they have been attempting to diminish the weight given to European developments, just as Dubnow had sought to reduce the excessive emphasis which Graetz had given to the Jews of Germany, in favor of Poland and Russia. Periodizations of the modern age which are exclusively Europe-centered have therefore become subject to considerable challenge.

With all of these difficulties, is there any value in setting a definite terminus for the beginning of modern Jewish history? I would argue that there is not, unless stimulating discussion with some new theory be itself a value. Any endeavor to mark a border-line which will be meaningful for all Jewries and embrace the origin or rise to normative status of all—or even most—of the characteristics of Jewish life as it presently exists seems to me bound to fail. Yet, one must begin somewhere in relating the Jewish history of most recent times. In practice it is, therefore, probably best to begin with the seventeenth century where, according to nearly all views today, many of the elements that become constitutive of later Jewish life first made their appearance to any degree. But the conventionality of so doing must be fully realized. For, looking further backward, it is possible to attest certain apparently modern developments in some form even in earlier centuries, just as some scholars have tried to dismantle the Renaissance by carrying its various elements back to the Middle Ages.[16] Surely, the Golden Age of Jewish life in Islamic Spain and certain of the communities of sixteenth-century Italy possess significant characteristics of modernity when held up against eighteenth-century Poland. On the other hand, there remains a vast difference between the degree of modernity in evidence before the mid-eighteenth century and that apparent thereafter. One can neither ignore the seeds of later development by suggesting a seventeenth-century "traditional society" little touched by change until a century later, nor, contrariwise, suggest that modernity has arrived along with its first harbingers.

What the Jewish historian can legitimately do—and must do—is to set the forces of continuity (which are never absent) against those of change and to analyze their relative progress and interaction. For most recent times, this means tracing a transformation of Jewish life that proceeded gradually, and sometimes fitfully, from West to East, from class to class, and in which various constituent elements—economic, social, and intellectual—underwent differing degrees of change. The scholar may find crucial points of development which he can legitimately regard as watersheds for a *particular* Jewry, but their limited importance must always be born in mind. Rather than being concerned with the impossible task of determining the precise bounds of a single "modern period" for all Jewries, it would be best to focus on the process of *modernization*[17] in its various aspects, tracing it from one area of Jewish settlement to another and trying to determine its dynamics. (To what extent, for example, does it operate by diffusion and to what extent is it explainable by an internal dialectic within each Jewry?)

Finally, there remains the question of the differing perspective between Jewish historians in Israel and in the Diaspora. If the modern period, or the process of modernization, is defined in whole or in part by Jewish life led as a minority group participating in a non-Jewish society and subjected to the ambiguities and ambivalences of that situation, then the establishment of the State of Israel—as Dinur asserted—has put an end to such Jewish modernity, at least for the Jews in Israel. In fact, the entire Zionist movement can then be seen as essentially postmodern, a reaction spurred by antisemitism to the integration favored by the Haskalah. But if Diaspora Jews are essentially living the heritage of the Jewish enlightenment while Israelis draw sustenance from the roots of Zionism, then we have the anomalous situation where Diaspora Jewry today lives in one period of Jewish history while Israeli Jewry lives in another. From the Israeli viewpoint, this suggestion that the Diaspora remains mired in an earlier period while Jewish history has marched on to its next stage is strangely reminiscent of Lessing's, Hegel's, and, later, Toynbee's viewpoint on the failure of the Jews to advance along with the history of the world. According to its Zionist variation, Diaspora Jews have stubbornly refused to make the called-for dialectical transition from Haskalah to Jewish nationalism.

For the future of Diaspora Jewish existence, such a conception must be as unacceptable on ideological grounds, as it is for historiography on account of its serious distortion of demographic realities. Yet there is no avoiding the obvious fact that many—though by no means all—of the commonly accepted characteristics of Jewish modernity do not apply to the State of Israel. Those which result from minority status are notably absent. Thus, there is a basic bifurcation that necessarily exists between that portion of the Jewish people which lives exposed to the complexly interacting forces of assimilation and antisemitism and the other portion which enjoys a high degree of political independence and the ability to shape education and culture. In order to employ a single concept of modernization which will embrace developments leading simultaneously toward today's Diaspora Jewry and toward Jewish existence in the State of Israel it is, therefore, necessary to include within it both the forces that have operated in the direction of integration into non-Jewish society and those equally modernizing influences—such as a modern separatist nationalism drawn largely from European models—that have driven in the direction of disengagement. Jewish nationalism must be seen not as postmodern, but as part of the modernization process itself.

A single concept is possible, moreover, because the division created by the opposing forces has not become complete. Although the integrative pattern still dominates Diaspora existence today, elements of Jewish national identity are noticeably present as well. By the same token, Israeli society is so influenced by the cultural and intellectual currents of the West that it hardly makes sense to declare that its center of gravity lies within a specifically Jewish sphere like that of pre-modern Jewish communities. If, therefore, modernization (which results in modernity) were conceived in terms of novel elements of both integrative and disjunctive character, it could meaningfully be used to characterize a basic process which has led to both of the forms of Jewish existence today: that of the Diaspora and that of the State. The conceptual unity of Jewish history would thus be preserved, even down to the present.

Notes

1. See George H. Nadel, "Periodization," *International Encyclopedia of the Social Sciences* (New York, 1968), 11:581–85.
2. *Neuere Geschichte der Israeliten* (Berlin, 1846), 1:7.
3. *Kitvei Rabbi Nahman Krochmal*, ed. Simon Rawidowicz (Berlin, 1924), 112.
4. See his anonymously published *Briefwechsel einer englischen Dame über Judentum und Semitismus* (Stuttgart, 1883).
5. *Geschichte der Juden* (Leipzig, 1870), 11:3.
6. In this view, as he himself acknowledged, Dubnow was anticipated by Martin Philippson, *Neueste Geschichte des jüdischen Volkes*, 3 vols. (Leipzig, 1907–11). From a Marxist perspective it was later adopted by Raphael Mahler, *Divrei Yemei Yisrael* (Merhavia, 1969), 22.
7. *Israel and the Diaspora* (Philadelphia, 1969), 79–161.
8. *The Messianic Idea in Judaism* (New York, 1971), 125–26, 140–41.
9. *Toldot Am Yisrael Mi-Yemei Ha-absolutism ad Lehakamat Medinat Yisrael* (Jerusalem, 1968), 2.
10. *Toldot Am Yisrael Ba-et Hahadashah* (Tel Aviv, 1969).
11. *A Social and Religious History of the Jews* (New York, 1965), 9:v.
12. E.g., Azriel Shohet, *Im Hilufei Tekufot* (Jerusalem, 1960).
13. See Barukh Mevorah's review of Shohet's book in *Kiryat Sefer* 37 (1961–62): 150–55.
14. "Neue hebräische Veroffentlichungen zur Geschichte der Juden im deutschen Lebenskreise," *Bulletin des Leo Baeck Instituts* 4 (1961): 67–73.
15. *Tradition and Crisis* (New York, 1961), 227, 245. See the criticism of Shmuel Ettinger on the original Hebrew edition in *Kiryat Sefer* 35 (1959–60): 12–18.
16. Wallace K. Ferguson, *The Renaissance in Historical Thought* (Cambridge, Mass., 1948).
17. Cf., Richard Bendix, "Tradition and Modernity Reconsidered," *Comparative Studies in Society and History* 9 (1967): 292–346.

CHAPTER 2

Reflections on Jewish Modernization

It is hard to think of a better illustration of the fragmentation in contemporary intellectual discourse, which some characterize as typically postmodern, than the multiple ways in which we employ the concept "modern" and its derivatives "modernization" and "modernity."[1] A glance at the literature reveals the extent of the divergence. Once the fundamental decision is made that "modern" does not simply mean the most recent age regardless of content but that the term has a substantive, rather than (or in addition to) a chronological meaning, the tendency is to define it within the discourse of a particular discipline. Since "modernization" first began to appear as a technical term in the 1950s, its meanings have continually expanded.[2] For economists it is the process whereby preindustrial economies become industrialized and it is closely linked to the spread of capitalism. For sociologists and anthropologists it involves shifts in the web of relationships among the members of a society. Social psychologists explore "individual modernization," concentrating on the transformation of dispositions and behavior patterns.[3] And for philosophers and social theorists the key element is the appearance of rationalization or subjectivity.[4]

Although historians endeavor to look more broadly at all these elements of change, they too are inclined toward one or another characteristic depending on their focus or approach to history. They may point to rapid technological advance, the rise of the centralized state,[5] the emergence of individual freedom, urbanization, secularization, or the idea of progress as essential to modernization. To such disciplinary distinctions the Israeli sociologist S. N. Eisenstadt, one of the pioneers of modernization theory, has added the elements of time and geography: modernization takes different forms in twentieth-century Asia and Africa than it did in eighteenth-century Europe.[6] As a result of this multivocality, general discussions of modernization become difficult, and the more so when one considers the charged opinions held with regard to the relative value of modernization, which in a polemical context usually turn on the human price that is paid for industrialization, for the free exercise of instrumental reason, or for the religious void created by what Max Weber famously called the "disenchantment of the world."

Such disagreements and debates have their counterparts in Jewish studies, where some theologians have made Jewish modernity their whipping boy and some historians declared it an age gone by. It thus seems desirable, and even urgent, to reflect upon just what Jewish modernization means in the hope of thereby clarifying and particularizing its use. From the historian's perspective, it seems best not to begin with a definition but to work at the task inductively, first raising the issue of Jewish specificity in the process of modernization and then gathering evidence for such multifaceted change as we might term Jewish modernization.

While in some parts of the world and in certain strata of the Jewish population modernization has long been complete, in others it is still ongoing. As the beginning of the process cannot be precisely and uniformly located for all Jews, neither can its conclusion.[7] Here, however, point of origin or conclusion is not my subject, but rather characteristics of form and matter. I shall endeavor to adduce them by focusing on the Jews of Germany, realizing that the characteristics and dynamics may differ for Jewish modernization elsewhere in Europe and in the Arab world.

In reflecting on the subject of Jewish modernization I found myself repeatedly driven back to asking a very unsettling question: Does the quarry really exist? Perhaps there is no distinguishably Jewish modernization at all but only a process whereby Jews increasingly participate in the modernization of the societies in which they dwell. If this is so, then the object of study needs to be defined as a changing relationship rather than as an internal development. In other words, modernization becomes a concomitant or effect of integration, which is the more fundamental process, and the name we give it could just as well—and perhaps better—be Westernization or Europeanization. Understanding the phenomenon in this way would make the Jewish relation to modernity parallel to that of developing countries whose modernization consists in large measure of their adaptation to Western models in such diverse areas as political and social structure and the arts and the sciences. The challenge of modernization, seen in this light, is essentially external and thus differs from the internal challenge that it raised for those nations that began the process. Unleashed by relatively sudden exposure rather than inner ferment, the shift is also likely to be more abrupt.[8]

Jewish modernization in this sense is strikingly characterized by Jürgen Habermas's phrase: "a leap into a foreign history."[9] The German Jews in the late eighteenth century (to focus now on them) perceived the environment as currently more friendly to their aspirations than ever before and attributed this change to cultural processes that had been at work for some time among the Western European nations. These processes had set non-Jews far ahead of Jews, who did not participate in them. But now a moment of opportunity had arrived—and not only because enlightened circles began to welcome Jewish participation. In the words of the Berlin Jewish intellectual Saul Ascher: "At present, since the nations have arrived at a firm point in their *Bildung* and for some time have, as it were, been standing still, they have left us time gradually to catch up with them."[10] In other words, Ascher is suggesting here in 1792 that the advancing locomotive of culture has halted for a short while, giving the Jews an opportunity to leap on board the train and join with non-Jews in the ride to the stations that lie ahead. About two decades later, the same image of an advancing and more embracing culture, to which the Jews have yet to attach themselves, recurs with a note of greater urgency in Israel Jacobson's dedicatory address at the synagogue he founded in Seesen: "All around us the Enlightenment is enlarging its scope," says Jacobson admiringly. "Should we *alone* get left behind?"[11] Collective progress, traveling together in the direction of moral improvement and rational behavior, will, Jacobson is certain, have the added benefit of closer relations between Jew and Gentile.

These texts, then, would indicate that modernization for the Jews begins with the desire to join and ultimately become full partners in the endeavor to shape the new European culture. But this is Jewish modernization only in the sense of attachment by Jews to a modernization process that has neither its origins nor its end point in the Jewish sphere. Is this the whole story or only part of it? I would argue that it presents one of a number of perspectives, namely the one that is located within the general culture and provides the view of Jews modernizing because the culture to which they are attaching themselves is in the process of transformation from medieval values and institutions to those different ones that characterize the eighteenth century, especially its enlightened elite. Modernization here implies a process whereby individual Jews leave the Jewish community and Jewish identity behind. But there are other relevant perspectives, as well, in which the adjective "Jewish" preceding "modernization" means more than that it is Jews who are running to catch the train.

Let us note first the lively sense among Jews that a break has occurred in their own history as a result of the shift in attitude toward them that has accompanied general enlightenment. Jewish existence is about to be transformed. "A new chapter in the history of the Jews has begun," writes Joseph Wolf introducing the journal *Sulamith* in 1806. It is an age "that is beginning to tell of happy events and with every advance it becomes yet brighter, yet more delightful."[12] Wolf believes that for the individual Jew the new era is one in which Jews may enjoy greater self-esteem because for the first time they are esteemed by others as human beings. Even more ecstatic are the editors of the journal *Erbauungen*, which was published especially for Jewish youth. "O glorious present!" the editors exclaim in 1813. "O still more glorious future!"[13]

Such optimism is, of course, to be understood primarily as a hopeful response to the first indication of Jewish emancipation in France, Holland, and Germany. But it is more than this. It is also evidence of a shift in mentality that fits into the pattern of modernization in general: the sense of an epochal new beginning and of ongoing progress from the present into the future.[14] Adoption of the idea of progress, of the concept that the new is likely to be better than the old, involved a revolution in European thinking. It began with the seventeenth-century *querelle des anciens et des modernes* over the relative value of ancient and modern writers and then spread to the more general question of intellectual progress. In Germany Lessing acclaimed the advance of science, which explained the world and humanity more accurately and reliably than the poets and philosophers of ancient times.[15] As the dispute took its course in Germany, the old educational establishment, the teachers of poetry and rhetoric, championed the ancients while the proponents of the moderns were the physicians, natural scientists, and enlightened theologians.[16] Progress in the sciences, the latter group held, could also be the paradigm for progress in individual and social morality since the scientific worldview emancipated its adherents from superstition and prejudice.

It was this idea of progress that gave modernization its salvific, even messianic character. When Jewish writers at the end of the eighteenth century boast of the growing number of Jews who are physicians and scientists they are not simply making an apologetic point, but indicating to the world that Jews recognize the redemptive role of nontheological knowledge. Among Jews the traditional attitude that ascribed authority to religious texts in direct proportion to their antiquity, i.e., to their proximity to Sinai, gave way to the contradictory notion that intellectual advance made possible an ever closer approximation of the truth. In 1799 Mendelssohn's disciple David Friedländer confided to a more traditionally oriented relative: "I value the Rambam where he philosophizes, I value Bachya, I value the Kuzari, but I also know that our newer writers have presented the matters that count more adequately, more thoroughly, and more clearly."[17] The modernists among Jews (die Neuen, as they were called) accepted this progressivist view. They tailored it to the specifications suggested by their sense of having entered a new, more enlightened and scientifically progressive age. The traditionalists (die Alten), by contrast, resisted it.

The scientific worldview was itself seen as the product of enlightenment (understood as a personal possession rather than as an age). From the perspective of individual orientation such enlightenment was the principal characteristic of modernization. In a famous essay[18] Kant defined it by the imperative: sapere aude! Those who dared to gain wisdom on their own, Kant held, would free themselves from all tutelage and would refuse the imposition of every authority except that of the state within its proper sphere. Although Moses Mendelssohn defined Aufklärung differently from Kant, he had already drawn out the implications of the Königsberg philosopher's personal autonomy principle. In his Jerusalem he argued for complete religious freedom within Judaism, thereby encouraging individual Jews to make their own decisions in regard to practice and belief without fear of rabbinical or communal censure. For his part, Friedländer could rejoice that the rabbis, who, he was certain, still lived in the twelfth century, were now "thank God, bereft of all power."[19] For him and others, modernization, understood as enlightenment in the Kantian sense, represented an emancipation from the tutelage of rabbis[20] and parnasim (communal officials). Thus modernization in the Jewish sphere, as in the non-Jewish, came to mean the religious autonomy of the individual.

There is also a sense in which modernization, for Jews as for Christians, meant secularization.[21] The freedom from religious controls, which was the product of governments dismantling the old Jewish community structures, allowed individuals to expand the secular spheres of their existence: to devote less time and concentration to specifically religious matters. It also stimulated some to develop worldviews in which the Jewish religion played only a minor role or no role whatever. But seen differently, modernization for Jews and non-Jews meant a displacement of the sacred rather than its abandonment. Human tasks performed under the paradigm of universal progress take on the mantle of sanctity. For Jews, Jewishly oriented activities that are understood to further that progress, whether in education or in religion, are similarly sacralized.

The application of the idea of Jewish modernization to the economic sphere raises its own paradoxes. Jews were encouraged to leave behind their ghetto occupations as peddlers and petty traders by training their children to become farmers and artisans. Governments and their spokesmen even at times made such a transformation prerequisite for emancipation. Yet if economic modernization is understood as the advance of industrial capitalism, then Jews were being asked to distance themselves from it. Here adaptation to the surrounding society was interpreted to mean "normalizing" or "productivizing" the Jews' current occupational structure, a process which, if it had in fact taken place, would have removed Jews from those areas of the economy that were the most progressive. But in general they stubbornly chose to go instead to the universities and to develop modern capitalistic enterprises, both of which enabled them to play a disproportionate role in reshaping the German economy. Jewish modernization, in this instance, was Jews, in refusing to adapt, positioning themselves to play an outsize role in the ongoing modernization of their environment.

The counterpart of Jewish modernization as individual participation in the modernizing general culture and society is the turn toward modernizing Jewish institutions. It is the importation of modernity into the Jewish realm. With regard to Germany one thinks first of the schools. The *maskilim*, the Jewish enlighteners, recognized that enlightenment and general culture were more easily implanted at an early age. The educational institutions which they created, patterned on non-Jewish schools, were to serve as vehicles for the transformation of attitudes no longer deemed appropriate. The secularly trained teachers completely rejected the old paradigm of the traditional pedagogue, the *melamed*. Rather they saw themselves as incarnations of the "enlightened Jew" whose task it was to transmit a blend of Jewish and non-Jewish values to his pupils. Since for a time these schools were permitted to enroll Christian children, they also served to bring Jew and non-Jew closer together in childhood. But they were nonetheless Jewish institutions, supported and administered by Jews. As such, they constituted evidence of a modernization process within the Jewish sphere, not attachment to one outside of it. One can point similarly to the new voluntary organizations, from the Gesellschaft der Freunde of 1791 to the Verein für Cultur und Wissenschaft der Juden of 1819 that engaged in nontraditional activities—late burial of the dead in the one case and critical scholarship in the other—but did so within a Jewish social or intellectual milieu. The official Jewish community, as well, modernized in the sense that it adapted to the new situation in which it was no longer a legally recognized corporate entity, but only a *Gemeinde*. Like the Christian communities,[22] it moved in the direction of becoming a mere collectivity of individuals whose autonomous consciences served as the ultimate source of religious authority. In this process ties within the Jewish community became less organic and more voluntary. Modernization transformed the community from *Gemeinschaft* into *Gesellschaft*.[23]

The official task of this *Gesellschaft* was understood to be that of a *Religionsgesellschaft*,[24] serving the religious needs of its members. However much Jews continued to be separated and to separate themselves for social purposes or for the task of extending their emancipation,[25] it was only the religious distinction that Jews and non-Jews alike recognized as permanent. Since there was no room here for a secular Judaism, it was religious modernization which became crucial in the German context.

As Mendelssohn was the great proponent of Jewish modernization through integration into a modernizing culture and society, so was he the most active propagator of the modernization of Judaism through its rationalization. That is not to say that Mendelssohn saw himself as a reformer of Judaism. Quite the contrary, Mendelssohn argued that Judaism had all along been a religion of reason and hence, one might say, modern before the modern age. But in interpreting Judaism in strictly rational terms he in fact placed before his contemporaries a view of it that differed from the common understanding among Gentiles and Jews alike. Especially non-Jews had great difficulty in accepting the idea that Judaism might be inherently more in consonance with the Enlightenment than was Christianity and hence better suited to the new age.

But, of course, Mendelssohn's harmonization of Judaism with the Enlightenment extended only to its religious philosophy, not to its practice, which Mendelssohn did not attempt to rationalize. He thus formulated a Judaism that was modern in the universality and rationality of its doctrines but disregarded modernity in its observances. It was this decision by Mendelssohn to leave the realm of greatest Jewish particularity untouched that proved most problematic for many among the enlightened Jews of the following generation.

The problem lay not only in the increasingly felt hindrance that observance of the law provided to the desire for social and political integration. It lay also in the notion that religious modernization was moving away from both particularity and ceremony. By the end of the eighteenth century, enlightened circles in Germany were speaking more of religion in generic terms than of particular religions, a mode adopted also by the modern Jewish educators in their catechisms. With respect to the diminished significance of ceremonial observance in religion, it was the voice of Kant that spoke the loudest. For Kant the new religious community was not the church but the amorphous collective of all those who regarded themselves as bound by moral obligation. Rational religion did not require priests or sacraments; it did not even require churches, except as instruments to inculcate virtue.[26] Among a growing number of enlightened German Jews Kantianism was understood as modern religion. For some it became a rationale for leaving Judaism, but it also raised the question of whether Judaism could be moralized in practice just as Mendelssohn had rationalized it in theory.

It is this association of religion with the inculcation of moral virtue and the sense of moral obligation that helps to explain the rapid spread of edifying sermons, delivered in the vernacular (and hence comprehensible also to women), not only within a context of liturgical reform but in communities that otherwise remained orthodox. More broadly, rituals in general now had to be reinterpreted within the moral framework of religion. What set the early religious reformers apart from the traditionalists was their willingness to instrumentalize religious practice, to ask whether a particular ritual was *zweckmässig* in heightening religious consciousness.[27] They created a filter, as it were, through which only those practices passed that were religiously useful because they were effective means for what the reformers deemed to be the higher ends of religion. Whether or not a particular observance passed through the filter had also to do with its aesthetic attractiveness. This attention to internalized aesthetic criteria was more broadly represented among German Jews than ideological reform and can be seen as a constituent element of a religious modernization that increasingly set Western Jews apart from fellow Jews in the East even before the emergence of an ideologically grounded movement for religious reform. An apt illustration is this passage from a conservative work, published in 1813, which advocates only formal changes:

> Our coreligionists in Poland, Moravia, and other places may find our suggestions pointless and they are right because the main reason for

the necessity of reform for us is the dissonance between our advanced culture and the religious service, which has remained behind. But this reason unfortunately does not yet exist for our coreligionists. We have attended the devotions held in large communities in Poland and found that they are completely appropriate for them. They are edified by a kind of speaker that we can't bear to hear and are moved to tears by singers who don't move us at all.[28]

Thus German Jewry, across a broad spectrum, became conscious of possessing sensibilities that set it apart from Jews to the east and that were increasingly reflected in the way it conducted its religious life. Modernization was coming to encompass not only the Jew but also Judaism. The impetus in each instance arose from the outside, from the larger society, itself engaged in the continuing process of modernization. But this drive toward modernization did not simply produce the desire of the individual to jump on board but also the wish to create a parallel modernization of the Jew as Jew and of Judaism as a religion that, in drawing on its own resources, had nothing to fear from modernity.

We may finally ask: Is Jewish modernization, seen from the perspective of the present, a process of Jews becoming what they are today or only what they were yesterday? Were its instigators blinded by the bright flame of the Enlightenment, which drew them toward it at their own peril? We live in an age that possesses both renewed respect for tradition and diversity and mistrust of universal claims, a time whose principal imperative Jean François Lyotard has called a "war on totality."[29] It is therefore not surprising that Judaism and thought about Judaism should reflect these attitudes. Does that mean the process of modernization has ended and that of "postmodernization" begun? If so, then perhaps a new bandwagon is moving by and it is time for Jewish thinkers to jump on board.[30] Yet it remains to be seen whether new ways will be found once more to domesticate this new process within Judaism—or, alternatively, whether modernity in some chastened form remains viable and may yet survive both outside Judaism and within it.[31]

Notes

I would like to thank Barry Kogan, David Myers, and David Sorkin for the suggestions they gave me upon reading the manuscript. An earlier version of this essay was delivered as part of a panel on "Modernization of the Jews" at the meeting of the Association for Jewish Studies in Boston in 1994.

Especially in the last chapter of his *Zakhor*, where he deals with the impact of historical distance (clearly a product of modernization) upon Judaism, Yosef Hayim Yerushalmi has provided new impetus for reflection on Jewish modernization.

1. If one adds the term "modernism" one hits upon the further paradox that this term is sometimes used to refer to a late-nineteenth-century movement in the arts which some would understand as the emergence of postmodernity. See Barry Smart, "Modernity, Postmodernity, and the Present," in Bryan S. Turner, ed., *Theories of Modernity and Postmodernity* (London, 1990), 18.
2. Jürgen Habermas, *The Philosophical Discourse of Modernity. Twelve Lectures*, trans. by Frederick Lawrence (Cambridge, Mass., 1987), 2.
3. Alex Inkeles and David H. Smith, *Becoming Modern: Individual Change in Six Developing Countries* (Cambridge, Mass., 1974); Alex Inkeles, *Exploring Individual Modernity* (New York, 1983). The individual also serves as the focus in Peter Berger, Brigitte Berger, and Hansfried Kellner, *The Homeless Mind: Modernization and Consciousness* (New York, 1973).
4. See, for example, David Kolb, *The Critique of Pure Modernity: Hegel, Heidegger, and After* (Chicago, 1986); Lawrence E. Cahoone, *The Dilemma of Modernity: Philosophy, Culture, and Anti-Culture* (Albany, 1988).
5. In choosing the process of political modernization in order to establish an interpretive framework, one historian explained his decision by remarking that "intellectual developments are too amorphous to be amenable to comparable categorization." C. E. Black, *The Dynamics of Modernization: A Study in Comparative History* (New York, 1966), 90.
6. See the volume edited by Eisenstadt, *Patterns of Modernity. Vol. 1: The West* (New York, 1987).
7. See the introduction to my *Ideas of Jewish History* (New York, 1974), 1–42, and my "Where Does the Modern Period of Jewish History Begin?" Reprinted as chapter 1 of this volume.
8. Black, *Dynamics of Modernization*, 8; François Bourricaud, "Modernity, 'Universal Reference' and the Process of Modernization," in ibid., 12–14.
9. Jürgen Habermas, *Philosophical-Political Profiles*, trans. Frederick C. Lawrence (Cambridge, Mass., 1985), 26.
10. Saul Ascher, *Leviathan oder Ueber Religion in Rücksicht des Judenthums* (Berlin, 1792), 11.
11. *Sulamith*, 3:1 (1810): 309.
12. Ibid., 1:1 (1806): 6.
13. *Erbauungen*, 1 (1813): 7. For the heightened sense of the significance of present and future in the Jewish Enlightenment, see Shmuel Feiner, *Haskalah ve-historyah: toldoteha shel hakarat avar yehudit modernit* (Jerusalem, 1995), 55–76.
14. Habermas, *Philosophical Discourse of Modernity*, 8.

15. See Lessing's "Gedicht über die Vorzugsfrage," in Peter K. Kapitza, *Ein bürgerlicher Krieg in der gelehrten Welt. Zur Geschichte der Querelle des Anciens et des Modernes in Deutschland* (Munich, 1981), 207–10.
16. Ibid., 430.
17. Ludwig Geiger, "Ein Brief Moses Mendelssohns und sechs Briefe David Friedländers," *Zeitschrift für die Geschichte der Juden in Deutschland* 1 (1887): 271.
18. "Beantwortung der Frage: Was ist Aufklärung?" It originally appeared in 1784 and is conveniently reprinted along with Mendelssohn's essay and other relevant material in Norbert Hinske, ed., *Was ist Aufklärung? Beiträge aus der Berlinischen Monatsschrift* (Darmstadt, 1977), 452–65.
19. Geiger, "Ein Brief," 268.
20. A radical non-Jew, in reference to the tutelage of the rabbis, employed a metaphor of maturation: "The child eventually becomes an adult and outgrows the rod. Why not the Jew?" [Andreas Riem], *Leviathan oder Rabbinen und Juden* (Jerusalem [Leipzig], 1801), viii.
21. David Martin, "Secularization: The Range of Meaning," *The Religious and the Secular* (New York, 1969), 48–57.
22. Reinhard Koselleck, "Aufklärung und die Grenzen ihrer Toleranz," in Trutz Rendtorff, ed., *Glaube und Toleranz: Das theologisiche Erbe der Aufklärung* (Gütersloh, 1982), 258.
23. On the restructuring of the Jewish community see David Sorkin, *The Transformation of German Jewry, 1780–1840* (New York, 1987), 107–23.
24. *Zur Judenfrage in Deutschland* 1 (1843): 213.
25. Sorkin, "The Ideology of Emancipation," in his *Transformation of German Jewry*, 13–104.
26. Koselleck, "Aufklärung und die Grenzen ihrer Toleranz," 270–71. Even marriage as religious rite came under attack in the *Berlinische Monatsschrift*. "Enlightened people don't require all those ceremonies," one writer declared. Cited in Hinske, *Was ist Aufklärung*, xxxvii.
27. Thus Jacobson at the Seesen dedication complains "that our religious service hitherto has ailed on account of numerous useless elements [*Zwecklosigkeiten*.]" *Sulamith* 3:1 (1810): 309.
28. [Abraham Muhr], *Jerubaal oder über die religiöse Reform der Juden in preußischen Staaten* (Breslau, 1813), 27. Muhr's general attitude to reform is best expressed in this passage (10): "In our opinion, one may not tear down that which is old simply because it is old in order to build something new in its place even if in principle it seems better. We can't determine the consequences of our ideas in their execution and modern trumpery could easily displace the old but supportive columns that get torn down."
29. Jean-François Lyotard, *The Postmodern Explained: Correspondence, 1982–1985* (Minneapolis, 1993), 16.
30. For example, Arnold M. Eisen, "Rethinking Jewish Modernity," Albert T. Bilgray Lecture, Tucson, Ariz., Apr. 1992.
31. Perhaps in the form of a synthesis between premodern and modern

elements. See David Ray Griffin, ed., *Sacred Interconnections: Postmodern Spirituality, Political Economy, and Art* (Albany, 1990), xi. Among the latter would certainly be criticism which, as Foucault notes, requires continuing faith in the Enlightenment. Paul Rabinow, ed., *The Foucault Reader* (New York, 1984), 50.

CHAPTER 3

The Emergence of
Modern Jewish Historiography:
Motives and Motifs

The modernization of European Jewry was a gradual process that spread from individuals to communities and from one social class to another. It traveled from city to small town and from central and western Europe eastward. Among its component elements were economic redistribution, acculturation, secular education, and religious reform. Scholars have examined each of these elements and their interrelation. They have also recognized the appearance of a new historical consciousness that began to play a crucial role in the formation of modern Jewish identity. Recently, the shifting relation of Jews to their history has received much attention, both in general surveys and in specific studies.[1] Yet the emergence of a fresh historical awareness, after centuries in which historical interest was at best limited, deserves further consideration, for the process was by no means simple and straightforward. As Jews began to attribute major significance to history in general and to Jewish history in particular, they faced issues that were not speedily or uniformly resolved: What was the purpose of historical study? What history should be learned? How was the study of history related to Jewish religion and its possible reform? And perhaps most important, should the study of Jewish history principally serve to liberate the Jew from tradition by historicizing it or create a new attachment to the past by reconceiving it as a model or anchorage for the present? These questions emerge especially among German Jews during the periods of the Enlightenment and Romanticism. The answers given reflect both the intellectual milieu and the specific historical situation of the Jews.

I. The Value of Historical Knowledge

Although Moses Mendelssohn, the first prominent and articulate modern Jew, on one occasion complained of his boredom with history, his first biographer, Isaac Euchel, felt constrained to point out, in 1788, that his subject's secular education had begun with historical studies. That remark, in turn, served as a good excuse for parenthetically explaining to his Hebrew readers just what history was and why Jews should study it. He wrote:

> [History consists of] the events that take place in every state, and in truth knowing it is of great benefit, since it is filled with the occurrences that happened to human beings in general and to particular individuals at various times. From it one can learn to walk in the way of one's country, to compare situations, times, nations, and persons— with regard to laws, religions, and customs. In the end one strengthens his ability to distinguish between truth and falsehood as well as to improve his moral qualities. One is able to adapt his own inclinations to the virtues of upright men, the performers of great deeds, whose life histories he has found in these narratives—and many other such benefits.[2]

Euchel had written about Mendelssohn so that this first notable Jew to be recognized as a man of outstanding European culture could serve as a model to members of the contemporary generation seeking their own blend of Jewish identity and modernity. Mendelssohn, he claimed, "led us on the path of truth and showed us the way of virtue; he illuminated the road before us. My brothers, let us hold to this path ourselves, turning neither to the left nor to the right. . . . May his life serve as our example, his teaching as our eyes."[3]

When Euchel wrote his biography, Mendelssohn had been dead only two years. Many of his readers had known the celebrated Berlin Jewish philosopher personally; all knew something about him. To study his life was therefore no recovery of a forgotten past but the attempt to preserve, strengthen, and extend the impact that Mendelssohn had made on the Jewish collectivity in the last generation. However, Euchel and the other maskilim[4] were likewise interested in repossessing a more distant Jewish past that was either misunderstood or little known. They began with the Bible, surprisingly a source mostly unfamiliar to the average Jew apart from the Pentateuch, the Prophetic selections read on Sabbaths, and those books or verses (especially Psalms and the Five Scrolls) that were part of the liturgy or holiday worship. When the maskilim devoted special attention to the Bible in their Hebrew periodical, *Ha-Me'asef,* they were seeking not only to dwell upon their own classical literature, as non-Jewish scholars were carefully exploring the Greek and Roman Heritage, but also to bring to awareness a work of broader horizons that they could set against the narrower, legal focus of rabbinic writing. Moreover, biblical history could be easily exploited for didactic purposes. It was simply necessary to recast the historical account and stress the moral lessons that could be derived from it. As the new Jewish pedagogy departed from the law-oriented study of traditional texts and took on a moralistic cast, biblical history became a treasure trove of positive and negative exemplars.[5]

Yet the value of the biblical period as a model for the present was limited by its setting. It represented an age when Israel possessed its own land, its own political and social institutions. Modern diaspora Jewish existence required as exemplars individuals who had combined adherence to Judaism with full participation in the non-Jewish world around them. Such exemplars were scarce in the history of Ashkenazi Judaism, the tradition that was the particular heritage of the Central European Jews. They were rather to be found among the Sephardim, the Iberian Jews and their descendants, who never fully abandoned the openness to secular culture that was their legacy since the time they lived under relatively tolerant regimes in Islamic Spain. Thus the regular column in the periodical of the German maskilim that was entitled "History of the Great Men of Israel" was devoted to (aside from Mendelssohn) such Sephardi figures as the medieval philosopher-legist Moses Maimonides; the widely learned Joseph Delmedigo of seventeenth-century Crete; and the Dutch rabbi, Manasseh ben Israel, who not only enjoyed extensive correspondence with Christian scholars but displayed political skill in seeking the readmission of the Jews to England. Mendelssohn appeared as an exception among the Ashkenazim, but not in the parallel Sephardi tradition. To draw upon Sephardi models meant to widen the past of German Jews, bringing to awareness figures very different from the prominent rabbinical authorities, whose names made up the chain of recent tradition. Creating a new tradition of the religious but worldly required shifting its course away from the most immediate to a more distant channel.

From prominent Sephardim, who were consistently and wholeheartedly Jews, historical interest spread to figures at the periphery of Jewish existence. Isaac Orobio de Castro, for example, was for most of his life a Portuguese Christian intellectual and a prominent physician, whose medieval knowledge brought him a professorship and then a rectorship at the University of Toulouse. But on suspicion of being a secret Jew, a Marrano, Orobio had been subjected to tortures by the Inquisition, and eventually he joined the Jewish community in Amsterdam. Uriel Acosta was similarly of Marrano origin, but unlike Orobio, he could not make a permanent transition to the normative Judaism of the seventeenth century and eventually took his own life. What these figures, and others like them, represented to Jewish writers of the Haskalah was the gray area at the boundary of Judaism, a vicinity that attracted their attention as their widening interests drove them away from prevalent norms. While they could not identify with the headstrong Acosta, they could sympathize with him and with others who had been victims of intolerance, whether inflicted by the Inquisition, as upon Orobio de Castro, or by Jews, as upon Uriel Acosta.[6]

Both the moralistic, didactic purpose of the Haskalah's use of history and its interest in Sephardi Jewry continued into the early nineteenth century, even when the subject matter ceased to be predominantly biographical. Shalom Cohen carried them remarkably far in an article analyzing causes for the expulsion of the Jews from Spain in 1492.[7] Although he compiled explanations given by various writers, Jewish and non-Jewish, Cohen's point was not to settle on one interpretation, let alone to propose his own. His chief purpose was to present the expulsion as a morality tale in which the evil of intolerance resulted in divine retribution. Spain's position in the world had declined since it expelled its Jews. Indeed, Napoleon had recently devastated and taken possession of it. Addressing Spain in the second person, Cohen admonished it to repent: "Banish hatred from your heart and do not presume that the gates of heaven are open to the adherents of your faith alone." Since he was writing in Hebrew and thus for Jews alone, Cohen's motive could only have been to hearten his coreligionists with evidence that hatred of Jews ultimately breeds calamity. And likewise, by implication, tolerance redounds to the benefit of nations. That was a lesson from history which Jews, then seeking emancipation, could use to justify their quest for political and social integration.

Among the earliest modern Jewish historians Marcus Fischer, who lived in Vienna and in Prague during the early nineteenth century, is of particular interest. He wrote studies in Hebrew both on general history and on Jewish subjects. And he was familiar with the best-known historical writings of his day. At the beginning of his history of the Jews in North Africa he placed a citation from the German historian August von Schlözer in which the non-Jewish writer had attested to the multiple values deriving from a study of the history of the Jews. It seems to be the first instance where a Jew recognized that his own writing was part of the larger enterprise of historiography; and like Schlözer, he was at pains to point out its moral value. Each nation, Fischer argued, had had its historians who sought to show that truth, justice, and virtue brought prosperity and victory, while corruption resulted in increasing troubles, sometimes to the point of extinction. The Jews too had possessed their historians in ancient times who had undertaken that task, but much of their work was lost, and more recently Jews had sorely neglected a history filled with countless tribulations. The Jewish historian in the present had no choice but to rely on what gentiles had written. At least he could be critical of his sources, following those that seemed the most reliable.[8]

Fischer's critical senses, however, competed with more powerful inclinations. His desire to present a history of Prague Jewry was so strong that he created one out of whole cloth. Not only did he forge a chronicle of events running from 1271 to 1743, he tailored it to fit his ideology. Fischer was inclined to a liberal interpretation of Jewish law, and the chronicle that he allegedly only translated provided ample evidence of community ordinances that could serve as enlightened precedents. Moreover, his medieval Jews effectively refuted the charges of nineteenth-century critics regarding Jewish character. They were both industrious and fully loyal to their rulers. In Fischer's chronicle the effort to reveal a Jewish past for the sake of present-day instruction reached its extreme: the invention of that past in the form thought to be of the greatest value.[9]

II. Using the Past to Demolish the Present

The reverse side of using the past to provide precedents was its employment for the sake of destroying encrusted contemporary norms. This was the purpose of those enlightened Jews in Berlin who approached the brilliant but erratic Solomon Maimon with the request that he translate into Hebrew selected scholarly works, which they would then print.[10] One suggested that historical studies would be especially useful since they would enable tradition-bound Jews to discover the origins of their religious doctrines and their subsequent degeneration. Their readers would come to understand that the causes for the fall of the Jewish state and for the following persecution and oppression lay in the people's ignorance and opposition to every reasonable institution. The study of history, as some of the more radical German maskilim saw it, would liberate their fellow Jews, especially the benighted ones in Poland, from the shackles of a tradition that they had never before examined critically. They would come to realize that their plight was of their own making. Historical study would serve not as a source of pride but as a rebuke. Some of his Berlin friends therefore proposed to Maimon that he translate Jacques Basnage's history of the Jews from French into Hebrew. In the end, however, they could not agree that historical study was the most effective tool for breaking the grip of the past. David Friedländer then suggested beginning with works espousing natural religion and natural morality, for these were the proper end of all enlightenment. In effect, Friedländer was saying that modernization could best be advanced by purposefully neglecting study of the divisive and unedifying past for the sake of unhistorical knowledge that united Jews with non-Jews in their common rationality. Maimon himself shared that view, though he was unenthusiastic about the value of teaching natural theology or morals. He thought it best to begin Jewish reeducation with mathematics. That discipline was as intellectually challenging as talmudic study, and its truths less arguable. But Maimon was also persuaded that in fact there was no real Jewish history to study since the Jewish nation scarcely ever possessed any political relations with other civilized nations and, aside from a few fragments regarding prosecutions, there were no historical sources on the Jews since Josephus. Even more, Judaism since the Talmud had not undergone any internal changes, and hence was not historical. If periodization separated epochs that were essentially different, then the contemporary period of Jewish history had begun over a thousand years ago. It had continued on to his own time, and would continue "to all eternity (*si diis placet*) down to the arrival of the messiah."[11] Maimon clearly had no hope that Judaism could reenter history. Individual Jews could be modernized, but only by stepping outside their community and becoming part of the history of the European nations. Maimon's object was to create an awareness of incongruity between the European and the Jewish present. Others would then follow his own example and consider their personal existence likewise to lie outside the bounds of Judaism.

Yet some who shared Maimon's desire to be free of tradition, if not to depart entirely from the sphere of Judaism, were convinced that historical study could help demolish prevalent norms and still leave a usable residue. Peter Beer, a Bohemian Jewish pedagogue inspired by Mendelssohn but far more radical, frankly expressed his view that exclusion of the Jews from European society had produced a "pernicious esprit de corps and loathsome selfishness" which are inimical to the good of the state.[12] Beer wanted to reeducate Jews in such a way that their sense of Jewish solidarity would be diminished, hastening their political and cultural integration. To his mind, that required using the hammer of historical study to shatter the perceived unity and solidity of Jewish tradition. To that end, Beer wrote not a unitary history of the Jews or of Judaism, but a history of Jewish sects.[13] By reviving interest in Samaritans, Hellenizers, Essenes, Sadducees, and Karaites, Beer was able to challenge the association of Judaism with Pharisaism, whose extension was the rabbinism that reigned in his time. By explicating other norms within the boundaries of Jewish history, he challenged the universal validity of the rabbinic one. Pharisaism, too, was only one sect among others. Of course as long as Jews continued to regard themselves as heirs of the Pharisees, they would have difficulty fully accommodating their religion to civil life. Fortunately, enlightenment would bring about the end of rabbinism.[14] But since the Jews had not always been rabbinites, it followed that rabbinism was not the only possible basis of Judaism and therefore efforts then being made by governments and individuals to "improve" the Jews were not, after all, doomed to failure. Contra Maimon, the present period of Jewish history did not have to last until the advent of the messiah.

Beer was apparently the first Jewish writer to use historical study for the purpose of tearing the scarlet thread of Jewish continuity. But in so doing he made it possible to remain within the variegated landscape of the Jewish legacy that he described. Whereas Maimon, insisting that contemporary Judaism was inherently incapable of change, was forced to go beyond its limits, Beer was able to reach back beyond sectarianism to present a new norm. He declared himself an adherent of the "pure Mosaic faith," which had preceded sectarian division. If Jewish history was discontinuous and divided, then the leap back to the Israelite epoch could be seen as the return to an earlier common ground. Moreover, the ancient Mosaic faith was likewise the basis of Christianity, and it presented fewer obstacles to political integration. Pharisaism was indeed a decline from Mosaism, but reascent was possible. In addition, Mosaism for Beer was not simply one historical manifestation of Jewish religion. Properly understood, it was the *Urreligion* that by its very nature could never fall victim to sectarianism. While all later expressions of Judaism were subject to historical vicissitude, Mosaism possessed principles but no history. Beer saw it as the universal faith transcending both time and denominations.

The use of Jewish historiography to undermine the acceptability of prevalent religious norms continued well into the nineteenth century. The movement for religious reform in Judaism, which burgeoned in Germany during this period, employed historical criticism to loosen the hold of various orthodox beliefs and practices by demonstrating their late importation into Jewish tradition. Gershom

Scholem was not far off the mark when he called the leading theoretician and scholar of the Reform movement, Abraham Geiger, "the most talented of all the destructive scholars."[15] Geiger himself had once written that one primary purpose of Jewish historical scholarship was "to prove that everything that presently exists at some point came into being and [therefore] possesses no binding force."[16] He and other religious reformers did indeed employ their considerable scholarly skills to show that change and variety had been indigenous to Jewish history. While orthodox understanding insisted that historically successive layers of tradition were essentially one in content and of divine origin, Geiger argued that the Bible, Mishnah, and Gemara represented fresh stages of religious development. Succeeding generations had sought to reconcile the contradictions between them, but what had happened in fact was that the sages of the Mishnah had read their ideas back into the Bible, and those of the Gemara had done the same with Mishnah. A tradition that for theological reasons rejected development had dogmatically excluded it.[17] But Geiger, unlike Beer, did not proceed from a disassembling of Jewish history to plucking out one phase and ascribing to it alone universal and ongoing validity. Instead, he could, like non-Jewish scholars, use his recognition of all historical phenomena as timebound and subject to change for the purpose of furthering religious reform. It became possible for him to identify with the totality of the Jewish tradition as a developing entity destined to produce ever-changing norms. Moreover, as a student of German idealist philosophy, he attributed such development less to external causes than to the "spirit" of Judaism active within the Jewish collectivity.[18]

III. External Influences

Although the internal Jewish agenda provided the major impetus for the emergence of modern Jewish historiography, both the increased prominence of historical studies in Germany beginning in the late eighteenth century and the attention paid by non-Jewish historians to Jewish history were also significant factors.

Motives that determined Jewish maskilim to turn to historical studies had their equivalents among German *Aufklärer*. The German Enlightenment, like its Jewish derivative, was intent on shattering restrictive norms by expanding experience to embrace the variants presented by preceding centuries and thus broaden the range of possibilities for the future. It too sought to liberate itself from a confining present and saw historical study as a necessary prologue to reform.[19] Enlightenment historians, like their seventeenth-century predecessors, dwelt on the role of individuals in history. Like the maskilim, they too looked for exemplars and some were willing even explicitly to intrude their own views. August von Schlözer, for example, saw it as part of the historian's task to be the moral judge of the characters who populated his narrative.

It was further characteristic of eighteenth-century historiography that it lacked an integrative scheme, that it produced piles of bricks rather than architecturally designed buildings.[20] If Jewish historians wrote similarly, pasting together accounts but falling short of achieving organic unity, it was clearly because they had as yet no other model. Isaac Marcus Jost, the first modern Jewish writer to attempt a comprehensive history of the Jews, remained very much in the tradition of *Aufklärung* historiography although he lived in the period of Romanticism. Jost's writings (to which we shall return) lacked unity of conception. Although later critics attributed this characteristic to his failure to conceive of the Jews as a single people, it was no less due to the models that he had before him during his student years in Göttingen.

To varying degrees, however, Jewish historians by the end of the second decade of the nineteenth century were influenced by the transition from earlier Enlightenment thought to historicism. As historiography became less rhetorical and more *wissenschaftlich*, more dedicated to objectivity and less an instrument for moral instruction, its use for exemplary purposes fell into mild disrepute. The purpose of historical writing was now to present the fruits of serious research.[21] Leopold Zunz and the circle of young men who formed the Verein für Cultur und Wissenschaft der Juden in Berlin in 1819 were determined that study of the Jewish past undergo a similar *Verwissenschaftlichung*. They too refused to limit the scope of their study to exemplars of the values they sought to establish in the present and they cast away the rod of moral judgment.[22] In an often quoted sentence from his earliest work Zunz clearly separated his own purpose from that of his Haskalah predecessors: "Here we are setting up the whole of Jewish literature in its fullest compass as an *object of research*, without worrying whether the total contents should be or can be also a *norm for our own judgments*."[23] Consequently, Zunz chose to study the medieval Jewish history of the Ashkenazim, explicitly refusing to make one of its central figures, the exegete Rashi of Troyes, into an exemplar of broader culture.[24]

German historicism was influential for Jewish historiography in another important respect. In its attack upon eighteenth-century ideas of natural law and eternal truths, historicism not only created a greater sense of the fluidity of truth, it also individualized and particularized it. Moses Mendelssohn, the adherent of natural religion, could not conceive of a Judaism whose basic doctrines had been conditioned by the particular historical experience of the Jews. Two generations later, scholars like Abraham Geiger were intent on investigating the sources of a presumed development attributable at least in part to the vicissitudes of Jewish history. The individualizing trend led Geiger and others to seek the particular essence of Judaism that set it apart from other faiths.

A different kind of external influence came from gentile historians of the Jews who had acquired claim to the subject by default. The first writer in modern times to attempt a comprehensive history of the Jews was the French cleric Jacques Basnage. As a Protestant who had fled France after the revocation of the Edict of Nantes, Basnage possessed uncommon sympathy for the Jews as victims of religious persecution. But often, he argued, they were themselves responsible for their fate. In the fashion of seventeenth-century historiography, Basnage set himself up as a trial judge for each instance: "The Christians ought not to think it strange that we very frequently acquit the Jews of several crimes whereof they are not guilty, since justice requires it. . . . But as our design is neither to offend, nor to flatter them, [the Jews] ought not to be surprised that we declare against them when the facts appear well attested."[25] Their sins had therefore doubtless provoked God's wrath, but its measure seemed inexplicably beyond their just desserts. That the Jews nonetheless survived was indeed a miracle that evoked astonishment and refuted the deist denial of divine providence. Basnage was amazed that, despite all of the persecutions that they suffered, Jews could still be found in so many parts of the world. But that survival—in a situation of oppression—was for Basnage rather an indication of divine disfavor than of grace. Their preservation was for the sake of their eventual conversion, a project Basnage felt should be vigorously carried forward, in part by ridiculing the Talmud and other rabbinic works.[26] Basnage thus combined extraordinary knowledge of the Jews' history and some sympathy for their plight with adherence to traditional supersessionist dogmas regarding Jewish persistence following the Incarnation. The Jewish historian of the nineteenth century, Heinrich Graetz, praised Basnage for calling attention to Jewish history, but faulted him for making it no more than the history of a church and of recurrent victimization.[27] For Basnage the two were in fact related. On account of their stubborn beliefs the Jews had suffered. In rejecting Christ they had become objects of history, not its creators.

Later Christian writers drew generously from Basnage. Among them was Hannah Adams of Boston, the earliest American woman historian. Her history of the Jews, first published in 1812, heralded its theme on the title page of the first volume with a quotation from Deuteronomy: "And the Lord shall scatter thee among all people from one end of the earth even unto the other—and among these nations thou shalt find no ease, neither shall the sole of thy foot have rest."[28] Like Basnage, Adams was fascinated by the cruelty the Jews had endured during their extended wanderings. At intervals she "sighed" over their fate. But even more than Basnage, she made the Jews responsible for their "wretchedness and depravity." And while Christians, in persecuting Jews, had been unfaithful to "the fundamental precepts of the gospel," Jewish shortcomings were directly attributable to their religion. The history of the Jews was of great significance for Christians, she believed, since it portrayed "the lineal descendants of the chosen people of God, forfeiting their inestimable privileges by rejecting the glory of Israel and involving themselves in the most terrible calamities."[29] Jewish history, in short, was an argument for the truth of Christianity.[30]

It is not surprising that Adams's history—with her approval—became a tract for converting the Jews. In 1818 the London Society for Promoting Christianity Amongst the Jews republished it with some changes to make it suit conversionist purposes even better. In 1819 it appeared in German translation in Leipzig, the first comprehensive history of the Jews down to the nineteenth century to be published in the German language. The anonymous translator added a prologue in which he held out the prospect of emancipation but only if the Jews themselves would change their customs, institutions, and way of thinking, for example moving their sabbath to Sunday. But he personally thought a study of the Jewish past would reveal that in fact the Jews had never changed for the better. Good fortune simply made them arrogant.[31]

Thus if new interest in historical studies served positively as a spur for young Jewish scholars to emulate the university historians with serious scholarly efforts applied to their own historical legacy, the writings of Christians on Jewish history that now came to their attention served the same end negatively. To the educated public Basnage and Adams represented the best and most complete histories of the Jews. Their portrayal of the Jews as pitiable victims whose lot was as much the result of their own fixed beliefs and characteristics as of medieval intolerance made Jewish history a tale of passivity, corruption, and incorrigibility. Its study could neither inspire Jewish readers nor further the cause of Jewish political acceptance among non-Jews. The first Jewish historians were thus not only reestablishing historical inquiry among Jews, mostly dormant since Josephus, but also seeking to recapture the field from gentile writers who had used it for their own purposes.

IV. Isaac Marcus Jost and Heinrich Graetz

The remarkable survival of the Jews despite all their tribulations, which had so inspired the Christian historians, seemed to less theologically oriented observers not at all certain to continue. With German Jewry's emergence from its spiritual and cultural ghetto, beginning in the late eighteenth century, and the rising hope of emancipation, the barriers that had marked off the Jews and created their separate historical existence were falling away. Those young Jews most exposed to German culture, the university graduates, were least certain about Jewish continuation. Even the young philologist Leopold Zunz justified Wissenschaft des Judentums as rendering a final accounting for a literature that had reached the end of its history.[32] His contemporary Eduard Gans, a student of Hegel, was yet more persuaded that Judaism could no longer retain its independent existence under the new condition of integration. At best, it would continue "as the current lives on in the ocean."[33] Given the apparently destined end of Jewish history—and the clear practical advantages of being a Christian—Zunz at one point considered conversion and Gans was in fact converted. Isaac Marcus Jost, a member of the same Berlin circle, did not, as far as we know, weigh that possibility. Perhaps that was mainly because of his conservative disposition, but it was also the result of his continuing faith that the egalitarian principles of the Enlightenment would emerge anew after the Romantic reaction. His *History of the Israelites*, the first comprehensive history of the Jews written by a Jew in modern times, was predicated on that faith.[34]

Jost had begun his university studies in Göttingen in 1813, where he was especially drawn to the prominent historian and biblical scholar Johann Gottfried Eichhorn. Encouraged by Eichhorn, he began to gather material for his extraordinarily ambitious project.[35] When the first of his nine volumes appeared in 1820, Jost explicitly acknowledged the political intent of his history. He was writing as much for non-Jews as for Jews in the hope that an honest portrayal of the Jewish past, one that was theologically unbiased, would help government officials come to a fair conclusion regarding the Jewish capacity for living under conditions of emancipation. Consequently, in his history he was always at pains to point out how Jews were loyal and useful subjects of the states in which they lived. Later historians and critics have focused on this aspect of Jost's historiography. They have also pointed out that his writing lacked drama, that in dividing the history of the Jews by areas of settlement he obscured the degree of unity among Jews everywhere, and that even his use of the term "Israelites" in the title of his work was indicative of its apologetic tone. Yet Jost's history was markedly more favorable to the Jews than the work of the Christian writers. He could write with considerable feeling at least about those epochs of the Jewish past with which he readily identified. His account of the Jewish expulsion from Spain is not atypical of the various aspects of his writing:

> Aside from a few weaklings, [the Jews] all decided to give up their possessions to their fatherland for the sake of their religion and rather to perish than to abandon it. It was a heroic decision which simultaneously inspired more than 300,000 souls (according to others, 800,000), although they were scattered everywhere! Doubly praiseworthy, since the Jews, whose number and influence could easily have ignited a civil war—which held out nothing more dreadful than what the large emigration caused them to fear—nonetheless refrained from any agitation or stirring up of emotions. Even though many of them had attracted the contempt and hate of non-Jews on account of their usury and the obstinacy of their community, such a decision surely wipes out all the hostile feelings that one harbored against Judaism and opens the way for high regard and admiration. No longer could one accuse of avarice those who exposed all of their possessions to threatening dangers in order to seek a homeland in unfamiliar lands, where they could pray to an imageless God. One could no longer declare wicked those who rejected an easy way out to maintain a respected status for themselves and their families in order not to change their faith, no longer scorn as servile spirits those who were able to raise themselves so high above everything mundane.[36]

As Jost himself realized, his pioneer effort was necessarily faulty. Important sources were not available to him.[37] His first concern was to render an account of the external history of the Jews, the shifting relations between the Jews and the governments under which they lived. Only in his later writings did he turn more to the Jews' religious and cultural history. With all of its shortcomings, however, Jost's audacious *History of the Israelites* aroused broader interest among Jews and non-Jews than did the more narrowly specialized, though more erudite, writings of his contemporary Leopold Zunz. Jost, at least initially, was principally a political historian determined to present with utmost accuracy and dispassion the vicissitudes of Jewish status in a broad, well-ordered, and encompassing narrative. He wanted to create a perspective for viewing the entire expanse of Jewish history. Zunz, by contrast, was more interested in the detailed working of the inner parts, the creativity, that was, of course, to some extent explicable by the external events.

Jost was the first historian to stress the interrelatedness between the history of the Jews and the nations in which the Jewish diaspora was lodged. Hence he argued that the study of Jewish history was of great value for understanding general history. But he went further: Jewish history, he claimed, "is not an independently subsisting whole, rather an aspect of the history of the most important nations and states with which the Jews have come into contact."[38] In effect, therefore, there was no history of the Jews that possessed unity and continuity. The historian of the Jews simply pieced together what were elements in the histories of other groups.

The first critic to take fundamental issue with Jost's approach was Abraham Geiger. Geiger agreed with Jost that the history of the Jews consisted of fragments from the historical contexts in which they lived. But he insisted that while this was true for the *Jews* it was not true for *Judaism*. Indeed, what was remarkable about the Jews was that they had managed to survive without the external support of unifying national institutions. It was their religion that had created connections both in time and in space. Jewish history, properly understood as essentially a history of the Jewish faith, thus gained independent standing. Its object, he argued, was "an historical entity that stands entirely alone and allows of no parallels, that just for that reason must be explained in terms of itself alone." Under the influence of post-Enlightenment philosophical thought, Geiger believed such understanding was possible because of the existence within Judaism of a rational principle of development whose changing manifestations the historian could expect to trace. Although, as noted above, Geiger was determined to use historical criticism to demolish prevalent norms, he was intent as well on using history to establish a new foundation for Jewish identity. What he termed the "religious genius" of the Jews became the explanatory principle for Jewish creativity as well as the basis for continuity in Jewish history.[39]

Heinrich Graetz, the most important Jewish historian of the nineteenth century, embarked on a middle course between those of Jost and Geiger. His eleven-volume *History of the Jews* (1853–76) sought to do equal justice to their political history and to their spiritual legacy,[40] which required defining the object of Jewish history more broadly than did his contemporaries. For Graetz, as for Jost, the external history of the Jews remained a tale of imposed suffering, though his sympathies were invariably with the victims. But for the inner history of the Jews, it was not Geiger's religious genius that served as the unit of historical continuity but rather the Jewish *Volks-seele* (collective soul) with its broader cultural as well as religious modes of expression. That concept also made it possible for him to draw together diverse Jewish historical experiences which, in Jost's writing, had remained anchored in their particular contexts. Instead of simply piecing together histories of individual communities, he was able to give Jewish history an unprecedented unity without making that unity dependent upon the prevalence of a single idea. The object of Jewish historiography became, as Graetz put it, both corporeal and spiritual, political and religious/moral.[41]

However, neither Graetz's focus on the collective soul of the Jewish people nor his greater appreciation for the breadth of Jewish creativity made him a romantic or an historicist. Like Jost and Geiger, Graetz was a rationalist who could muster little sympathy for Jewish mystical movements. Like writers of the Enlightenment, he remained a critic and judge of his material, unwilling or unable to penetrate those phases of the Jewish past with which he could not identify. He followed an even older tradition in his occasional ascription of historical events to the intervention of "the finger of God" and his ultimate explanation for the Jewish people's sufferings as divine chastisement for its sins. Only later, in Eastern Europe, where Jewish nationalism fully displaced Jewish religion for some of the religiously disaffected, did a strictly secular Jewish historiography emerge.

Like the maskilim, Graetz focused on individuals. Some historical characters play the same exemplary role in his writings as they do in the earlier biographies. But more important, Graetz's extensive attention to life histories contributes to the drama of his writing. Historical characters appear as foils for one another: the false messiah Shabbetai Zevi and the philosopher Baruch Spinoza in the seventeenth century; the rationalist Moses Mendelssohn and the mystical founder of Hasidism Israel ben Eliezer in the eighteenth. Graetz also liberally strews his accounts with villains: the assimilationists, the antisemites, and especially the apostates who turned on their erstwhile coreligionists.

Although an effort has been made to find Rankean influence on Graetz's historical writing,[42] his chief motivation was not to apply criteria derived from German scholarship to Jewish sources, as had been true for the young Zunz. By the time that Graetz began to write his history in the second half of the nineteenth century,

Wissenschaft des Judentums was, though insufficiently recognized, certainly well established. Thanks to the work of a small cadre of dedicated scholars and the broad outlines established by Jost, knowledge of the Jewish past was no longer as fragmented as it had been earlier. It was chiefly internal considerations that impelled Graetz to undertake Jost's project anew. Jewish consciousness had eroded significantly for two generations since the onset of cultural integration and of the fitful process leading to complete civil equality. In its more integrated organization of material, its biographical focal points, and its vivid, dramatic presentation, Graetz's history served to draw together and find roots for a Jewish identity battered and diminished by modernity. It therefore resorted to the Jewish past not in order to break norms, broaden enlightenment, or gain political or intellectual acceptance, but rather to regain a sense of Jewish separateness by revealing the separate historical path of the Jews.

In the last volume of his history, Graetz reflected on the work of his predecessors and indicated implicitly where his own approach differed. Modern Jewish historiography had had to begin with a past that was disfigured and misconstrued. Heaped up memories had been preserved only piecemeal and imperfectly. Christian scholars had patched together their particular kind of account. Then Jost had snatched away Clio's pen from Christian hands and undertaken to give the fragments a different configuration. It was Jost's great achievement to have furnished "a guide to the labyrinth." But his predecessor had remained an apologist who could seldom convey enthusiasm for his subject and did not see it whole. According to Graetz, "he tore the heroic drama of many thousands of years into nothing but tatters."[43]

In fact, however, Jost did not tear a coherent fabric asunder. Rather he loosely stitched together sources that he found unconnected, leaving the differences among various phases of the Jewish past clearly apparent. Graetz declared that his own approach was entirely different; not accumulative but dialectical—and hence fully integrative. Modernity for the Jewish people, Graetz argued, had not brought about the end of Jewish history but a remarkable resurrection: "a people arose out of the night of the grave, the only one that the annals of human memory attest."[44] Modern scholarship had given the impetus to self-examination, hence to self-discovery, and finally to heightened self-consciousness. In awakening the people to its past, it had deepened its sense of self and founded its claim to further historical existence. To write about the Jewish past, in Graetz's view, was thus a way to re-create the Jewish people even as

German historians were unearthing their history to create a German national identity. As historicism in Germany came increasingly to center upon the German legacy and to act as a force for German unity, so did Graetz come to view study of the Jewish past as a tool for reversing the declining salience of Jewish identity in a community by then well on the road to social, cultural, and political integration. It was this motive, carried further to national consciousness and divested of its close religious connection, which came to prominence in Eastern Europe toward the end of the nineteenth century.

Notes

1. The general works include Nathan Rotenstreich, *Tradition and Reality: The Impact of History on Modern Jewish Thought* (New York, 1972); *Ideas of Jewish History*, ed. Michael A. Meyer (New York, 1974); Lionel Kochan, *The Jew and His History* (New York, 1977); and Yosef Hayim Yerushalmi, *Zakhor: Jewish History and Jewish Memory* (Seattle and London, 1982).

2. Isaac Euchel, *Toledot rabenu he-hakham Moshe ben Menahem* (Berlin, 1788), 123. Cf. the article, signed only with initials, in *Ha-Me'asef* 1 (1784): 9–14, 25–30, which not only contains an extended argument for the usefulness of studying ancient history but attempts to assimilate basic historical epistemology, apparently learned from some contemporary non-Jewish source, to traditional Jewish categories.

3. Ibid., 112–13. On Euchel see Shmuel Feiner, "Isaac Euchel—'Entrepreneur' of the Haskalah Movement in Germany" [Hebrew], *Zion* 52 (1987): 427–69.

4. The maskilim were the proponents of Jewish enlightenment, especially through the cultivation of secular disciplines such as science, philosophy, and literature. Their movement was called the Haskalah.

5. Thus, for example, Peter Beer, in his *Toledot yisra'el* (Prague, 1796), not only provided a retold account of biblical history in place of the traditional text but also added suggestions for teachers and students as to what moral lessons they could draw from the events.

6. Markus Fischer, "Orobio," *Sulamith* 4:1 (1812): 417–24; S. Löwisohn, *Vorlesungen über die neuere Geschichte der Juden* (Vienna, 1820), 92, 94–98; Reuven Michael, "The Contribution of *Sulamith* to Modern Jewish Historiography" [Hebrew], *Zion* 39 (1974): 86–113.

7. *Ha-Me'asef,* 9:1 (1810): 20–32, 43–48, 72–80.

8. Marcus Fischer, *Toledot yeshurun tahat mahadi ve-imam edris* (Prague, 1817); Ruth Kestenberg-Gladstein, *Neuere Geschichte der Juden in den böhmischen Ländern* (Tübingen, 1969), 275–83.

9. S. H. Lieben, "Die Ramschak Chronik," *Jahrbuch der Gesellschaft für Geschichte der Juden in der Čechoslov Republik* 1 (1929), 369–409. As Lieben

points out, Fischer was not alone in forging historical documents. In 1818 the Bohemian writer and librarian Václav Hanka published the fake Königenhofer manuscript, which he had claimed to discover. Within the Jewish community there was likewise a previous instance. As early as 1793 Saul Berlin, like Fischer, the enlightened scion of a rabbinical family, had published a bogus collection of medieval responsa, entitled *Besamim rosh*, that made the fourteenth-century rabbinate appear remarkably lenient.

10. Solomon Maimon, *Lebensgeschichte*, 2 vols. (Berlin, 1792–93), 2:232–36.
11. Ibid., 1:163.
12. Peter Beer, *Kelch des Heils* (Prague, 1802), 266–67.
13. *Geschichte, Lehren und Meinungen aller bestandenen und noch bestehenden religiösen Sekten der Juden und der Geheimlehre der Cabbalah*, 2 vols. (Brünn, 1822–23). Quite apart from its ideological interest, the work is important as the first comprehensive historical study of the Jewish religion by a modern Jew. Cf. Reuven Michael, "Peter Beer (1758–1838)—Author of the First Monograph on Jewish Sects" [Hebrew], *Proceedings of the Ninth World Congress of Jewish Studies* B-2 (Jerusalem, 1986), 1–7.
14. Unlike Fischer's history of the Jews of North Africa, which carried a subscribers' list headed by the Prague rabbis, Elazar Fleckeles and Samuel Landau, Beer's writings provoked the wrath of traditional Jews.
15. Gershom Scholem, *Luaḥ Ha-Aretz* 4 (1944–45), 101–2.
16. Letter to Joseph Dérenbourg, Nov. 18, 1836, *Allgemeine Zeitung des Judentums* 60 (1896): 165.
17. Abraham Geiger, "Über selbständige Mischnaerklärung," *Literur-Blatt zum Israelit des 19. Jahrunderts* (Dec. 14, 1845), 25.
18. Cf. my "Abraham Geiger's Historical Judaism," in *New Perspectives on Abraham Geiger*, ed. Jakob J. Petuchowski (Cincinnati, 1975), 3–16.
19. Cf. Peter Hanns Reill, *The German Enlightenment and the Rise of Historicism* (Berkeley, 1975), 214.
20. Hermann Wesendonck, *Die Begründung der neueren deutschen Geschichtsschreibung durch Gatterer und Schlözer* (Leipzig, 1876), 128, 149; Reill, *German Enlightenment*, 29, 45–46, 101, 214. Even Barthold Neibuhr's critical and erudite history of Rome has been described as less a narrative than "a string of dissertations." (G. P. Gooch, *History and Historians in the Nineteenth Century* [London, 1913], 22.) The same was true for the historical work of Leopold Zunz, the founder of Wissenschaft des Judentums.
21. Jörn Rüsen, "Von der Aufklärung zum Historismus: Idealtypische Perspektiven eines Strukturwandels," in *Von der Aufklärung zum Historismus: Zum Strukturwandel des historischen Denkens*, ed. Horst Walter Blanke and Jörn Rüsen (Paderborn, 1984), 40; Hans Erich Bödeker et al., "Einleitung: Aufklärung und Geschichtswissenschaft," in *Aufklärung und Geschichte*, ed. Hans Erich Bödeker et al. (Gottingen, 1986), 15–21.
22. Georg G. Iggers, *The German Conception of History: The National Tradition of Historical Thought from Herder to the Present*, rev. ed. (Middletown, Conn., 1983), 8–9.

23. Leopold Zunz, *Etwas über die rabbinische Litteratur, nebst Nachrichten über ein altes bis jetzt ungedrucktes hebräisches Werk* (Berlin, 1818), 5 (emphasis Zunz). Cf. Leon Wieseltier, "*Etwas über die jüdische Historik*: Leopold Zunz and the Inception of Modern Jewish Historiography," *History and Theory* 20 (1981): 135–49. Some of Zunz's own later work nonetheless displayed an obvious present-minded subjectivity.

24. See my *The Origins of the Modern Jew: Jewish Identity and European Culture in Germany, 1749–1824* (Detroit, 1967), 177–78.

25. [Jacques] Basnage, *The History of the Jews from Jesus Christ to the Present Time*, trans. Thomas Taylor (London, 1708), ix. On Basnage see Miriam Yardeni, "New Concepts of Post-Commonwealth Jewish History in the Early Enlightenment: Bayle and Basnage," *European Studies Review* 7 (1977): 245–58; Lester A. Segal, "Jacques Basnage de Beauval's *l'Histoire des Juifs*: Christian Historiographical Perception of Jewry and Judaism on the Eve of the Enlightenment," *Hebrew Union College Annual* 54 (1983): 303–24.

26. Basnage, *History of the Jews*, 755–56. Peter Beer followed Basnage in preferring Karaites to Rabbinites.

27. *Geschichte der Juden von den ältesten Zeiten bis auf die Gegenwart* 10 (Leipzig, 1868), 315–18.

28. Hannah Adams, *The History of the Jews, from the Destruction of Jerusalem to the Present Time*, 2 vols. (Boston, 1812). On Adams see Anita Libman Lebeson, "Hannah Adams and the Jews," *Historia Judaica* 8 (1946): 113–34.

29. Adams, *History of the Jews*, 2:325.

30. Ibid., 2:330.

31. Hannah Adams, *Die Geschichte der Juden von der Zerstörung Jerusalems an bis auf die gegenwärtigen Zeiten*, 2 vols. (Leipzig, 1819), 1:vii, xiii. See the critical review in the Jewish journal *Sulamith* 6:1 (1820–21): 180–81. The reviewer had hoped that Adams's book could serve as a usable history text in Jewish schools.

32. Zunz, *Etwas über die rabbinische Litteratur*, 3.

33. Salman Rubaschoff, "Erstlinge der Entjudung: Drei Reden von Eduard Gans im Kulturverein," *Der Jüdische Wille* 1 (1918): 113.

34. I. M. Jost, *Geschichte der Israeliten seit der Zeit der Maccabäer bis auf unsre Tage*, 9 vols. (Berlin, 1820–28). It was later followed by his *Neuere Geschichte der Israeliten von 1815 bis 1845*, 3 vols. (Berlin, 1846–47), which included one volume devoted to cultural history. The most extensive study of Jost is the Hebrew volume by Reuven Michael, *I. M. Jost, Founder of Modern Jewish Historiography* (Jerusalem, 1983). See also his "Jost, Graetz and Dubnow on the Singularity of Jewish History" [Hebrew], in *Transition and Change in Modern Jewish History: Essays Presented to Shmuel Ettinger* (Jerusalem, 1987), 501–26, and the earlier evaluation by Salo W. Baron, "I. M. Jost the Historian," *Proceedings of the American Academy for Jewish Research* 1 (1928–30): 7–32. For a different interpretation of Jost from that given here see Ismar Schorsch, "From Wolfenbüt-

tel to Wissenschaft: The Divergent Paths of Isaak Markus Jost and Leopold Zunz," *Leo Baeck Institute Year Book* 22 (1977): 109–28.

35. [Wilhelm] Friedentahl, "Dr. I. M. Jost: Eine biographische Skizze," *Jahrbuch für Israeliten* 19 (1861): 142.

36. *Geschichte der Israeliten*, 7:83–84.

37. See his letter in *Kerem Hemed* 9 (1856): 133.

38. I. M. Jost, "Beitrag zur jüdischen Geschichte und Bibliographie," *Wissenschaftliche Zeitschrift für jüdische Theologie* 1 (1835): 358.

39. See Geiger's review of Jost's history in *Wissenschaftliche Zeitschrift für jüdische Theologie* 1 (1835): 170–82; 2 (1836): 505–16; and his *Das Judentum und seine Geschichte* (Breslau, 1864), 27–36.

40. Work on Graetz includes the essays by Shmuel Ettinger and Reuven Michael in Zvi Graetz, *Darkhe ha-historiyah ha-yehudit* (Jerusalem, 1969), and the introduction by Ismar Schorsch in Heinrich Graetz, *The Structure of Jewish History and Other Essays* (New York, 1975). Other items are listed in Stephen L. Sniderman, "Bibliography of Works about Heinrich Graetz," *Studies in Bibliography and Booklore* 14 (1982): 41–49.

41. Heinrich Graetz, *Geschichte der Juden* 1 (Leipzig, 1874), xxxi–xxxiii.

42. Salo Baron, "Graetzens Geschichtsschreibung: Eine methodologische Untersuchung," *Monatsschrift für Geschichte und Wissenschaft des Judentums* 62 (1918): 5–15; Hans Liebeschütz, "Jewish Thought in Its German Background," *Leo Baeck Institute Year Book* 1 (1956): 217–21. For a contrary view, see F. I. Baer, "On Our Historical Studies" [Hebrew], *Magnes Anniversary Book* (Jerusalem, 1938), 35.

43. *Geschichte der Juden* 11 (Leipzig, 1870), 448–57.

44. Ibid., 448.

CHAPTER 4

Heinrich Graetz and Heinrich von Treitschke: A Comparison of Their Historical Images of the Modern Jew

In 1870 the Jewish historian Heinrich Graetz published volume 11 of his *Geschichte der Juden,* which brought his magnum opus down to the most recent period of Jewish history. Well over half of its nearly 600 pages were devoted to the Jews of Germany, though at the time they made up little more than a tenth of the world Jewish population. Nine years later, in the summer of 1879, the German historian Heinrich von Treitschke read Graetz's work in preparing volume 2 of his own multi-volume opus, *Deutsche Geschichte im Neunzehnten Jahrundert* (1878–94). He was appalled and angered by what he found: Graetz's writing represented in the form of historical narrative just those attributes which explained, and almost justified, the virulent antisemitism then spreading in Berlin. Only a few weeks after reading Graetz, Treitschke lent his own voice to the chorus of protest against an allegedly ruinous Jewish influence in Germany and held Graetz up as the best example of Jewish adherence to anti-German and anti-Christian attitudes. The dispute which ensued drew in leading German Jews as well as Theodor Mommsen, Treitschke's colleague at the University of Berlin. In recent years the public debate of 1879–81 has received ample scholarly discussion.[1] Much less attention, however, has been given to analyzing Graetz's historiography with the intent of explaining why it should so have provoked Treitschke. And no one, to my knowledge, has attempted to compare Graetz's historical image of modern German Jews with the quite extensive historical treatment Treitschke himself accorded to the same figures in the volumes of his history.

Such a comparison is especially intriguing because, however

differently they regarded the modern Jew, Graetz and Treitschke were remarkably alike in the manner of their historiography. For neither man was historical scholarship merely an antiquarian discipline. They both wrote as much or more to educate and inspire as to add to historical knowledge.[2] Graetz disdained the work of his predecessor, Isaac Marcus Jost, precisely because it was so disconnected and bloodless. His own writing, in contrast, breathed a partisan commitment to Jewish revival within the modern world. No less enthusiastic and abundantly apparent in his historical work was the Saxon Treitschke's intense commitment to his adopted Prussia: to the values it represented and to its self-assigned hegemony in Germany. Each man wrote with glowing passion, believing that historiography itself could play a significant role in the formation of contemporary attitudes and loyalties. For Graetz, as for Treitschke, history was not driven by impersonal forces. The Jewish past, Graetz held, was a "many thousand year heroic drama" (*Heldendrama*) in which great men struggled to overcome obstacles and villainies. Collectively, the Jews were a *Heldenvolk*, a heroic people which, with God's help, valiantly battled for survival against its foes.[3] So too Treitschke wrote history more as heroic drama than as dispassionate analysis. Prussia, the champion of genuine Germanic values, had been singled out to play its decisive role against an odious France, and was destined to unite a fragmented Germany.[4] In each man's work great individuals, embodying national ideals, draw the reader's identification and stand as models for emulation. Neither Graetz nor Treitschke hesitated to cast judgments upon historical characters. On the contrary, praise and blame, adulation and condemnation, determined according to their own ideological criteria, seemed to each of them an integral part of the historian's task. Indeed, it was precisely because these two men had so similar a commitment to employing history for directing present and future that their opposing historical images of modern Jews in Germany conflicted so violently. Let us then examine these images in some detail.

For Graetz, modern Jewish history begins in the eighteenth century with Moses Mendelssohn. Emerging from the medieval ghetto, Mendelssohn became a celebrity in Berlin on account of his masterful German prose, his literary criticism, and his popular philosophical writing. Yet we are reminded that he remained an observant Jew who resisted all attempts to deprive him of his Jewish loyalty. Graetz devotes almost two full chapters, nearly a hundred pages, to Mendelssohn's life and achievements. The reason for this centrality is quite apparent. Mendelssohn's biography, Graetz tells us, was "paradigmatic" for the history of the Jews in modern times, for their upward struggle from lowliness and disdain to a new level of self-consciousness and self-respect. By showing them the possibility of integrating modern culture with Jewish identity, Mendelssohn liberated his fellow Jews from their largely self-imposed isolation. Personally, he freed himself of the uncouth manners and narrow intellectual preoccupations of the ghetto. He overcame the ugly Judeo-German jargon and rejected the "perverse, unruly mode of thought" which characterized talmudic *pilpul.* He gained an aesthetic sensitivity absent from the world of his childhood. All of this, however, did not distance Mendelssohn from Judaism. On the contrary, it opened the possibility for understanding the earliest sources of Judaism, especially the biblical literature, in their remarkable simplicity and truth. Mendelssohn's transformation from ghetto to modern Jew, as Graetz pictures it, is essentially external. He successfully shook off all the disfiguring excrescences which had attached themselves to Judaism during the centuries of its isolation, revealing its true values. Thus he prepared the way not for assimilation but for revival and rejuvenation.[5]

Because Mendelssohn sought to integrate modernity into Judaism rather than sacrificing his Jewish identity to it, he aroused the dismay of non-Jewish writers who believed modernity compatible with Christianity alone. It is in stubbornly resisting the enticement of men like the Swiss pastor Johann Caspar Lavater to draw him to Christianity that Graetz's Mendelssohn becomes heroic and the model for succeeding generations. Fortunately, however, he did not have to confront a wholly hostile and seductive non-Jewish world. Graetz provides Mendelssohn with a German counterpart, Gotthold Ephraim Lessing, no less a liberator and regenerator of his own people. "He was," says Graetz, "the first free man in Germany, freer perhaps than the royal hero Frederick [the Great]." The friendship which developed between Mendelssohn and Lessing is not less paradigmatic for Graetz than the figure of Mendelssohn himself. It represents the origins of that mutually fructifying dialogue between equals that German Jewry always hoped for but failed to achieve. Not surprisingly, Graetz dwelled at length upon Lessing's play *Nathan the Wise.* For what *Nathan* represents to Graetz is not merely Lessing's high regard for Mendelssohn, who might have gained his virtue as the result of his exit from an enclosed Jewish society, but gentile recognition that a *medieval* Jew, immersed in his own heritage, could be freer of prejudice than his Christian contemporaries. Even the most enlightened spirits of the eighteenth century—Graetz adds to make sure the point is not lost—still needed to liberate themselves from prejudices with which Nathan was not burdened.[6]

Lessing's message fitted well into Graetz's conception: Mendelssohn did not have to learn tolerance from Christians; it was inherent in his own tradition.

Interestingly, Heinrich von Treitschke fully shares Graetz's high regard for Moses Mendelssohn. But he draws a very different portrait. Mendelssohn appears in Treitschke's history as the first talented German Jew to successfully transcend his ingrained Jewish heritage and thus contribute significantly to German culture. To be sure, he remained loyal to the religious beliefs of his ancestors and resisted Lavater's attempts to convert him, but what mattered is that he liberated himself from Jewish *national* characteristics. Unlike others who followed him, Mendelssohn did not seek "to drench the German world in Jewish ideas."[7] His contribution was made as a German, not as a Jew, indeed despite his Jewish origins. Vis-à-vis his fellow Jews, Mendelssohn's self-appointed task, as Treitschke saw it, was not to revive Judaism, but to win his coreligionists for German culture. Thus Mendelssohn is as paradigmatic for Treitschke as he is for Graetz, except that here he appears as the first model of successful Germanization, striking proof that Jews can emancipate themselves from their origins, that they can cross the divide from Jewishness to Germanness. For Treitschke this was a liberal, and certainly a nonracist position. But, of course, it left no room for dialogue.

Mendelssohn fell into the first of five categories of modern Jews which Treitschke had enumerated in his dispute with Graetz.[8] He was among the "very many estimable, good patriots" who had emerged within German Jewry since the eighteenth century. They were to be distinguished, in turn, from "the multitude of unadulterated Orientals," the best example of which was Graetz himself; a swarm of homeless international journalists; large cosmopolitan financial powers, such as the Rothschilds;[9] and finally, from the "generally harmful elements" making up the unassimilated Jewish lower class.

Treitschke's history presents us with some further examples, following Mendelssohn, of Jews who clearly belong to the lone acceptable category. Among them, not surprisingly, are men who converted to Christianity, leaving behind all Jewish associations. Friedrich Julius Stahl, the dogmatic proponent of a Christian state which would exclude Jews from political rights, was "the only great political mind among all thinkers of Jewish blood." Fellow Jews, Treitschke noted, soon ceased to count him among their own—and, indeed, Graetz makes no mention of him whatever.[10] In the same category was Moses Mendelssohn's grandson, Felix. Although Richard Wagner had declared that Felix Mendelssohn's Jewish origins made his music incapable of touching heart and soul,[11] Treitschke was full of admiration for the composer precisely because he regarded Mendelssohn's work as so German. He described the man as "a German from tip to toe." Like his grandfather, Felix Mendelssohn also served Treitschke as evidence that a Jew can achieve true fame in Germany only when he allows his consciousness to dissolve fully and without qualification into the stream of German life. To his honor, Mendelssohn had rescued Germany from the pernicious moral influence of another Jew, Giacomo Meyerbeer, in whom Jewishness and adulation of the French joined to produce a most undesirable foreign import.[12]

Conversion, however, even in the generations after Moses Mendelssohn, was not a prerequisite for gaining Treitschke's positive evaluation. The German historian wrote briefly but favorably of Israel Jacobson and David Friedländer, early leaders of the Jewish Reform movement, because they sought to create "a worthier form of religious service," one which also reduced religious differences between Christians and Jews.[13] He gave more attention to Gabriel Riesser, the great champion of Jewish political equality in Germany. Treitschke described Riesser as a noble and honorable man, dedicated to his German fatherland. He paid him the high compliment of declaring that this moderate liberal possessed deeply German sensitivities (*grunddeutsch empfand*), a tribute he likewise extended to Moritz Veit, the Berlin publisher, politician, and Jewish communal leader. If all Jews had been like Riesser, Treitschke concludes, Jewish emancipation in Germany would not have been problematic.[14]

Treitschke's favorable assessment of the religious reformers and of Riesser may well have been a direct response to the very different portraits of these men drawn by Graetz. During his polemic with the Jewish historian, Treitschke had attacked Graetz for deprecating Jacobson's institution of German prayers and confirmation and belittling Riesser for merging fully into the life of "the country where by chance he was born."[15] For Treitschke, the reformers and Riesser represent a continuation of the assimilation process which Mendelssohn had begun. For Graetz, however, for whom Mendelssohn's heroic virtue lay precisely in his resistance to assimilatory enticements, these men marked an anti-Mendelssohnian trend. They gave in—as he had not—to the temptation of allowing themselves to be fully absorbed by the Christian and German world around them. They did not speak as Jews in fruitful encounter with their surroundings but as men who sought to melt into their environment. In matters of religion Graetz drew the line between decorum and vernacular sermons, which he found acceptable adaptations rooted in Judaism, and more specifically Christian or German intrusions into the religious service. As for Riesser, Graetz shared Treitschke's view that this Jewish politician felt himself far more German than Jew. But for Graetz Riesser's inner transformation set him sharply apart from Mendelssohn.[16] In fact for Graetz it made him less a Jew than two highly talented individuals who had both converted to Christianity: the political journalist Ludwig Börne and the poet Heinrich Heine. Riesser received only a few pages in Graetz's history; Börne and Heine an entire chapter.

Graetz recognized that he needed to justify devoting so much attention to these two men. Rhetorically he immediately asked: "Do Börne and Heine also belong to Jewish history?" His answer was unqualified: "Indeed they do! Not only did Jewish blood flow in their veins, but also Jewish sap coursed through their nerves." Christianity, Graetz insisted, had no right to claim them, nor, fully, did Germany. Paradoxically, these converts were more Jewish, more in the Mendelssohn tradition, than Friedländer, Jacobson, or Riesser. Like Mendelssohn they made their contribution to Germany as Jews and like him resisted the pressures to undergo an inner transformation. Their conversions to Christianity were about as external as when Mendelssohn gave up the old Judeo-German dialect. Each remained rooted in Jewish history. Börne's writing, Graetz contended, recalled the Prophets and the Psalms; Heine's style was comparable to Ibn Ezra, Al-Harizi, and Immanuel of Rome. As he put it: "The varied and attractive blossoms of the Börne-Heine spirit shot up from Jewish soil and were only watered by European culture." Like Mendelssohn and Lessing they were liberators, except that by this time these Jews no longer needed to free themselves from the ghetto; they could instead set out to liberate the Germans from the double yoke of political and social immaturity.[17]

In order to sustain this image of Börne and Heine, Graetz was forced to explain away a great deal of contradictory evidence. Börne, especially, had harsh things to say about Judaism, which long before Marx he had associated with the most egregious features of capitalism.[18] But for Graetz such virulent critique was but a temporary, uncharacteristic lapse induced by the evil influence of the Christian theologian Friedrich Schleiermacher and his soul-mate, the salon Jewess Henriette Herz. Even if Börne did not consciously regard himself as a Jew, he was one in spite of himself. "He did not realize," Graetz says, "how much his inner being, the truthfulness of his nature, owed to Judaism." Once again Graetz speaks of Börne's "Jewish blood," a racial element which is as prominent in Graetz, the Jewish historian, as in Treitschke, the antisemite.[19] Graetz can even muster understanding for Börne's conversion, undertaken in the honest, if illusory, hope that his detractors would not thereafter be able to discount his critiques of German life as coming from a Jew. Graetz has some difficulty, however, in coming to terms with Börne's later and apparently sincere attraction to Catholicism. The best he can say to excuse it is that the poisonous seed implanted by Schleiermacher and Herz once again sprouted forth. But it also gives Graetz occasion to remark that Börne, for all of his virtues, was as a Jew and a writer considerably less than Heinrich Heine. He lacked Heine's depth and sense of history.

To be sure, Heine also became a Christian and made some rather sardonic comments about Jews and Judaism. But self-criticism, where not the product of self-hate, was after all a Jewish quality, and besides, at least some of Heine's scorn was reserved for the imitativeness of the Jewish religious reformers. Heine had indeed lost his faith in the God of Israel, but that once again was the result of a pernicious external influence, in this case the philosophy of Hegel. Unlike Börne, Heine possessed a sense of history and identified himself with the *Leidensgeschichte* of Israel. Despite his opportunistic conversion, he maintained a lifelong antipathy against Christianity and felt guilt about officially forsaking Judaism. Heine did once call Judaism "a misfortune,"[20] but increasingly his underlying love for his heritage broke forth, until toward the end of his life he returned to Judaism in all but name. Graetz's enthusiasm for the late Heine even waxes theological: "The spirit of Jewish law and of Jewish history had indeed come upon this errant son of Israel and revealed to him what few before him had grasped in depth and none depicted so luminously." Together, Börne and Heine reduced German hatred of the Jews because they proved the Jewish capacity to contribute richly to German letters, as much, Graetz insisted, as any non-Jew in their generation. Their writings also brought Germany and France closer together, helping to prepare the messianic age of reconciliation among nations. That union, to Graetz, was the Jewish national vocation, to which both Börne and Heine had remained faithful. They were thus modern Jews in the best sense, bringing their own national spirit to bear upon the larger world without allowing it to fully absorb them.

Treitschke's historical image of Börne and Heine corresponds with the one drawn by Graetz in that for him too they remained lifelong Jews.[21] But for Treitschke these two men represent a radical departure from Mendelssohn. They were Jews who sought to impose their foreign ideas upon Germany—and that at a time when a disunited and insecure German nation was most vulnerable to deleterious influence. Unlike the French and English, the Germans had not yet been able to create a firm national character capable of resisting subversive notions of state and society. Yet it was just at this time that there occurred what Treitschke called a Jewish "invasion" (*Einbruch*) of the inner sanctum of German culture, a "pollution" of the German essence. The chief culprits of this foreign intrusion were, of course, Börne and Heine.

In fairness to Treitschke it must be noted that, even late in life, when he had long forsaken liberalism and was generally regarded as an antisemite, he did not allow ideology to fully overwhelm his sense of judgment. He did not demonize Börne and Heine in the manner of later antisemites; in fact he expressed some admiration for the achievements of each one. But the completed images are nonetheless repugnant. Börne, despite his conversion, retained the "racial pride of the chosen people." Despite his efforts to write as a German, his German national feeling was like a graft that did not take hold. He remained a stranger, a Jew more French than German. His style was clearly un-German, he lacked soul, he could only imitate. Worst of all, and most ominous, Börne corrupted the German youth, which believed his criticisms of Germany, and so came to despise their own patrimony. Like Graetz, Treitschke recognized the greater genius of Heine, but it lay not at all in his Jewishness. The young Heine, Treitschke generously admits, did capture something of the German soul. But this was Heine at his least political and least Jewish—the Heine who wrote some fine lyrics in his *Buch der Lieder* and refashioned the song of the Lorelei. The later Heine, more Jewish and more French, was bereft of the German muse. He lacked any sense for the sacred, despised Christianity, and fell victim to the rank heresy of setting the sovereign individual above the state. Full of admiration for France, Germany's archenemy, Heine resonated with French *esprit* but was barren of German *Geist*. Above all, he remained a Jew, an Oriental, though of a peculiarly modern type. No longer fully rooted in Judaism, Treitschke's Heine absorbed influences from the outside, but was never able to enter fully into any tradition. He could only flit back and forth from one opinion or mode of sensibility to another. He never gained inner unity. Neither fully German nor fully French, receptive but not creative, he was a virtuoso of form who lacked substance.

There remains one modern Jew toward whom both Graetz and Treitschke harbored ambivalence. Rahel Varnhagen, the most intellectually gifted of the Jewish salonieres, drew the praise of each historian for her insight, truthfulness, and gentle character. For Graetz, her effervescent, winged spirit could be attributed to the "talmudic blood" which flowed in her veins. Despite her strayings and her baptism, she too, like Heine, returned, though only in the final hour when on her deathbed she confessed to the personal significance of her Jewish origins. But like the other "sinful" Jewish women of her circle, she lived her life by values Graetz could not identify as Jewish. Once again it was a Christian who had led her astray: "The seducer of this 'little woman with the large soul,' (as she was called) was Goethe. His poetry and worldly wisdom, his pagan ideas, became Rahel's Bible. . . ." Graetz himself recognized Goethe's greatness, but he set him alongside Fichte as the two leading German intellects whose desire to exclude the Jews from an essentially post-Christian society marked a new state in the history of antisemitism. That Rahel should have become a devotee of Fichte and the most effective popularizer of Goethe placed her on the side of Judaism's enemies. Her admiration for these men was as much or more a betrayal of Jewish loyalty as was her later baptism.[22]

Treitschke's problem with Rahel was a different one. His own veneration for Fichte and Goethe was so great that he felt most uncomfortable with the knowledge that a Jewish woman should have become an exponent of their ideas, and in the case of Goethe even deserved credit for bringing his contributions to the attention of cultured circles in Berlin. Like Graetz, Treitschke sensed residual Jewish characteristics in Rahel. But he defined them differently. Alongside her amiable qualities, Treitschke thought it necessary to note, Rahel also possessed "a half unconscious and for that reason boundless vanity," so that in admiring the finest German poet she was really only gratifying her own ego and comforting herself for a felt lack of creativity. Too much in the enemy camp for Graetz to claim her, to Treitschke's historical eye she remained self-centered and spiritually barren, imbued with typically Jewish qualities which kept her separate and apart from the men she admired—the men who represented Treitschke's Germany.[23]

We know that when Treitschke read the eleventh volume of Graetz's history, he "could scarcely find words to express his disgust." He was especially infuriated by what he perceived as the author's intense detestation of Christianity and Germanism: "The man shakes with glee every time he can say something downright nasty against the Germans."[24] Treitschke was not wrong about Graetz's feelings. While preparing the volume in 1868 Graetz had written to his friend the proto-Zionist Moses Hess: "I am looking forward with pleasure to scourging the Germans and their leaders—Schleiermacher, Fichte, and the whole wretched Romantic school."[25]

Treitschke was not only revolted by Graetz's work when he first read it, he was forced to go through it again carefully to marshal quotations in the course of the subsequent public dispute. The volume seems definitely to have played a role in his progress toward antisemitism, and its negative emotional impact must have remained with him even after the dispute was over. So too, I would contend, did the images of modern Jews which he found on its pages. To be sure, Treitschke remained sufficiently a liberal to allow that some Jews could become fully Germans. He would not allow that such a favorable trend was not characteristic of at least some men of Jewish origin, and hence the desire to find it already in Mendelssohn. But Graetz confirmed Treitschke in the notion that those modern Jews associated with France, with individualism, or with acerbic critique of Germanic and Christian values were still Jews in essence and acting from innate, Jewish characteristics which they themselves may not have fully appreciated. Graetz and Treitschke agreed that modern Jews could either be absorbed by German culture or interact with it from the independent position that Treitschke called "neo-Jewish."[26] They differed on which individuals belonged to each category and which type should become the paradigm.

Notes

1. The principal sources are gathered in Walter Boehlich, ed., *Der Berliner Antisemitismusstreit* (Frankfurt am Main, 1965). See the studies by Sigurd Graf von Pfeil, "Heinrich von Treitschke und das Judentum," *Die Welt als Geschichte* 21 (1961): 49–62; Hans Liebeschütz, "Treitschke and Mommsen on Jewry and Judaism," *Leo Baeck Institute Year Book (LBIYB)* 7 (1962): 153–82; idem, *Das Judentum im deutschen Geschichtsbild von Hegel bis Max Weber* (Tübingen, 1967), 157–219; and Michael Meyer, "Great Debate on Antisemitism: Jewish Reaction to New Hostility in Germany, 1879–1881," *LBIYB* 11 (1966): 137–70. For an annotated listing of studies dealing with Graetz's historiography see Stephen L. Sniderman, "Bibliography of Works About Heinrich Graetz," *Studies in Bibliography and Booklore* 14 (1982): 41–49.
2. Simon Bernfeld, "Dorshe reshumot," *Ha-Shiloah* 2 (1897): 397–98. Yet there is no apparent common personal or intellectual influence. Treitschke studied at Bonn where he came under the tutelage of the political historian Friedrich Christoph Dahlmann. Graetz attended the University of Breslau where the most significant influence on him was a historian of philosophy, Christlieb Julius Braniss.

3. Heinrich Graetz, *Geschichte der Juden* (Leipzig, 1870), 11:456; Boehlich, *Der Berliner Antisemitismusstreit*, 251.

4. Antoine Guilland, *Modern Germany and Her Historians* (New York, 1915), 254–325; Andreas Dorpalen, *Heinrich von Treitschke* (New Haven, 1957), 218, 286.

5. *Geschichte der Juden*, 11:311–13, 27, 41. Graetz finds some of the Mendelssohnian qualities also in his contemporary, Elijah, the Gaon of Vilna. In a more favorable milieu than Poland, he notes, Elijah would likewise have been able to work for the rejuvenation of his fellow Jews. However, he possessed the defect of slavishly venerating the Kabbalah, which Graetz believed was an aberration of Judaism. (Ibid., 118–21.)

6. Ibid., 36–38.

7. Heinrich von Treitschke, *Deutsche Geschichte im Neunzehnten Jahrhundert*, 5 vols. (Leipzig, 1878–94), 3:703. Cf. idem, *Politik. Vorlesungen gehalten an der Universität zu Berlin*, ed. Max Cornicelius (Leipzig, 1897), 276.

8. Boehlich, *Der Berliner Antisemitismusstreit*, 79.

9. Of the Rothschild firm Treitschke wrote that "it was not German, as had been those of the Fuggers and Welsers, but manifested from the start the cosmopolitan character of modern Judaism." (*Deutsche Geschichte*, 2:164–65.)

10. Ibid., 5:55, 414–16. To Treitschke it was quite obvious that "a living sense of politics must remain foreign to a people which centuries ago had lost its national state."

11. Richard Wagner, *Das Judenthum in der Musik* (Leipzig, 1869), 25.

12. *Deutsche Geschichte*, 4:454–55, where Treitschke revels in the irony of it: "Thus a German of Jewish extraction led our cultured society back to the old traditions of its national art precisely in the days of the Paris *Deutsch-Juden*." Felix Mendelssohn had the additional virtue for Treitschke of having already been appreciated as a child by no less a figure than Goethe (ibid., 2:44–45.) The very qualities which endeared Mendelssohn to Treitschke, however, made him odious to Heinrich Heine. See S. S. Prawer, "Heine's Portraits of German and French Jews on the Eve of the 1848 Revolution," in Werner E. Mosse et al., eds., *Revolution and Evolution in German-Jewish History* (Tübingen, 1981), 359–66.

13. *Deutsche Geschichte*, 2:417.

14. Ibid., 5:632.

15. Boehlich, *Der Berliner Antisemitismusstreit*, 40–41.

16. *Geschichte der Juden*, 171–73, 412–15, 470–73. Graetz held it against Riesser that he did not join Moses Montefiore and Adolphe Cremieux, as the representative of German Jewry, on their trip to the Near East in 1840 on behalf of the falsely accused Jews of Damascus (ibid., 551).

17. Ibid., 368–407.

18. On this subject see now Orlando Figes, "Ludwig Borne and the Formation of a Radical Critique of Judaism," *LBIYB* 29 (1984): 351–82.

19. *Geschichte der Juden*, 373. Already on the first page of his preface to the volume Graetz refers to the Jews interchangeably as *Stamm, Volk,* and *Rasse*.

20. It is at least curious and ironic that Treitschke should have used just this term—*Unglück*—to describe how many Germans in 1879 felt about the Jewish presence in their midst (Boehlich, *Der Berliner Antisemitismusstreit,* 11). While it is most likely a coincidence, one wonders whether Graetz's citation of Heine's personal reference (*Geschichte der Juden,* 400) may not have led Treitschke to pick out this particular expression. Later "Die Juden sind unser Unglück" became the motto of the Nazi newspaper *Der Stürmer.*

21. For Treitschke on Börne and Heine see *Deutsche Geschichte,* 3:705–14; 4:419–27, 440–43; 5:378–82; *Politik,* 295; Boehlich, *Der Berliner Antisemitismusstreit,* 84–85; Max Cornicelius, ed., *Heinrich Treitschkes Briefe* 2 (Leipzig, 1913), 229–30.

22. *Geschichte der Juden,* 179–81, 245–49.

23. *Deutsche Geschichte,* 2:44–45; 4:428–29. Cf. Sophony Herz, "Treitschke's kritische Haltung gegenüber Berthold Auerbach, Rahel Varnhagen und Fanny Lewald," *Jahrbuch des Instituts für Deutsche Geschichte* 1 (1972): 132–39.

24. Franz Kobler, *Jüdische Geschichte in Briefen aus Ost und West: Das Zeitalter der Emanzipation* (Vienna, 1938), 426–27; Boehlich, Der Berliner Antisemitismusstreit, 42.

25. Heinrich Graetz, *Tagebuch und Briefe,* ed. Reuven Michael (Tübingen, 1977), 287. Further on in the same letter Graetz writes: "We must above all work to shatter Christianity" (*das Talui-thum*).

26. Boehlich, *Der Berliner Antisemitismusstreit,* 83.

CHAPTER 5

Jews as Jews versus Jews as Germans: Two Historical Perspectives

The historiography of modern diaspora Jewries is burdened by methodological problems that are the specific consequence both of these Jewries' modernity and their diaspora status. Until modern times Jewish communities, with rare exceptions, constituted religiously and culturally self-contained units whose internal autonomy was established by political contract and which were related to the outside world mostly by economic ties. There were few religious or cultural differences among Jews living in Poland, Germany, or Eastern France. The principal distinction among them was between Ashkenazim (Yiddish-speaking Central and East European Jews) and Sephardim (Jews of Iberian origin). Jews in German lands considered themselves Jewish, not German, and they were similarly regarded by non-Jews. Consequently, general historians of Medieval Central Europe have treated the Jews in terms of ongoing political and economic relationships as well as of outbreaks of hostility. Historians of Medieval Jewry have added to these externals the closed inner circle of communal and religious life.

Beginning in the eighteenth century, however, the lines began to blur. Increasingly, Jews identified themselves with the countries in which they lived and with the culture of Central and Western Europe. German Jews became differentiated from Jews in England and France, and especially from the still self-contained Jewish communities in the East.[1] As they ceased to live wholly within a Jewish cultural orbit, they entered German history as an internal element. It therefore became necessary for historians of the Jews to treat this modern German Jewry within its German and European cultural context, differentiating it and comparing it with Jewish communities elsewhere. And it became necessary for historians of Germany to deal with the Jewish element within, not outside of, German culture. Thus the Enlightenment and its political concomitants established a new location for German Jewry, one that removed the clear distinction between German and Jew even as it created distinctions among the various communities of the Jewish Diaspora. It became difficult to differentiate Jews as Jews from Jews as Germans. What are the consequences of this situation for the historiography of German Jewry?

For Jewish historians it became necessary to note the increasing differences between German Jews and those in other lands: their adoption of the German language, their religious reform, their participation in German culture, their rise to bourgeois status. They were also forced to note that as these processes went forward they were accompanied by a general diminution in Jewish consciousness as Jewish identity shrank to make room for other identifications. They therefore saw it as their task to trace a constricting circle of Jewishness as assimilation spread within German Jewry and—aside from chronicling the course of antisemitism and Jewish defenses against it—to concentrate on vicissitudes within the remaining Jewish sphere: the Jewish communities and their various activities, Jewish religious thought and ideologies. Reflecting their own narrower view of the nature of Jewishness, some nineteenth-century historians of the Jewish experience went so far as to single out the religious element as the one permanently differentiating feature. Others kept a broader perspective that included the Jewish community as historical agent, although that community now lacked the coercive authority of its medieval forbear. Beyond these domains lay the most problematic area: the role of individual Jews whose degree of Jewishness now varied along a spectrum from Orthodoxy at the one extreme to merely residual elements remaining beyond apostasy on the other. Later Jewish historiography also sometimes tended to view the Jewish experience in Germany through the lens of the Holocaust. German Jewry seemed the best lesson for Jews elsewhere in the perils of self-delusion.

From the viewpoint of German history, modern Jews have been seen quite differently. When it did not ignore them almost entirely or treated them as mere objects of legislation, nineteenth-century general German historiography regarded most German Jews as recalcitrant for daring to retain elements of Jewish differentiation.[2] More recent writing on German history in general has been interested in analyzing the effects of Jewish integration, economically, politically, and culturally, upon German society and the reaction of German society to that integration. Like its Jewish counterpart, it has also focused on the Jews largely from the perspective of the Holocaust. But in this instance that has been less an attempt to explain the Jewish failure to anticipate it than to see the persecution of the Jews within the larger context of Nazism and seek an explanation of why the German people did not sufficiently resist it. German historians down to the present have given little attention to the continuing inner life of the Jews in Germany from the eighteenth century onward. Those who deal with German Protestantism and Catholicism ignore the Jewish religion and the workings of the Jewish community as if these somehow remained foreign to the German scene.[3] On the other hand, cultural historians do deal with those Jews whose cultural influence has been the broadest. Yet such individuals are often far removed from Judaism, and it seldom seems to matter much, if at all, whether they are converts to Christianity.

In short, historians of the Jews have been mainly interested in German Jews as Jews while modern German historians have been interested in them as Germans.

However, it seems that neither perspective does justice to the phenomenon in its totality. German Jews as Jews and German Jews as Germans may be the two sides of a coin, but obverse and reverse images must adhere to each other. Can the two perspectives be brought together?

The difficulty of that task becomes apparent from a few examples. Moses Mendelssohn, the eighteenth-century philosopher and first prominent modern German Jew, has *prima facie* significance for Jewish as for German history. For the former he represents the first clear articulation of a boundary between a new European/German identity and a Jewish one. Because his internalization of Enlightenment values could be understood as an extension of purview, with his Jewishness—in religious terms—remaining intact, he became a paradigm for Jewish Orthodoxy. Because he was the first German Jew highly regarded by non-Jews for his cultural achievements he became no less a paradigm for non-traditional Jews. As the perceived fountainhead of Jewish acculturation, Mendelssohn's importance for German history is likewise beyond dispute, since without that acculturation the individual and collective influence of Jews in Germany would have been negligible and the reaction to Jews very different. The change in Jewish political and economic status, though not directly related to Mendelssohn and beginning somewhat later, was the concomitant of that acculturation.

It is in the post-Mendelssohnian period that the perspectives diverge.[4] Here those individuals who assume the greatest importance in the inner life of the Jewish community—who are the most Jewish in their identity and in their spheres of influence—are not the Jews of interest to historians of Germany since they were little noticed by non-Jews. This clearly holds true for religious developments and those individuals associated with them. The establishment in Germany of a modern orthodoxy, a conservative middle path, and a religious liberalism slowed the process of assimilation. Each of them maintained a publicly acknowledged form of Jewish distinctiveness and even destiny. From the viewpoint of Jewish history, their significance is of the first order. Yet almost all overviews of German history ignore them completely, an omission which seems unjustified on two grounds. First, it indicates a failure to recognize that such figures as Samson Raphael Hirsch, Zacharias Frankel, and Abraham Geiger assume an importance for Jewish history that extends beyond the realm of what is often called the "inner history" of German Jewry: their formulations of Jewish identity had consequences for Jewish-Gentile relationships as well. Second, and more important, it implies the questionable assumption that what goes on mainly within German Jewry is not of consequence for German history, somewhat in the way France becomes important for German historians only in terms of its relations with Germany. But if Jews in Germany from the late eighteenth century onward did indeed become Germans, then surely their inner history is also a part of German history.

Similarly, the development of Wissenschaft des Judentums, like the modernization of Judaism, is a topic almost exclusively discussed from the perspective of Jewish history. Historians of Germany deal with the rise of scientific scholarship generally and with its influence on Christianity. Radicals like David Friedrich Strauss and adherents of the Tübingen School receive attention on account of the challenge they presented to Protestantism in the *Vormärz*. But the parallel effect of the critical study of Jewish sources on Judaism and indirectly on Jewish identity in Germany, that stemmed originally from the circle of Leopold Zunz in the early nineteenth century and widened in succeeding decades, is not noted outside the circle of Jewish historiography.

Although the history of antisemitism in Germany is common to both historiographies, the history of Jewish responses to it is not. The monograph literature on the largest of all Jewish organizations in modern Germany, the Centralverein deutscher Staatsbürger jüdischen Glaubens, is considerable, yet the mention of this organization—to say nothing of its leadership—has remained absent from even the thickest general histories of modern Germany. I could, likewise, find no reference to the Reichsvertretung der deutschen Juden, the representative organization of German Jewry during the 1930s, nor to its remarkable leader, Rabbi Leo Baeck. Antisemitism is judged an important part of German history; its effect on the Jews and their reaction to it is not.

The same, finally, can be said for the history of German Zionism, a subject likewise much studied in recent years but similarly absent from the standard general works on German history. It is of course possible to justify this omission—and those mentioned above—by noting the small percentage of Jews in Germany. In the case of German Zionism, moreover, the movement initially attracted only a very small proportion of this already small number. But for German Jewry Zionism became increasingly important as antisemitism grew stronger, and by the Nazi period it had come to play a very important role. Moreover, by that time Zionism had become a significant consideration for those planning to rid Germany of its Jews.

These phenomena—religious and intellectual developments, communal organizations and strategies, and Jewish ideologies— almost without exception have been left to historians of the Jews; they have been considered a part of Jewish history, but either outside of German history or too insignificant for inclusion in any but specialized studies. If at all aware of them, German historians relegate such matters to the history of Jews acting as Jews within, but not as part of, Germany.

In general, historians of Germany have given the most attention to those Jews furthest removed from Jewishness. Their motives for this preference have been at once deplorable and justifiable. The prevailing conception in German historiography until recent times, that Jews could not be fully German and yet remain Jews in any significant sense, necessarily led to their inclusion only when they had been willing to give up Jewishness entirely, or nearly so. It was not possible for a writer like Heinrich von Treitschke, for example, to regard a fully conscious Jew as a major contributor to German life. More justifiable is concentration on Jewishly peripheral figures simply because in most instances those individuals who achieved the greatest importance for German history were subjectively removed from the inner circle of Jewish life, and often they were converts. Yet there were figures of some importance within the German cultural orbit whose Jewishness—however unorthodox—remained personally and positively significant. Einstein, Freud, and Kafka would be the most outstanding names, but one could add the philosopher Hermann Cohen, the painter Ludwig Meidner, and quite a few others. In such cases, their Jewishness was more than a point of origin and thus deserves more than passing attention.

Still, as noted above, the history of the modern German Jews does describe a curve of decreasing Jewish differentiation, if that differentiation is measured by adherence to indigenously Jewish traditions. But to accept that as the whole picture is to ignore a remarkable phenomenon to which George L. Mosse has repeatedly called our attention: the coming into existence of a new type of differentiation, grounded not in Jewish tradition but in the very experience of acculturation and emancipation itself.[5] Mosse has provided an influential new criterion for historically significant Jewishness that extends beyond community involvement but does not descend to racial considerations. He has argued that acculturating German Jews, beginning in the eighteenth century, developed a lasting attachment to the particular form of *Bildung* that was paradigmatic in the German Enlightenment. They continued to cherish its ideals of toleration, rationalism, and optimism long after most segments of German society had abandoned them. Thus this attachment, which was originally the result of a desire to be like their fellow Germans, came increasingly to distinguish the German Jews from them and form a sort of Jewish identity that was non-Jewish in content but nonetheless marked them as Jews regardless of their closeness or distance from Judaism. The role of *Bildung* in German-Jewish history is clearly of importance both from the side of Jewish history as acculturation and from the side of German history as a significant cultural orientation, rooted in a segment of the German population, and running counter to powerful trends that culminate in the Nazi period.

It is clear also that Jews who converted to Christianity might carry their anachronistic attachment to Enlightenment values with them into their new faith and thus preserve, at least for a time, the residue of a phenomenon that was the product of a collective response of German Jews to their intellectual environment at the beginning of their integration into it. Jewish history does indeed extend beyond the line of apostasy. However, contrary to still common practice, it would seem difficult on these grounds to designate as significantly Jewish the orientation and accomplishments of any decidedly anti-Enlightenment figure, such as the Jewish-born theoretician of the German-Christian state, Friedrich Julius Stahl. Indeed, by any but racial criteria, Stahl stands outside German-Jewish history.[6]

Yet it is remarkable how little significance most writers, Jewish and non-Jewish, have attached to the fact of apostasy, assuming that conversion does not extinguish racial characteristics. Writing about Jewish actors in 1927, Arnold Zweig described them collectively as Mediterranean types whose organ of thought was the ear and whose organ of speech was their bodies. Whether they identified themselves as Jews or Christians did not matter. On the stage they always remained "Jews."[7] More remarkable, in the collective volume entitled *Juden im deutschen Kulturbereich,* which, though originally prepared in the early 1930s was still being revised until its first public distribution in 1959, the editor Siegmund Kaznelson stated that his criterion for inclusion was descent rather than religious affiliation not only as a counterthrust to antisemitic minimization of Jewish achievement, but also "not to expose ourselves to the—justified—reproach of not paying attention to clear biological and historical facts."[8] Specifically, Kaznelson's criterion for determining the participation of the "Jewish element"[9] in German culture was one Jewish parent. In an appendix he added names of individuals often thought to be Jewish but who, in fact, did not meet this minimal racial standard.[10]

A more recent Gentile compiler of short biographies of notable German Jews, Walter Tetzlaff, limited his purview to *Volljuden,* since "half Jews could as well be counted for the other side." But he did include all the baptized without distinction, justifying his decision by what he regarded as the Jews' own definition of themselves as a people rather than a religious denomination.[11] Joseph Walk, in his biographical compilation of twentieth-century German Jews, offered a yet different criterion for including baptized Jews and *Mischlinge*: they were also affected by the Nazis' anti-Jewish measures.[12] Although Tetzlaff's and Walk's criteria may have some justification in biographical dictionaries, they possess only limited validity for a synthetic history, which must also determine the degree to which baptized Jews still consider themselves Jewish and whether their attitudes and accomplishments show any evidence, not only of response to racial antisemitism, but also of identifiable, if residual Jewish influences. Germans treated as Jews by the Nazis, who are no longer such by their own or any other legitimate identity criteria, remain Jews in no sense but that of the oppressor.

Where, then, do the German Jews fit properly into the framework of German historiography? I think at four kinds of junctures. The first are those where Jews have been most often mentioned: when they became the objects of emancipation and the victims of antisemitism. Their acceptance or rejection, as Golo Mann and others have pointed out, clearly reveals much about the state of German society[13] and, as Fritz Stern has noted, also about the German ambivalence to modernity.[14] The Jews' response to changing attitudes, I would add, also reveals something about their self-perceived role in German society. A second kind of juncture occurs with regard to individuals whose contribution to German society or culture is in some way traceable to Jewish influence. Merely to mention the Jewishness of a leading figure in passing, as is commonly done in general works, has little value when a cogent argument, however brief, is not made for its explanatory role—if only to block the reader's flight to a racial explanation. Third, some attention should be given to inner Jewish developments in terms of demographic and identity shifts, the effects of emancipation, the course of acculturation, religious reform, intellectual and ideological developments, and community activity.[15] Hajo Holborn's history of Germany pioneered in introducing discrete sections on the Jews, but antisemitism remained the focal point of his treatment, inner developments sandwiched between references to outer rejection.[16] The first attempts of which I am aware to do justice in a balanced way to the inner life of the Jews in a brief history of modern Germany have come in the excellent summary sections devoted to them in recent works on the nineteenth century by Thomas Nipperdey[17] and Reinhard Rürup.[18] Yet what remains lacking even in their work is the fourth juncture: the mention of relevant parallel phenomena among the Jews and within Judaism when such matters as historical criticism or religiously motivated political activity are discussed for German Protestantism and Catholicism.[19]

Clearly the expansion of Jewish history is also necessary, although I have not dwelt on it here. The history of the Jews in Germany cannot be fully understood without frequent reference not only to the German political context but also to parallel social phenomena among other minority groups[20] and to religious developments within Christianity. This becomes the more important as Jewish integration proceeds during the nineteenth century and in most instances the Jew as Jew gives way more and more to the Jew as German. The composition of the image is altered as German elements merge with or displace Jewish ones.

Where does that leave the historian whose treatment of the German Jews is not intended exclusively either for the framework of German history or for that of Jewish history? Clearly it involves a consideration of both contexts and the shifting location of German Jewry within each of them.[21] It means trying to determine how Jews in different ways and to various degrees became Germans and what the outcome of that process was for themselves, for Jews elsewhere, and for Germany.[22]

Notes

1. For a description of this process see Jacob Katz, "From Ghetto to Zionism: Mutual Influences of East and West," in Isadore Twersky, ed., *Danzig: Between East and West: Aspects of Modern Jewish History* (Cambridge, Mass., 1985), 39–48.
2. Michael A. Meyer, "Heinrich Graetz and Heinrich von Treitschke: A Comparison of their Historical Images of the Modern Jew," *Modern Judaism* 6 (1986): 1–11.
3. Gordon Craig, for example, in his *Germany, 1866–1945* (New York, 1978), devotes a great deal of attention to antisemitism and to the Holocaust, but when dealing with religion mentions only Jewish numbers— and that in the uninformed belief that the 567,884 German Jews in the 1890 census were all "orthodox" (181). When Craig expanded upon the subject of religion in modern Germany in a chapter especially devoted to it in his later volume, *The Germans* (New York, 1982), he limited his discussion there to Protestantism and Catholicism. The Jews appeared in the same volume segregated and separated in a chapter entitled "Germans and Jews."
4. Thus James J. Sheehan, in his *German History, 1770–1866* (Oxford, 1989), devotes two full paragraphs to Mendelssohn (178–79), but is silent on the Jewish Enlightenment that followed, although he deals with its Catholic counterpart. His sections on religion in the nineteenth century deal with Protestantism and Catholicism, but not with Judaism.
5. See especially his *German Jews Beyond Judaism* (Bloomington, Cincinnati, 1983).
6. Yet Franz Schnabel, in his *Deutsche Geschichte im neunzehnten Jahrhundert*, 2nd ed., 4 vols. (Freiburg, 1948–51), three times refers to Stahl's Jewish origins (vol. 2, pp. 36, 249; vol. 4, p. 539), while not mentioning the religious identity of men who remained Jewish their entire lives, like Ferdinand Lassalle and Berthold Auerbach. His fourth volume, which bears the subtitle *Die religiösen Kräfte*, does not discuss the Jewish religion at all. A chapter on Stahl is included in Manfred Treml and Wolf Weigand, eds., *Geschichte und Kultur der Juden in Bayern. Lebensläufe* (Munich, 1988), 117–20.
7. Arnold Zweig, *Juden auf der deutschen Bühne* (Berlin, 1927), 22–23.
8. Siegmund Kaznelson, ed., *Juden im deutschen Kulturbereich. Ein Sammelwerk* (Berlin, 1959), 1043–44.
9. Ibid., xii.
10. Thus Nahida Remy, who was born non-Jewish but then converted to

Judaism and wrote on Jewish subjects, is relegated to the appendix. Stahl, however, appears six times in the text.

11. Walter Tetzlaff, *2000 Kurzbiographien bedeutender deutscher Juden des 20. Jahrhunderts* (Lindhorst, 1982), i. In this compilation it is half-Jews who are relegated to the appendix, with a notation as to which parent was Jewish.

12. Joseph Wolk, *Kurzbiographien zur Geschichte der Juden, 1918–1945* (Munich, 1988), vii.

13. Golo Mann, *Deutsche Geschichte des 19. und 20. Jahrhundert* (Frankfurt a. Main, 1958), 466–67.

14. See especially his *The Politics of Cultural Despair: A Study in the Rise of Germanic Ideology* (Berkeley, 1961).

15. These categories are absent and the Jews treated only as objects in the widely circulated volume by Hellmut Diwald, *Geschichte der Deutschen* (Frankfurt a. Main, 1978).

16. Hajo Holborn, *A History of Modern Germany, 1648–1840* (New York, 1964), includes a section entitled "The Status of the Jews" (285–88) plus separate treatments of Moses Mendelssohn and of Jewish emancipation. There is virtually nothing on inner Jewish developments after Mendelssohn. His *A History of Modern Germany, 1840–1945* (New York, 1969), collects Jewish material under "The Jewish Question" (277–80), beginning and ending with antisemitism. Later references to Nazi persecution do not include how German Jews dealt with such animosity.

17. Thomas Nipperdey, *Deutsche Geschichte, 1800–1866* (Munich, 1983). The section which gathers almost all of Nipperdey's references to German Jewry suggests an external approach in its title, "Das Problem der Minderheit. Die Juden" (248–55). However, it includes a full page on inner reorientation.

18. Reinhard Rürup, *Deutschland im 19. Jahrhundert 1815–1871* (Göttingen, 1984). His section on the Jews (105–9) bears a title similar to Nipperdey's: "Minderheiten. Die Juden." Rürup, the best versed in Jewish history among historians of Germany, here not only relates the emancipation of the German Jews to the emancipation of the bourgeoisie, but also draws comparisons between German Jewry and Jews in other lands.

19. The one volume of which I am aware that contains such integration, at least to a limited degree, is a book already a generation old: Koppel S. Pinson, *Modern Germany: Its History and Civilization* (New York, 1954). Thus Pinson, for example, in dealing with intellectual life in the Weimar period, relates the Jewish thinker Martin Buber to a trend among Protestants and Catholics to seek out the mystical foundations of religion and ethics (456–57, 461).

20. The Huguenots are one such group. See Stefi Jersch-Wenzel, *Juden und "Franzosen" in der Wirtschaft des Raumes Berlin/Brandenburg zur Zeit des Merkantilismus* (Berlin, 1978).

21. This is the composite goal set for the Leo Baeck Institute's synthetic

history of the Jews in German-speaking lands since the seventeenth century. The collaborative four-volume work, edited by Michael A. Meyer and Michael Brenner, has appeared in Hebrew, English, and German.

22. After this essay was written, two relevant evaluations of German-Jewish historiography appeared in *LBI Year Book* 35 (1990): Moshe Zimmermann, "Jewish History and Jewish Historiography: A Challenge to Contemporary German Historiography," 35–52; and Reinhard Rürup. "An Appraisal of German-Jewish Historiography," xv–xxiv. In a broadly based survey Zimmermann differentiates between what he terms "exclusive" and "inclusive" approaches, noting that most German-Jewish historiography remains exclusive, i.e., unintegrated into German history. Especially interesting in Rürup's appraisal is his detection of ambivalence on the part of German historians toward stressing differences that marked Jews off within German society. While expanding upon such differences pays tribute to the special role of Jews in German society, it also serves to stress their otherness—a consequence that seems to some undesirable against the background of Nazi antisemitism. Rürup persuasively argues that neglecting the peculiarities of Jewish distribution in the various sectors of German life falsifies reality. From the standpoint of a historian of modern Germany, he also maintains that the approaches of Jewish history and German history are both legitimate and both necessary. Beyond that mutual recognition, of course, lies the task of integrating the two.

CHAPTER 6

The Question of Continuity in Jewish History

Some years ago, when David Ben-Gurion was visiting the West Coast of the United States, the president of the University of California at Los Angeles hosted a luncheon in his honor. At this festive meal, which took place just after Ben-Gurion had delivered a lecture to university students, I was seated next to the eminent historian of the United States, George Mowry. The subject of our conversation, following Ben-Gurion's presentation, was Jewish history. To my surprise, Mowry expressed his view that, in fact, there was no such thing as Jewish history. One could speak of the history of the Kingdom of Israel in ancient times and the history of the state of Israel in modern times, but all that occurred between the one period of sovereignty and the other was nothing more than aspects of the history of other peoples. In his opinion, there was no continuous history of the Jews, but only two separated stretches of history with a yawning temporal gulf between them.

One could perhaps ascribe the view of the gentile historian to ignorance of the Jewish past. But, in fact, there are scholars who know Jewish history very well who are similarly convinced that it lacks continuity. In a number of the writings of Jacob Neusner the expression "Jewish history" appears in quotation marks, for example in his statement that "there is no single, unitary 'Jewish history.' "[1] And in his biting critique of H. H. Ben Sasson's *A History of the Jewish People* he writes: "The utter chaos produced by the unitary and linear theory of 'Jewish history' is perhaps the book's best demonstrated proposition."[2] Neusner admits that with regard to particular periods and places it is permissible to use the expression

"Jewish history," but he negates the possibility of arriving at a general conception according to which it would be possible to write the history of the Jews in all periods and in all lands. Thus Jewish history breaks apart for him, as well, into separated clusters without continuity between them.

The problem of historical continuity is not unique to Jewish historiography. It exists, as well, for the history of any people that experienced changes in its nature, whether such changes occurred during the course of an extended process or rapidly during a revolution. But in such instances the difficulty is not that severe. It is certainly true that the intellectual world of a contemporary Englishman is far distant from that of his medieval progenitors. But the changes occurred gradually, first affecting the enlightened and afterwards gradually penetrating the consciousness of wider sectors of the populace. There is no clearly marked rupture between England of the Middle Ages and England of modern times. In the second instance—a rapid or revolutionary change which affects an entire people—a rupture is indeed apparent. France after the Revolution is not the same as France before it. But the rupture occurred only in certain areas of the life of the French nation, even if it had ramifications for other areas as well. Some elements remain stable and it is these that provide continuity since they are only tangentially, or not at all, affected by the revolution. For example: territorial concentration, common language, occupational distribution, and cultural heritage. An analysis of Russian history, to take another example, may well lead to the conclusion that the continuous elements, those existing during both the imperial era and the Soviet period, outweigh in significance the break caused by the Russian revolution. It largely depends on the relative weight that a particular historian gives to the various elements.

For Jewish history the problem is far more severe. The non-changing elements that exist for other peoples do not exist for the Jews. There is no single territorial concentration, no single spoken language, no single political framework. The problem of continuity appears with regard to both space and time. In the same period Jews dwell in various lands, speak different languages, and their Jewish identity finds a variety of expressions both with regard to the institutions they support and the intellectual world they build for themselves. In the course of time, such far-reaching changes have occurred that it becomes questionable whether there is at all anything essential in common between King Alexander Yannai and the Jews of the United States, between the author of the medieval *Book of the Pious* (*Sefer Hasidim*) and the secular Jew living in the state of Israel.

The problem of continuity arises in the consciousness of the modern Jew who desires to define his Jewish identity historically. If he wants to determine norms for his life in accordance with Jewish tradition, he soon discovers that Jewish tradition possesses uniformity neither of beliefs nor of practices. In order to create a connection with it he must attach himself to certain lines of development and detach himself from others. His desire to create a consistent, historically grounded Jewish identity requires negation no less than affirmation. He is unable to avoid existential decisions such as to negate the Diaspora or to affirm it, to deny Judaism as a religion or to accept the yoke of the commandments. Likewise the historian, if he or she is a Jew looking for personal meaning in Judaism and striving for some goal, which in her or his view represents the aim of Judaism, in reality builds a new universe that is attached only to certain elements of the tradition and not to the entirety of the Jewish past. Such selectivity is surely justified as long as it is undertaken consciously. A severe problem arises, however, when the claim is made that the affirmed past is the entire past or that it represents "the true Judaism," while contradictory elements either do not exist or may be relegated to insignificance. Jewish historians, in their desire to create continuity between the past and their own Jewish identity, have ignored contrary phenomena or negated them. At the very least, they have consigned them to the margins of Jewish history. Again and again Jewish self-definitions have been projected back upon the past and have shaped its image.

Until modern times the problem of continuity was not so severe. Only during the first half of the nineteenth century and under the influence of general intellectual trends did historical consciousness penetrate the intellectual world of Jewish thinkers. The need began to be felt for an approach to the Jewish past which was not that of the preacher or polemicist, who chooses from it what is useful for a particular purpose, but rather of the historian who intends to understand it in its totality, without applying his research to any practical end. Well known is Leopold Zunz's pronouncement in his pamphlet *Some Words on Rabbinic Literature:* "Here we are presenting Jewish literature in its fullest compass as a subject for research without concern for whether its entire content needs to be, or can be, also a norm for our own decisions." Following the Jewish Enlightenment, Zunz's generation in Central Europe was also more aware of the rupture between itself and its past. This rupture was so severe in his view that he sometimes cast doubt on whether it would at all be possible to heal it, whether there was, in fact, any continuity between past and present. In addition, the emancipation of the Jews in the West brought them inside a non-Jewish historical process and raised the question: What now is the relevant past of the Jew in the West from which he is to draw—the Jewish past, from which in numerous respects he is alienated, or the European past that he has adopted as his own?

As long as Jews did not identify with the surrounding society and did not internalize its values, the continuity between their lives and those of their ancestors was essentially guided by a single idea: the faith that God has chosen the Jewish people from among all the nations and that God fulfilled the covenant with His chosen people throughout the generations. Divine providence is directed first and foremost toward Israel and there is no event in Jewish history that cannot be explained by this special relationship between God and the people. From this theological point of view, the variety of Jewish life in various periods and in different places did not damage historical continuity. Ever since Sinai the covenant served as a scarlet thread tying the generations together. Seen in this way, the history of the Jews is simply a religious and moral drama in which the Jewish people seeks to be faithful to the covenant and yearns for the coming of the Messiah.

During the nineteenth century, as well, significant efforts were made to establish continuity in Jewish history on the foundation of the relationship between God and the Jewish people. Outstanding among them is Nahman Krochmal's Hebrew book *Guide to the Perplexed of the Time*. To be sure, the relationship here is newly attired in garb borrowed from idealistic philosophy, and God acts within history as "Absolute Spirit," not from a position of transcendence. But even for Krochmal, despite all the vicissitudes through which Israel passes, divine providence does not allow historical continuity to be broken. As a historian, Krochmal was aware of these vicissitudes, but he was able to encompass them within a schematic framework. Each people passes through a cycle composed of three periods: budding, blossoming, and wilting. At the end of the cycle the history of that people, as an independent historical entity, likewise comes to an end. Only the traces of its culture continue to live in the history of other nations. The people of Israel likewise passes through the same periods, but on account of God's special providence it is not condemned to extinction like other peoples. The end of one cycle invariably gives birth to the next. God assures the existence and continuity of the people. Despite all the vicissitudes, Israel cannot vanish, for, in the last analysis, it is not the master of its own history. Its destiny to be an eternal people is determined from on High.

Krochmal was not the only one who made continuity in Jewish history dependent upon divine providence. What singles out his view is the rigid scheme within which providence operates. That scheme relieved him of the need to prove through empirical history that there was any unchanging element present in every period and to make continuity dependent upon its presence.

Other thinkers in that generation, during the first half of the nineteenth century, refrained from placing Jewish history into a framework that would determine its course in advance. But they too were influenced by the reigning perplexity with regard to history, and especially by the gulf between the past and the present that seemed so very deep. Whereas Krochmal sought to solve the problem by means of an encompassing system, they attempted to isolate a single component which, by empirical research, could be shown to represent the ever-present essence of Judaism.

For the Association for Culture and Scientific Study among the Jews, established in Berlin in 1819, the determinative component was the idea of the unity of God, signified by God's Hebrew name which, in their view, symbolized the unity of all Creation. When this conception was revealed to the Jewish people, it became its representative and guardian in history. Influenced by idealistic philosophy and their own sense of history, the members of the Association admitted that this idea was at first not fully grasped, not even by the Jews themselves. For these young men, as also for Krochmal, rational comprehension was not determinative. It was sufficient that the idea dwells within the people and gradually develops within its consciousness in order for it to bridge all of the historical vicissitudes and to turn every generation into a link in the chain of tradition. However, in contradiction to Krochmal's conception, there is no promise here for the future. The idea, which pulsates within Judaism, is capable of being passed on to humanity as a whole, turning Judaism into no more than a component of human culture and thereby depriving it of its uniqueness. It would live on, but—to use Eduard Gans's metaphor—only like a current in the ocean.

Likewise in the writings of Rabbi Abraham Geiger the religious principle was to constitute the connection between the generations. In his view, the changes that occurred in the political and social status of the Jews did not create a tear in the historical fabric since faith in the one God, which is the source of morality, always remained strong. To be sure even faith did not remain static; it developed over the course of history and created external forms in accordance with time and place. But therein, Geiger believed, lay its power to persist. As he envisaged it, "Israel is not like a rock that endures for millennia, rigid and unaltered, only to be shattered when the winds of change pass over it." However, even if the externals of faith were flexible, its essence was fixed and there was, for example, no room in it for mysticism or for any principle that stands in contradiction to human reason. Thus this consistent faith provides continuity with the past and also unites Israel in the present in spite of all the currents that flow within it and despite the fact that a growing percentage of Jews in the West have already ceased to observe the commandments. Geiger's attempt failed, however, in that he did not sufficiently distinguish between his own rationalistic religious Judaism, of which he sought to find examples in the Jewish past, and the broader historical Judaism, which embraces a variety of religious phenomena that cannot be subsumed under a single theological conception.

Critics of Geiger's historiography today would doubtless also emphasize that he failed to ascribe adequate importance to the national element in Jewish history. In his opinion that element was not of the essence, but only a transient form. A contemporary historian might explain Geiger's view as resulting from the particular conditions of the nineteenth century. Yet even in the twentieth century the same tendency persists to make continuity dependent upon the religious factor, which in its essence remains unchanged.

The historian Yitzhak Baer certainly did not negate Jewish nationality, but for him, as well, the link between the generations is provided by an unchanging religious essence, whose origins lie at the beginning of Jewish history. "The nation entered the gateway of history as a religious community," he wrote, "as a community that arose to realize particular religio-social ideals in this world. . . . The character of the nation is permanent and fixed from the start by certain tendencies of the monotheistic faith: clinging to the one God and equality and freedom in human society."[3] These ideals, according to Baer, "are grounded in the soul of the nation and are not easily subject to change." Baer calls these beliefs "eternal teachings" whose source is the Hebrew Bible and which contain the secret of the people's survival. Alongside them are secondary teachings which, according to Baer, serve the Jew intellectually or morally, such as the obligation to believe in Creation out of nothing and to extirpate idolatry. The first set, concerning social justice "obligate every generation and every era." But this does not hold true for the latter set "whose significance is determined by temporal conditions."[4] Jacob Fleischmann has already analyzed the subjective distinction between essential and accidental that Baer makes in the first chapter of his book *Israel among the Nations*.[5] However, in a lecture that Baer gave at the World Congress of Jewish Studies in 1947 he came yet closer to the characteristics of idealist historiography. In that lecture he even adopted Krochmal's idea of cycles, albeit not according to the same division into periods. There he concludes: "The unity of the history of the Jewish people will persist also in the future if this period of transition [the modern age] will conclude with a new period of youthfulness that continues with the realization of the historical trends of the previous periods out of purity of heart and devotion of soul and out of those same yearnings for the transcendental world without which there is no life and renewal for any people in the world."[6] And in his well-known booklet *Galut* Baer concludes that there is a power which raises the Jewish people above the realm of causal history. Thus Baer's philosophy of history—though not necessarily his specific work as a historian—remains within a metaphysical framework that assures continuity.

In opposition to this tendency to make continuity dependent upon some form of religious essence there emerges in the nineteenth century the inclination to find continuity in the spirit of the nation. Zunz had already criticized Geiger's historical conception because it contracted Jewish history to the sphere of the religious idea, to the history of Jewish theology. According to Zunz, it was incumbent upon modern Jewish scholarship, above all, to liberate itself from theology and provide ample room for every piece of literary creativity produced by a Jew, whether it be in the sphere of religion or any other. However, for Zunz the object of Jewish history remained the realm of spiritual and intellectual creativity. The subjects of his research are the great writers, and Jewish history consists essentially of the history of literature.

In the writings of Heinrich Graetz the center of gravity moves from the religious idea and the work of literature to a sphere that lies between idea and nationality. Likewise for Graetz, no less than for Geiger, there is a normative Judaism which is eternal and creates a connection between one period and the next. Any phenomenon that contradicts it, such as mysticism, in his view becomes a deviation from the norm, which Graetz likewise believes to be a rationalistic conception of God with an emphasis upon the moral commandments. However, according to Graetz, the religious idea is not the bearer of history. Unlike Geiger, he did not write the history of an idea, but neither did he write the history of a people. He wrote the history of the collective soul, the *Volksseele*, of the Jewish people.

Yet for Graetz, as well, the unchanging religious idea, anchored in the soul of the people, remains the thread that connects the generations.

The first historian openly and specifically to take issue with idealist historiography was Simon Dubnow. As a secular Jew living in Russia, he was able to call attention to a fact that his predecessors refused to consider: there is no single religious idea that consistently characterizes Judaism. In his words: "In the history of Judaism . . . there is no single definite idea which runs through all periods like a silk thread."[7] In rejecting idealist historiography, Dubnow also rejected its principle of continuity. Yet he too was convinced that there can be no integral Jewish history without an unchanging foundation. He therefore found it necessary to discover a different connection in place of the ideal one. And indeed, according to Dubnow's philosophy of Jewish history, there exists a "national thread" that creates a connection between periods and between Jewish diasporas.[8] The people of Israel itself is the basis for continuity and the subject of Jewish history. Beliefs changed over the course of time until in the modern period some Jews even rejected the basic principles of the Jewish faith. Yet that did not remove them from Jewish history. What did not change was the people's national consciousness, its character as a nation, even if that consciousness found expression in various ways. Thus Dubnow was able to include secular Jews within the historical continuum. The same was not true, however, for those Jews who defined Jewish identity exclusively as belonging to a religious community and denied Jewish peoplehood.

The national element likewise predominates in the writings of Ben Zion Dinur. But here something new is added that is not present as a fixed and determinative factor in Dubnow's writing: the connection with the land of Israel. The centrality of the land of Israel in Jewish consciousness unifies the various diasporas and provides continuity for the history of the Jewish nation. This connection, according to Dinur, began as early as Abraham and it stands out in every period. It likewise determines the character of the present age in Jewish history, which Dinur called the period of struggle for independence, the establishment of the state of Israel, and the beginning of the ingathering of the diasporas. Zion has become the scarlet thread.

From the standpoint of historiography, there are obvious defects and distortions in every attempt to solve the problem of continuity in Jewish history by fixing upon a single element. The result, necessarily, is the neglect or denigration of elements that stand in opposition to it. Just as in Graetz's historiography Jewish mysticism is treated with contempt and in Geiger's historiography there is no room for a secular Judaism, in the writings of Dubnow and Dinur German Jewry of the nineteenth century, for example, appears as a deviation from the norm. It possesses only negative significance with regard to the historical continuum. On the other hand, any phenomenon that strengthens the scarlet thread receives a positive evaluation and more extended treatment than is warranted by actual influence. With the intent of preserving the purity of the emphasized element of continuity, all varieties of this approach tend to reduce the significance of external influences and to view the connecting element as a factor whose dynamics is basically internal: it was Abraham who discovered monotheism, or: Zionism arose from internal ferment and not from the influence of foreign national movements. Yet another effect of this approach is the tendency to place the element of continuity within an eschatological framework and to judge historical phenomena, especially those in recent times, according to whether they drive forward in a particular direction that is determined in advance. Messianism, whether in its religious or its secular form, is certainly a most important element in Jewish history, but it is clearly not a proper criterion for the historian.

If, then, there is no scarlet thread, is it perhaps necessary to agree with Mowry and Neusner that there is no single and integral Jewish history? Neusner, indeed, is persuaded that any effort to determine continuity will be in vain. It is his view that a continuous history exists only for Judaism and not for the Jews. Although he is willing to recognize variations that Geiger and Graetz ignored or rejected, and although his approach is entirely secular, it nonetheless represents a return to the religious definition of the nineteenth century. Continuity is to be found only in the realm of religion and the proper locale for the study of the Jewish past is, consequently, in the department of religion and not in the department of history. This viewpoint, however, not only removes Jewish nationality from the historical continuum but also has difficulty in finding continuity in the realm of religious ideas on account of internal oppositions within Jewish religious thought.

In view of all these efforts to solve the problem of continuity in Jewish history—efforts that did not succeed in encompassing all phenomena and in evaluating them in a balanced manner—is it necessary simply to despair of the project? Indeed, if we endeavor to isolate a single thread that passes through the entire length of Jewish history, the effort, I believe, is bound to fail. However, if we change the image—if we employ a metaphor that I suggested some years ago and imagine not a thread but a *rope* as the model for historical continuity—we may be able to create a more useful tool for historical understanding.[9] A rope is composed of many strands, none of which stretch from one end of the rope to the other, yet the rope does not pull apart since each strand overlaps others. The strands may be understood to represent the various elements that characterize Jewish history, such as—to use Dinur's list—the national, the religious, the social, the territorial, the linguistic, and the political. One strand may be thicker than another at a particular time; it may also gradually change its hue. It may tear and cease to exist further in the life of the entire people or of a portion of it. But as long as all of the strands do not tear at the same time historical continuity is not damaged. The rope in its entirety stands for the people of Israel, the word "people" here possessing a meaning that itself changes in accordance with the composition of the rope at any particular time and in any particular place of Jewish settlement.

Every model has its defects and shortcomings, and surely they exist in this one as well. But I would submit that it fits the Jewish historical reality better than any other that we may employ in seeking to solve the intractable problem of continuity.

Notes

1. Jacob Neusner, Review of Michael A. Meyer, ed., *Ideas of Jewish History,* in *History and Theory* 14 (1975): 218.
2. Jacob Neusner, Review of H. H. Ben-Sasson, *A History of the Jewish People,* in *American Historical Review* 82 (1977): 1031.
3. Yitzhak Baer, *Yisrael ba-amim* (Jerusalem, 1955), 14–15.
4. Ibid., 16.
5. Jacob Fleischmann, "The Problem of Objectivity in Jewish Historiography" (Hebrew), *Iyyun* 9 (1958): 108–10.
6. Yitzhak Baer, "The Unity of Jewish History and the Problem of Its Organic Development" (Hebrew), *Gilyonot* 24 (1950/51): 216.
7. Simon Dubnow, *Nationalism and History* (New York, 1961), 94.
8. Ibid., 330.
9. Michael A. Meyer, ed., *Ideas of Jewish History* (New York, 1974), 40–41.

PART II

The Jews
of Germany

CHAPTER 7

The German Jews:
Some Perspectives on Their History

Memories are like rocks that we dig out of the shallow waters of a stream. At one time the stones had jagged edges, but gradually the river has worn them smooth. So too our minds, in recalling, wear away the details, the contradictions, the ironies of what we once learned and leave only the smooth message that is easily remembered and easily conveyed. Young minds, learning from the recollections of others, sometimes receive only the worn-away form of the transmitted memory. If they want to know the jagged original, they must restore it on their own.

Our tendency to simplify, to stereotype, is never more pronounced than when we have a point to make and want to make it most forcefully: the less qualification, the stronger the message. For actively identifying Jews in America today no message rings more loudly than the call for Jewish survival, both physical and spiritual. The Holocaust, the rapid rate of Jewish identity loss in the Diaspora, these have created a felt need not only to look for some guiding star but also to fasten upon a ghost from the past, a historical phantom that will frighten contemporaries sufficiently to drive them from its own unfortunate path. The history of German Jewry, I believe, has come to play such a negative role. Popular consciousness has cut away the jagged edges so that the smooth memory which remains may serve the dominant Jewish purpose of our day. But to have done that, I would argue, has been no service either to history or to American Jewry.

The history of the German Jews is popularly perceived as an object lesson in the perils of naïveté and assimilation. Naively, Jews in Germany believed that they had nothing to fear in the "land of thinkers and poets." Later, in Eastern Europe, the Holocaust rolled forward so quickly the Jews there were in no position to escape. But in Germany eight years intervened between Hitler's rise to power and the beginning of the deportations in 1941. Why did the German Jews not save themselves? Why did they—who saw Hitler from up close—not warn their fellow Jews of what he might be capable? Because the Holocaust is so troubling for Jews and for many gentiles, there has been a tendency to see German Jewish history from a Holocaust perspective, even as some historians have explored the history of Germany in general from that point of departure. Likewise, in popular consciousness the German Jews have become the paradigmatic examples of assimilation. During the Weimar period their intermarriage rate paralleled that of Jews in the United States today; it was believed that German Judaism faced the prospect of disappearance by absorption. To speak of German Jewry, therefore, has been more to utter a warning than to claim a legacy.

I do not, in reaction, see it as my task to exculpate the German Jews, to wage a polemic or set forth an apologetic on their behalf. But I do believe that historians must try to preserve the jagged edges, even if that makes it more difficult to generalize. German Jewry has passed into history, its unevenly shaped legacy squeezed into the mold of popular myth. Perhaps looking back upon that legacy from a few discrete angles of vision may help to restore its complexity, its ambiguity, and its individuality.

If it is true that history is full of ironies—as I believe it is—then the history of German Jewry has had more than its share of them. And that particular angle of vision may be among the most enlightening. Let me elaborate two such ironies which seem the most basic and the most striking. The two are interrelated.

German Jews have been called "pioneers of modernity." And, indeed, they have taken pride in that designation. If modernity is characterized by an ability and a willingness to leave tradition aside and employ new, more effective, efficient, or compelling means to achievement in the economy, in the sciences, and in the arts, then there can be no doubt that German Jews played a role in modernization vastly disproportionate to their numbers.

It was also dangerous. Modernization was by no means regarded as an unequivocal good in German society. Innovation necessarily rests upon implicit or explicit criticism of current practice and belief. It unsettles, it uproots, it paints an uncertain picture of the future. The widespread fear of rapid change in Germany could easily be mobilized by right-wing ideologues and politicians who marked the Jews as rootless cosmopolitans, men and women without any sense of tradition. Having entered German society rather late and under the influence of the Enlightenment, they could appreciate only the dictates of reason; they lacked understanding for the "deeper" concerns of the heart. The most modernistic Jews had broken themselves off like a branch from their own tree of Judaism. Few Germans were willing to graft them onto theirs. Instead, they decried the Jews collectively for lacking all reverence for tradition, for knowing only how to destroy. They were "an agent of decomposition" that might dissolve the old but was incapable of creating a sense of continuity between the old and the new.

The first irony—and it is a double one—should then be apparent. For the German Jews to have pioneered modernity is, in retrospect, a noteworthy distinction. But its effects in context were doubly negative: the most outstanding pioneers were, for the most part and to varying degrees, non-Jewish Jews; and as symbols of modernity, the German Jews aroused more anxiety than gratitude—with negative consequences for themselves.

It is therefore not surprising that most German Jews felt deep ambivalence about the most radical in their midst and hesitated to take credit for them. At the same time they sought to convince non-Jews of their ability to become part of that German tree, even if somewhat belatedly. Whether they were religiously Orthodox or Reform, German Jews during the nineteenth century took on the manners and mores of the Germans around them. As more and more of them became urban and bourgeois, they adopted the characteristics of their class in nearly every respect. Jewish men pursued the regnant work ethic; Jewish women played the role of leisured matron. Only in religion, in the preservation of a few family traditions, and in their greater interest in the arts did Jewish families stick out from others of their class. Increasingly, as they began to behave more and more like Germans, they felt that in fact they were Germans. What few realized, however, because it was so difficult an idea to accept was a second irony: the more they came to resemble the Germans the more they were perceived as a a threat to German society.

The message they had received was never entirely clear. Since the beginning of the quest for Jewish emancipation in Germany, Jews had been told repeatedly that they would gain equality once they had given up those characteristics which could not be harmonized with being German citizens. The after-effects of life in the ghetto would have to be shaken off: the concentration in a few occupations, the Judeo-German speech, the religious and ethnic exclusivism. The most enlightened spirits among the Germans encouraged the Jews in that direction, holding out promises of reward. But early on there were also contravening signals. In Prussia, the government prohibited religious reforms, in part because of the fear that a Jewish religion too much like the Christian would be inappropriately attractive to non-Jews. When, after two generations of Jewish acculturation in Germany, antisemitism reared its head again with a vengeance in the last decades of the nineteenth century, it was not aimed solely at the recent immigrants from Eastern Europe, the *Ostjuden*, or at the minority of fully observant Jews. On the contrary, the new racial antisemitism directed its most virulent thrusts against the Jews furthest removed from Judaism, those less easily discernible as Jews and hence the more insidious threat to Germanism. What the German Jews could not know—because it was usually kept secret from them—was that even their alleged friends, the liberals who wished them well, harbored secret hopes for their eventual disappearance as a distinct entity within German society. That was as true toward the end of the nineteenth century, when German Jews had achieved full political equality, as it was at the very beginning of that process a hundred years earlier.

Some German Jews, of course, chose to throw off the burden of discrimination once and for all by converting to Christianity. Scholarship has shown correlations between waves of discrimination and apostasy. Conversion usually removed disabilities in the professional sphere, but it seldom removed social barriers. The converts, at least in the first generation, were regarded as baptized Jews, not Christians, or even wholly Germans. Nor were their accomplishments regarded as springing from German soil. The talented poet Heinrich Heine presents the most prominent example. Few German writers possessed such a remarkable intuitive understanding of German ways—and of German foibles—as did this baptized Jew. Yet non-Jewish Germans often balked at including his work within the German canon. He was a virtuoso of the German language, but he remained an intriguing outsider.

What was true of converts was the more true of German Jews who chose—however minimally—to retain their identity. By the beginning of the twentieth century few of them remained Orthodox; the vast majority opposed the Zionist movement from its origins until the rise of Hitler; and they observed Jewish customs only minimally. Yet large numbers of them joined in the defense of Jewish rights, and their social circles—even in the most assimilated families—continued, by choice or by lack of choice, to be almost exclusively Jewish. They remained different in another way as well, one linked more to Jewish fate than to Jewish heritage. Because they had entered German society under the aegis of Enlightenment rationalism and universalism, they remained true to these principles even after they had been abandoned by a society in quest of its unique German soul. Not that all Germans became romantics or entirely abandoned the Enlightenment, but Jews remained faithful to it with an ardor that rendered them distinctive. Their dedication to universalism preserved their particularity.

Irony heaped upon irony: the German Jews sought to escape animosity through assimilation, but the assimilation only brought increased animosity, and that animosity in turn—where it did not induce escape through conversion—led to increased awareness of themselves as Jews. Not, as Jean Paul Sartre believed, that antisemitism makes the Jew, but in Germany it did have the effect of bringing Jewishness to the surface. Marked as Jews from the outside, some of the most assimilated were forced to confront their Jewishness. They came to realize that they were regarded as Jews *in spite of* themselves. If so, they concluded, they would be Jews—*out of spite.*

The talented Viennese novelist Jacob Wassermann may serve as an example of these trends in a single life. His Jewishness was the product of rejection by non-Jews; he noted its lack of positive content. Wassermann was neither religiously nor nationally Jewish. Yet his greatest admirers were his fellow Jews. A Christian friend told him that the German and Jewish spirits would never mix. Much as he tried to write as a German for Germans, Wassermann came to realize, he would always be regarded as a Jewish writer. He once noted down what he regarded as typically Jewish faults that shamed and disgusted him, as well as virtues that he found worthy of praise. But in the last analysis, Jewishness was not something rejected or chosen on account of its deleterious or beneficent influences. It was, he felt, a fate he could not overcome. There was no choice but to accept the reality of antisemitism. Well-intentioned efforts to exorcise the prevalent sense of Jews as strangers were all in vain. As a Jew he would necessarily suffer on its account—though, reflecting his persistent primary identification, he admitted that antisemitism grieved him more as a German than as a Jew.

The ironic angle of vision has set us above our subject, wryly smiling down upon it with the knowing glance of one who sees more broadly than can those with only limited views below. It will be well now to complement it with a comparative perspective set on the same level: Germany and the United States, German Jews and American Jews.

That antisemitism became far more endemic in Germany than in the United States has many explanations. But it seems to me of primary importance that whereas Germany became a nation in rebellion against the values of the Enlightenment, which it persistently deemed foreign to the German spirit, the United States enshrined them in the fundamental documents of its nationhood. The idea of tolerance in this country may at first have been an import from abroad, but Jefferson and his associates never considered it foreign to the nascent American character. It was present at the birth of the nation and, though occasionally violated, it was never cast out. American antisemitism could not easily claim to be the true Americanism.

It strikes me as further worthy of note that public discourse about Jews in the United States has consistently been put in terms of "Jews and Christians," not "Jews and Americans." In fact, the latter formulation seems exceedingly strange. In Germany, however, despite the German Jews' frequent (though not entirely ingenuous) protests that Jewishness was strictly a religious identity, the terms of distinction were different. Of course, in certain contexts one spoke there also of Judaism and Christianity, but the prevailing categories were *Judentum* and *Deutschtum*, Judaism and Germanism. The pairing typical for the United States makes Jews and Christians equally Americans, "American" being primarily a political category. Jews are seen as separate on account of their religion (or alternatively distinguished from other ethnic groups like Latinos or Irish Americans), but they share equally in Americanism. The other conception assumes that Judaism and Germanism are fundamentally different manifestations within the same cultural category. Merging them—if possible at all—changes the character of each. And since Germanism was closely related to German citizenship, this perceived cultural difference could have political consequences. Still today historians speak regularly of *Deutsche und Juden*, but I know of none who use the terminology "Americans and Jews."

In the German language there are two words for Germans, *Deutsche* and *Germanen*. The latter is usually translated as "Teutons" and has a racial connotation, though it also appears in such forms as *Germanistik*, the study of German culture. German Jews never claimed to be *Germanen*. In fact, during the first virulent outbreak of German chauvinism in 1815, a Jewish writer roundly condemned what he called "Teutomania." But the very existence of that special designation to which Jews did not aspire left open, so it seemed to them, the racially unburdened name of *Deutsche*. When German Jews came under renewed attack during the last quarter of the nineteenth century, one of their leading personalities, Moritz Lazarus, argued that *Deutschtum* was essentially a subjective category. It was not a matter of birth but of education and of the will to be German. Later the leading German Jewish philosopher at the beginning of the twentieth century, Hermann Cohen, defined the German spirit as "the spirit of classical humanism and true cosmopolitanism." Since it was therefore fully in harmony with the universal message of the Hebrew prophets, Germanism could not be the antagonist of Judaism. The two were fundamentally alike, both pointing to the messianic goal of human redemption. Cohen's wishful and unhistorical thinking rested upon his definition of Germanism as an idealized Kantianism and finding the essence of Judaism in a selective reading of Second Isaiah and Micah. In the United States too, Jewish leaders, like Isaac Mayer Wise, for example, idealized Americanism and universalized Judaism, but their formulations were not as far removed from historical reality. They did not have to fight against a narrower conception of Americanism that excluded the Jews.

Language reveals another no less significant difference. It was not uncommon in Germany to speak of non-Jewish Germans as a *Wirtsvolk*, a host people, vis-à-vis the Jews. It was as if the Jews had been invited to dwell as guests in a house that was not their own and their remaining there was dependent on good behavior. The landlord could always evict the tenant. A related image pictured the Jews as adopted children, set apart from the natural offspring of the German people. This view of the relationship produced the popular saying with regard to the Jews: *Stiefkinder müssen doppelt so brav sein* ("stepchildren have to be twice as good"). Both of these notions— host and guest, parent and stepchild—have been absent in America, which prides itself on being a nation of immigrants where categories like "indigenous" and "autochthonous" apply only to Native Americans and where Jews are not perceived as outsiders and latecomers to a fully shaped peoplehood.

The relations between Judaism and Christianity also differed in the two countries. During the second half of the nineteenth century liberal American Christians associated themselves with their Jewish counterparts in a Free Religious Association. Rabbis and ministers exchanged pulpits. Later, Jews and Christians joined in common social justice ventures. Such phenomena were unheard of in Germany. Jews and Christians in Germany certainly collaborated as individuals in cultural and philanthropic activities, but Christianity and Judaism neither addressed each other in dialogue nor made common cause. Judaism in Germany did not enjoy the same public status as did Christianity. Very few Germans held that toleration of the Jewish religion was anything more than a necessary concession to those who were born Jews. They surely did not believe that they had anything to learn from Judaism, and it was for that reason that the doctrine of the "mission of Israel," an idea widely held among even highly assimilated German Jews that Jewish monotheism was religion at its highest and relevant not only to Jews, so rankled German Christians.

The comparative perspective, then, somewhat softens the view gained by the ironic one. German Jews faced a situation vastly different from that of their coreligionists in the United States. It is not as if there was a sudden turnabout from tolerance in the style of America to Nazi annihilation. Since the early nineteenth century German Jews were engaged in an ongoing struggle to create and sustain tolerance in a country that did not have a fundamental commitment to it. They hoped for the triumph of the "good Germany," perhaps exaggerating its influence, though it was by no means a chimera. When Gabriel Riesser, the great Jewish champion of political equality, wrote in favor of complete Jewish emancipation in the 1830s, he argued—cogently and effectively—that German values, not foreign ones, required opening doors to German Jews. That the narrower exclusivistic Germanism won out was not a foregone conclusion and it did not happen all at once. Even after Hitler came to power, it was—at least for a time—possible to believe that the tide could be reversed. All that was fully clear in 1933 was that assimilation had proven fruitless.

There is a third angle of vision worthy of our attention, the perspective of influence. What have Jews elsewhere learned from German Jewry? There have, of course, been the negative lessons to which I referred at the beginning: the consequences of self-delusion and the perils of assimilation. However much I may deplore the oversimplification upon which they rest, I can scarcely deny their influence. If Diaspora Jews are more wary, less naïve today than they were two generations ago, it is not alone because of the Holocaust, but because in German Jewry they see a Jewry much like their own, which was insufficiently on guard and overly trusting. Its example does serve as a warning. Likewise, if the prospect for Jewish cultural survival remains troubling for identifying American Jews, it is, in part, because the more knowledgeable among them recall the rapid progress of assimilation in Germany and here too perceive an admonition from the past.

Yet if Jews elsewhere, especially in the United States, view German Jewry entirely in this light, they fail to recognize how much their own Jewish life and institutions have followed the German Jewish model. There is a distinctly positive angle of perception which requires elaboration.

However problematic the Jewish role in radical modernization proved to be for Jews and gentiles alike in Germany, in various compromise formulations modernization became the pattern for Jewish existence wherever Jews emerged from the ghetto or, as in the United States, where Jews began their historical existence free of medieval constraints. Thus the German Jewish philosopher of the eighteenth century Moses Mendelssohn became the paradigmatic modern Jew, proving through his cultural contribution to Germany that Jews could live fruitfully within two civilizations. It was Mendelssohn who demonstrated through his own life that adopting the values of an enlightened society did not conflict with preserving the tenets and practices of an enlightened Judaism. The movement of Jewish enlightenment (the Haskalah), which he spurred, stressed the universalism and rationalism that he believed inherent in Jewish tradition. The impetus of the Haskalah was irresistible. From Berlin and Königsberg it spread to Vienna and Prague, to Galicia, and finally to Russia. American Jews too were influenced by Mendelssohn and could more easily follow his example in a society and culture hospitable to diversity. Even when Zionism came to challenge the universal dreams harbored by the Haskalah as unrealistic, it adopted its this-worldliness. And although Zionism was not popular among German-speaking Jews, it remained peripheral until Theodor Herzl, himself a product of the German Jewish milieu, used capacities and experiences gained as a Jew in Budapest and Vienna to turn it into a world movement.

It was also in Germany that Jewish periodical literature began, first in Hebrew with *Ha-Measef* in 1784, then in German with *Sulamith* in 1806. These periodicals served to ease German Jewry into modernity and they became models for similar journals elsewhere. In 1837 Rabbi Ludwig Philippson founded the *Allgemeine Zeitung des Judentums,* a weekly Jewish newspaper that served the important function of creating a sense of Jewish solidarity not only among German Jews but also with Jews elsewhere in the world. It too was a model, not least for American publications like Isaac Leeser's *Occident* and Isaac Mayer Wise's *Israelite.*

Yet more significant has been German Jewry's religious influence. It was in Germany that the modern rabbinate as we know it today first developed. Early in the nineteenth century the notion that rabbis should have an advanced secular education was controversial in conservative Jewish circles, as was the idea that rabbis should deliver regular sermons in the vernacular or play the role of pastor. But these innovations gradually made their way even into German Orthodoxy. They spread westward to France and England, even to some circles in Eastern Europe, and they have become givens for the American rabbinate.

Despite the relatively small proportion of Jews of German origin within American Judaism today, its denominational division—with the exception of the isolationist wing of Orthodoxy and Reconstructionism—rests upon ideologies developed in modern Germany. However much American Reform Judaism was a response to its particular social context, the basic principles it has espoused since the middle of the nineteenth century are those put forth by Abraham Geiger and the other German Reformers—the idea of progressive revelation, the historical critical approach to Jewish tradition, the centrality of the Prophetic literature. Similarly, Conservative Judaism remains committed to the concept of a flexible, historically interactive Jewish law that was espoused in Germany by Zacharias Frankel. And modern American Orthodoxy has for many years drawn upon the writings of Samson Raphael Hirsch, especially his idea that belief in the divinity of the Written and Oral Law, along with practice of all prescribed rituals, does not conflict with full participation in the political and cultural life of a modern nation. Only as much of American Orthodoxy in recent years has begun to distance itself from the intellectual environment and withdraw into a self-contained traditional Jewish world has Hirsch's influence declined.

It seems remarkable also that among religious thinkers most influential among Jews today German philosophers and theologians continue to be so disproportionately represented. To be sure, there are also non-Germans—one thinks of Rav Kook and Joseph Soloveitchik on the Orthodox end of the spectrum, Abraham Joshua Heschel and Mordecai Kaplan on the side of religious liberalism. But it is hard to imagine modern Jewish thought today without Hermann Cohen's messianism, Martin Buber's theology of dialogue, Franz Rosenzweig's religious existentialism, and the German-born Emil Fackenheim's theology of contemporary Jewish historical experience. It is surprising—and perhaps troubling—that the state of Israel has yet to produce a native-born religious thinker of equivalent standing.

German Jewry also developed a kind of Jewish commitment concerned above all with the protection of Jewish rights and defense against calumny. In 1893 the German Jews created an organization to combat antisemitism which they called the Central Union of Ger-

man Citizens of the Jewish Faith. In 1906 American Jews did the
same when they created the American Jewish Committee and again
in 1913 when they formed the Anti-Defamation League of B'nai
B'rith. Even as the Central Union became the largest and most influential Jewish organization in Germany, so did the various Jewish
defense organizations in the United States rapidly gain a major representative role among American Jews. In America, as in Germany,
contributing to the fight against prejudice became for many, especially nonreligious Jews the principal expression of their Jewishness.

With the burgeoning of Jewish studies in American universities during the last thirty years yet another German Jewish innovation has increasingly gained attention: Wissenschaft des Judentums,
the disciplined study of Judaism and of the Jewish people. Modern
Jewish scholarship, which differed from the earlier form of Jewish
study on account of its critical approach to texts, emerged in Berlin
during the second decade of the nineteenth century. Its most significant early figure was Leopold Zunz, a man whose extraordinary
attainments made him eminently qualified for a university chair,
though he received none since Jews and Judaism were considered
unworthy of such an honor. In Germany, Zunz remained on the
periphery. In America, however, the man who wanted to emancipate Jewish scholarship from the odium of theology appears now as
the earliest model for university scholars of Judaica, and Wissenschaft des Judentums, once rejected in the land of its birth, is today
represented in some fashion at nearly every institution of higher
learning.

A fourth and last perspective would seek out the nature of what
has been called the "German Jewish spirit." Were there particular
qualities that characterized most German Jews, qualities that can be
distilled and whose influence followed German Jews abroad? At the
risk of impressionism and subjectivity, let me venture at least a ten-
tative reply. Perhaps it is best to begin with what could be regarded
as a negative—German Jews, on the whole, lacked fervor. Their en-
thusiasms were well tempered; they seldom let themselves be swept
away by their emotions. Most were limited by the inhibitions of a
bourgeois ethos which they clung to out of a sense that it was important for their own security. But there was another side to the
same coin: German Jews were seldom fanatics. Of course, they had
their internal arguments—and these could be sharply expressed, especially between Zionists and anti-Zionists—but there was always
respect for the rules of the game. Very few German Jews were chau-
vinists either as Germans or as Jews. Remarkably, it was leading

German Zionists who had settled in Palestine, men like Arthur Ruppin, Samuel Hugo Bergmann, Martin Buber, and Ernst Simon, who played disproportionately prominent roles in the movements for reconciliation with the Arabs that arose in Jerusalem beginning in 1925.

One must note, too, the great value German Jews placed on education and culture. They flocked to the universities in far greater relative numbers than non-Jews. And while the quest for a higher secular education became characteristic for Jews in Eastern Europe as well, it was especially pronounced in Germany. There it was bruited about that "doctor" is the typical Jewish first name. German Jews were also patrons of the arts far out of proportion to their numbers. The aspiration to be a cultured person was perhaps the most common distinguishing Jewish characteristic. It made German Jews immigrating to America in the mid-nineteenth century often feel that the country was a wasteland of higher culture and that its rough-hewn popular culture was nigh insufferable. Still eighty years later, when America possessed considerably more intellectual sophistication, there were numerous German Jews among the refugees fleeing Hitler whose advanced scientific and cultural skills gained them access to American university positions and wide influence in American cultural life.

Finally, German Jews—with exceptions to be sure—possessed a devotion to doing things in a proper and orderly way that often made them the butt of ridicule, especially in Israel. If they were assigned a broken seat on a railroad train, for example, they would rather suffer the discomfort than move to the empty seat across the aisle. Their ingrained obedience to authority—a product of exaggerated Germanization—may have made them easier victims when the Nazis assumed power. Yet from their own point of view, their faith in the authority of law and even their excessive formality, stiff as it might sometimes be, was an expression of their human dignity. It was, I believe, that quiet, resolute dignity which helped sustain German Jews during the persecutions of the 1930s and which Rabbi Leo Baeck, German Jewry's great leader in its final hour of trial, was able to assert and to reaffirm in others even in the concentration camp at Theresienstadt. That remarkable dignity, which transcended humiliation, is also part of the legacy of the German Jews.

CHAPTER 8

"Scripture or Spirit?": The Revelation Question in German-Jewish Thought of the Nineteenth Century

In the spring of 1844 in the town of Köthen in Anhalt, Gustav Adolph Wislicenus, minister of the Neumarktskirche in Halle, gave a lecture to a gathering of Protestantische Freunde which he entitled "Scripture or Spirit?" Later published as a pamphlet,[1] Wislicenus's lecture drew extraordinary attention. Here was a Protestant clergyman formulating in the most succinct and radical fashion the disjunction that had received more subtle expression in the writings of leading theologians and extended learned treatment in the recent work of historical critics. In his lecture Wislicenus issued a veritable declaration of independence from the authority of the Bible, not alone from its letter, but from its spirit as well. For the spirit of Scripture was faithfully conveyed in its letter and it conflicted with the spirit now alive in contemporary humanity. Thus the Bible could no longer serve as a norm for belief. Scripture was to be replaced by the world spirit—that "Holy Spirit," according to Wislicenus, which had once manifested itself in the Bible but had moved beyond it. "Thus the spirit has also created the Bible," he maintained, "but not in order to halt with its word, rather to use it in order to drive itself onward. The spirit has not spoken in these writings in order to divest itself of its inner creative freedom and to become the servant of a transient form of itself." Scripture thus represented no permanently authoritative revelation. Its message, in relation to the present, could be seen only as a more primitive manifestation of a spiritual force which revealed itself progressively in history.

Wislicenus and his circle represented the extreme in Protestant theology of the mid-nineteenth century. More typical for the popu-

lar thought of the period in Germany were the views of Karl Gott-
lieb Bretschneider, whose *Compendium of the Dogmatics of the
Evangelical Lutheran Church* appeared in a fourth edition in 1838.
What Wislicenus held to be true of all revelation Bretschneider ap-
plied only to the Old Testament. He declared pre-Christian religious
institutions to be imperfect and intended only for a limited time.
The New Testament was the norm for Christian judgment of the
Old. Schleiermacher had put it even more strongly, calling the Old
Testament simply a "superfluous authority for Christian dogmatics" and finding the sole revelation to lie in the person of Christ.[2]
For Bretschneider the Christian revelation was unparalleled, and it
had not been exceeded. A member of that school which was known
as rational supernaturalism, he maintained against orthodoxy that
the Holy Scripture was not itself in its totality revelation, but that
revelation was to be found in it. Scripture testified to "the unmedi-
ated and supernatural influence of God" which, coming from outside the human spirit, acted to enlighten it. It is the scriptural
revelation which serves as norm for judging the truth of any later
claims to revelation. Like so many religious intellectuals of the nineteenth century—Christian and Jewish—Bretschneider accepted Lessing's famous concept that religious history was an "education of
humanity," but for him this education was brought about through
the influence of revelation on history. Reason did not develop independently; it had to be trained by scripture. The task of reason could
never be to replace scriptural revelation, but only to purify it, enno-
ble it, and make it fruitful.

The scripture versus spirit controversy, which rent German Christianity, had its counterpart within German Jewry. In some respects
the latter conflict was a reflection of the former. German Jews too
had been influenced by the *Zeitgeist*; those with a university education had read Kant, Hegel, and their disciples. They had observed
Christian attempts to meet the challenges of Enlightenment rationalism, idealistic philosophy, and historical criticism. But whereas the
Christian tradition faced the challenge of secular thought from the
position of a politically and culturally entrenched worldview, Judaism was forced to undergo intellectual confrontations during a period when Jews had still not achieved full political and social
equality and when cultural bias against Judaism, originating in both
religious and secularized circles, remained very strong. While the
intellectual basis of Christianity was being shaken, Judaism was undergoing a much more profound crisis of self-doubt, one which
went beyond religious issues to the existential question of how and

whether to maintain Jewish identity while partially integrated into a milieu radically different from the ghetto and scarcely appreciative of the Jewish faith. Jewish consideration of the problem of revelation in nineteenth-century Germany cannot therefore be divorced from the total situation in which Jews found themselves socially and politically as much as religiously and intellectually.

In this analysis my interest is not primarily in the purely theoretical side of the revelation question. I shall not be concerned with evaluating the role of concepts of revelation within encompassing theologies, nor do I intend to trace the influence of particular philosophical systems upon Jewish thinkers. I shall instead focus on a comparison of concepts of revelation in three representative Jewish theologians who wrote during the second third of the nineteenth century: Samson Raphael Hirsch (1808–88), Samuel Hirsch (1815–89), and Abraham Geiger (1810–74). Each of the three was an influential rabbi, active in the practical life of his community and known beyond it. Each tried to shape modern Jewish life in accordance with his own paradigm. Samson Raphael Hirsch was the founder of Neo-Orthodoxy, a movement which attempted to integrate a strictly orthodox form of Judaism with a wholehearted participation in German culture. Samuel Hirsch (no relation to the first Hirsch) was a representative of the radical wing of the Jewish Reform movement. He served as a rabbi in Dessau and Luxembourg before migrating to America where he and his son, Emil G. Hirsch, became leading figures in the establishment of Reform Judaism in the United States. Abraham Geiger, rabbi in Wiesbaden, Breslau, Frankfurt-on-the-Main, and finally in Berlin, was the most outstanding representative of Jewish religious liberalism in Germany. Possessing profound scholarship and considerable practical ability, he was able to gain broad acceptance for his initially radical, but in the course of time increasingly moderate views. As we shall see, each of the three put forward a doctrine of revelation which reflected the scripture-spirit conflict even as it attempted to deal with the specific situation of modern Jewry.

The starting point for any consideration of Jewish concepts of revelation in the nineteenth century must be a thinker of the eighteenth, Moses Mendelssohn (1729–86).[3] Influenced by the universalism and rationalism of Enlightenment thought, Mendelssohn responded by stressing similar characteristics in Judaism. He urged that in its basic tenets Judaism was wholly assimilable to natural religion, that it possessed no dogmas, and that it was not a "revealed religion" which provided truths necessary for salvation and otherwise unavailable. Religion, in Mendelssohn's view, merely gave sanction to obligations which reason itself required. As he himself put it: The eternal truths "could not have been inspired through direct revelation. . . . The Supreme Being has revealed them to all rational creatures through actions and concepts; He has inscribed them on their souls with a script that is legible and intelligible at all times and in all places."[4] Thus there was no religious barrier between Jew and gentile, at least none erected from the Jewish side. Jews and Christians could share a natural religion, independent of historical experience, which alone was necessary for human bliss. This deep religious bond would make possible integration of the Jews into German culture and society despite external differences—all this on the assumption that Christianity could transcend its revealed dogmas, which some of the Christian "neologians" were in fact setting out to do.

Yet Mendelssohn did not entirely abandon the concept of a supernatural revelation. He simply excluded all doctrine from it. For Mendelssohn, as is well known, God at Sinai gave to ancient Israel a "revealed legislation." For Mendelssohn, the Pentateuch is a divine book composed essentially of laws, ordinances, rules of conduct, and prescriptions. In addition, the Torah contains rational truths and religious precepts. But these can be learned from outside the Torah as well. The revealed laws are related to the doctrines as body is to soul; God favored the Jews by presenting them with practical means for keeping religious truths alive in their minds. These laws, in their totality, are incumbent upon Jews in every generation whether they can fathom them rationally or not. Given supernaturally by God, they can be abrogated by Him alone. Mendelssohn thus confined revelation in Judaism to its law, which distinguishes Israel from the rest of humanity. It is incumbent upon Jews to obey it, but it is not necessary for the salvation of humanity. It is directed to the will, rather than to the mind. Through his reason the Jew as human being participates in the great tasks of modern society; through submission to God's law, revealed specifically to a single people, he remains set apart, the member of a particular religious minority.

During the half century which separates Mendelssohn's death from the first writings of Samson Raphael Hirsch, the Enlightenment Jewish philosopher's narrow concept of revelation produced ramifications unintended by its author. Among Mendelssohn's disciples were those, like David Friedländer (1750–1834), who refused to accept the divinity of the law, regarding it rather as a human and historical product. They were left with only adherence to natural religion for which, they soon realized, Jewish tradition was as superfluous as it was detrimental to emancipation. Those who chose to continue believing that the law was revealed supernaturally by God found little in Mendelssohn's writings to encourage them. It seemed as if the law were a burden imposed on God, which Jews were forced patiently to bear. By the 1830s, religious sentiment and spiritual creativity seemed to many at odds with a law that was often obeyed in rote fashion or not obeyed at all. Lay reformers had sought to make largely cosmetic changes in the worship service which they hoped would lead to a reinvigoration of Jewish religion at least in the synagogue. But they averted their eyes from the decay of religious practice taking place generally in the daily lives of individual Jews.

No one was more troubled by this situation than the young Samson Raphael Hirsch.[5] An opponent of religious reform, he nonetheless recognized that orthodoxy had been unable to cope with its new environment. Its leadership condemned innovation while proving itself incapable of propagating traditional belief and practice in the idiom of the cultural milieu which Jews were increasingly adopting as their own.

To no small degree Hirsch's success in rejuvenating orthodoxy was owing to his recognition of the inadequacy of Mendelssohn's doctrine of revelation. In Hirsch's thought, Torah is given the breadth and significance which Mendelssohn had denied it. For Hirsch the revelatory content of Torah is not alone law; it is a teaching (*Lehre*) about man's life on earth. The teaching encompasses the law but it extends beyond it. It is the paradigm of a complete religious life, an ideal fully realizable only eschatologically, but serving in its specifics to educate the Jewish people to its universal task until ultimately it becomes the general pattern for all mankind. Hirsch agreed with Mendelssohn that Judaism has no dogmas, but he believed that its revelation did have noetic content. Underlying the duties which God commands are revealed truths about man, nature, and history. Revelation creates the basis for spiritual life in the broadest sense. The latter could not exist without the former.

Hirsch regarded Mendelssohn as continuing a venerable but nonetheless misguided tradition. Like Maimonides before him, Mendelssohn did not stand wholly within Judaism seeking to build it spiritually upon its own foundations. Unlike those medieval writers whom Hirsch admires in this regard—Judah Halevi and Nachmanides—Mendelssohn was more concerned about harmonizing Judaism with contemporary non-Jewish thought than with interpreting it out of itself. Consequently he had narrowed Judaism excessively and failed to justify its particular significance in broader human terms.

Hirsch agreed fully with Mendelssohn that the authority of the revelation rested upon its supernatural character, the dramatic events at Sinai witnessed collectively by the Israelites in the desert. Whether or not it was fully comprehensible to the human mind, it was binding in its totality until such time as God would rescind it. Like nature, it was a given. But Hirsch undertook to create what we might today call a hermeneutics of the literature of revelation. He sought to show his readers from a purely human perspective that there was no conflict between scripture and spirit, for spirit—the best of the modern spirit—was contained within scripture, which in turn originated in the spirit of God. The task which Hirsch set for himself and his generation of Jewish religious leaders was simply "to grasp with the spirit that which one should respect" and to show the error of those who believed Judaism was a "spiritless phenomenon." The result would be different from the work of the first generation of reformers—not merely a "polishing of the exterior frame," but a recovery of the spirit of traditional Judaism and hence an assurance of its viability in the new age.[6]

For Hirsch the spirit of Judaism was not to be equated with the *Zeitgeist*. The revelation at Sinai is perfect and in no need of supplementation, let alone dialectical advance. It does not enter into history but stands above it, rendering judgment upon the imperfections of society. Thus reform can only be of the Jews, not of the Jewish teaching. The task is to bring about a "realization of that eternal ideal within and in conjunction with contemporary circumstances; education, raising the age to the Torah—but not bringing the Torah down to the level of the age, lowering the peak to the flat surface of our lives."[7] The revelation was never dependent upon any human factor, also a culturally primitive and religiously backward people could not have become its recipients. When the Torah says God spoke, it is God's words which are revealed, not a vague inspiration to which Moses gave substance. Were the latter the case, then the revelation would immediately be relativized and historicized. It would lose its absolute character. Hirsch explicitly recognizes this danger. He writes: "Were the 'Word of God,' which Moses and Israel transmitted to us as spoken by Him, mediated in any way in its transmission by Moses' and Israel's *conception* of it, we would have to make room for the possibility that this Word, as we have it, was limited by the mental capacities, insights, and views—by the entire level of culture—of the people and the man who conveyed it to us."[8]

Thus Hirsch must reduce the role of Moses in the revelation to absolute passivity. Moses was not a great legislator as others have pictured him. He was merely a vessel. The revelation was not "from Israel and from Moses," but rather "to Moses and to Israel did He speak His Word." Thus the revelation is superhuman; it is sui generis and cannot be placed in any developmental sequence of religious doctrines. The Jewish religion, like all religions, has a history, but the Torah, as revelation, has none. It follows that historical criticism cannot legitimately be directed to the Torah since its very premise is the false assumption that Torah is a human creation reflective of a particular cultural and religious situation. Nor can reformers argue that it belongs to another age, for it belongs to no age and to every age. It is, Hirsch insisted, eternal.

For Hirsch, literal divine revelation extends not only to the totality of the Pentateuch, but beyond it to the Oral Law which later gained written form in the Talmud. It was the latter which was under the most severe attack by historical critics and reformers who questioned its Sinaitic origins and rejected its apparent irrelevancies. Hirsch's defense of the Oral Law is to argue that an attack upon its authority is in effect an attack upon scripture for our knowledge of the Written Law's divinity depends upon the reliability of the same rabbinical chain of tradition which transmitted the Oral Law. Moreover, Hirsch argues, nearly every word of scripture presumes an oral elaboration without which it remains incomplete. In his Pentateuch commentary, Hirsch went so far as to suggest that scripture represented nothing more than "brief memoranda" that presume the complete teaching, which is oral. The Pentateuch was "only a crutch for the memory and a corrective for doubt."[9] Like notes taken on a lecture, the Pentateuch would jog the memory to recall the totality of the teaching. While other religions have adopted the written revelation from Judaism, Hirsch argues elsewhere, "they have lacked the key and consummation of the oral revelation."[10]

Hirsch's defense of the Oral Law was the more imperative since its status as Sinaitic revelation had been challenged not only by reformers and secular critics but also by the conservative positive-historical school of Zacharias Frankel (1801–75) and Heinrich Graetz (1817–91). In his Darchei Hamishnah (1859), Frankel had shown great admiration for the early rabbis, but in his very respect for them he had trespassed the bounds of orthodoxy. He had made them religious innovators, not mere transmitters of the oral teaching. Frankel allowed that the rabbis had created their own elaborations of the Torah's statutes and had in addition promulgated laws which were wholly the product of their own minds. For Frankel, so Hirsch argues, "the tradition is only something transmitted, not something received; its first transmitters searched for and invented it."[11] Similarly Graetz, in his *History of the Jews*, had made the ancient rabbis into personalities whose individual qualities of character determined the laws associated with their names. They were not simply bearers of the tradition, but its creators, and thus the talmudic teaching, rather than being a faithful reflection of Sinaitic revelation, became "nothing but the product of the character and psychological talents of those particular personalities."[12] When the volume of Graetz's history dealing with the biblical period appeared some years later, Hirsch must have been even more disturbed to find that Graetz made Moses likewise into a creator of the Jewish faith, and—with the apparent exception of the Ten Commandments—not merely a passive recipient of the divine word.[13]

Hirsch's insistence upon the absolute externality of revelation and his denial of any human component in it is understandable in light of his aforementioned concern to escape historicization. However, it not only set Hirsch at odds with non-orthodox Jewry, it set him very much against the temper of the times. Ever since Kant formulated the dilemma in the eighteenth century, religious thinkers had been forced to grapple with the conflict between God's will as represented by scripture and the autonomy of the human spirit, which Kant argued was essential to higher religion.[14] Hirsch's stand on this issue is unequivocal. The revelation is wholly heteronomous. It stands in opposition to human inclination and it demands obedience. "To revere God," says Hirsch, "means—to obey God." With regard to none of the duties which it imposes does the Torah require our recognition of its purpose in order for it to be binding. For Hirsch there is no counterpart of the external God within the human being which must validate the content of revelation by its assent. In fact the opposite is the case: Israel's resistance to the law of God "is the most certain criterion for the divine origin of this law, which did not arise *out of the people*, but came *to* it. . . ."[15] If contemporary Jews oppose observance of the law—however they may justify their attitude intellectually—their opposition in fact simply indicates that the revelation still stands far above the religious level of the age. Furthermore, their argument is invalid: obedience to the law need not crush the spirit, for as traditional religion in the West—whether Christian, Muslim, or Jewish—has always held, true spiritual freedom lies in subordinating man's will to God's.

Such a conception of freedom, however, stood in the starkest opposition to that promulgated by the Enlightenment. By the thirties it seemed to liberal thinkers, Christian and Jewish, that either traditional religious doctrine would have to be sacrificed or the autonomy of the human spirit, the latter being the very hallmark of modern man. For Samuel Hirsch, the reformer, this conflict lies at the base of his reinterpretation of Judaism.[16]

According to this Hirsch, Christianity had as yet failed to realize the full gravity of the problem. Catholicism, though less authoritarian than in the past, continued to be grounded in heteronomy and thus remained in fundamental conflict with the principles of the modern age. Protestantism had laid claim to the principle of autonomy of the spirit, but in fact had merely exchanged the authority of the entire ecclesiastical tradition for that of the first three centuries, the authority of the papacy for the authority of a book. In Judaism, Samson Raphael Hirsch likewise represented a failure to come to terms: seeking to persuade fellow Jews to observe the law, though the ultimate reason for its observance remained simply its divine origin.

For Samuel Hirsch, revelation in the normal sense of the word necessarily implies the infringement of human autonomy. The human spirit becomes enslaved to an authority which lies outside itself. "Indeed," says Hirsch, "today one regards such a God, Who speaks only in riddles and despotic decrees, as a false deity." On the other hand, what the human spirit is able to discover through its own efforts requires no revelation. Remarkably, Hirsch makes the critique of revelation into an argument for Judaism, or at least for Judaism as he conceives it. Christianity, he claims, requires revelation; Judaism does not. The reason is the Christian doctrine of Original Sin. If man's faculties have been corrupted by sin, then he requires for his salvation a divine will set in opposition to his own. But Judaism, which lacks the doctrine of Original Sin, needs no such confrontation. Therefore Hirsch can agree with Mendelssohn that "Judaism has neither a revealed God and teaching nor a revealed mystery and dogma." It is not a revealed religion. Nothing was taught at Sinai which could not be arrived at by the autonomous human spirit. As a reformer, Hirsch further holds, this time against Mendelssohn, that Judaism also has no revealed *legislation*. Its ceremonial laws are merely symbolic acts whose continuing significance must be measured by their appropriateness to the spirit and task of the modern age. To his mind, it was religiously counterproductive for Jews to spend their spiritual energies in attempting to force meaning into outworn practices.

Yet Hirsch is unwilling to dispense entirely with the conception of revelation. While rejecting supernaturalism, he allows for what he calls the "natural revelation dwelling in every human being," which all—presumably because there is no barrier of innate sinfulness—are able to follow. But this seems an extraordinary expansion of the term far beyond common usage. What I believe Hirsch has really done is to do away with the concept of revelation in any meaningful sense and to compensate for it by an implicit greater emphasis on two other concepts: creation and redemption.

The reason that revelation is either religiously unacceptable or superfluous is that God created man in His image, endowing him with uncorrupted rational faculties capable of recognizing truth. Likewise, the quest for freedom, characteristic of the modern age, represents a positive human aspiration to imitate God. The capacities instilled in man at the beginning require no external illumination or redirection of man's will. Creation does not require the correction of revelation. At the same time, Hirsch is not a deist, nor is he unaware that it is precisely the specificity of the revelation at Sinai which marked the Jews as a separate people. In the absence of such a revelation, the identity of the Jew is apt to be lost and Jewish religious ritual to become wholly meaningless unless God is active in history as redeemer and Israel is assigned a special role in the redemption of humanity. Drawing upon Hegelian thought, Hirsch asserts the existence of an independent world-spirit which stands above the nations and their strivings. Hirsch identifies this world-spirit with the personal God of religion Who demands of man only that he develop his spiritual capacities and Who, educating and forming him, ever vigilantly attends his spiritual life.

For Hirsch, Judaism like no other religion represents this redemption process. It is, he says, the "religion of history." Scripture for Judaism is not a book of revelation but a book of history. It is the history of a people's education while at the same time serving as a historical model and exemplar for all other history. It warns of the consequences of sacrificing the quest for spiritual freedom to hedonistic desires while pointing out the benefits of true devotion to the life of the spirit. Christianity, as a religious denomination, must look always back to its origins in the past and define itself according to its own confession of faith. It is "a completed teaching, a given revelation." Judaism, for Hirsch, has no confession of faith and no specific point of origin. Its focus is not at all upon the past but upon the universal future of humanity. Therefore, says Hirsch, Judaism feels itself so closely related to the worldview of the present age. In fact, Judaism simply provides religious motivation. The task of the modern age is for the Jew a religious task. Without a specific doctrine or law, separated only by its historical symbols, Judaism testifies to the "sanctity of history."

The position of Abraham Geiger on revelation manifests the same concerns evidenced in the thought of Samuel Hirsch.[17] Like Hirsch, he too, from the beginning of his career, could not accept a wholly external God who imposes His will upon man. Moral acts, Geiger holds in agreement with Kant, can have value only if they stem from an inner moral impulse, "if they flow directly out of the striving for self-ennoblement . . . and the veneration and love of God."[18] For Geiger, no less than for Samuel Hirsch, obedience is not morality. Unless the human being is himself convinced of the rightness of his act, that act has no religious or moral significance. A duty performed without reflection is a lifeless deed. Geiger goes even further: an act done without autonomous assent is actually destructive of moral consciousness. The relation of God to man is not like that of a parent whose child is expected to obey merely out of regard for father or mother. God's will, as transmitted through tradition, must be examined by the human being in order to determine whether the external word matches the word within, whether the received will of the God of historical revelation is in conformity with the divine in man. There cannot remain an unresolved conflict between historical revelation and rational assent. For Geiger the divine within in effect becomes judge of the teaching conveyed in the name of the external God. Obedience is appropriate only to the former, to the moral sense implanted by the Creator God. The teaching is not to be blindly adopted or obeyed but to be appropriated and internalized to the extent that it can be made to resonate upon the moral consciousness. As a reformer, Geiger was particularly concerned to apply this viewpoint to ceremonial regulations, finding their observance incumbent upon the Jew only if they served to invigorate religious and moral sensitivities. Seemingly conjoining two contradictory concepts, Geiger arrived at what he terms "a freely chosen obedience mediated by inner understanding."[19]

To the believer in an external inscrutable God, Geiger's respect for the divine within appeared as a mask for mere obedience to the human self. The only way Geiger could deal with such an accusation was through a doctrine of individual religious experience whereby reflection points to an inner presence not wholly equatable with the human spirit even as it is directly related to it. The human spirit must attest to the divine spirit.[20] For Geiger God is indeed the root of the human spirit without Whom the great spiritual endeavors of individuals and peoples would not be possible. All higher strivings in art and science are a revelation of spirit since they bring spiritual development beyond its actual level to the realization of a greater potential. Religion represents the endeavor to reach the higher level, "the impetus toward the all-encompassing unity which the person as a whole, following the nature of his spirit, surmises to be the foundation of all being and becoming, the source of all earthly and spiritual life. . . ."[21] As "primordial spirit" and "source of spirit" God stands at the beginning; as the fulfillment of spiritual striving He stands eschatologically beyond historical time. The human being is spirit from God's spirit, but the two are not the same.

Geiger thus seeks to avoid the equation of the human with the divine. Yet God's presence in religious experience seems quite independent of scripture. What remains here of the authority of the Bible? Is not scripture simply absorbed into the stream of spiritual history, relativized, and, like any other ancient text, made a fit object of historical criticism? Taken as whole, the Written Torah is for Geiger no more to be regarded as a direct verbal communication from God to Israel than is the Oral Torah embodied in the Talmud. Bible and Talmud are both human documents. On grounds of scholarship as well as the desire for reform, Geiger concluded early in life— though he hesitated to express his view openly—that the Bible was not in itself divine, that historical research would show how it had gradually taken shape, how it reflected the historical circumstances of its time. He criticized Samson Raphael Hirsch for plucking the Bible out of the stream of history. The historical scholar could not allow such a procedure. He might recognize a common spirit at work in the Bible but he had also to recognize the inevitable process of growth and decline as well as the influence of external circumstances. Geiger himself, in his magnum opus, *The Original Text and Translations of the Bible* (*Die Urschrift und Uebersetzungen der Bibel,* 1857), tried to show how the gradual establishment of a fixed text of the Bible was directly influenced by shifting perceptions over a long period of time.

Yet, unlike Samuel Hirsch, Geiger in the final analysis did not allow Scripture to be merely the reflection of a spiritual history. One reason at least seems to have been a polemical need to set Judaism above Christianity and thus justify its perpetuation despite political and social pressures. For had Geiger accepted a wholly evolutionary scheme, he would then have had no reply to critics of Judaism— Christian theologians and philosophers—who regarded it as an inferior religion transcended by Christianity. The more critical Christian scholars had particularly stressed the spiritual hiatus between the two faiths. Having stripped Christianity of its miraculous elements and come to regard it as a human creation, they were reluctant to root it too deeply in Judaism lest it be robbed of its originality. Schleiermacher was particularly concerned to stress the shadow sides of Judaism, so that Christianity, in purely natural terms, would appear to represent a major discontinuity. Orthodox theologians, for their part, might regard Christianity as the perfected revelation, but at least had to regard Judaism as an equally genuine revelation, even if a temporary one. Both rationalist and orthodox Christian writers regarded Judaism as superseded by the new faith. However, by raising the biblical revelation out of the stream of history, Geiger could make it tower over both what precedes and what follows it.

In the latter portion of his life Geiger developed a concept of revelation clearly at variance with more radical reformers such as Samuel Hirsch. While the Bible continued to be for him a human document, it conveyed a historical revelation which was not explicable by the natural course of spiritual development. For Geiger this revelation, which stands at the beginning of Israel's historical existence, is of the One God Himself.[22] Monotheism is not an idea to which humanity would have been able to raise itself. Yet it was so overwhelming that it dominated Judaism and spread outward from it.

Like the Talmud and like Maimonides, Geiger makes revelation dependent upon the spiritual preparation of the prophet, though, in contrast to Maimonides and following Judah Halevi, he holds that the prophet is only an organ of the people. The prophet expresses a collective religious genius shared by the people as a whole. The Jews, for Geiger, are the "people of revelation." But revelation does not rest upon genius alone. In a rather early set of lectures Geiger speaks only of a "sudden exaltation,"[23] but later, using language that recalls Bretschneider, of "the Power that fills everything illuminating individual spirits so that they broke through their finite bounds. . . ."[24] There is no compulsion of the human spirit in this concept of revelation, but the spirit is so radically transformed that the event cannot be explained otherwise than by an external source. It is not the specific will of God which Scripture attests, but the self-revelation of God as the author and goal of all spiritual striving. Borne through history by the Jews, this revelation of the one God perpetuates itself through the centuries on account of its inner truth.

Even as Geiger sets the revelation reflected in scripture apart from the religious ideas of ancient Near Eastern peoples who preceded Israel, so does his periodization of Jewish history bring revelation to an end with biblical times. The age of revelation is followed by the periods of Tradition, Legalism, and Criticism.[25] Whether within Judaism or outside of it, the basic truth revealed in Scripture can in the course of history only be better comprehended; it cannot be superseded.

We may then conclude that within modern Judaism the scripture-spirit conflict arose for reasons rooted in philosophy, in historical criticism, and in the minority position of the Jews. Like Christian theologians, their Jewish counterparts were compelled either to deny that heteronomy was religiously inferior to spiritual autonomy or to devise a concept of revelation which was not characterized by obedience to a higher teaching not fully comprehended by the human spirit. In the course of the nineteenth century historical criticism increasingly undercut the authority of texts hitherto regarded as revealed. In Judaism one could stand one's ground, as did Samson Raphael Hirsch, and insist upon the revealed character of both the Oral and the Written Law; one could hold that *Wissenschaft* might only interpret the sources, not question their status as faithful transmitters of Sinaitic revelation. Alternatively one could, with Zacharias Frankel, make a sharp distinction between the written and oral traditions, subjecting the latter, but not the former, to historical study. With Samuel Hirsch one could absorb even scripture wholly into the historical development of spirit. Or, finally, one could with Geiger regard the Bible as a human document, but one which conveyed an elevated doctrine of God to be characterized as revelation on account of its inexplicability by the natural slow process of spiritual development. These intellectual considerations must in turn be understood in the context of a Jewry rapidly integrating into German society, a Jewry whose religious leaders in their concern to preserve Jewish identity, each in his own way sought to present a concept of revelation which would set Judaism apart, even as its adherents participated more and more in the non-Jewish world around them.

Notes

1. Gustav Adolph Wislicenus, *Ob Schrift? Ob Geist? Verantwortung gegen meine Ankläger*, 2d. ed. (Leipzig, 1845).
2. See the note in K. G. Bretschneider, *Handbuch der Dogmatik der evangelisch-lutherischen Kirche* (Leipzig, 1838), I, 179.

3. On Mendelssohn see especially Alexander Altmann, *Moses Mendelssohn: A Biographical Study* (Tuscaloosa, Ala., 1973); also Michael A. Meyer, *The Origins of the Modern Jew: Jewish Identity and European Culture in Germany, 1749–1824* (Detroit, 1967), 11–56.

4. *Jerusalem, oder über religiöse Macht und Judentum* (Berlin, 1783), II, 112.

5. General studies of Hirsch include Noah H. Rosenbloom, *Tradition in an Age of Reform: The Religious Philosophy of Samson Raphael Hirsch* (Philadelphia, 1976) and Pinchas E. Rosenblüth, "Samson Raphael Hirsch: Sein Denken und Wirken," *Das Judentum in der Deutschen Umwelt 1800–1850*, ed., H. Liebesschütz and A. Paucker (Tübingen, 1977), 293–324. Directly related to our topic is Pinchas Paul Grünewald, *Eine jüdische Offenbarungslehre: Samson Raphael Hirsch* (Bern, 1977).

6. See especially *Neunzehn Briefe über Judentum* (Altona, 1836), 91–100; *Horeb, Versuche über Jissroels Pflichten in der Zerstreuung* (Altona, 1837), x, 27–28; *Gesammelte Schriften*, 6 vols. (Frankfurt am Main, 1902–12), I, 90.

7. *Neunzehn Briefe*, 84.

8. *Gesammelte Schriften*, III, 165.

9. *Der Pentateuch, übersetzt und erläutert* (Frankfurt am Main, 1920), I, 149; II, 123.

10. *Gesammelte Schriften*, I, 103.

11. Ibid., VI, 408, 413.

12. Ibid., V, 322.

13. Heinrich Graetz, *Geschichte der Juden*, I (Leipzig, 1874), 20–58.

14. For a contemporary Jewish discussion of the dilemma see Emil L. Fackenheim, "The Revealed Morality of Judaism and Modern Thought: A Confrontation with Kant," *Quest for Past and Future: Essays in Jewish Theology* (Bloomington, Ind., 1968), 204–28.

15. *Pentateuch*, II, 197.

16. My analysis of Samuel Hirsch is based primarily on the position he put forward in his short work, *Die Reform im Judenthum und dessen Beruf in der gegenwärtigan Welt* (Leipzig, 1844), from which the citations in the text are taken. For a study of Hirsch's earlier major work, *Die Religionsphilosophie der Juden* (Leipzig, 1842), see Emil L. Fackenheim, "Samuel Hirsch and Hegel," *Studies in Nineteenth-Century Jewish Intellectual History*, ed. Alexander Altmann (Cambridge, Mass., 1964), 171–201. Much work on Hirsch has been done by Gershon Greenberg. See especially his "The Historical Origins of God and Man: Samuel Hirsch's Luxembourg Writings," *Leo Baeck Institute Year Book*, XX (1975), 129–48. Greenberg has shown that Hirsch's position on theological issues changed considerably during the course of his life.

17. A bibliography of secondary literature on Geiger is contained in *New Perspectives on Abraham Geiger*, ed. Jakob J. Petuchowski (Cincinnati, 1975), 55–58.

18. *Wissenschaftliche Zeitschrift fur jüdische Theologie*, IV (1839), 1; cf. ibid., 314–18.

19. Ibid., 11.
20. Letter to M. A. Stern, 28 Dec. 1858, *Nachgelassene Schriften*, 5 vols. (Berlin, 1875–78), V, 229–30.
21. *Das Judentum und seine Geschichte* (Breslau, 1910), 10.
22. In his evaluation of the work of the Jewish theologian Solomon Ludwig Steinheim (*Jüdische Zeitschrift für Wissenschaft und Leben*, X, [1872], 285–92), Geiger distinguished between "das Offenbarwerden Gottes," which he believes to be the true meaning of revelation in Judaism and "das Offenbarmachen, die Mitteilung der Lehre an das Ohr," which is Steinheim's conception. Here Geiger criticizes Steinheim for holding that the truth of revelation is supported by its contradiction of reason. To Geiger's mind, this is a Christian point of view, not a Jewish one.
23. *Nachgelassene Schriften*, II, 6.
24. *Das Judentum*, 35.
25. *Nachgelassene Schriften*, II, 63–64.

CHAPTER 9

Jewish Scholarship and Jewish Identity: Their Historical Relationship in Modern Germany

While the development of modern Jewish scholarship and the formulation of various modes of modern Jewish identity have both been popular subjects of study, they have usually been treated separately.[1] Only a few studies have dwelt on their relationship, and those only within the context of a relatively brief period; as yet consideration has not been given to a longer view. How did these two elements of modern Jewish history relate to one another over a span of time sufficient for the perception of change? This essay examines the question by focusing upon the development of Wissenschaft des Judentums in Germany from its inception in the early nineteenth century until the eve of the Holocaust. As it will become evident, modern Jewish scholarship was variously perceived as undermining, ignoring, or revitalizing Jewish identity. Moreover, not only did Jews recognize the far-reaching significance of the relationship; Christians did as well, and they responded accordingly. To trace the relationship between Jewish scholarship and Jewish identity, then, is to gain a significant perspective from which to view both the external and the internal history of Jews in modern Germany.

Both of the concepts to be dealt with here are modern in origin. Identity, in the psychosocial sense in which it is relevant for the present subject, has become a popular tool of analysis only in this generation, largely through the theoretical work of Erik Erikson. Studies of personal and collective identity have gained popularity at a time when crisis and confusion attend individual maturation and hinder the formation of group self-definition. But for the Jews, the identity question did not await the twentieth century. They were forced to confront it as they emerged from a physical and spiritual ghetto into a non-Jewish environment that was deeply ambivalent about taking them into its midst, and that to varying degrees demanded they alter the identity that had characterized them in the past. Hitherto, turned inward both by exclusionary pressure from the outside and by their own religiously grounded sense of superior worth, Jews had not needed to mark off their Jewishness; they possessed no non-Jewish identifications. Only when they began to feel that they were European or Germans as well as Jews did Jewish identity become problematic.

Even more obviously does scientific scholarship enter Jewish history only in modern times, despite the fact that it has its analogues in traditional Judaism. Jews, of course, have always given great honor and respect to their scholars, and even during medieval times they were characterized by an extraordinary degree of male literacy. But there is a vast difference between study, *talmud torah* (or in Yiddish and German, *lernen*), on the one hand, and Wissenschaft des Judentums, on the other. To study the classical texts is a religious commandment in Judaism; it is *melekhet shamayin* (literally, the work of heaven).[2] Such study was for a clearly defined purpose—to discern the will of God speaking through the text of Torah and Talmud—and thus the sanctity of the house of study, Moses Maimonides noted in the twelfth century, exceeds even that of the synagogue.[3] The truth was understood to reside in the text itself, not in the mind or methodology of the scholar. Modern Wissenschaft, in contrast, brought to Jewish scholarship a critical element that was not inherent within its own tradition. It separated the present from the past and introduced the concept of development. To varying degrees, it also secularized what had previously been regarded as wholly sacred. Not surprisingly, it was soon perceived as a grave threat to the faith of those who were most traditional; a threat that extended, moreover, to their very identity as religious Jews.

For other Jews more receptive to the intellectual world of the nineteenth century, the application of scientific scholarship to Judaism in the form of critical historical research became a necessary means for assuring the survival of Judaism outside a ghetto. These Jews believed that Wissenschaft des Judentums could liberate them from the old ways and suggest new paths more compatible with modernity; while unbinding the old ties, it would rebind with new ones. Yet even among non-Orthodox Jews, Wissenschaft des Judentums raised doubts and fostered disputes with regard to its consequences for Jewish identity. By the beginning of the twentieth century it had become the object of severe critique not only by

Orthodox Jews but also by some of the scholars themselves, by proponents of religious revival and by Zionists. As for Christian scholars, with few exceptions they viewed it all along with mistrust, or else sought to use it for the purpose of weakening Jewish identity. The relationship between Jewish scholarship and Jewish identity was thus both complex and ambiguous.

In focusing on Wissenschaft des Judentums, it is important to recall that the initial assault upon the untroubled identity of premodern Jews actually arose from the Haskalah, the Jewish response to the German Aufklärung. It was in the age of Moses Mendelssohn (1729–86) that the most acculturated German Jews were forced into the realization that their traditional way of life conflicted with their aspirations to be accepted and to feel at home in gentile society. That society was now more willing to accept them into its midst as Jews—provided they would give up most of the ties of solidarity that had bound them together until then. Mendelssohn had argued that Judaism, properly understood, did not conflict with the tenets of the Enlightenment, that it was in fact more rational and tolerant in its beliefs than was Christianity. Therefore, he argued, commitment to the ideals of the Enlightenment need not damage loyalty to Judaism. But Mendelssohn, like most men of the Enlightenment, did not think in historical categories. It was not until two generations later, when historical consciousness came to replace rationalism as the key to understanding human reality, that scientific historical study rather than the reconciliation of Judaism with reason became the crucial task for those who sought a means of justifying the persistence of Judaism in the modern world.

The group of young men who formed the Verein für Cultur und Wissenschaft der Juden in 1819 were convinced that science, broadly conceived, was the principal intellectual characteristic of the modern age. In order to survive in this milieu, Jewish identity had to be made consistent with it. The canons of critical scholarship taught in German universities, where a number of them were students at the time, would have to be applied to the sources of Judaism. One result would be a clearer understanding that Judaism had changed over the centuries: that in its present configuration the pristine idea of Judaism lay hidden beneath later accretions. The overthrow of rabbinism and the emergence of religious reform would be a necessary and important product of Wissenschaft. As Immanuel Wohlwill put it in the opening article of Leopold Zunz's *Zeitschrift für die Wissenschaft des Judenthums* (1822): "The freer, scientific attitude forces its way through the weed-infested underbrush of ceremonialism, grown mechanical and mindless through millennia of habit—and it perceives, still present within, the same divine idea, just as it had once clearly revealed itself."⁴ So too, it was believed, the political emancipation of the Jews in Germany, which had been set back during the period of reaction following the defeat of Napoleon, would gain renewed impetus from objective studies of the Jews. But although the members of the Verein thus considered carefully what they regarded as the beneficent practical effects that the new Jewish scholarship would have on Jewish life, what they sought above all else was to show that Wissenschaft and Judaism were not intellectually incompatible—an aim that recalled Mendelssohn's earlier efforts to reconcile Judaism and rationalism.

It was the immediate goal of the Verein to raise Judaism to the level of Wissenschaft, which, according to Wohlwill, was "the standpoint of European life." Only on this level could Judaism survive in the modern world. But Wissenschaft was first of all criticism. To employ its tools meant to undermine the unity and sanctity of Jewish tradition. Its first stage was necessarily demolition. Only once the building, which had been constructed on a foundation that could not withstand critical analysis, crumbled could some of its bricks be used to build a new structure on more durable foundations.

German Jewry, however, was by no means agreed that Judaism required a new lodging built by Wissenschaft. As the seeds planted by the Verein began to sprout in critical studies and in scholarly institutions during the course of the nineteenth century, Wissenschaft des Judentums represented for some a force that shored up Jewish identity and made it viable for modern Jews. But for others it was a force that needed to be severely kept in check. Untrammeled, they feared, Wissenschaft would run rampant over all that Jews held sacred.

At one end of the spectrum stood those modern Jews whose limited internalization of modernity excluded Wissenschaft des Judentums entirely. German Jews who were adherents of the Neo-Orthodoxy of Samson Raphael Hirsch welcomed both the opportunity to become German patriots and the literary culture that Germany and Europe offered them. But they rejected vehemently any and every attempt to apply the tools of historical criticism to those sources that constituted the religious foundations of Judaism. The revelation contained in Torah and Talmud remained by its very nature beyond the reach of literary or historical analysis: It was by definition and unassailably God's word. Hirsch did believe there was a legitimate *jüdische Wissenschaft*, but what he meant by the term when he used it positively was not the application of the same scientific criteria to Jewish sources that others had applied to the sources of ancient Greece or Rome. He meant rather the uniquely Jewish Wissenschaft that had been practiced by Jews throughout the millennia; in fact, nothing other than a continuation of *talmud torah,* the reverent study of the sacred texts.

But Hirsch was not one to be satisfied with defending the bastion of tradition. He sallied forth as well to do battle with modern scholarship over its own objectives. He argued that, if Wissenschaft des Judentums had hoped to rescue Jewish identity from the forces of assimilation, it had failed badly. Whereas *lernen* had been everyone's Jewish task (or at least that of male Jews), Wissenschaft des Judentums was necessarily elitist. Its influence was limited to those few who engaged in it and the not much larger circle that read the scholarship they produced. The true Jewish scholarship, Hirsch argued, had been a *Wissenschaft des Lebens,* a living scholarship; it had taught traditional Jews how to lead their lives and it was also the *Wissenschaft der Juden* in the sense that it belonged uniquely to Jews. What modern scholarship might have accomplished—that is, giving new form to the old conceptions—it had failed or refused to do, instead calling the religious conceptions themselves into question and thereby undermining Jewish faith, the only basis for Jewish identity.

But the most pernicious effect of Wissenschaft des Judentums, according to Hirsch, was that it legitimized abandonment of Orthodoxy. He wrote of critical scholars in 1862: "In all of this they see only the all too welcome scholarly legalization of the break with Jewish law that in practice they undertook long ago for themselves and their children."[5] In other words, Wissenschaft des Judentums was a palliative for guilty consciences. Or, put more kindly: Even when Wissenschaft only raised doubts, without drawing conclusions, its effect was to influence parents to withhold their children from traditional Jewish education. Because it suspended commitment it broke the transmission from one generation to another. Or, put yet another way, the new form of study, unlike the old, did not complement religious acts; it replaced them. For some of the scholars, Wissenschaft des Judentums had become the principal basis of their Jewishness. For them the practice of Judaism itself had become secondary to studying *about* Judaism through the alien lens of Wissenschaft. For Hirsch, the result was at best a vicarious Jewish identity. The new scholars no longer recited the religious poetry of the synagogue; they only studied it.

Hirsch and his supporters were especially fearful of Wissenschaft des Judentums at its most conservative, for then its pernicious influence was difficult to detect. In 1859, for example, Zacharias Frankel had published his *Darkhei hamishnah*, an important scholarly work on the ancient rabbis. Though showing great respect for the ancient sages, Frankel had ventured the view that, despite the explicit insistence of the Talmud, there were laws in the Mishnah that did not originate at Sinai but were innovations of the rabbis themselves. From the Orthodox point of view, such questioning of the revelational status of the Oral Law was tantamount to undermining the foundations of traditional Judaism and therefore abetting the erosion of Jewish consciousness.[6] To the eyes of the Orthodox, the Jewish Theological Seminary in Breslau, headed by Frankel since its creation in 1854, was a particularly insidious source of contamination for German Jewry. Its teachers and students were generally observant of the rabbinic commandments no less than of those in the Pentateuch—but in accepting historical criticism of rabbinic texts, they had created a cleft between belief and practice that was bound to widen.[7]

The Orthodox camp itself, however, was not entirely monolithic, and Wissenschaft des Judentums was not rejected out of hand by all Orthodox scholars. Ezriel Hildesheimer, who in 1873 became the first director of the Rabbinical Seminary for Orthodox Judaism in Berlin, believed that Torah and Wissenschaft could exist side by side. Although Hildesheimer and his colleagues never questioned the Sinaitic origins of the Written and Oral Law, they produced scholarly historical writings, published critical editions and compiled bibliographies. Hildesheimer's associate, David Hoffmann, was even willing to cite the work of non-Orthodox scholars and to allow that the form of the Mishnah—though not the content of its laws—was determined by the ancient rabbis themselves. The Orthodox rabbinical seminary in Berlin thus allowed a discipline foreign to Judaism to enter rabbinical training. Much criticized on that account by Hirsch, its faculty represented the most liberal position in German Orthodoxy.[8]

Wissenschaft had a firmer hold at the Jewish Theological Seminary in Breslau. Frankel himself humanized the talmudic literature, while his colleague, the historian Heinrich Graetz, freely emended the verses of Psalms. Yet Frankel drew the line at Pentateuch criticism. The Five Books of Moses remained beyond the grasp of Wissenschaft, a kernel of direct divine revelation that Frankel would not allow to be dissected into disparate sources. Insulated from the more open atmosphere of the university, the Breslau seminary let in as much Wissenschaft as Frankel and his colleagues believed would enhance its status and strengthen Judaism, while shutting it out

from the inner sanctum, which they believed had to remain invio-
late. The seminary employed on its faculty only men who were in
basic agreement with Frankel's conception of Judaism,[9] and its statutes specified that if a teacher left the standpoint of positive and
historical Judaism or "taught in a manner that endangered the
above mentioned point of view" he was subject to dismissal without
compensation.[10] Scholarship without faith, Frankel was convinced,
would lead in Germany, as it had in ancient Alexandria, to the complete loss of Jewish identity.[11]

Yet Frankel also believed that Wissenschaft, properly applied,
was absolutely essential to Jewish survival in that it could reveal the
inner life of the Jews, their spiritual activity through the generations,
thus creating a bridge between past and present. Without scholarship, he wrote, there could be no Judaism, for "it decays when the
love of its scholarly study disappears."[12] Not surprisingly, Frankel's
own writings and those published in the renowned *Monatsschrift für
Geschichte und Wissenschaft des Judentums* during the years that he
was its editor concentrated on the inner, religious history of the
Jews, especially as revealed in the rabbinic literature—an area of
research that stressed those elements that made the Jews unique and
provided the basis for their continuing religious separateness in
Germany.[13]

In focusing on religious history, the Conservative Frankel followed much the same path as did Abraham Geiger, the most important intellectual leader of the Reform movement in Germany and
one of the greatest modern Jewish scholars. Like Frankel, Geiger
saw himself as a theologian and the task of Wissenschaft des Judentums as principally theological. His research as well sought to reveal
the spiritual creativity of the Jews, to rehabilitate the reputation of
the Pharisees from the distorted image presented in the New Testament and to provide a more variegated historical basis for a religious Jewish identity.

Where Geiger differed from Frankel was in his willingness to
apply Wissenschaft to all Jewish texts, even to the Pentateuch, and
in his intentional use of it for the purpose of religious reform. Although he claimed never to depart from the canons of unprejudiced
historical scholarship, Geiger freely admitted that, unlike most other
scholars, "I was always concerned to study thoroughly the kernel
[of Judaism] and to draw results from it for reform."[14] For Geiger,
Wissenschaft des Judentums demonstrated the historical flexibility
of Judaism and hence the possibility of reshaping it once more in a
manner that could sustain Jewish identity in the modern world.[15]

The overtly present-minded religious rationale for Wissenschaft des Judentums, shared by Frankel and Geiger though differently understood by them, is almost absent in the later work of Leopold Zunz, perhaps the foremost of all nineteenth-century Jewish scholars. After his early disappointment with religious reform and a brief failed attempt to serve as rabbi for the progressive segment of the Jewish community in Prague, Zunz increasingly withdrew to Wissenschaft des Judentums as a kind of refuge from the present. He disliked the use of Jewish scholarship for the purpose of advancing particular religious conceptions, whether by Jews or by Christians. In his *Zur Geschichte und Literatur* he wrote in 1845: "Our Wissenschaft therefore needs first of all to emancipate itself from the theologians and raise itself to the level of historical understanding."[16] Jewish scholarship became for Zunz an end in itself: To be a Jewish scholar was his way of being Jewish. Increasingly, as he grew older, Zunz occupied himself with the Jewish past almost to the exclusion of contemporary Jewish affairs. He ceased to read Jewish newspapers. He knew well the work of the medieval Jewish poet Kalir but was not familiar with the poetry of Y. L. Gordon, the leading Hebrew poet of his own time.[17] His most fervent wish was to see Wissenschaft des Judentums gain entry into a German university where it could flourish freely, unaffected by the sectarian purposes of rabbis and seminaries.

Zunz's extraordinarily erudite disciple, Moritz Steinschneider, went even further in dissociating Jewish scholarship from Jewish identity. Steinschneider's scholarly concern was to show the cultural influence of Jews in Islamic lands during the Middle Ages by bringing to light their long-forgotten works. It was recognition of the Jewish contribution to Western civilization by the scholarly world that Steinschneider sought, not any internal Jewish goal.[18] Consisting of dry data, his works lacked historical imagination and were virtually unreadable. But Steinschneider took pride in the fact that they were wholly untendentious and free of all sentimentality. In an age of positivist historiography, he held high the ideal of objectivity, of "pure" research uncontaminated by present-minded considerations. He refused to join the faculty of any Jewish institution or become a member of any Jewish scholarly association. For him, as for Zunz, Jewish scholarship in a purely Jewish setting meant the creation of a new intellectual ghetto.[19]

However, the German academic establishment would not allow Jewish scholarship to expand from Jewish institutions into the fully public sphere of the university. Not only did it refuse to grant it the status of a recognized discipline, those gentile scholars who dealt with its subject matter did so in a manner that could only discourage Jews from identifying with their tradition. Internal Jewish ambivalences about critical scholarship were thus complicated by the negative verdict upon Judaism passed by leading non-Jewish scholars.

Zunz and Steinschneider both longed for a professorship at a German university. Zunz repeatedly petitioned the Prussian government to create such a position but to no avail. He was especially hopeful in 1848, when he believed that the prevalent liberal spirit would make it possible. But the reply he received used the newly created political situation as an argument against such a position: "A professorship that would be established with the ulterior motive of supporting and strengthening the Jewish organism in its particularity, in its alienating laws and customs, would contradict the purpose of the new freedom that levels stubborn differences. It would mean a special concession to the Jews, an abuse of the university."[20] In other words, Jewish scholarship could not be allowed to enter the University of Berlin lest its presence there serve to perpetuate a differentiated Jewish identity in Germany. Zunz, perforce, remained a *Privatgelehrter*, a scholar consigned to working on his own.[21]

Of course, German universities could not ignore Jewish studies entirely. Hebrew and Old Testament were well established in theological faculties, and in the nineteenth century there was also increasing interest in postbiblical Jewish literature. Yet scholars who dealt with the literature of the Jews, such as Julius Wellhausen and Friedrich Delitzsch, denigrated the object of their study—and sometimes also the reputations of Jewish scholars outside the universities whose learning exceeded their own.[22] The most vicious such scholar was the antisemitic orientalist at the University of Göttingen, Paul de Lagarde. Although he and his students perforce drew heavily upon the works of the Jewish scholars, they attacked them for overvaluing the objects of their research. Zunz was a particular target of their venom; according to Lagarde, he and other Jewish scholars demanded "admiration for things that, like the poems of the Jewish Middle Ages translated by Zunz and Zunz's translation itself, fill us either with irresistible sarcasm or with disgust."[23]

Similarly, the German historian Heinrich von Treitschke attacked the last volume of Heinrich Graetz's *History of the Jews* (1870) because its author had evaluated his material by internal Jewish standards rather than by the German criteria Treitschke himself employed when he dealt with such figures as Heinrich Heine and Ludwig Börne. Graetz had indeed written his history to implant deeper identification in his Jewish readers, just as Treitschke's *German History* (7 vols., 1915–19) was intended to inspire greater German loyalty. Yet although their romantic historiography was remarkably similar, Graetz could not effectively defend his views against the Berlin professor, and even fellow Jews turned against him for his alleged Jewish chauvinism.[24]

Where antisemitism was absent among Christian scholars of Judaism, missionary intent took its place. Hermann Strack, professor of oriental languages at the University of Berlin, was a friend of the Jews who had defended them against the ritual murder libel. But when he founded the Institutum Judaicum at the university in 1883, his purpose was not only to advance scholarship but also to win Jews over to Christianity. In a lecture he delivered in 1906, Strack attempted to reveal the basis of the Jews' loyalty to their faith so that it would be easier to undermine it.[25] The Institutum Judaicum founded by Franz Delitzsch at the University of Leipzig three years earlier served similar purposes.

Thus, Jews who studied at German universities found their religion represented either by antisemites or by missionaries. The German university was prepared to weaken Jewish identity, but in no way to sustain it. The hope of gaining recognition for Jewish practitioners of Wissenschaft des Judentums by the German academic establishment was repeatedly disappointed throughout the nineteenth century and early twentieth centuries. Only here and there was a Jewish scholar allowed to give a course or two without benefit of a regular professorship.[26]

By the beginning of the twentieth century Wissenschaft des Judentums in Germany was clearly in decline. Its greatest scholars had passed from the scene. It remained outside the universities and, of most immediate significance, the connection between Wissenschaft and Jewish identity had become ever more tenuous. Jewish scholars were mostly following the paradigm of Zunz and Steinschneider. They dwelt on minutiae at the expense of exploring larger ideas and concepts; an obsession with uncovering new facts had replaced the original scholarly endeavors to discover the Jews' inner spirit. Looking back upon the evolution of Wissenschaft des Judentums even as early as 1879, Ludwig Philippson wrote: "If we look more closely at the course of its development down to the present, we will have to admit to ourselves that in fact it became only historical research and this historical research, in turn, became microscopic."[27] It was felt that Wissenschaft des Judentums was far more concerned with what clothing the medieval commentator Rashi might have worn than with the content of his writings.

Heinrich Graetz's history had been exceptional. Its popular

style had won entry for it into thousands of Jewish homes, and in translations its influence had spread throughout the Jewish world.[28] Although deficient in methodology and objectivity, it had linked scholarship with identity more effectively than any other single work. But by the end of the nineteenth century no equivalent works were being produced. Jewish scholarship had become an elite occupation, not in the sense that its practitioners enjoyed a high degree of prestige but because they wrote in such a specialized and recondite fashion that only those few who shared their background and interest could fully appreciate and derive benefit from their work. Jewish scholars had adopted the standard to which Max Weber called attention in a famous lecture: "Today any truly definitive and sound achievement is always—a specialized achievement."[29] In seeking to meet the standards of scholarship, Wissenschaft des Judentums had almost completely severed its link to Jewish life. It was wholly determined by its object, not only by the subjective desires of those who engaged in it.

In the period after the First World War, criticism of this conception of Wissenschaft des Judentums emerged from three independent sources. It came first of all from within its own circle of scholars. The historian Ismar Elbogen, who taught at the Hochschule für die Wissenschaft des Judentums in Berlin—the Jewish institution most open to theologically unconstrained scientific research—fully accepted the universal standards of scholarship, noting that "the special character of our scholarship results only from the material, not from the method or mentality of the scholars." But he also declared of Wissenschaft des Judentums:

> Even though it considers the most careful historical and philological treatment of the sources and determination of the facts among its tasks, it does not engage in these for their own sake nor in order to revive dead literary monuments, but rather to reveal the foundations on which the present can be built. Its goal is and remains *living Judaism*. That must be the focal point at which all the rays are aimed, the leading idea that ties a unifying bond around the multiplicity of sources and scholarly inquiries.[30]

Elbogen argued for what he called a "reorientation of our scholarship,"[31] by which he meant redirecting scholarly endeavor from adducing new (but relatively insignificant) facts to uncovering roots in the Jewish past that would strengthen Jewish identity in the present.

A second source of criticism came from the small circle of Jewish intellectuals who were seeking to revive religious faith and commitment to Judaism among those Jews most estranged from Jewish life. The leading spirit in this group was the Jewish theologian Franz Rosenzweig. Whereas Steinschneider had held the view that the task of Jewish scholarship was simply to recover the Jewish past, scholarship and education being two distinct areas of activity,[32] Rosenzweig argued that "the teacher and the scholar must be the same person."[33] Speaking at the opening ceremony for the Freies Jüdisches Lehrhaus, the institute for adult study that he established in Frankfurt in 1920, Rosenzweig deliberately reintroduced the premodern term *lernen*.[34] In his view, Wissenschaft des Judentums had proven its inadequacy to sustain Jewish identity: Specialized scholarly works would not bring the highly assimilated Jews of Germany back to Judaism. That goal could be achieved only by leading them gradually back to the center, to the basic texts of the Jewish religion.

Lernen, Rosenzweig maintained, was the proper mode of such study, although it had to be informed by Wissenschaft rather than employing the old uncritical method of the yeshivah. Rosenzweig proposed an Akademie für die Wissenschaft des Judentums whose members would be both scholars and teachers. Shortly thereafter, such an academy did come into existence, and although it did not fully correspond to Rosenzweig's concept, the goal of its various scholarly projects was similar. As the historian of Jewish philosophy Julius Guttmann set it forth, the task of the academy was to lead back to the sources of Jewish life: not to indicate a particular direction but to create self-understanding; not to engage in apologetics or edification but to reveal "the force and content of Jewish spirit and life."[35] Jewish scholars increasingly turned their attention to the history of Jewish philosophy, seeking to analyze and interpret the systemized expressions of the Jewish spirit. They repeatedly called upon the Jewish community to support their work, which they saw as serving the purpose of Jewish survival.[36]

The most severe critique of Wissenschaft des Judentums came from the Zionists. As early as 1902, the foremost proponent of cultural Zionism, Ahad Ha'am, had complained that Jewish scholarship had become only a "monument to our spiritual enslavement."[37] Later, a fellow Zionist, the great scholar of Jewish mysticism Gershom Scholem, made a similar point by quoting a remark attributed to Steinschneider: "The only task we have left is to provide the remnants of Judaism with a worthy burial."[38] Rather than erect memorials, the Zionists sought to revive the dead, and Zionism in Germany soon began to make use of Wissenschaft des Judentums for its own ideological purposes.

In 1904, the sociologist and Zionist leader Arthur Ruppin published a book entitled *The Jews of Today*. Expanding the scope of Wissenschaft des Judentums to include statistical demographic studies, Ruppin set out to show that Jewish identity in the diaspora was progressively eroding and would soon disappear entirely. His tables demonstrated that the modern religious identity that Geiger and Frankel had sought to shape through Wissenschaft des Judentums had been unable to withstand the pressures of assimilation. In fact, it had abetted assimilation through its secularization of the sacred literature.[39] Ruppin pointed to the increasing number of apostasies, dissociations from the Jewish community, and mixed marriages. Although few Central and West European Jews were willing to admit it, only the influx of Jews from the East had prevented their numbers from diminishing severely. Since few Jews were willing to give up modern culture, the only basis for continued Jewish identity, he believed, was a national one distinguished by ethnic unity and common language. In Ruppin's hands, Wissenschaft des Judentums became diagnosis, prognosis, and remedy—all from a Zionist perspective.

Yet Zionism also shared in large measure the positive program set forth by Elbogen and by Rosenzweig. Scholem later defined its purpose as "the recognition of our own character and history," and beyond that "to fathom what is alive in Judaism; in place of antiquarian literary history, to undertake a phenomenologically penetrating, objective examination."[40] In fact, that goal was not unlike the one initially set forth—but not fully achieved—by the founders of Wissenschaft des Judentums in Germany more than a hundred years earlier.

During the Weimar period, Jewish scholarship also enjoyed a slightly more favorable reception in German universities. At the recently founded university in Frankfurt, Martin Buber taught as honorary professor for general religious studies, and Nahum Glatzer received a teaching assignment in Jewish religious studies and Jewish ethics. Other universities employed Jewish scholars on a part-time basis.[41] In Berlin, a most amazing transformation of attitude to Jewish scholarship occurred in 1925 when a prominent biblical scholar at the university, Hugo Gressmann, took over the Institutum Judaicum three years after the death of Hermann Strack. Under its new director the institute was wholly divested of any missionary intent. But Gressmann went further, beyond toleration to an extraordinary respect for the integrity of Jewish tradition. He believed that there were valuable insights regarding the inner spiritual life of the Jews that Jewish scholars, knowing their tradition from within, would be uniquely able to offer students at the university. He was persuaded that "true objectivity always presumes love, and for that reason the Jewish scholar always has an advantage with regard to the Jewish religion; necessarily, he must know it better than the Christian scholar." Moreover, Gressmann insisted, to study Judaism was to deal with a religion that "has proven itself to be a living force down to the present time." Gressmann organized a series of lectures under the auspices of the institute in the academic year of 1925/ 1926 in which leading Jewish scholars were called upon to convey the dynamics of Jewish religious creativity for Christians as well as for Jews. In introducing the series, he explicitly asked that his listeners regard these lectures "as a recognition of Jewish scholarship."[42] Until his early death in 1927, Gressmann was also a member of the governing body of the Pro-Palästina Komitee, a group of Christian supporters of Zionism.

For German Jewry the reassessment of Wissenschaft des Judentums by Jews and by gentiles came late in its history. There was not sufficient time for it to influence Jewish identity. Nazism introduced its own Wissenschaft des Judentums in the form of *Rassenforschung* (racial research), and, one by one, the Nazis closed down the institutions of Jewish learning. In 1936, the Zionist Jewish newspaper *Jüdische Rundschau* sent a set of questionnaires to Jewish scholars concerning the state and future of Jewish scholarship in Germany. The replies testified to a state of crisis. One scholar after another was finding refuge outside of Germany; there were "deeply felt gaps." Nevertheless, Viktor Aptowitzer wrote from Vienna: "It is a Jewish obligation to prevent Jewish scholarship from perishing in Germany." And Ismar Elbogen in Berlin replied resolutely: "It is clear that the severe emotional convulsion that we contemporary Jews have experienced must also affect scholarship. It alters one's mental attitude, pushes certain problems to the fore. But it must not impinge upon the goal of all scholarship, the search for truth."[43] Only a few years later Wissenschaft des Judentums would come to an end in Germany when the Hochschule (now demoted to the rank of Lehranstalt) für die Wissenschaft des Judentums, the last Jewish scholarly institution allowed to operate, was forced to close in 1942 and its last teacher, Leo Baeck, was deported to Theresienstadt.

Was the German Jewish experience typical for other Jewries? Certainly the erosive effect of historical criticism upon Jewish belief, and hence upon Jewish religious loyalty, affected all Jews who encountered it. What differed was the percentage of Jews exposed to its canons: in Russia, a relatively small proportion during the nineteenth century; in the West, nearly all Jews. Moreover, in Eastern Europe at the turn of the century, the solution for modernizing Jews more frequently entailed the substitution of a secular Jewish identity for a religious one, whereas in Germany, religion and critical scholarship were harmonized in one manner or another. In addition, the especially large role that scholarship played in German culture made the issue of its relationship to Judaism more important than elsewhere; it could not be pushed aside.

The situation of contemporary Jewry in the United States differs sharply. For the first time in the diaspora, Jewish scholarship is amply represented—by Jews—in the universities, and this at a time when upwards of 90 percent of young Jews receive higher education. If Jewish scholarship, as practiced by both Jews and non-Jews in Germany, served to undermine and to alter as well as to sustain Jewish identity, it would seem that in the United States it is now in a position to strengthen it greatly. But if it does so, it will be through those forms of accommodation that emerged in response to the earlier challenges first presented in Germany.

Notes

1. A somewhat different version of this essay in the German language appeared in Julius Carlebach, ed., *Wissenschaft des Judentums. Anfänge der Judaistik in Europa* (Darmstadt, 1992), 3–20.

2. Cf. Isador Twersky, *Introduction to the Code of Maimonides* (New Haven and London, 1980), 170–71.

3. See his *Mishneh Torah*, hilkhot talmud torah 4:9.

4. Leopold Zunz, *Zeitschrift für die Wissenschaft des Judenthums* 1 (1822): 15–16.

5. Samson Raphael Hirsch, "Wie gewinnen wir das Leben für unsere Wissenschaft?" *Jeschurun* 8 (1862): 89.

6. Gottlieb Fischer, "Herrn Dr. Z. Frankel's hodogetisches Werk über die Mischnah," *Jeschurun* 7 (1861): 197–98.

7. Esriel Hildesheimer, "Harav 'Azriel Hildesheimer zaẓal 'al Rav Zekhariyah Frankel zal uveit-hamidrash lerabanim bebraslav," *Hama'ayan*, Tishrei 5713 (1952): 65–73.

8. Mordechai Breuer, "Hokhmat yisrael: shalosh gishot ortodoksiyot," in *Jubilee Volume in Honor of . . . Joseph Soloveitchik* (Jerusalem and New York, 1984), vol. 2: 856–65; idem, *Jüdische Orthodoxie im Deutschen Reich, 1871–1918* (Frankfurt, 1986), 168; David Ellenson and Richard Jacobs, "Scholarship and Faith: David Hoffmann and His Relationship to *Wissenschaft des Judentums*," *Modern Judaism* 8 (Feb. 1988): 27–40.

9. M. Brann, *Geschichte des jüdisch-theologischen Seminars in Breslau* (Breslau, 1904), 48–52.

10. *Statut für das jüdisch-theologische Seminar, Fraenckel'sche Stiftung* (Breslau, 1854).

11. Zacharias Frankel, "Ueber palästinische und alexandrinische Schriftforschung," *Programm zur Eröffnung des jüdisch-theologischen Seminars, 10 August 1854* (Breslau, 1854), 42.

12. Zacharias Frankel, "Einleitendes," *Monatsschrift für Geschichte und Wissenschaft des Judentums* (hereafter, *MGWJ*) 1 (1852): 5.

13. Ismar Schorsch, "The Emergence of Historical Consciousness in Modern Judaism," *Leo Baeck Institute Year Book* 28 (1983): 429.

14. *Nachgelassene Schriften* 2 (Berlin, 1875), 27.

15. For more detail see Michael A. Meyer, "Jewish Religious Reform and Wissenschaft des Judentums: The Positions of Zunz, Geiger, and Frankel," *Leo Baeck Institute Year Book* 16 (1971): 19–41.

16. Leopold Zunz, *Zur Geschichte und Literatur* (Berlin, 1845), 20.

17. Paul Mendes-Flohr, ed., *Hokhmat yisrael* (Jerusalem, 1979), 26.

18. Moritz Steinschneider, "Die Zukunft der jüdischen Wissenschaft," *Hamazkir: Hebraeische Bibliographie* 9 (1869), 76–78.

19. Gotthold Weil, "Moritz Steinschneider," *Jüdische Rundschau* 8 (Feb. 1907): 53–55.

20. S. Maybaum, "Die Wissenschaft des Judentums," *MGWJ* 51 (1907): 655. The faculty, in its report to the minister, also noted that the presence of a chair for Wissenschaft des Judentums might have the undesirable effect of attracting more Jewish students to the university. L. Geiger, "Zunz im Verker mit Behörden und Hochgestellten," *MGWJ* 60 (1916): 340.

21. The resentment Jewish scholars felt at their exclusion despite superior knowledge is evident in David Kaufmann, "Die Vertretung der jüdischen Wissenschaft an den Universitäten," in his *Gesammelte Schriften*, vol. 1, ed. M. Brann (Frankfurt, 1908), 14–38.

22. Michael A. Meyer, *Response to Modernity: A History of the Reform Movement in Judaism* (New York, 1988), 202–4.

23. Paul de Lagarde, "Lipman Zunz und seine Verehrer," *Mittheilungen* 2 (Göttingen, 1887), 159–60. So, too, one of Lagarde's students found it necessary to write of Zunz in his doctoral dissertation: "The continual admiration of one's own people seems unjustified." Ludwig Techen, *Zwei Göttinger Machzorhandschriften* (Göttingen, 1884), 17. David Kaufmann came to the defense of Zunz with his "Paul de Lagarde's jüdische Gelehrsamkeit," in his *Gesammelte Schriften*, 207–57.

24. Michael A. Meyer, "Heinrich Graetz and Heinrich von Treitschke: A Comparison of Their Historical Images of the Modern Jew," chapter 4 in this volume.

25. See Hermann L. Strack, *Das Wesen des Judentums. Vortrag gehalten auf der Internationalen Konferenz der Judenmission zu Amsterdam* (Leipzig, 1906). Strack also reviewed Techen's work favorably. Excerpts from his review are in Kaufmann, "Paul de Lagarde's jüdische Gelehrsamkeit," 213.

26. Alfred Jospe, "The Study of Judaism in German Universities Before 1933," *Leo Baeck Institute Year Book* 27 (1982): 295–319.

27. *Allgemeine Zeitung des Judentums* 43 (1879): 706–7.

28. Ismar Elbogen, "Hokhmat yisrael: sekirah," in *Devir: Maasaf 'iti lehokh-mat yisrael* 2 (annual [1923]), 12.

29. Max Weber, *Wissenschaft als Beruf* (Munich and Leipzig, 1919), 10.

30. Ismar Elbogen, "Ein Jahrhundert Wissenschaft des Judentums," *Festschrift zum 50 jährigen Bestehen der Hochschule für die Wissenschaft des Judentums in Berlin* (Berlin, 1922), 142.

31. *MGWJ* 62 (1918): 84.

32. M. S. Charbonah [Moritz Steinschneider], ed., *Herev be-tsiyon oder Briefe eines jüdischen Gelehrten und Rabbinen über das Werk Horev* (Leipzig, 1939), x.

33. Franz Rosenzweig, "Zeit ists . . . Gedanken über das jüdische Bildungsproblem des Augenblicks (1917)," in his *Kleinere Schriften* (Berlin, 1937), 73.

34. Franz Rosenzweig, "Neues Lernen: Entwurf der Rede zur Eröffnung des Freien Jüdischen Lehrhauses," in ibid., 94–99.

35. Julius Guttmann, "Jüdische Wissenschaft: Die Akademie für die Wissenschaft des Judentums," *Der Jude* 7 (1923): 489–93.

36. See, e.g., Hermann Vogelstein, "Das liberale Judentum und die jüdische Wissenschaft," *Liberales Judentum* 9 (1917): 61–65.

37. Ahad Ha'am, "Die Renaissanse des Geistes," in his *Am Scheidewege* 2 (Berlin, 1916): 124.

38. Gershom Scholem, "Wissenschaft vom Judentum einst und jetzt," in his *Judaica* (Frankfurt, 1963), 152–53, based on *Jüdische Rundschau* 8 Feb. 1907, 54.

39. Arthur Ruppin, *Soziologie der Juden*, vol. 2 (Berlin, 1931), 185.

40. Scholem, "Wissenschaft vom Judentum einst und jetzt," 148, 163–64.

41. Jospe, "The Study of Judaism in German Universities Before 1933," 311–12.

42. Hugo Gressmann, ed., *Entwicklungsstufen der jüdischen Religion* (Giessen, 1927), 1–12. On Gressmann and on the participation of Jewish scholars in the second edition of *Die Religion in Geschichte und Gegenwart*, see Leonore Siegele-Wenschkewitz, "The Relationship Between Protestant Theology and Jewish Studies During the Weimar Republic," in Otto Dov Kulka and Paul Medes-Flohr, eds., *Judaism and Christianity Under the Impact of National Socialism* (Jerusalem, 1987), 143–47.

43. *Jüdische Rundschau* 41, no. 27/28 (3 April 1936), 9–10.

CHAPTER 10

German Political Pressure and Jewish Religious Response in the Nineteenth Century

Wer ein Jude ist, ist es immer gegen sein Vorteil

LEO BAECK, 1905

Jewish existence in the modern world has been endangered by two contradictory perils: hatred of the Jews, which led to mass extermination in the Holocaust, and acceptance of the Jews, which has led to massive loss of Jewish identification. Yet neither of these attitudes necessarily produces a destructive effect. Anti-Jewish policies and agitation have at times shored up collective will and brought forth determined efforts at Jewish apologetics and defense; freer environments have allowed Jewish creativity to flourish. The interplay of these two forces is nowhere more clearly revealed than in the modern history of German Jewry, which highlights the negative and positive valences of each as they appear in ever changing combinations. Modern antisemitism developed ideologically largely in a German context and no major Jewish community was as well advanced on the road of annihilating its own identity as was Weimar Jewry in the 1920s. But periods of antisemitism also forced German Jews into renewed self-consciousness and in an environment of relative toleration they achieved remarkable cultural productivity.

During the nineteenth century these two opposing forces were brought to bear not alone on German Jews but also on their expression of the Jewish faith. What began as a general religious reform movement among Jews at the beginning of the century and had become a distinctive religious orientation—Liberal Judaism—by its end encountered each of the forces, experiencing their positive and their negative effects. A look at German Jewish religious development within its political context may help us to understand how the external forces operated, how Jews inclined to a modernization of their faith responded to them, and perhaps, by way of analogy, implicitly suggest strategies for Jewish survival today.

The following words were written by the first great champion of Jewish emancipation, Christian Wilhelm Dohm, in 1781: "This anxious and petty spirit of ceremonialism, which has insinuated itself into the Jewish religion, will surely once again vanish as soon as the Jews are given a wider sphere of activity and accepted as members of political society, making its interests their own. Then they will appropriately reform their religious system and its laws; they will return to the freer and nobler ancient Mosaic law and find authority in the Talmud to apply and explain the law according to changed times and circumstances."[1] Dohm here expressed an expectation; he did not set forth a condition. He genuinely believed that once the Jews were relieved of the restrictions and disabilities which weighed so heavily upon them, it would follow almost necessarily that the Jewish religion, appropriate to the circumstances of the ghetto but not to those of a politically integrated religious community, would of itself undergo a metamorphosis that would render it more appropriate to its new context. But the boundary between expectation and requirement is a thin one. The philosopher Immanuel Kant was clearly standing on the other side of the line when in 1798 he expressed his conviction that Jews and Christians could become brothers in faith provided that the Jews would purify their religious ideas and cast aside their outdated ritual. Kant suggested that if they would take on a faith resembling the ancient religion of Jesus—as had indeed already been proposed by the enlightened Jew and Kantian, Lazarus Bendavid—they would soon become learned and well behaved, worthy of all the privileges of citizenship.[2]

Whether as expectation or as condition, the message conveyed by Dohm, Kant, and the other Enlightenment figures who shared their view could not be lost on those Jews who increasingly sought civic and political integration. Well into the nineteenth century German governments, legislatures, and individual writers repeated it: Jews are potentially acceptable, but Judaism in its inherited form is not. It seemed as if there were a price to be paid for emancipation in the coin of Jewish religious belief and practice. Not surprisingly, it has often appeared to historians of the Jews that the movement for religious reform was at bottom a persistent effort to deliver an acceptable down payment for so highly valued a commodity.[3] Yet a careful study of the relation between German political demand and Jewish religious response reveals that it was far more complex. For the message which Germany conveyed to its Jews during the course of the nineteenth century was not consistently that of Dohm and Kant, and the Jewish response was far from acquiescent. Much has been written about Jews and German politics on the one hand[4] and about the development of Jewish religion in Germany on the other.[5] But there has been much less consideration of the connection between them. As we shall see, the relationship was in some respects quite ironic.

Let us begin by noting that the initial reforms of Jewish religious practice came not in anticipation of attaining political aspirations but directly following complete or substantial emancipation. The first congregation to make principled changes in its liturgy was Adath Jeshurun, established in Amsterdam a few months after the Batavian Republic granted complete civil and political equality to the Jews of Holland in 1796. Indeed, it was emancipation which broke the authority of the community elders, making possible the independent activity of the reformers.[6] Likewise, the religious reforms instituted by Israel Jacobson in Westphalia followed a decree which in 1808 granted the Jews equality.[7] And in Prussia the establishment of a modified religious service came three years after the Prussian Emancipation Edict of 1812. To be sure, Jewish equality in Prussia and in the other German states remained incomplete throughout most of the nineteenth century, especially with regard to state offices, and informal discrimination was never absent. However, insofar as religious reform was initially prompted by political considerations, it seems to have been more a response of adjustment to a new situation, of gratitude for rights given, than of payment for goods not yet delivered.[8] Moreover, the weight of political considerations in a religious reform movement, as against the influence of newly internalized religious and aesthetic values deemed to be in conflict with tradition, should by no means be exaggerated. After all, those individuals whose Jewish allegiance had eroded almost completely had no compunctions about converting to Christianity.

To their surprise and shock Jewish religious reformers very soon discovered that most governmental authorities were suspect of their projects. Even before the post-Napoleonic reaction swept across Central Europe, rulers preferred that Judaism remain untouched by religious ferment. The enlightened King Jerome of Westphalia, who had initially given his sanction to the religious reforms carried out by a Jewish consistory, apparently became uneasy about them once they were put into effect. When the head of the consistory, Israel Jacobson, approached him during a regular audience in court, the king ungraciously accused him of propagating sectarianism and turned away without awaiting Jacobson's reply.[9]

In Prussia the situation faced by Jewish reformers was simply exasperating. Immediately after the Edict of 1812, David Fried-länder, Mendelssohn's disciple and at the time an Elder of the Berlin community, published an encompassing program for Jewish religious and educational reform.[10] Three years later a modernized Jewish service was established in Berlin for those members of the community who felt alienated from the traditional worship in the community synagogue. It included some prayers in German, an organ, a choir, and an edifying German sermon. This "temple," as it was called, attracted surprisingly large numbers. But after a brief and rather tumultuous history, it was forced out of existence—not because traditional Jews in the community refused to tolerate it, but because Frederick William III and his ministers saw it as dangerous to established religion generally, possibly attractive to gentile worshipers, and as deflecting Jews from the only true salvation which lay in Christianity.[11] From 1823 onward for eighteen years no religious innovation of any kind was tolerated among the Jews of Prussia. In the age of Metternich and the Holy Alliance, renewed political and civil restriction of the Jews went hand in hand with a policy to ossify their religious institutions. Even as late as 1851, when Frederick William IV granted the title of Silesian *Land-Rabbiner* to the orthodox rabbi of Breslau, Gedaliah Tiktin, he wrote in his decree: "To be sure he has no right to the title, but I am inclined to grant it to him so that the direction which he represents might, for political reasons, gain the desired added strength."[12] The message conveyed by government policy in Prussia was thus the opposite of that delivered by Dohm and Kant. It said that the authorities do not want religious reform because innovation of any kind represents a danger to the state; the Jew who wishes to win favor is best advised to demonstrate that in religious matters, as in political ones, he is decidedly conservative.[13]

This attitude toward the Jewish religion was justified in the *Vormärz* period especially by those German writers who advocated the idea of the Christian state.[14] It is a curious fact that the chief theoretician of this political conception was a convert from Judaism, Friedrich Julius Stahl, and that he was not the only Jewish apostate to advocate the close union of church and state.[15] Yet it is not at all surprising that such converts should be especially disdainful of Jewish religious reforms. In the first place, any sign of religious vitality in the Jewish community would represent a threat to the very principle of Jewish moribundity on which they had made their own major life's decision. The doctrine of historical development within a religious spirit that retained its unique identity could be applied properly only to Christianity, not to Judaism. The latter was essentially and unalterably a religion of adherence to the letter of an unchanging law. Stahl insisted that from a Christian point of view an exclusivistic orthodoxy—the only "genuine" Judaism—was distinctly preferable to a philosophically oriented, modernized Jewish faith. If he did not favor legally prohibiting the latter, it was only because he believed it inherently unstable and hence a likely bridge to Christianity.[16]

Constantin Frantz, one of the advocates of the Christian state who was not a Jew, transmitted a considerably more ambiguous message. He seems to set forth a condition for equality: Jews are to compose a new Jewish creed for Christian inspection and judgment. Only then will the state be able to determine what their potential status should be. Meanwhile, it should not interfere with Jewish affairs by either encouraging or obstructing religious change. Yet it is clearly not Frantz's final intent to give approval to what he derisively terms "so-called reforms," since they only serve "the great Babylonian whore" of reason. He finally conveys his true intention within the contours of an age-old myth still very much alive in the nineteenth century. It is the legend of Ahasuerus, the eternally wandering Jew, which Frantz conjures up for his readers. Condemned to roam about the earth for rejecting the messiah, the Jewish people can never find peace. It wants to mingle among the peoples and snuff out its peoplehood, but it cannot—not until the Second Coming of Christ. Thus efforts at Jewish religious reform and cultural integration—no matter how sincere—must always and necessarily be found wanting. They are futile attempts to escape a myth which the Jewish people must live out until the end of days.[17]

In general, proponents of the Christian state proclaimed their respect for what one of them called "historical orthodox Judaism."[18] Since they opposed Jewish political equality, it was obviously in their interest to prefer that expression of Judaism which, on the basis of the Talmud and Jewish liturgy, they could most easily stigmatize as setting its adherents apart from the body politic and from their fellow Germans of the Christian faith. Any other form was inauthentic and might easily lead to materialism or atheism. Frederick William IV's desire to return the Jews to the status of a separate corporation, first set forth in 1842 and then largely embodied in the Prussian Jewry law of 1847, must be seen as the practical counterpart to this theoretical tendency. Jewish political segregation could be justified if one could point to a (largely distorted) image of an alien and unchanging orthodoxy as the only "authentic Judaism."[19]

* * *

From relatively freer thinkers came a different message. They were willing to grant political emancipation to the Jews without conversion—but only if they would eliminate virtually all those elements of their religion which set them apart. In 1831 a commission report was presented to the Diet of Baden which favored equality of Jews with Christians according to certain explicit conditions: they would have to abandon Hebrew (called their "national language"), forego circumcision of their sons ("a sign of their national segregation"), give up adherence to dietary laws, transfer their sabbath to Sunday, and either purify or abandon the Talmud. All this they would have to do during a period of ten years before they would be eligible for complete political equality.[20] Not surprisingly, Baden Jewry—with apparent unanimity—rejected the offer. In fact the government's pursuit of this policy, though later moderated, seems in practice rather to have discouraged than encouraged religious change. The Jews of Mannheim, among the most acculturated in Baden soon declared in a petition that they were foregoing even those religious reforms which they themselves favored lest they give so much as "the appearance of thereby desiring to purchase political equality."[21]

In its deliberations the Baden Diet had been influenced by the thinking of H. E. G. Paulus, a liberal professor of theology and philosophy at Heidelberg, who emphatically set forth the view that Jews should be required to make a collective commitment to religious reform if they desired emancipation. It would be a mistake for the Baden government to give special privileges to individual Jews who no longer practiced traditional Judaism, since favoring them would encourage selfish interest and serve to further isolate their brethren.[22] Yet twenty-four years earlier, in 1817, Paulus had himself publicly favored emancipation for those Jews who met his conditions. Those whom he then called the "better" individuals should be singled out, he thought, encouraging others to forsake their particularism.[23] It was Paulus's earlier view which was echoed by Karl Streckfuss, a Prussian official of relatively liberal spirit, who in 1833 favored almost complete equality, but only for those Jews who were "ripe" for it. Such ripeness consisted mainly of an occupational shift into economically more productive occupations, but there was a religious aspect to it as well. In terms of Judaism it meant less complete adherence to ritual law, universalization of the messianic idea, and giving Jewish children religious instruction within gentile schools. Streckfuss's liberalism was expressed in the suggestion—never carried out in Germany—to establish teaching positions for Jewish theology at several universities. But as a Prussian official he had to support the king's will that Jewish dissidents might not have their own religious service.[24] The effect of Streckfuss's liberalism was therefore to encourage defection from religious observance without the promise of freedom to develop new modes of religious expression. In terms of religion, his proposal was more an invitation to dismantle Judaism than to reform it.

Radical writers, highly critical of the Christian state and of Christian tradition generally, not surprisingly proved to be no less critical of Judaism.[25] They too conveyed a message hovering between extreme demands and outright rejection of the Jews unless they gave up their identity entirely. Friedrich Wilhelm Ghillany, who gained notoriety by trying to prove that human sacrifice was commonly practiced in ancient Israel, was willing to forgive latter-day Jews the sins of their ancestors provided they would give up their messianic hope, the practice of dietary laws, and circumcision. If those so inclined would then separate themselves from the traditionalists, rebuild their religion on the love of neighbor commanded in Leviticus, and rearrange their religious worship accordingly, they would possess a well founded claim to emancipation and—Ghillany assures them—Germany will not refuse to grant it.[26] The left-wing Hegelian Bruno Bauer offered no such hope. Even enlightened Jews, he believed, could never completely rid themselves of particularism. They might claim they were not a nationality, might not be observant, but they were firmly committed to an independent Jewish future; they refused to give up their identity as Jews.[27] For Bauer, Jews would have to transcend Judaism completely before they could claim equality. *Les extrêmes se touchent.* Christian conservatives and anti-Christian radicals joined in opposing Jewish aspirations as long as Jews remained Jews, while liberals, with their conditionalism, offered only demeaning compromises.[28]

German Jewry thus found itself with no obvious political ally in its quest for equality. Yet liberalism, grounded in principle in the universal egalitarianism of the French Revolution, seemed to offer the best hope, especially after it awoke to new life in Germany following the 1830 July Revolution in France. It was after all in the liberal camp where those few intrepid champions of unconditional and complete equality for the Jews could be found.[29] For non-traditional Jews, as we shall see, identification with liberalism was the more natural since in sentiment and practice they had left behind much of Jewish particularity and could attach themselves easily to a larger common cause. Yet while liberals could not without violating their principles demand conversion, they could and did—as we have seen—insist on reforms as the individual or collective prerequisite. In short, they demanded a price, mostly in terms of economic realignment and cultural integration, but also in specifically religious matters. How then did Jews who were themselves committed to Jewish religious reform feel about striking the bargain proposed to them by the liberals?

Unquestionably there were German Jews who thought the religious demands set forth by liberal writers and by German governments had some justification. Although privately held views are difficult to assess and certainly cannot be determined by the insinuations of religious opponents, it would be most surprising if among those Jews who were most secularized there were not some who were predominantly interested in their own political advantage. A portion of them, having without overt pressure given up most Jewish observances, already conformed to the required pattern. What is worthy of note, however, is that in the documentable public arena, private motivations were buried beneath an eloquent chorus of moral outrage. The overwhelming response was not that the price was too high but that the state simply had no right to make religious demands in the first place.[30] This was the position not only of traditional Jews, who might be expected to resist any abrogation of religious practice, but conspicuously of men who identified themselves with the movement for reform. Let us illustrate.

Gabriel Riesser, the most prominent of all advocates of Jewish emancipation, was an active member of the Hamburg Temple, who did not feel bound by the ceremonial laws of Judaism. By culture, education, and sentiment fully Germanized, he was nonetheless frustrated in his career plans by anti-Jewish restrictions. Yet Riesser never sought exceptional status, neither for himself nor for other Jews in a similar situation. From the first, he rejected any intrusion of state power into matters of Jewish conscience and conviction as decidedly unjust. According to Riesser, the state had as little right to forbid religious beliefs and practices as it had to impose them. It could demand only that Jews perform the obligations incumbent upon all citizens—and this they had done in every instance. Riesser consistently demanded complete equality with Christians for all Jews, not for an "enlightened aristocracy," and he implicitly called into question the good faith of states and individuals who wanted to differentiate between them. How ironic, he noted, that in those places where the Jews had on their own done the most to modernize their schools and synagogues they suffered the worst inequities. How absurd for the Prussian official Karl Streckfuss, whose government had suppressed all religious progress, to condemn the existing religious worship while brushing aside as deists those who sought to improve it.[31]

That religious reform must have nothing to do with political pressure of any kind was stated most forcefully in Riesser's periodical *Der Jude* by Carl Weil, a communally active Jew and a liberal publicist. "Judaism will and must develop historically," he wrote in 1831, but the decision must be made from within Judaism. "Reform must flow out of the hearts of its adherents, if religious salvation is not to be huckstered away for worldly justice."[32] Weil's implication is a bitter one: the states which were trying to improve the Jews morally by discouraging the mercenary mores of the petty trader were asking them to enter into a thoroughly disreputable and venal bargain!

Johann Jacoby was also not taken in by the call for reform. A Königsberg Jew who like Riesser was destined to play a significant political role in Germany, Jacoby questioned whether the German states in fact wanted Jewish reform. Since they were in any case intent on keeping Jews out of positions of public authority, they required a Judaism which could most easily be stigmatized as alien and unyielding. Jacoby realized that what Jews believe and practice really was not the issue at all. At least in Prussia, exclusion of the Jews from political authority was an absolute. The state therefore thought it best to blunt the egalitarian argument by preventing religious assimilation. Orthodoxy provided a much more effective "pretext for discrimination."[33]

A similar suspicion of state policy and an outright rejection of conditional emancipation is heard a decade later among Jewish religious leaders, themselves advocates of some degree of reform. Zacharias Frankel, the most conservative of the prominent non-orthodox rabbis, insisted on an absolute separation of the political and religious realms. Emancipation was for him a matter of justice, Jewish reform purely a matter of religion. Each of these two endeavors had to reach its goal independently of the other. Jews must seek full equality without any conditions. In fact, the more independent reform endeavors remained of external circumstances, the more honorably would emancipation be achieved.[34] Abraham Geiger, the outstanding theoretician of a more thoroughgoing religious reform which was fundamentally at odds with that of Frankel, did not disagree. For him too the Jewish question was not a test of the Jews but the true test of German liberalism—one which it had failed badly. Repeatedly leading liberals had proven that on this one issue they were false to their principles. Jewish emancipation, according to Geiger, would come not when the Jews changed, but when a victorious liberalism would rise to a genuine acceptance of its own ideology.[35]

The slow progress of religious reform during the 1840s led to the formation of splinter groups in a number of German cities. Organized by laymen who issued radical programs, these societies set themselves apart religiously from their communities. The most prominent such group was formed in the Prussian capital. Its leaders propounded the idea of a German Jewish church whose religious existence was but an element in the spiritual life of the state. Seemingly, no group had more reason to claim a special right to emancipation. Yet their literature gives no hint of it. To the contrary, perhaps because they were most suspect, they most loudly proclaimed their innocence. Sigismund Stern, one of the leaders of the group, said he would reject on the spot any right tied to acceptance of a reform. In fact, he would sooner return to antiquated customs than win privileges which would exclude fellow Jews who were attached to traditional practice. Along with every other Jewish public figure, Stern held that the state could only ask that Jews do their duty as citizens. Orthodox Jews no less than reformers had repeatedly proven their loyalty and expressed their attachment to Germany as their *Vaterland*. If national exclusiveness was the complaint, there were no grounds for it anywhere in contemporary Jewry.[36]

The proponents of conditional emancipation thus met a united front of refusal to barter religious freedom for political equality. As Jews gradually freed themselves from the medieval heritage of loyalty to constituted authority, some of them came to realize that the path to complete emancipation required shaking the political foundations upon which the philosophy of conditionalism rested.

The years leading up to the Revolution of 1848 witnessed a shift in the external forces operative upon German Jewry. Liberalism was gradually purging itself of its worst prejudices; politically conscious Jews were entering its ranks. While pressures for conformity had created mostly resentment and rejection, increasing acceptance without conditions drew individual Jews outward into broader identifications. The leading defenders of Jewish rights now entered the general political arena where Jewish emancipation became only one objective within the framework of programs which they urged as liberals or as democrats. Although until the revolution political activism was rare among German Jews, with its outbreak sizeable numbers participated eagerly, or at least lent it their sympathy.[37] In many places rabbis and Jewish community leaders were drawn into the maelstrom of political activity. They served as electors and as representatives in local assemblies, wrote and preached in favor of the cause, and in some instances suffered the consequences during the reaction which followed. A larger purpose inclusive of Jewish aspirations, but also transcending them, aroused German Jewry to unprecedented political enthusiasm. As Jews, they were excited by the revolution because they believed a secular more representative state would surely abolish all of the restrictions, especially in the various areas of government service, which still kept them from the enjoyment of complete equality.

Although Heinrich Heine once suggested in a satirical poem that among Hamburg Jews the traditionalists were conservatives and the Temple members democrats,[38] it is in fact not possible to draw any hard and fast parallels between religious orientation and political persuasion during the tumult of 1848.[39] Orthodox Jews were not necessarily political conservatives, and radical reformers were not necessarily radical democrats. Samson Raphael Hirsch, the founder of Neo-Orthodoxy, became a liberal.[40] Leopold Zunz, who at the time of the revolution was an observant Jew and a disdainer of religious reforms, participated ardently and prominently among the radical democrats in Berlin. On the basis of his own bitter experience, Zunz sensed that only a state thoroughly purged of Christian exclusivism would allow the Jewish literature to which he devoted his great scholarly talents to enter the academy.[41] Rabbis and community leaders were generally less inclined to radicalism. In Berlin both the religiously conservative rabbi, Michael Sachs, and the relatively more flexible community leader Moritz Veit adopted a moderately liberal position.[42] So did Zacharias Frankel and Abraham Geiger, though the latter for a time called himself a democrat.[43] The political positions of both Frankel and Geiger may have been influenced by their commonly held belief in religious progress through historical evolution, a belief which led each of them to criticize more radical reformers for failing to take the claims of tradition sufficiently into account.[44] Though in his youth much inclined to revolutionary religious change, by mid-century Geiger had adopted a policy of compromise in religious affairs in order to prevent disunity and to maintain a rootedness in history. The reaction which followed the suppression of the revolution seemed to confirm the position of historically oriented Jews like Frankel and Geiger that too much change too quickly brought regression rather than progress.

The religious leadership of German Jewry must also have realized that the widening cause of political liberalism, which increasingly attracted Jewish participants, was becoming a "secular

substitute faith"[45] for Judaism. The equation of Judaism with political liberalism had already appeared in the writings of Riesser and
Jacoby as early as the 1830s. Though their self-respect did not permit
them to abandon Judaism, each of them interpreted its significance
in terms of the larger human struggle represented by the liberal
cause. For Riesser Judaism was to be understood in the spirit of
Moses and the Prophets as "a teaching of hope, of the future, of
development, not of faith in past events." And the future increasingly came to mean the larger future of all humanity. Both Riesser
and Jacoby interpreted the Jewish messianic faith to refer to a universal goal. For Riesser it was "belief in the power and eventual
triumph of justice and goodness." For Jacoby it was "the truth
which ever more forcefully shakes old outdated prejudices and
medieval dogmas and which sooner or later will make us free."[46]

Initially Jacoby had directed his attention to specifically Jewish
concerns. He helped to put forward a plan of moderate religious
reforms in Königsberg and later associated himself with the Berlin
reform group. He then believed that Judaism was destined to become the universal religion and that in freedom it would experience
a spiritual rebirth. Still in 1848 he remained conscious of his specific
obligations as the only Jew on the Committee-of-Fifty at the Pre-
Parliament in Frankfurt.[47] But gradually the Jewish cause and the
liberal cause became one. Using a striking image, Jacoby once wrote
to a Christian friend: "We are all languishing in a huge prison. You
are allowed to walk around freely within it while I and my co-religionists are shackled to the floor with heavy chains."[48] Jacoby was
not satisfied to throw off the shackles. He knew that the prison had
to be destroyed. In the course of time Jewishness receded from Jacoby's increasingly socialist consciousness as the enchained lower
classes came to appear eminently more deserving of his concern
than an upwardly mobile bourgeois Jewry. When his friend and fellow radical Aron Bernstein hailed Jacoby as a prophet of old, Jacoby
did not respond with a Jewish reference.[49] Riesser's Jewish self-consciousness remained relatively higher. Even after 1848 he devoted
himself to Jewish matters, though in the enthusiasm of the revolution he was so carried away as to urge mixed marriages.[50]

The leading Jewish parliamentarians of the second half of the
century did not stand on Jewish ground at all. The liberal Ludwig
Bamberger was reminded of his Judaism only by the antisemitic diatribe of Heinrich von Treitschke. Eduard Lasker, who was originally
destined to be a rabbi and who had been an admirer of the young
Heinrich Graetz and a visitor at the Breslau rabbinical conference in
1846, later in life rarely mentioned his Jewish background. He en-

tered into Jewish affairs only when out of liberal principles he sponsored the *Austrittsgesetz*, encouraging separatist Jewish communities and thereby weakening collective Jewish institutions.[51]

The easy slide from a universalized Judaism into a nonconfessional political liberalism may be more readily comprehensible if we compare their courses of development.[52] Liberalism in Germany, like Jewish religious reform, arose out of a rapid disruption of traditional loyalties. Like the Jews who were thrown into non-Jewish society by state centralization and Enlightenment ideology, Germans during the Napoleonic era were forced to reorient themselves to a profoundly changed situation. The reforms of Stein and Hardenberg did not find a continuation in the restorationist 1820s, but the progressive forces which had been unleashed could only be restrained, not destroyed. Similarly, once Jews had begun the process of acculturation, universalizing their religious ideas and setting their worship into line with prevailing aesthetic sensibilities, there could be no return to the earlier mentality of the ghetto. Political restraint only temporarily dammed up the flood. As liberalism broke loose in the 1840s after a period of inner gestation, so too, following a theoretical interlude during the 1830s, did religious reform begin to express itself more forcefully and dramatically in the following decade. For Jewish liberals the two could for a time go hand-in-hand, especially as liberals generally tended to see political activity in spiritual terms. Like Jewish religious modernists, they were convinced that history was on their side, that sooner or later they were destined to win out. But it was precisely the spiritual, even messianic element in political liberalism that increasingly wore away the particular identity of those Jews whose ideals closely approximated those of the liberals and who had cast off the particularizing laws and ceremonies of Judaism. In the period after the reaction of the 1850s, liberalism and modern Judaism became so closely identified that the term "liberal Jew" could eventually embrace both a political and a religious orientation. As we shall see, by the first years of the twentieth century, this continuing identification aroused Jewish religious leaders to fear for the survival of a positively religious and distinctively Jewish Liberal Jewry. And yet, for most non-orthodox Jews political liberalism did not entirely crowd out a commitment to Jewish faith. Indeed, the fact that many liberal Jews chose to remain Jews in more than a nominal sense soon caused them to be singled out for special opprobrium in a new wave of anti-Jewish hostility.

* * *

Until the achievement of full political equality for the Jews in Germany, as embodied in the constitution of the German Reich, their opponents fought in various ways to slow down the process of emancipation or at least to limit it to Jews divested of Judaism. After 1871 they sought to reverse the emancipation or to minimize its effect. The antisemitic movement which arose at the end of the decade was split between those who opposed Jews on Christian religious grounds and those who rested their case on racial arguments.[53] For both, the Jewry which was now before their mind's eye differed greatly from that of the thirties and forties, when an earlier generation had sought to stigmatize it. A higher proportion of German Jews was now highly urbanized, well-to-do, culturally assimilated; and most of them were no longer orthodox. An attack on talmudic Judaism could have little credibility in 1880 when only a minority of Jews in Germany governed their lives in accordance with its statutes and subscribed fully to its worldview. Antisemites were therefore unable to hide any longer behind the pretense that the Jews needed to be "improved" by stripping them of particular elements of belief and observance. The secular Jews, and those who on account of their continued religious association with Judaism were called adherents of *Reformjudentum*, were now perceived to be the major threat to German society.

During the course of the nineteenth century the German Jewish religious leadership had developed a concept called the "mission of Israel," the idea that Judaism possessed a moral and religious task in relation to the nations of the world and that ultimately it would become the world religion. The doctrine was common to all branches of German Jewry,[54] but it assumed a particularly prominent role among Reform Jews where it was not balanced by an equivalent inward focus upon Jewish observance. Reform theologians had given pride of place to the Jewish mission in their desire to preserve a sense of Jewish purpose, a reason for Jewish survival, and an argument against conversion. But perhaps without realizing it, they had also placed a new weapon into the hands of the antisemites.

Adolf Stöcker, the Prussian court preacher, was a latter-day advocate of the Christian state, willing to tolerate Jews but believing they could become fully German only by conversion. Like his contemporary, the historian Heinrich von Treitschke, Stöcker held that Jews enjoyed equality in Germany by the good will of a generous Christian nation. But instead of displaying proper gratitude by accepting the notion that Christianity had spiritually superseded Judaism, they insisted that their religion still had a positive role to play in the world. Stöcker was not far wrong when he claimed that Jewish modernists had read liberal principles of tolerance and religious freedom backward into Jewish history. They had done so, of course, in the attempt to stress the modernity of Judaism and its compatibility with progressive thought. But for Stöcker such Reform Judaism had to represent a false Judaism. The real Judaism, he insisted, was decrepit; the new one was not the Jewish religion at all. Yet regrettably, "even the most liberal reformer wants to remain a Jew." The court preacher therefore made a new demand directed at the very heart of the ideology which sustained non-orthodox Jews in their Judaism: If Jews want to maintain their political equality in Germany, then, among other things, they must "renounce the arrogant belief that Judaism will be the religion of the future, since it is so utterly the religion of the past."[55] Most German Jews could hardly have responded to Stöcker's demand to cut out the very heart of their religious faith without collapsing their Jewish identity into simple ethnicity—and the latter was a questionable category in a state intolerant of cultural diversity.

The secularist writer Wilhelm Marr, founder of the Anti-Semitic League, represents the other branch of late nineteenth-century antisemitism. Unlike Stöcker, Marr did not seek to convert the Jews, since to his mind Jewishness was a racial characteristic which baptism could not wash away. But he too had reason to devote special attention to Reform Jews, for their Jewishness was the least apparent. They were mainly unobservant; they did not believe in the revelatory status of the Talmud or even of the Hebrew Bible. But they were Jews nonetheless. They circumcised their sons and, while they were happy to engage in a critical discussion of Christianity, they were remarkably sensitive when an outsider attacked Judaism or cast aspersions upon the Jews. Their Judaism was amorphous, not clearly defined. "The Reform Jew," says Marr, "is a creature of which one never knows where the Jew begins and where he ends. . . . God save German representative institutions from Reform Jews. Better the most orthodox Polish rabbi!"[56]

Since the antisemitic barrage came at that point in German history when the alliance between Bismarck and the parliamentary liberals had just broken down and since Jews were prominent in the liberal parties, it is not surprising that antisemitism was linked to antiliberalism.[57] A few years earlier the veteran antisemite Constantin Frantz had already associated the National Liberal party with "Jewish domination."[58] Liberalism now became "Jewish liberalism" as represented especially by Eduard Lasker and Ludwig

Bamberger. The connection seemed to make sense. Even if most liberals were not Jews, most Jews were certainly liberals.

The sentiments of Stöcker, Marr, and those who thought as they did were institutionalized in antisemitic parties and elaborated in the press. Yet if the antisemitic intent was to break the "arrogant" spirit of the Jews, the effort surely failed. As in the case of earlier verbal attacks, Jews hastened to respond, stressing their Germanness but also refusing to accept the antisemites' critique of Judaism.[59] Ironically, the general effect was not to weaken Jewish self-consciousness but to strengthen it. Alienated Jews, who had entered fully into the German political and intellectual milieu, spoke out as Jews—though sometimes a bit abjectly. The *Centralverein*, formed in 1893, drew together the largest body of German Jews ever united in a single organization in order to defend their interests against calumny and discrimination.[60] It was only after the antisemitic pressures shoring up a sense of Jewish solidarity began to diminish that the ever more pronounced identification of non-orthodox Judaism with the liberal worldview began to reveal its damaging consequences for liberal Jewish religion.

By the end of the nineteenth century the designation "Reform Jew" in Germany was generally used to refer only to the extreme separatist position represented by the *Reformgemeinde* in Berlin. Those non-traditional Jews who remained in the unified Jewish communities now called themselves adherents of "Liberal Judaism." Beginning in the 1890s they formed national organizations of liberal rabbis and laity; they competed against Orthodox and Zionist parties in community elections. In their German political attitudes they tended to favor the left-wing liberal parties while Orthodox Jews were more often supporters of the Catholic Center or of the Conservatives. Those Jews who were socialists were usually also atheists and either dropped out of the Jewish communities or played no active role in them.

That the majority of German Jews who were religious liberals should support the parties of political liberalism is not surprising. The principles of liberalism had always mandated Jewish emancipation even if in practice liberals had not always lived up to them. Moreover, liberalism in politics demanded the same opposition to outdated forms and inherited dogmas which set liberal Jews apart from their orthodox rivals. Positively speaking, they shared a commitment to historical development and progress.

Yet for religiously committed liberal Jews, the association soon began to appear problematic. No one saw the issue more clearly than Felix Goldmann, a liberal rabbi who served first in Oppeln, then in Leipzig, and who was among the most active spokesmen of the *Centralverein*. In 1910 Goldmann wrote a perceptive article in the periodical *Liberales Judentum* which well sums up the relationship between political and Jewish liberalism as it existed on the eve of the First World War.[61] As Goldmann saw it, the positive role political liberalism had played and was playing in terms of Jewish rights was rapidly being negated by its deleterious influence on the Jewish religion. The political liberals might be champions of Jewish rights, but they acted to diminish Judaism. They did not recognize Judaism as a living element in German culture and they were not concerned with sustaining it. Liberal principles demanded that religion be regarded as a private matter, yet the liberals were willing to tolerate state support of Christian institutions. They salved their consciences by failing to support equivalent appropriations for the Jewish religion. Their double standard served to weaken Judaism.

The worst effect of the liberal connection was its influence on the attitudes of the Jews themselves. Religiously indifferent members of the community persisted in calling themselves liberal Jews, by which they meant only that they were committed to progressive political attitudes and vaguely Jewish universalism. Excluded from fraternities at universities, Jewish students declared their own fraternities open to all. Holding high the banner of liberalism, most Jews opposed confessional elementary schools. Unlike Christian liberals, their Jewish counterparts were willing to sacrifice Jewish interests for the sake of the larger cause. Not surprisingly, Orthodox Jews made the claim that Liberal Judaism was tantamount to complete religious assimilation. Liberal rabbis and committed laity were forced to develop guidelines for Jewish belief and practice in the hope of breaking the bond perceived to exist between liberalism and religious indifference.[62] The political ally of Jewish emancipation once again posed the principal threat to the vitality of the Jewish religion.

Thus by the early years of the twentieth century the problematics of Jewish religious existence and evolution in a society not wholly committed to religious pluralism lay clearly exposed. German rulers, officials, and intellectuals, antisemites and liberals alike, nearly all expected—and some demanded—that Judaism disappear from the religious horizon. The message was mixed because some sought to bring it about slowly, others more speedily; some with a carrot, others with a stick; some by urging or even demanding religious reform, others by prohibiting it. Initially the Jews were confused, baffled by what was demanded of them. Most soon came to realize that unconditional and complete emancipation could come about only if Germany itself underwent fundamental change. To their distress it never changed completely. Jews ultimately attained equality, but Judaism remained condemned to oblivion. The exclusive doctrines of the Christian state gave way to an inclusive liberalism which by its erosive force proved to be more damaging to Jewish identity than were either conditional terms of emancipation or anti-semitic attempts to reverse it. The erosion had become extreme by the end of the Weimar period when exclusivism returned in its most vicious and destructive form.

Yet throughout their modern history German Jews displayed remarkable resistance to the pressures, rising up against the idea that their religious beliefs and practices should be determined by political considerations. To give modern expression to their religious faith, to enable it to withstand both repressive and erosive forces, they created forms of religious Judaism which were transplanted to American soil and took root here: Modern Orthodoxy, Conservative Judaism, Reform. Jewish survival in any modern diaspora context demands a similar or greater capacity to develop and strengthen a Judaism able to resist those external forces which serve either to restrain it or to dissipate it. Here, as in other respects, the experience of German Jewry presents both a warning and a model.

Notes

My colleagues, Barry Kogan and the late Jakob J. Petuchowski offered helpful comments on the manuscript of this lecture.
1. Christian Wilhelm Dohm, *Ueber die bürgerliche Verbesserung der Juden* (Berlin and Stettin, 1781), 143–44.
2. Immanuel Kant, "Der Streit der Facultäten," *Sämmtliche Werke*, ed. K. Rosenkranz and F. W. Schubert, X (Leipzig, 1838), 307–8.
3. Simon Dubnow, *Weltgeschichte des jüdischen Volkes*, IX (Berlin, 1929), 110–11; Y. Zvi Zehavy, *Tenuat Hahitbolelut Beyisrael* (Tel Aviv, 1942), 23; Ismar Schorsch, *Jewish Reactions to German Anti-Semitism, 1870–1914* (New York, 1972), 7, 9, 13; Raphael Mahler, *Divre Yeme Yisrael: Dorot Aharonim*, VII (Tel Aviv, 1980), 123. Cf. Ahad Ha'Am in *Al Parashat Derakhim*, IV (Berlin, 1930), 38. The contrary view has been expressed, without documentation or illustration, by Yehezkel Kaufmann, *Golah Venekhar*, II (Tel Aviv, 1930), 44–45, 247, and in 1939 by Julius Guttmann, "Die geistige Erbe des deutschen Judentums," reprinted in *Bulletin des Leo Baeck Institute* 58 (1981), 5.
4. Especially to be singled out is the valuable work of Jacob Toury, which

has been immensely helpful for the preparation of this lecture. In particular, see his *Die politischen Orientierungen der Juden in Deutschland* (Tübingen, 1966); *Mehumah Umevukhah Bemahapekhat 1848* (Tel Aviv, 1968); and "Die Revolution von 1848 als innerjüdischer Wendepunkt," in *Das Judentum in der Deutschen Umwelt 1800–1850*, ed. H. Liebeschütz and A. Paucker (Tübingen, 1977), 359–76. See also Ernest Hamburger, *Juden im öffentlichen Leben Deutschlands* (Tübingen, 1968).

5. For example, Max Weiner, *Jüdische Religion im Zeitalter der Emanzipation* (Berlin, 1933) and Heinz Mosche Graupe, *Die Entstehung des modernen Judentums: Geistesgeschichte der deutchen Juden 1650–1942* (Hamburg, 1969; Eng. trans.: New York, 1978).

6. Mahler, I (Merhavia, 1961), 235–44.

7. Jacob R. Marcus, *Israel Jacobson: The Founder of the Reform Movement in Judaism* (Cincinnati, 1972), 52–106.

8. This is the sentiment animating Eduard Kley's Foreword to the prayerbook of the Berlin temple: *Die Deutsche Synagoge*, ed. E. Kley and C. S. Günsburg, I (Berlin, 1817). Cf. for England: Bill Williams, *The Making of Manchester Jewry, 1740–1875* (Manchester, 1976), 259.

9. Isaac Marcus Jost, *Geschichte des Judenthums und seiner Sekten* III (Leipzig, 1859), 326.

10. David Friedländer, *Ueber die durch die neue Organisation der Judenschaften in den Preussischen Staaten notwendig gewordene Umbildung* (Berlin, 1812).

11. Michael A. Meyer, "The Religious Reform Controversy in the Berlin Jewish Community, 1814–1823," *Leo Baeck Institute Year Book (LBIYB)* XXIV (1979), 139–55.

12. Ludwig Geiger, ed., *Abraham Geiger: Leben und Lebenswerk* (Berlin, 1910), 94. Cf. Herbert Strauss, "Pre-Emancipation Prussian Policies towards the Jews 1815–1847," *LBIYB* XI (1966), 132.

13. Rarely did German states impose synagogue reforms forcibly upon all the Jews in their domain. One prominent exception was the Grand Duchy of Saxe-Weimar, which in 1823 issued an edict that required its 1,400 Jews to conduct their religious services only in German and a year later stipulated that any Jews desiring a concession from the government would have to bring evidence of having attended such worship regularly. But the decree was mainly limited to the language of prayer, and it was in no way linked to any prospect of general emancipation. Views differ as to the attitude of the *Landesrabbiner*, Mendel Hess—an extreme religious radical—to this decree after he assumed the chief rabbinical position in the Grand Duchy in 1828. Jost insisted that Hess protested energetically against such religious compulsion. But Hess's position may well have been inconsistent. See Isaac Marcus Jost, *Geschichte der Israeliten*, X:1 (Berlin, 1846), 226–32 and X:3 (Berlin, 1847), 227 note. And see the discussion in Jakob J. Petuchowski, *Prayerbook Reform in Europe* (New York, 1968), 126–27.

14. Jacob Katz, *From Prejudice to Destruction: Anti-Semitism, 1700–1933* (Cambridge, Mass., 1980), 195–202; Ismar Schorsch, "The Religious Pa-

rameters of Wissenschaft—Jewish Academics at Prussian Universities," *LBIYB* XXV (1980), 10.

15. Toury, *Orientierungen*, 19–20.

16. Friedrich Julius Stahl, *Der christliche Staat und sein Verhältniss zu Deismus und Judenthum* (Berlin 1847), 42–55; Wolfgang Bernhard Fränkel, *Die Unmöglichkeit der Emanzipation der Juden im christlichen Staate* (Elberfeld, 1842), 126; and anonymously Paulus Cassel (see Katz, 211) or another convert in Hermann Wagener, ed., *Das Judenthum und der Staat* (Berlin, 1857), 37.

17. Constantin Frantz, *Ahasverus oder die Judenfrage* (Berlin, 1844), 34–37, 47. Cf. in Wagener, where the Ahasuerus legend occurs on 70–71. A year earlier Karl Streckfuss had used the same legend in support of an opposite position. In the course of a decade, since he first broached the subject of Jewish emancipation, Streckfuss had become convinced that if all external restrictions on the Jews were removed, their sense of solidarity would rapidly disintegrate. Then, he concludes, "Ahasuerus . . . will silently lay down his weary head to eternal slumber." See his *Ueber das Verhältniss der Juden zu den christliche Staaten. Zweite Schrift unter diesem Titel* (Berlin, 1843), 120.

18. Wagener, Vorwort.

19. Immanuel Ritter writes of Wagener: "He wants his Jews authentic and to stamp the authentic ones as sworn enemies of Christianity." See his *Beleuchtung der Wagenerschen Schrift* (Berlin, 1857), 10.

20. Wagener, 59–60; Reinhard Rürup, *Emanzipation und Antisemitismus* (Göttingen, 1975), 53, 56–57.

21. Cited by Rürup, 153.

22. H. E. G. Paulus, *Die jüdische Nationalabsonderung* (Heidelberg, 1831), 6–7. In Paulus's formulation, there can be no *Verbesserungen* in Jewish status without a moral and religious *Besserung* of the Jews (90).

23. Idem., ed., *Beiträge von jüdischen und christlichen Gelehrten zur Verbesserung der Bekenner des jüdischen Glaubens* (Frankfurt a.M., 1817), Vorwort.

24. Karl Streckfuss, *Ueber das Verhältniss der Juden zu den christlichen Staaten* (Halle, 1833).

25. Nathan Rotenstreich, "For and Against Emancipation: The Bruno Bauer Controversy," *LBIYB* IV (1959), 3–36. Shmuel Ettinger, *Ha'antishemiut Ba'et Hahadashah* (Tel Aviv, 1978), 89–98; Katz, 159–74.

26. Friedrich Wilhelm Ghillany, *Die Judenfrage* (Nuremberg, 1843), 42–47.

27. Bruno Bauer, *Die Judenfrage* (Brunswick, 1843), 28–29, 76–77.

28. In practice, the policy of German states with regard to religious reform during the thirties and forties could be quite inconsistent. In Bavaria, official sentiment gravitated slowly toward the orthodox Jews. Following the example of Baden, the Bavarian diet in 1833 considered granting Bavarian Jews full political rights provided that they would make religious concessions. The government itself at first gave its approval to the elimination of certain prayers from the liturgy and called for district synods to discuss revision of Jewish beliefs and practices. But later it

insisted that rabbis in the state be strict adherents of "all genuine Mo-saic doctrines and ceremonies and discountenance all destructive neol-ogy"; it forbade the ceremony of confirmation and refused to permit any Bavarian rabbis to attend the reform-minded Frankfurt rabbinical conference of 1845. See *Der Jude* I (1833), 202; *Allgemeine Zeitung des Judenthums* IX (1845), 450; *Sinai* I (1846), 94; David Philipson, *The Reform Movement in Judaism* (New York, 1930), 76–78.

29. A good example is Karl Wilhelm Christian Weinmann, a deputy to the Bavarian Chamber from Munich. His views on Jewish political equality are in *Der Jude* I (1832), 203–5.

30. Ismar Schorsch notes that this was already the view of Moses Mendels-sohn. See his "On the History of the Political Judgment of the Jew," *Leo Baeck Memorial Lecture 20* (New York, 1976), 12.

31. Meyer Isler, ed., *Gabriel Riesser's Schriften*, II (1867), esp. 12–14, 139 note, 169 note; *Der Jude* II (1833), 99, 102; Moshe Rinott, "Gabriel Riesser—Fighter for Jewish Emancipation," *LBIYB* VII (1962), 24.

32. *Der Jude* I (1832), 201–3.

33. Johann Jacoby, *Ueber das Verhältniss des Herrn Streckfuss zur Emancipation der Juden* (Hamburg 1833), 16.

34. *Zeitschrift für die religiösen Interessen des Judenthums* I (1844), 224–27, 330–37.

35. *Wissenschaftliche Zeitschrift für jüdische Theologie* V (1844), 150, 199–202. While Geiger and his associates believed that rabbinical authority should allow for maximal participation in German social and political life, they were by no means oblivious to the continuing weight of Jewish religious obligation. When the Breslau rabbinical conference in 1846 was discussing the issue of whether Jews should feel free to work in government service on the sabbath, M. Levy, a teacher of religion in Breslau, seriously questioned whether, under present circumstances, the Jewish sabbath should yield to the state. The state, he thought, was as yet but a dim likeness of what it ideally should be. Jewish observance of the sabbath contributed to creating a messianic momentum in which the state might eventually come closer to realizing its own moral idea. See *Protokolle der dritten Versammlung deutscher Rabbiner* (Breslau, 1847), 199; cf. 202–3.

36. *Reform-Zeitung. Organ für den Fortschritt im Judenthum* I (1847), 44, 58. An unpublished manuscript, written by Samuel Holdheim during his tenure as rabbi and preacher of the Berlin *Reformgemeinde*, succinctly delineates the political situation of this most radical reform circle. Un-dated and written in Hebrew characters (which I have transcribed into modern German orthography), this brief reflection may have been in-tended for delivery during the particular sabbath or New Year service during which the Sacrifice of Isaac is read from the Torah. It was proba-bly written during the 1850s. I am grateful to Professor Jonathan Hel-fand for providing me with a copy from the Archives of the Leo Baeck Institute in New York (AR 3644/4). It reads as follows:

Die geschichtlichen Erinnerungen des Judentums sind so zu sagen die Geschichte der Selbstopferung Israels um seines Geistes willen und darum mit dem Ursprung seiner Geschichte mit dem Opfer Abrahams nahverwandt. Ein sehr treffliches Wort haben hierüber die Alten ausgesprochen

כל מצוה שמסרו ישראל נפשם עליהם נתקיימה בידם

[Cf. B.T. Sabbath 130a]. Diejenigen Gottesgebote, um deren Willen Israel den Opfertod nicht scheute, haben die Religion in ihm erhalten. Ich erinnere Euch, meine Freunde, an die erste Zeit, als wir unsre Gemeinschaft gründeten, als wir das Land unsrer Geburt und unsres Wirkens für unsre Heimat für unser irdisches Vaterland erklärten und auf die Sammlung der Zerstreuten in Palästina zur Wiederaufrichtung eines nationalen jüdischen Reiches verzichten zu müssen erklärten, was war es, wessen unsre Gegner uns beschuldigten? Bürgerliche Ehre, bürgerliche Gleichstellung, materielle Wohlfart, das ist der ausschliessliche Gegenstand Eures Strebens, Euch als die heimischen Kinder des vaterländischen Herdes, uns als die Fremden darzustellen, das und nicht Gottesfurcht ist das Ziel Eures Strebens. Nun, meine Freunde, das Blatt hat sich gewendet. Wir werden wegen unsrer religiösen Bestrebungen erst recht als die Fremden und Verstossenen bezeichnet. Wenn wir dessen ungeachtet unsre religiösen Bestrebungen dennoch mit Eifer und mit Opfer verfolgen, so geben wir Zeugnis vor Gott und der Welt, dass nicht Irdischen [sic] sondern Göttliches unser Ziel sei. Darum ist der Boden, auf dem wir jetzt unser Heiligtum hinstellen, der heilige Boden Abrahams.

37. For a comprehensive analysis of the extent of Jewish participation see Toury, *Orientierungen*, 47–68. See also the essays contained in *Revolution and Evolution—1848 in German-Jewish History*, ed. W. E. Mosse, A. Paucker, and R. Rurup (Tübingen, 1981).
38. In "Deutschland. Ein Wintermärchen" (1844), *Heinrich Heine's Gesammelte Werke*, ed. G. Karpeles, II (Berlin 1893), 237, these two verses occur:

> Die Juden teilen sich weider ein
> In zwei verschiedne Parteien;
> Die Alten gehn in die Synagog',
> Und in den Tempel die Neuen.

> Die Neuen essen Schweinefleisch,
> Zeigen sich widersetzig,
> Sind Demokraten; die Alten sind
> Vielmehr aristokrätzig.

39. However, radical Protestants and Catholics easily combined critical rationalism in religion with clearly anti-government attitudes in politics. See Jörn Brederlow, *Lichtfreunde und Freie Gemeinden* (Wien, 1976).
40. Toury, "Die Revolution von 1848," 372. A loyalist account of the events of 1848, penned in Hebrew by a Baden Jew, is published in *Yivo Bleter* XLIV (1975), 144–45.
41. Letter of 17 March 1848 in *Leopold Zunz: Jude—Deutscher—Europäer*, ed. Nathan N. Glatzer (Tübingen, 1964), 266.

42. Ludwig Geiger, ed., *Michael Sachs und Moritz Veit. Briefwechsel* (Frankfurt a.M., 1897); idem, "Zum Andenken an Moritz Veit," *Monatsschrift für Geschichte un Wissenschaft des Judentums* LII (1908), 513–39.

43. *MGWJ* I (1852), 1–3; Ludwig Geiger, ed., *Abraham Geiger's Nachgelassene Schriften*, V (Berlin, 1878), 125, 196, 199.

44. Ismar Schorsch, "Zacharias Frankel and the European Origins of Conservative Judaism," *Judaism* XXX (1981), 344–54; Michael A. Meyer, "Abraham Geiger's Historical Judaism," in *New Perspectives on Abraham Geiger*, ed. J. J. Petuchowski (Cincinnati, 1975), 3–16.

45. Toury, *Mehumah*, 14.

46. *Riesser's Schriften*, II, 12, 89; Jacoby, *Streckfuss*, 13.

47. Edmund Silberner, ed., *Johann Jacoby Briefwechsel 1816–1849* (Hannover, 1974), 42, 72, 409. In addition to editing Jacoby's letters, Silberner has written a number of articles on Jacoby. See especially his "Zur Jugendbiographie von Johann Jacoby," *Archiv für Sozialgeschichte* IX (1969), 5–117, and "Johann Jacoby 1843–1846," *International Review of Social History* XIV (1969), 353–411. Also of interest: C. P. Jenkwitz, "Der Jude Johann Jacoby," *Gemeindeblatt der jüdischen Gemeinde zu Berlin*, 2 Sept. 1927, 212–13; Reinhard Adam, "Johann Jacobys politischer Werdegang 1805–1840," *Historische Zeitschrift* 143 (1930), 48–76.

48. *Jacoby Briefwechsel 1816–1849*, 56–57.

49. Edmund Silberner, ed., *Johann Jacoby Briefwechsel 1850–1877* (Bonn, 1978), 165, 168. Interestingly, Abraham Geiger tried to find Jewish characteristics in the work of Aron Bernstein. One of the initiators of the Berlin *Reformgemeinde*, Bernstein was a politically radical publicist who suffered imprisonment for the expression of his views during the 1850s. A prolific writer, he combined political journalism with popular scientific studies, biblical criticism, and the writing of novels which nostalgically recall Jewish life in the small towns of Prussia. According to Geiger, Judaism could become a "hidden power" in persons who devoted themselves to universal causes. Bernstein's enemies and friends never ceased to brand him a Jew, or specifically a *Reformjude*. They recognized—correctly, Geiger thought—that however far most of his work was removed from specifically Jewish matters, the "peculiarity of the Jewish spirit was unmistakably stamped upon it." For Geiger the peculiarly Jewish element consisted of the ability to treat both science and politics in a fashion that humanized them, regarding world and society in moral terms. See *Jüdische Zeitschrift für Wissenschaft und Leben* XI (1869), 223–26.

50. Toury, "Die Revolution von 1848," 365.

51. Tobias Cohn, "Eduard Lasker. Biographische Skizze," *Jahrbuch für die Geschichte der Juden und des Judenthums* IV (1869), 5; Joseph Gotthelf, "Dr. Eduard Lasker's Herkunft und Jugendjahre," *Deutscher Volks-Kalender . . . für Israeliten* (Brieg, 1885), 27–38; Gordon R. Mork, "The Making of a German Nationalist: Eduard Lasker's Early Years, 1829–1847," *Societas* I (1971), 23–32; James F. Harris, "Eduard Lasker: The Jew as National German Politician," *LBIYB* XX (1975), 151–77.

52. The similarities are apparent from reading of James J. Sheehan, *German Liberalism in the Nineteenth Century* (Chicago, 1978). See esp. 7–50, 159, 272.

53. Uriel Tal, "Religious and Anti-Religious Roots of Modern Anti-Semitism," *Leo Baeck Memorial Lecture 14* (New York, 1971); idem, *Christians and Jews in Germany: Religion, Politics, and Ideology in the Second Reich, 1870–1914* (Ithaca, 1975).

54. Michael A. Meyer, Response to Daniel Schwartz (Hebrew), *Zion* XLVI (1981), 57–58.

55. Adolf Stöcker, *Das moderne Judenthum in Deutschland, besonders in Berlin* (Berlin, 1880), 6–19. An English translation of the first part of the pamphlet is in Paul W. Massing, *Rehearsal for Destruction* (New York, 1949), 278–87.

56. Wilhelm Marr, *Der Weg zum Siege des Germanenthums über das Judenthum* (Berlin, 1880), 12–14. For Marr's relation to Riesser, whom he regarded as the foremost Reform Jew, see Mosche Zimmermann, "Gabriel Riesser und Wilhelm Marr im Meinungsstreit," *Zeitschrift des Vereins fur Hamburgische Geschichte* LXI (1975), 59–84.

57. Ludwig Bamberger, *Deutschthum und Judenthum* (Leipzig, 1880), 9–10; Toury, *Orientierungen*, 174, 183.

58. Constantin Frantz, *Der Nationalliberalismus und die Judenherrschaft* (Munich, 1874).

59. Walter Boehlich, ed., *Der Berliner Antisemitismusstreit* (Frankfurt a.M., 1965); Michael A. Meyer, "Great Debate on Antisemitism—Jewish Reaction to New Hostility in Germany 1879–1881," *LBIYB* XI (1966), 137–70.

60. Ismar Schorsch, *Jewish Reactions* 117–48; Jehuda Reinharz, *Fatherland or Promised Land* (Ann Arbor, 1975), 37–89; Sanford Ragins, *Jewish Responses to Anti-Semitism in Germany, 1870–1914* (Cincinnati, 1980), 45–103.

61. Felix Goldmann, "Religöser und politischer Liberalismus," *Liberales Judentum* II (1910), 61–64, 77–81, 112–15.

62. Michael A. Meyer, "Caesar Seligmann and the Development of Liberal Judaism in Germany at the Beginning of the Twentieth Century," *Hebrew Union College Annual* XL–XLI (1969–70), 540.

CHAPTER 11

"Wholly According to the Established Custom"?: The Spiritual Life of Berlin Jewry Following the Edict of 1823

The preeminence of Berlin in the history of Jewish modernity is beyond dispute. There Moses Mendelssohn first articulated a modus vivendi between Judaism and European culture, there social contacts between Jews and non-Jews flourished in the homes of Jewish *salonieres*, there Wissenschaft des Judentums was born and the first attempt at religious reform was made within a major Jewish community. All of this occurred during the last half of the eighteenth century and the first decades of the nineteenth. But then the situation changed radically. The Mendelssohnian solution failed as a universal model once natural religion gave way to less rationalistic forms of religiosity and enlightened Jews ceased to be traditionally observant.[1] The new nationalism during and following the Wars of Liberation reversed the tide of Jewish political and social inclusion. Jewish scholarship, excluded from the university, flourished only during the spare hours set aside for it by a few dedicated individuals. And religious reform was dealt a devastating blow when Frederick William III issued his well-known edict of December 9, 1823, prohibiting any innovation whatever in Jewish worship and requiring that Jewish practice remain "wholly according to the established custom." In every respect, except perhaps the economic, the Jews of Berlin had suffered a severe setback.

Not surprisingly, the important and fascinating developments within Berlin Jewry of the late eighteenth and very early nineteenth centuries have received much scholarly attention. But what of the period that followed, those dismal years of political reaction during which Berlin Jews collectively seem not to have produced anything worthy of mention, during which Jewish communities outside of Prussia became far more innovative, leaving Berlin and other Prussian communities behind? What characterizes this doubly "dark" age in the internal history of Berlin Jewry, illuminated neither by intellectual sparkle nor by an abundance of sources? Into what channels did its spiritual life now flow? What were the issues and noteworthy developments within the community during the 1820s and 1830s? These are the questions that I shall address.

The situation of Prussian Jews in the third and fourth decades of the nineteenth century was one of intense disappointment and frustration. Not only had they been excluded from anticipated positions in state service and academic institutions, but the government continued to regard their religion as merely "tolerated," denying it the recognition and public support enjoyed by Protestantism and Catholicism. Although the Jews of Prussia since 1812 benefited at least as individuals from a somewhat constricted emancipation, the treatment of Judaism as a religion remained much as it had been earlier—except, of course, that the enforceable authority which the community and its religious leadership enjoyed earlier had been gradually taken away.[2] Paragraph 39 of the emancipation edict, which held out the prospect of a reorganization of Prussian Jewish communities in keeping with civil equality and an improvement of Jewish education, remained a dead letter. The community lost its old mode of influence and gained no new one in return. Still in 1840 Moritz Veit noted that Prussian Jewry found itself in an extended state of "interregnum," waiting in vain for reorganization and recognition from above.[3] But the Prussian government repeatedly made it clear that its only interest in the Jewish religion was from a police point of view, especially to make sure that Jews did not split into sects. Frederick William III, who feared sectarianism also in Christianity and sought to curb it there, wanted to discourage religious ferment among Jews. Thus Prussian Jewry found itself in a situation where the regime both reneged on its own promise to help create modern forms of Jewish religious life and suppressed all attempts by Jews to do so on their own. According to Gabriel Riesser, most thoughtful Prussian Jews understood the 1823 order "as nothing other than an act of enmity against the tolerated religion, as arising from the effort to stifle Judaism in an impermeable envelope, tightly sealed off from the influx of life-giving fresh air, becoming ever more alien to contemporary forms; as an effort to let it petrify in its rigidity, depriving every living religious sentiment of sustenance in Jewish worship, and thereby forcing [the Jews] to seek a substitute in the bosom of the Christian church."[4] Riesser's contention is confirmed from Prussian government documents.[5] But where did such a correctly perceived policy leave Berlin Jews who were content neither to let Judaism remain in its ghetto state, and hence become more and more incongruent with their own lives lived within German society and culture, nor to accept the pressure for conversion? With the prohibition of modernized religious services both in the main synagogue and in smaller prayer houses in Berlin, only one public arena still remained open: the Jewish school. In the wake of the 1823 decree attention therefore came to focus on Jewish education. It was here that new conflicts now arose between traditionalists and reformers. And just as earlier, here too, the Prussian government played its role.

Only a few months after Frederick William's edict, in 1824, the Berlin Jewish community elected a new governing board, whose members made it their first priority to improve the school situation.[6] Heretofore Jewish children in Berlin had received their education from private tutors, in private schools conducted as business enterprises by individual educators, or, in the case of the poor, in the practically, and in large measure secularly, oriented Freyschule, founded in 1778 under the inspiration of Moses Mendelssohn and supported by individual donations. For years the Freyschule had been declining despite the best efforts of its director, Lazarus Bendavid. For a brief time some members of the Verein für Cultur und Wissenschaft der Juden had stepped into the breach by offering instruction without compensation. But their idealistic effort lasted for only about a year, ending in February 1823.[7] The new governing board now decided that the community itself should accept the obligation of providing Jewish education through a community school supported, at least in part, from its regular budget.[8]

That the new governing board of the community wished a community school not on the pattern of a traditional Jewish heder or talmud torah, but rather on that of the Freyschule, is apparent from the character of the individuals from whom they requested plans for the school. They were all modernists: Lazarus Bendavid, the director of the Freyschule; Isaac Levin Auerbach, who had been a preacher at the now defunct reformed services; David Friedländer, the veteran but radical disciple of Mendelssohn; and Leopold Zunz, who had likewise been a preacher at the Berlin services. They did not request a plan from the Vice-Ober-Land-Rabbiner Meyer Simon Weyl, envisaged no role for him in the governance of the school, and apparently did not even officially inform him of their intentions. The plan that was finally approved by the board called for a curriculum that would explicitly avoid the erroneous paths of rabbinism, which was identified with Polish Jews, and indifferentism, which it linked to religious naturalism—choosing instead a middle path, "the way of pure Mosaic-Prophetic religion."[9]

Weyl, however, had decided to act on his own. He prepared a plan for an institution of advanced Jewish learning that would train teachers and even rabbis. It would assure a new generation of Jewish leadership for all of Prussia that would not veer radically from the position of the old rabbinic Judaism.[10] Thus two new institutions were in the making during 1825, with distinctly conflicting purposes. Only a year after the king had given victory to the traditionalists in the area of religious worship, the lines between them and the modernists had been redrawn on the battlefield of Jewish education.

Both of these ventures required the approval of various government authorities and therefore also reopened the issue of whether it was in the state's interest to support traditionalists or modernists in the Berlin Jewish community. The King's position had not changed. In giving his approval to the new community school, he ordered his Minister of Religious and Educational Affairs, Freiherr von Altenstein, "to make absolutely sure that religious instruction in this institution follows Jewish dogma precisely and not, by virtue of departure from it, create a new sect, to which Jewry in recent times has a great propensity."[11] Altenstein's position was not very different from that of the king. He too opposed Jewish modernization, seeing it as a less desirable substitute for conversion.[12] If, nonetheless, the new community school received government approval, that was due in large measure to the efforts of one individual who enthusiastically advocated its approval in government circles: Johann Joachim Bellermann.

Bellermann was a noted Orientalist who taught at the Berlin University in addition to being director of the Gymnasium zum Grauen Kloster. He was also the government's special consultant for Jewish educational matters. Bellermann has invariably been portrayed as a great friend of the Jews, a liberal spirit who even left 10 Taler in his testament to support two poor students of the Jewish community school.[13] Earlier he had argued for allowing Christian children to continue studying in Jewish schools, an arrangement which the government prohibited in 1819, thereby contributing greatly to the decline of the Freyschule and other Jewish educational institutions.[14] Unlike the monarch and Altenstein, Bellermann supported the Jewish modernists and cultivated relations with their leading figures. At the same time he opposed Weyl's project. In a private notation for the files of the royal consistory, he declared it harmful because the curriculum would concentrate on post-talmudic texts, such as the sixteenth-century compendium of Jewish law, the *Shulchan Aruch*, which he branded a late work of low quality ("ein späteres Machwerk"), and because the proposed school would raise ever higher the barriers between Christianity and Judaism. When he was called upon to present his own version of a curriculum for the community school, he found even Zunz's proposal too rabbinic and one-sided. Bellermann, in fact, was little more of a religious pluralist than the monarch or Altenstein. He differed with them only on the means. In a memorandum to the consistory, written the day after he attended the dedication ceremony for the community school, he added a word about religious reform: "Whether the Jews may be permitted gradually to lay aside other irrational customs and numerous absurdities in marriage ceremonies, funerals, dietary laws, which have arisen from their twisted interpretations of the Talmud, I leave to higher determination. In my view, that is precisely the way to promote their conversion to Christianity."[15] In short, Berlin Jews had no one in authority who both respected them as individuals and sympathized with their desire to perpetuate their religion.

Underlying this battle over schools was the question of the authority of the rabbinate. In 1820 then elder of the Berlin community Ruben Gumpertz had supplied the government with a memorandum in which he reduced the rabbinical role to little more than the supervision of dietary laws. The Ministry of the Interior accepted Gumpertz's definition and made it the basis for policy.[16] Thus the rabbinate was left without the recognized right to take initiatives in the field of education. Although Weyl's project had already been approved by Altenstein's ministry, in the rivalry that now ensued, Weyl found it necessary to argue against the Gumpertz memorandum—which he did in a lengthy letter to Altenstein.[17] Here he counted among the rabbi's tasks not only ritual matters but also supervision of religious instruction and of the conduct of Jewish teachers. Accusing his opponents of spreading "Secten-Geist," he appealed to the man whom he regarded as his immediate superior ("unmittelbaren höchst gnädigen Chef") to order that in all matters concerning religious instruction and religious life the governing board of the community be prevented from acting without the agreement of the local rabbi.

Weyl's new school in fact consisted mainly of the old Talmud Torah, which was intended to feed into the new seminary.[18] The educational director was Jeremias Heinemann, now a religious conservative after serving earlier as one of the members of Israel Jacobson's Jewish consistory in Westphalia.[19] Weyl retained for himself the supervision of religious instruction. His school opened on October 18, 1825; and the community school two and a half months later. Not surprisingly, Weyl boycotted the opening ceremony of the latter, declining the invitation since he had been given no role in its creation. He must also have been disturbed at the identity of its director, Leopold Zunz, who was persona non grata with the Berlin rabbinate.[20]

Thus the Berlin community found itself with two very different educational institutions, neither of which was able to obtain sufficient financial support. In 1829 the two schools were united as the Jüdische Gemeindeschule Thalmud Thora, a boys' school[21] under the uninspired, compromise direction of Baruch Auerbach, the mostly inactive religious supervision of the Berlin rabbinate, and the pennypinching authority of the community's governing board. Altogether there were about one hundred students.[22]

Yet it was in this community school that some of the innovations earlier introduced by the Berlin Reform temple, that had been closed in 1823, received new life. On every Sabbath and holiday, after the presentation of a traditional liturgy, either Baruch Auerbach or his brother Isaac Levin Auerbach gave an edifying German sermon in the school's auditorium based on a scriptural passage, usually from the portion assigned to that week. A student choir sang Psalms in Hebrew in four-part harmony. Apparently the government looked the other way, allowing these exercises to continue despite at least one denunciation and persistent fearfulness that a new edict would abolish them. Although the exercises were intended primarily for the students, parents and other adults from all classes of Berlin Jewry and representing both sexes attended, filling the room to capacity. Riesser, who visited the services during the winter of 1832/33 reported: "It is moving to see how famished parents crowd around to share the meager spiritual sustenance of their children just so as not to languish completely in the state of deprivation into which they are placed."[23] Some hoped that these services would eventually give impetus to changes in the community synagogue, where the old disorder still reigned and German sermons were strictly forbidden. To be enduring, they thought, reform would in any case have to begin with the younger generation.[24]

During the 1830s even traditionalist Jews in Berlin began to reconcile themselves to formal innovations, such as the German sermon and the confirmation ceremony, provided they were conducted by Orthodox men and their content was not heretical. Just as Jewish traditionalists in Hamburg a decade earlier had found an externally modern but Jewishly pious religious leader in Isaac Bernays, so their counterparts in Berlin now found an equivalent in Salomon Plessner, who came to the Prussian capital from Breslau in 1830.[25] Every other week, on Saturday afternoons, Plessner gave German sermons at the old privately financed Beth Hammidrasch. In form his homilies were influenced by Christian models, but their content, for the most part, was Jewishly particularistic and wholly unobjectionable to the traditionalists.[26] Plessner was not only fully orthodox in belief and practice but somewhat of a mystic, who claimed personal divine inspiration for his interpretations of Scripture.[27] He was not a rabbi nor did he possess a doctorate, and he preferred to refer to himself as a teacher of religion (*Religionslehrer*) rather than as a preacher (*Prediger*). But in Berlin of the 1830s he became the kind of religious functionary for the more acculturated among the Orthodox that neither the aging rabbis, lacking fluency in German, nor the liberals, whose religious reputation was suspect, could be. This segment of Berlin Jewry called on Plessner to perform private confirmation ceremonies in their homes for both sons and daughters[28] and to deliver sermons at weddings.[29] Since these innovations came from within Orthodoxy, they aroused no significant opposition within the community nor fear of sectarianism on the part of the government.[30]

To some extent Wissenschaft des Judentums also revived in Berlin during the 1830s. In 1832 Leopold Zunz published his remarkably erudite *Die gottesdienstlichen Vorträge der Juden*, the first classic of modern Jewish scholarship. Two years later he began a series of public lectures on the Psalms, which drew an audience of about two dozen. Present were such diverse individuals as Salomon Plessner and the long-converted Eduard Gans.[31]

Yet despite these developments, the spiritual life of Berlin Jewry in the late 1820s and 1830s continued to suffer immensely from the political environment and from the Berlin Jews' own lack of common purpose. Prussian policy denied almost all public recognition to Jewish institutions. Rabbis and Jewish teachers were not given the tax privileges enjoyed by their Christian counterparts. In other German states their appointments received official government sanction, but not in Prussia.[32] An 1828 Prussian edict forbade Jews from giving their children Christian names. As late as 1836 another edict prohibited reference to Jews in official documents as of Mosaic or Old Testament faith—in fact by any term other than Jew or Jewish.[33] Prussian Jews felt that in one way or another they were perpetually being slighted, constrained, and pressured into conversion.[34] Zunz attributed the sad state of the Jewish schools in part to the "proselytism and spiritual pressure" appearing in various guises. These, he believed, created both abject institutions and abject people.[35]

The oppressive atmosphere motivated most parents to remove their children from the unfavored realm of Jewish educational institutions. Few sent their offspring to the community school, which acquired the reputation of being mainly for the poor, more charitable than educational in character. Less than one in ten of its pupils paid tuition, and most of its graduates found jobs as craftsmen or in other lower-class occupations.[36] Some children attended one of the private Jewish schools, of which there were more than a dozen in Berlin at the time. But all of the Jewish schools together accounted for only little more than one third of the Jewish school-age population.[37] The remainder went to non-Jewish schools, where the atmosphere was distinctly Christian and no Jewish teachers were allowed on the faculty. Various attempts to provide organized religious instruction for these children either inside or outside of school met with opposition and failure.[38] Not until 1856 did the Berlin Jewish community succeed in establishing a successful religion school for those children that attended public schools.

The parents who sent their children to non-Jewish schools had determined that their future, and the future of Jews in Germany generally, would be best served if the next generation possessed a common education and culture with Christians.[39] One Jewish educator, resentful of this attitude, decried what he called their "slavish adulation of everything Christian and the unfounded and unjust mistrust of Jewish teachers and educators simply because they are Jews."[40] Clearly Berlin Jews believed that culture, with all that it offered them, was to be found only outside the Jewish sphere. One either chose *Bildung* or one chose Judaism. The Jewish schools attempted to overcome this dichotomy, relating general culture to Judaism, so that the quest for *Bildung* would not seem to necessitate the abandonment of Judaism,[41] that, on the contrary, the child would gain general culture within a Jewish framework. But they were successful only to a limited degree with regard to those who attended and, of course, failed entirely to reach those who did not.

By the 1830s religious indifference was becoming ever more widespread among Berlin Jews, despite the influx of traditional coreligionists from Posen and elsewhere. Zunz put it bluntly: "Judaism here has about as much relation to religion as the fish catch at Stralau has to the Olympic Games."[42] Some contemporaries attributed such religious indifference among the cultured to the coercively imposed rigidity in religious practice. But it was also an attitude characteristic of many a Berliner and hence one in which they could share with similarly inclined non-Jews.[43] Most Berlin Jews who wanted to give expression to their Jewishness did so through philanthropy. Donations to Jewish as well as non-Jewish charities enabled them both to feel they were obeying an important Jewish imperative and to enhance the moral status of the community in the eyes of gentiles. Dozens of charitable societies and foundations dispensed funds or other assistance to Berlin's Jewish poor, whose numbers had increased greatly after the end of restrictions on new settlement.[44] One critic of Berlin's organized Jewish community had to admit that at least its care of the poor was exemplary.[45] Funds for Jewish education were much harder to come by. "They would rather build hospitals than found institutions of learning," groused a disheartened Zunz.[46]

The community governing board understood its task as simply "to administer and sustain"[47] existing institutions ("das Bestehende zu verwalten und zu erhalten"). Its members themselves rarely attended services and paid little attention to the nature of the ritual there. It was not until a relative outsider, Aron Hirsch Heymann, was elected Synagogenvorsteher in 1838 that some very conservative reforms were made in the services of the main synagogue. After considerable controversy, in which charges of sectarianism were once again raised, the auction of honors was abolished; a male choir of six to eight voices installed; decorum introduced through a Synagogenordnung and enforced by a specially appointed Ordnungs-Kommission; at least one member of the community board and Rabbi Öttinger mandated to be present at all Sabbath and holiday services; and—most controversial—the cantor dressed in a clerical robe, with a skull-cap replacing the earlier three-cornered hat.[48] This time the Prussian government only briefly paid heed when opponents within the community branded these reforms impermissible innovations.[49] But no changes were made in the liturgy itself and there were still no German sermons in the synagogue—indeed no Berlin rabbi who could speak proper German.[50]

The late thirties also brought some new and youthful blood to the community board. Among those now elected to it was Moritz Veit, a poet and liberal intellectual of moderate religious views. Veit gave impetus to a plan for the establishment of a proper teachers' seminary, which opened under the directorship of Leopold Zunz and with ten students in 1840.[51] Although Zunz and his staff were sufficiently suspect in Orthodox eyes to arouse severe criticism of the new institution, it produced a small number of graduates and persisted for almost a decade before falling victim to financial difficulties.[52]

Now too those Jewish intellectuals of Berlin who were not wholly alienated from Judaism felt the need to band together. Not since the demise of the Verein für Cultur und Wissenschaft der Juden in 1824 had there been a society of Jews in Berlin devoted to the propagation of culture among Jews. In November 1840 such a group was again formed, in part by those members of the old Verein who had neither left Berlin nor converted. Among them was Leopold Zunz, who became its first director. They were joined by others who came from the now more than seventy[53] Berlin Jews that possessed doctoral degrees. The Cultur-Verein's governing body included communal leaders such as Moritz Veit and the paid executive and legal counsel of the community Julius Rubo, as well as educators in the Jewish schools. Their purpose was slightly different from that of the old Verein. They did not endeavor to define Judaism anew, nor did they concentrate on Wissenschaft des Judentums. Rather they sought to encourage all forms of scholarly and artistic activity among Jews through stipends and other incentives. Yet like its predecessor, the group served as a focal point for the Berlin Jewish intelligentsia, now just at the time when a new liberal ferment was spreading throughout Prussia following the death of Frederick William III. The group also set as its task to work toward the goals of relating general culture to a Jewish environment, of raising the cultural level of the Jewish community, and of improving Jewish education. By 1843 it numbered more than two hundred members, some of them from outside Berlin. Since its members had differing religious views, religious reform was excluded from the agenda.[54]

At the same time that the Cultur-Verein was being formed, the governing board of the Jewish community was for the first time busy selecting a modern rabbi, one with advanced secular education, who would be able to preach in the synagogue and supervise Jewish education. In 1844 the choice fell on Michael Sachs, a religious conservative, who did not fully satisfy the now renewed quest for radical religious reform. In response there arose from among the members of the Cultur-Verein the Genossenschaft für Reform im Judentum. Spurred by the example of Catholic and Protestant radicalism among Deutsch-Katholiken and Lichtfreunde, it soon broke with the community and established an independent Reformgemeinde in Berlin.[55] To the minds of members of this group the rift between *Bildung* and Jewish religion could be sealed only by a wide-ranging theological and practical reform of the latter. In the political atmosphere of the mid-1840s they did not need to fear charges of sectarianism, even though their program was far more divergent from traditional Judaism than the mild changes that brought about the ban in 1823.

Thus, after about twenty years, Berlin Judaism was once again showing some life, seeking to regain the position of preeminence in the process of modernization that it had won in the days of Mendelssohn and lost during the dreary years of reaction.[56] But the energy now released in Berlin, as in other cities,[57] was largely centrifugal. The community which had held together religiously, in no small measure due to external pressure, now factionalized anew. Given the opportunity to modernize religiously once more, it soon contained a spectrum of actively espoused positions ranging from strictly Orthodox, through Conservative and Liberal, on to Reform. Given a freer atmosphere, the spiritual life of Berlin Jewry simply became more diverse. Religious pluralism among Jews, in Berlin as elsewhere, became a permanent feature of Jewish modernity.

Notes

1. Mendelssohn became a symbol rather than a model. See, for example, Isaac Levin Auerbach, *Toast auf das Wohl der jüdischen Gemeinde zu Berlin* (Berlin, 1829).
2. For an overview see Ismar Freund, *Staat, Kirche und Judentum in Preussen*, in *Jarhbuch für jüdische Geschichte und Literatur* 14 (1911): 109–38.
3. *Das jüdische Schullehrer-Seminarium in Berlin* (Berlin, 1840), 11.
4. Meyer Isler, ed., *Gabriel Riesser's Gesammelte Schriften*, 3 (Frankfurt a.M. Leipzig, 1867), 154. Riesser also noted that "nur in *Preussen* hat man alle Intelligenz, alle Aufklärung und alle Bildung von der Einwirkung auf den Gottesdienst ausgeschlossen, indem man ihnen jeden wirksamen Einfluss auf denselben unmöglich machte." Ibid., 173.
5. See the documentation in my *The Religious Reform Controversy in the Berlin Jewish Community, 1814–1823*, in *Leo Baeck Institute Year Book* 24 (1979): 139–55.
6. A school-by-school account of Jewish education in Germany is presented in Mordechai Eliav, *Jewish Education in Germany in the Period of Enlightenment and Emancipation* [Hebrew] (Jerusalem, 1960).
7. Leopold Zunz, *Sendschreiben des Vereins für Cultur und Wissenschaft der Juden an die Mitglieder der jüdischen Gemeinde in Berlin* (1823), in idem, *Gesammelte Schriften*, 2 (Berlin, 1876), 221–25.
8. For a detailed history of the school see Joseph Gutmann, *Geschichte der Knabenschule der jüdischen Gemeinde in Berlin (1826–1926,)* in *Festschrift zur Feier des hundertjährigen Bestehens der Knabenschule der jüdischen Gemeinde in Berlin* (Berlin, 1926). It absorbed most of the remaining teachers and students of the Freyschule, which then ceased to exist.

9. Ibid., 121. This plan was in large measure the work of J. J. Bellermann, on whom see below.

10. See the announcement in *Sulamith* 6:2 (1822–25): 373–78.

11. April 2, 1826, Moritz Stern Collection, Central Archives for the History of the Jewish People, P 17/548.

12. *Religious Reform Controversy*, 149–50. On Altenstein and the Jews see also Ludwig Geiger, ed., *Michael Sachs und Moritz Veit. Briefwechsel* (Frankfurt a. M., 1897), 30–32.

13. Gutmann, *Geschichte der Knabenschule*, 30 note. Bellermann also wrote a very gracious introduction to Ephraim Moses Pinner's *Compendium des Hierosolymitanischen und Babylonischen Thalmud. Ein Beitrag zur Geschichte der Israeliten und Eine Probeschrift der zu erscheinenden deutschen Uebersetzung des ganzen Thalmud* (Berlin, 1832). That he tried to further the careers of Jewish students in his Gymnasium is apparent, from the letter of recommendation he wrote for a David Rosenkranz in 1811 (in the Hebrew Union College Library, Cincinnati). See also Ludwig Geiger, ed., *Briefe von Lazarus Bendavid an J. J. Bellermann*, in *Zeitschrift für die Geschichte der Juden in Deutschland* (ZGJD), o.s., 4 (1890): 75–86.

14. Ludwig Geiger, *Geschichte der Juden in Berlin*, 2 vols. (Berlin, 1871), 2:235–38. In Heinemann's school Christian and Jewish children had studied "religion" together, with the Christian children having to learn specifically Christian doctrines on their own. *Jedidja* 1 (1817), 1:145 note. In the Freyschule there had also been combined religious services: "Kinder beider Confessionen, der jüdischen und der christlichen, stehen untereinander, beten, ohne an einander Anstoss zu nehmen, jene mit bedecktem, diese mit unbedecktem Haupte, zu unserm gemeinschaftlichen Schöpfer und Vater im Himmel . . . ," *Sulamith* 1 (1807): 2:138.

15. These two documents are from the Stern Collection P17/542. The first is undated; the second bears the date of November 30, 1826.

16. *Zur Judenfrage in Deutschland* (ZJD), 1 (1843): 213–16; Ludwig von Rönne/Heinrich Simon, *Die früheren und gegenwärtigen Verhältnisse der Juden in den sämmtlichen Landestheilen des Preussischen Staates* (Breslau, 1843), 146–49.

17. It is dated February 6, 1826, and is in the Stern Collection, P79/449.

18. On the school see Michael Holzmann, *Geschichte der Jüdischen Lehrer-Bildungsanstalt in Berlin* (Berlin, 1909), 1–31.

19. On Heinemann see Max Freudenthal, *Ein Geschlecht von Erziehern*, in *ZGJD*, n.s., 6 (1935): 146–54. Zunz's letters are replete with nasty comments about Heinemann, whom he utterly despised. See, for example, Nahum N. Glatzer, ed., *Leopold Zunz. Jude—Deutscher—Europäer* (Tübingen, 1964), 139, 142–43.

20. See the letter written by Weyl's successor, Jacob Joseph Öttinger, in 1834, which helped turn the community of Darmstadt away from offering Zunz a rabbinical position. Sigmund Maybaum, *Aus dem Leben von Leopold Zunz*, in *Zwölfter Bericht über die Lehranstalt für die Wissenschaft des Judenthums in Berlin* (Berlin, 1894), 32.

21. A girls' school came into existence in 1835.

22. Glatzer, *Leopold Zunz*, 144.

23. *Riesser's Gesammelte Schriften*, 3:156. See also Gutmann, *Geschichte der Knabenschule*, 36; Baruch Auerbach, *Die jüdische Gemeindeschule Thalmud Thora zu Berlin in ihrer fernern Entwickelung* (Berlin, 1833), 146–49; and *Allgemeine Zeitung des Judenthums (AZJ)* 1 (1837): 120. For a more critical view: *AZJ* 5 (1841): 159.

24. Meyer Isler, *Ueber jüdisches Schulwesen*, in *Der Jude* 1 (1832/33): 127.

25. On Plessner see Hartwig Hirschfeld, *Salomon Plessner*, in *Deutscher Volks-Kalender . . . für Israeliten* 32 (1885), 39–51, and idem, *Salomon Plessner*, in Elias Plessner, ed., *Biblisches und Rabbinisches aus Salomon Plessner's Nachlass* (Frankfurt a. M., 1897), 5–25.

26. For Plessner's own understanding of his homiletics see the preface to his *Belehrungen und Erbauungen in religiösen Vorträgen zunächst für Israeliten* 1 (1836): 2:vii–xviii. For positive and negative critiques of his printed sermons see *AZJ* 2 (1838): 337–38; 3 (1839): 387–88; 5 (1841): 215–16. By 1841 there was at least one other Jewish preacher active in Berlin. A contemporary report refers to a "Herr Lundsberg, ein jüdischer Theologe (der bereits seit einiger Zeit in einem der hiesigen Bethäuser mit Glück als Prediger fungirt und sich durch seine gemässigten und doch zeitgemässen Ansichten den Beifall der Bessern bereits erworben) . . ." *Israelitische Annalen (IA)* 3 (1841): 158. This was apparently Mayer Landsberg, later rabbi in Hildesheim.

27. See the fascinating impression Plessner made on Moritz Veit, in L. Geiger, ed., *Michael Sachs und Moritz Veit*, 8–9.

28. Salomon Plessner, *Confirmationsreden für die Israelitsche Jugend* (Berlin, 1839). The first printed confirmation talk he gave in Berlin dates from 1836. Confirmation ceremonies began to be held in the community school in 1830. An order by the Ministry of Interior to the local authorities in Minden had reaffirmed the prohibition of confirmations only a year earlier, in 1829. Jeremiah Heinemann, ed., *Sammlung der die religiöse und bürgerliche Verfassung der Juden in den Königlich Preussischen Staaten betreffenden Gesetze . . .* , 2nd ed. (Berlin, 1835), 317. Before the 1823 prohibition Heinemann had introduced a "Religions-Fest" for boys and girls in the private school which he directed at the time. *Jedidja* 1 (1817): 1:167–77; 2 (1818/19): 1:1–2, 207–16.

29. Plessner gave his first wedding sermon in Berlin in 1832. See his *Trauungsreden für Israeliten* (Berlin, 1839). Plessner's reputation was such that he was called upon to give wedding sermons outside of Berlin as well. Zunz too gave a wedding sermon on at least one occasion in 1837. Glatzer, *Leopold Zunz*, 197.

30. Certain innovations related to funerals, and eventually also funeral sermons, were permitted, at least in certain instances. When the community purchased land for a new cemetery near the Schönhauser Tor, it adopted a regulation for funeral processions that ensured that this display of Jewish religion in the public domain would be quiet and digni-

fied. However, no changes were made in the funeral liturgy. When Rabbi Öttinger dedicated the new cemetery with a German address in 1827, the police regarded it as a prohibited reform. *Sulamith* 7 (1830–33): 2:337–44; Geiger, *Geschichte der Juden in Berlin*, 1:164. Yet in 1834, at the request of the community governing body, Zunz gave a funeral oration at the grave of David Friedländer. Maybaum, *Aus dem Leben von Leopold Zunz*, 34.

31. Glatzer, *Leopold Zunz*, 176.
32. Heinemann, *Sammlung*, 428–40; idem, ed., *Ergänzungen und Erläuterungen* (Breslau, 1839), 230; Leopold Zunz, *Die gottesdienstlichen Vorträge der Juden* (Berlin, 1832), 464–67.
33. Heinemann, *Ergänzungen*, 215; Glatzer, *Leopold Zunz*, 189.
34. *Riesser's Gesammelte Schriften*, 3:125, 192–93. In fact, from 1822 to 1840 some 2,200 Prussian Jews converted to Christianity. Rönne/Simon, *Die früheren und gegenwärtigen Verhältnisse der Juden*, 108 note 1.
35. Glatzer, *Leopold Zunz*, 163.
36. *AZJ* 2 (1838): 212; *ZJD* 2 (1844): 416; Auerbach, *Die jüdische Gemeindeschule*, 166. Among contributors to the school was Professor Eduard Gans (ibid., 172).
37. *Sulamith* 7 (1830–33): 2:162; Geiger, *Geschichte der Juden in Berlin*, 2:244–45.
38. In 1827 Joseph Saalschütz, who would later become preacher and teacher in Königsberg as well as a notable Bible scholar, proposed to the Berlin community governing board a plan for a religious school that would meet eight hours a week for boys and four hours a week for girls. But the proposal was turned down since the board had just established the community school for boys and was planning one also for girls. Bestand 101: Akten der ehemaligen Jüdischen Gemeinde zu Berlin, in Jüdisches Historisches Institut in Polen, Akte 14 (obtained from Landesarchiv Berlin). When, beginning in 1843, the community tried to introduce Jewish religious instruction within the public schools, it met with opposition on account of their Christian character. Geiger, *Geschichte der Juden in Berlin*, 1:172; 2:246–47.
39. Cf. Jakob Auerbach, "Dr. I. M. Jost," *Jahrbuch für Israeliten*, 1861, 152.
40. Sigismund Stern, noted in *IA* 3 (1841): 157.
41. Gutmann, *Geschichte der Knabenschule*, 40–41. Cf. Glatzer, *Leopold Zunz*, 222.
42. Nahum N. Glatzer, ed., *Leopold und Adelheid Zunz: An Account in Letters, 1815–1885* (London, 1958), 68.
43. *ZJD* 1 (1843): 194; *AZJ* 2 (1838): 324.
44. For a listing with budgets see Friedrich Gustav Lisco, *Das wohlthätige Berlin* (Berlin, 1846), 365–403. Geiger estimated a threefold increase in the number of poor following the law of 1812. Geiger, *Geschichte der Juden in Berlin* 1:161.
45. Sigismund Stern in *ZJD* 2 (1844): 417.
46. Glatzer, *Leopold Zunz*, 211–12.

47. *ZJD* 2 (1844): 14.

48. Documents in Stern Collection, P17/549; Heinrich Loewe, ed., A. H. Heymann, *Lebenserinnerungen* (Berlin, 1909), 239–40; *AZJ* 3 (1839): 54, 247–48.

49. *IA* 1 (1839): 383–84; 2 (1840), 49–51; Glatzer, *Leopold Zunz*, 207. The government's order of December 31, 1839, that the cantor must go back to his old attire was reversed a few months later, after the community board submitted a petition. Stern Collection, P17/549.

50. As in the past, however, exceptions were made for special occasions. During a memorial service for Frederick William III, Rabbinats-Assessor Rosenstein gave an address, which a contemporary described as shaming the members of the community governing board on account of its lack of proper content and form. When the community celebrated the accession of Frederick William IV to the throne in the synagogue a few months later, its leadership called on Zunz to deliver what was later described as a "wahrhaft belehrende und erbauliche Predigt," in *IA* 2 (1840): 400.

51. See the addresses delivered by Veit and Zunz at the dedication ceremony in *Das jüdische Schullehrer-Seminarium,* 9–27.

52. Holzmann, *Geschichte der Jüdischen Lehrer-Bildungsanstalt,* 43–53. See the severe critique in *Orient* 2 (1841): 323–24. Zunz refused to accept any rabbinical or lay supervision of religious instruction or commit himself to an "externally religious" lifestyle. Maybaum, *Aus dem Leben von Leopold Zunz,* 62; Glatzer, *Leopold Zunz,* 217, 223.

53. *ZJD* 2 (1844): 124.

54. *IA* 3 (1841): 177–79; F. G. Lisco, *Das wohlthätige Berlin,* 391–92.

55. For its early development see my *Response to Modernity: A History of the Reform Movement in Judaism* (New York, 1988), 123–31.

56. For an overview of developments in various Prussian communities, see Isaac Marcus Jost, *Geschichte der Israeliten,* 10 (Berlin, 1846), 1:311–17.

57. Thus in a letter of S. M. Ehrenberg to I. M. Jost of December 15, 1841, we find: "Sonderbar dass in allen grossen Gemeinden jetzt offner Krieg der Partheien unter den Juden herrscht. So in London, Hamburg, Berlin, Breslau, und in Frankfurt . . . ," Glatzer, *Leopold and Adelheid Zunz,* 116.

CHAPTER 12

Jewish Political Leadership
in Nazi Germany

The situation of German Jewry from Hitler's rise to power in 1933 until its destruction is without parallel in Jewish history. In 1871 the newly established Second Reich had granted Jews, along with all other citizens, full political equality. Slightly more than sixty years later, the Third Reich withdrew that equality, rescinding the emancipation that had been granted by the Bismarck regime and reaffirmed by the Weimar Republic. The Jews of Germany, who had come to identify with their government, found themselves rejected by it. Not yet realizing the depth and ultimate consequences of that rejection, German Jewry nonetheless came to recognize that their situation required new and unprecedented forms of Jewish leadership. A Jewish community long riven across both religious and ideological lines was placed under growing pressure that released or augmented both centrifugal and centripetal forces. The result initially was a centralization of leadership to an extent hitherto unknown in German Jewry but also, for a time, a divisiveness based on the exacerbation of factional differences and conflicts that flared up repeatedly on the issue of where Jewish internal authority should be located.

In the course of a decade the tasks of Jewish leadership shifted, as did its relation to the Nazi regime. After an initial period of searching in vain for some sort of political accommodation, attention shifted to two objectives: planned emigration and the sustenance of Jewish life through education and social welfare. For a few years Jewish and Nazi goals ran parallel on the matter of emigration. At other times, they contravened each other—in the beginning when most Jews sought to remain at home in Germany and at the end when they sought to remain alive.

The principal leadership role within German Jewry from 1933 to 1943 was cast upon Leo Baeck: rabbi, theologian, officer in numerous Jewish organizations. It was extraordinary, especially in Germany, for a rabbi to assume so prominent a position. Yet he was uniquely qualified to combine a political leadership that frequently required confronting Nazi authorities with a spiritual leadership that became increasingly significant as despair deepened.

This essay is intended to take a fresh look at the nature and functioning of Jewish leadership in a period of increasingly deteriorating Jewish status and the invasion of Jewish life by external authority. It neither levels accusations nor offers exculpations but seeks only to arrive at a deepened understanding of motives and actions and the changing milieu in which they found expression.

The Creation of a Centralized Leadership

Although leadership in Central-European Jewry generally followed the Ashkenazi pattern of localized authority, political necessity could result in the investment of broad powers in a single individual. Thus in the sixteenth century Josel of Rosheim represented the collective interests of Jews in the German portions of the Holy Roman Empire. Josel was able to expand his authority to the point that he was referred to by such titles as "ruler of Jewry" (*Regierer der Jüdischkeit*) and "commander in general of the Jewish nation" (*Befehlshaber gemeiner jüd. Nation*). His role as *shetadlan*, intercessor with government bodies, on the imperial level was paralleled later in individual German states by court Jews, who were, however, not chosen by their Jewish constituents as Josel had been, but selected by ruling nobles and bishops on account of the financial services they rendered the regime. With centralization of government functions came the decline of the economic role of court Jews and thereby also their function as advocates for their coreligionists.

As Jewish political objectives in Germany moved from assuring physical and economic security to the political objective of emancipation, a new leadership emerged that was largely self-chosen. In Prussia it was David Friedländer and other Jews of his class who initially pressed for the amelioration of Jewish political status following the death of Frederick the Great in 1786. On the larger German scene, it was Gabriel Riesser who, by virtue of his essayistic skills, in the nineteenth century became the unelected but clearly foremost Jewish leader in pushing forward the Jewish quest for full political equality. It was only when emancipation had been achieved and was put under threat with the rise of political antisemitism in the late nineteenth century that the German Jews organized politically, creating the Centralverein deutscher Staatsbürger jüdischen Glaubens (Central Association of German Citizens of the Jewish Faith). It rapidly became the largest German-Jewish organization, although it represented an ideological position that excluded Zionists and most Orthodox Jews.

The Jewish communities in Germany had come together in 1869 to create a union of communities, the Deutsch-Israelitische Gemeindebund, but this loose organization did not attempt to exercise a political role. During the Weimar years some German-Jewish communities had banded together into more active regional organizations with varying degrees of cohesiveness. These too, however, were intended primarily to further social welfare activities.

The need for a broader representative body that could focus on political issues began to be more strongly felt even before Hitler came to power on January 30, 1933. It resulted at first in the creation of a very loose union of the regional organizations and then, almost immediately after the Nazi takeover, in a national body intended specifically to represent Jewish interests vis-à-vis the new regime. Based entirely upon the regional communal organizations, it was called the Reichsvertretung der jüdischen Landesverbände Deutschlands. Its weakness both in terms of its narrow base and of its unenterprising leadership rapidly became apparent.[1] Leo Baeck, who had been one of the chairmen, withdrew after a short time claiming that it consisted only of "an expanded Prussian state union or an expanded executive of the Berlin community."[2]

The question then arose as to whether a more effective representation to the government could at all be built upon the foundation of the Jewish communities or whether it had to include as well the ideologically based national organizations, in particular the Centralverein, the major Zionist organization (the Zionistische Vereinigung für Deutschland), and the association of Jewish frontline war veterans (the Reichsbund jüdischer Frontsoldaten [RJF]). These organizations had gained increased significance within German Jewry and, although they differed to varying degrees among each other in political orientation, collectively represented a new order within German Jewry. They were led by elites that were generally younger and less economically established than those which governed the local Jewish communities and the regional community associations. The new Reichsvertretung, which came into existence in the fall of 1933, for the first time attempted to encompass both orders within

German Jewry. The result was a much broader based organization but also one plagued with rivalry among the ideologically based organizations and with a long-standing power struggle between itself and the old community-based structure, especially the dominant community of Berlin, which contained fully one third of the Jewish population in Germany.

The Reichsvertretung der Deutschen Juden (after 1935: Reichsvertretung der Juden in Deutschland) was wholly a Jewish creation, although we now know that the Nazi regime during March–April 1933 was at least planning to create a central Jewish organization of its own to be governed by a *Judenrat* possessing police powers, and some Jews may have suspected that such efforts were afoot.[3] Once formed, its existence was simply announced to the Ministry of the Interior. Never granted any de jure recognition by the government and lacking the legal power to levy taxes upon its constituents, it was nonetheless recognized de facto as the collective representative body of German Jewry and initially allowed to exercise its functions without external interference.[4] Its growing budget, which was expended principally for social welfare, education, and vocational training, came in part from its constituents, but in large measure also from funds provided by the American Joint Distribution Committee and the British Council for German Jewry. The desire of these external charitable institutions to channel their funds through the Reichsvertretung strengthened its hand vis-à-vis the communities, which were not so favored. Nonetheless, its budget of 4.4 million marks in 1937 was only a small portion of the combined budgets of Jewish communities and organizations, which for that year was estimated at 25 million.[5]

Although the new Reichsvertretung was democratically constituted, its initiators had to consider just how much independence to grant its leadership. Was a democratic organization, dependent upon the consensus of its constituency, able to function effectively within a Nazi milieu where authority flowed from the top down? One of the founders, Rabbi Hugo Hahn of Essen, suggested that the communities, the community associations and the Jewish political organizations should all serve "the authoritarian leadership (*autoritären Führung*) as instruments of its will."[6]

Indeed, when first constituted, the Reichsvertretung was to represent a new departure in German-Jewish leadership. Whereas within the larger Jewish communities representation in their assemblies and on their executives was by party affiliation (Zionist, Liberal, Community-Orthodox), the Reichsvertretung was to be led by individuals chosen for their personal qualities regardless of affiliation, what one of the founders called a "cabinet of personalities."[7] However, it rapidly became apparent that the leadership of the Reichsvertretung could not locate itself above factional interests and that its composition required careful and periodically renewed attention to the shifting power structure within German Judaism. Thus, although it was not officially noted, the initial nine-man executive committee of the RV was carefully weighted according to geography, ideological affiliation, and religious orientation. Representation in the largely decorative advisory council was distributed in a like manner.[8] Only the president of the Reichsvertretung, Leo Baeck, and its executive director, Otto Hirsch, were chosen predominantly for their personal qualifications without explicit consideration of party affiliation.

Trying Old Tactics

Initially, the Reichsvertretung leadership believed that it might be possible to create some form of dialogue with the new regime or at least tease out an official statement reflecting the government's intentions with regard to the Jews. This intent was already apparent in the declaration that the old Reichsvertretung sent to the chancellor and various ministers on June 6, 1933. Referring to itself as the authorized representative of the German Jews, it requested an "exchange of views." Enclosed was a resolution, apparently drafted by Baeck, that was remarkable in two respects: it rejected apologetics, refusing once more to rehearse German Jewry's loyalty to Germany and long-standing relationship to German culture, and it assertively claimed the right to expect treatment according to law and on the basis of dignity. Less remarkably, it continued to argue in the old manner that such treatment would serve the good of Germany no less than that of the German Jews. Their request for an exchange of views—not surprisingly in retrospect—was summarily rejected.[9]

From time to time in the immediately following period the Reichsvertretung addressed the German regime in the language of protest. This occurred in January 1934 when its leadership complained of economic discrimination against Jews and argued that it served to harm German interests.[10] It occurred again, more strongly, in April and May of 1934 when *Der Stürmer* published its notorious ritual murder libel issue and Propaganda Minister Goebbels publicly accused the German Jews of fostering the boycott of German goods abroad.[11] The language of protest continued for a time longer, but by 1935 such remonstrances were simply published in the Jewish press for internal consumption, intended rather to vent Jewish feelings than to evoke any change in Nazi policies.[12]

Reactions to the new regime from the leadership of factional groups within German Jewry were in some respects reminiscent of responses to earlier excrescences of antisemitism. The Orthodox rabbinate declared the new trials of German Jewry punishment for the widespread abandonment of Sabbath observance and the dietary laws.[13] In the manner of Russian Jewry—which blamed lower officials, but not the czar, for anti-Jewish actions—the combined leadership of Separatist Orthodoxy wrote to the German chancellor of their firm belief that, even if isolated forces within German society sought the destruction of German Jewry, "neither the Führer nor the government of Germany would agree to such a development."[14] Ironically, on the opposite end of the religious spectrum, a leader of the Berlin Reform Congregation remained no less convinced that the Führer himself, and with him the German people, would do right by the "Jewish Germans," by which he meant those German Jews who were fully Germanized.[15] There was also the old willingness to take some of the blame for antisemitism. Thus the independent *Israelitisches Familienblatt* warned that the time might come when the dictates of Jewish solidarity would force action against "noxious" Jews whose business practices or dissolute lifestyles had provoked contempt. Less dramatically, Heinrich Stahl, the head of the Berlin Jewish community, argued that Jewish gatherings in public places need to be less conspicuous.[16]

There were, however, also new responses, in part because for the first time in Germany since emancipation the government itself was the source of antisemitism. Such, for example, was the attempt by the leadership of various Jewish factions to seek special treatment by pointing up areas of common ground. The Orthodox noted that they, too, opposed mixed marriages and conversions to Christianity.[17] The Zionists claimed that they, in particular, could well appreciate the significance of blood and race; believing that emigration was the ultimate Nazi goal, they declared their full cooperation.[18] On the other end of the political spectrum, the Jewish veterans belonging to the Reichsbund, which at this stage rejected emigration, proposed a special status for its members in view of their proven loyalty.[19] Searching desperately for a modus vivendi, Jewish leaders were initially ready to make voluntary concessions to the regime in the hope that there would be some response. Within the mainstream, the leader of German Liberal Judaism, Heinrich Stern, proposed that German Jews need not think that they could serve Germany only by occupying leading positions; they could serve, at least for the present, from the ranks. The Jews would accept a diminution of their equality, though they would not give up their hope eventually to regain it.[20]

The realization that any approach to the Nazi regime based on mutual respect was hopeless grew gradually among German leaders across the spectrum, more rapidly at the political center than along the edges. When the Nuremberg Laws officially reversed Jewish emancipation in September 1935, the Reichsvertretung and the Centralverein voluntarily altered their organizational names to substitute the words "in Germany" for "German." The Centralverein newspaper declared that to carry the banner of the association's old name under the new circumstances would be "quixotic."[21] The new statement of purpose the Reichsvertretung issued in the wake of the Nuremberg Laws marks this fundamental shift. No longer does the leadership make the case for Jews being Germans. It is now a matter of establishing some relationship between two wholly separate entities: the German people and the Jewish people, while seeking recognition for the autonomous leadership of the latter. Most likely written by Baeck, the statement calls on fellow Jews to develop a specifically Jewish manner and bearing as well as self-control and readiness for sacrifice.[22]

Internal Politics

Although the leadership elite of German Jewry recognized the unprecedented and crucial need for collective representation to the Nazi authorities, religious, ideological, and organizational divisions continued to create conflicts.

The most significant fissure lay between the rival claims to leadership of the national organizations of German Jewry on the one hand and the long-established community structure, especially the mega-community of Berlin on the other. The proponents of the Reichsvertretung had rapidly won over the Centralverein and the Zionists, but only reluctantly did the major communities go along, and only after speakers at a mass meeting in Berlin had declared the right of Berlin Jewry to possess the mantle of leadership.[23] Even after the prodding of the influential Max Warburg persuaded the Berlin leaders to lend their support to the Reichsvertretung, they looked repeatedly for opportunities to increase the relative influence of their community in relation to what they regarded as the "domination" of the Reichsvertretung by the national organizations.[24] In 1937, after threatening withdrawal, they succeeded, at least partially, in shifting the balance. Representing an "old guard" consisting of bankers, wealthy businessmen, and high civil-service officials,

they felt deprived of their right to leadership by the younger economically less well established and less experienced leadership circles of the national organizations. For their part the organizers of
the Reichsvertretung believed that this older elite lacked those qualities that had now become essential: broader perspective, diplomatic
skill, and political intuition (*Fingerspitzengefühl*).[25] No less disputed
were the activities of the Reichsvertretung in the areas of social welfare, education, and culture, domains historically anchored in the
communities.[26] As late as 1939, Heinrich Stahl sent a lengthy but
ineffectual memorandum to the Gestapo, severely criticizing the
work of the Reichsvertretung and requesting that the Berlin Jewish
community be entrusted with the collective leadership of German
Jewry.[27]

Among the major national organizations that formed the back-
bone of the Reichsvertretung, it was the Centralverein, and especially that wing of the organization that stood closest to the Zionists,
which carried the most weight. Leo Baeck and Otto Hirsch both belonged to this faction of the CV, which actively supported the work
of the Jewish Agency for Palestine. It was the Centralverein that vigorously defended the Reichsvertretung against the charges leveled
by Berlin. However, its influence declined in the mid-thirties as the
Zionist position seemed increasingly more adequate to the changing
reality.

Although the Zionists remained firm supporters of the Reichsvertretung, especially as its policies gradually fell into line with
Zionist ideology, their sense of growing influence led them to press
claims for greater power within its structure in parallel with similar
efforts in the community hierarchies. In 1936, after first claiming the
right to exclusive leadership of German Jewry, they were able to
attain 50 percent representation in the governing bodies of the
Reichsvertretung, and may thereby have prompted the revolt of the
Berlin community the following year. The principal issue between
them and the non-Zionists emerged, not on the issue of emigration,
but on the division of efforts and funds between emigration to Palestine and to other countries of refuge.[28] In calling the principal task
of the Reichsvertretung in 1937 "not much more than to supervise
and direct a necessary process of liquidation in the most economical
and productive manner," the Zionist paper *Jüdische Rundschau*, was
representing an increasingly common view.[29]

Since the founders of the Reichsvertretung intended to include
the Zionists from the start, those ideological factions in German
Jewry that were unable to make their peace with Zionism were critical of the project, at least initially. The Jewish war veterans group,

which at first sought to create a representative body consisting only of those who believed Germany to be "their permanent home and the goal of all their desires," nonetheless joined the Reichsvertretung at an early stage. Arguing that the Nazi regime would be more ready to listen to a frontline soldier from their conservative and patriotic group, they thereupon made their own unsuccessful claim to leadership.[30] A similar position was taken by those adherents of Liberal or Reform Judaism who were most opposed to Zionism. Although, like the veterans group, the Vereinigung für das liberale Judentum also attached itself to the Reichsvertretung in 1933, taking pride in the fact that Leo Baeck was "one of our own," it joined with the RJF and the Berlin community in supporting the latter's claims to greater power.[31] Far more critical was the attitude of the religiously extremist Reform congregation in Berlin. Its leadership refused to support the Reichsvertretung since it could not work together with Zionists, who did not share their self-conception as "Jewish Germans."[32] Similarly, those German-Jewish ideological factions not bound to a religious position that were furthest from Jewish nationalism would have no part of the Reichsvertretung. The Verband nationaldeutscher Juden went so far as to threaten legal action against the Reichsvertretung for giving the impression by its very name that it represented all German Jews. It charged that the Zionist leadership of the Reichsvertretung (by which they also meant Leo Baeck) was creating a new Jewish ghetto in Germany.[33]

The Separatist Orthodox likewise remained outside the Reichsvertretung, joining only during the last months of its existence in July of 1938. Objecting on religious, rather than ideological grounds to an organization spiritually under the influence of Leo Baeck and Martin Buber, they preferred to create their own representative body in 1934, the Vertretung der Unabhängigen Jüdischen Orthodoxie Deutschlands. Even in 1938 sentiment against joining an organization dominated by non-Orthodox Jews led one rabbi to brand such affiliation an act of apostasy, an *averah lishmad*.[34]

Of all the Jewish organizations the one that gave the most grief to the Reichsvertretung was the Staatszionistische Organisation in Deutschland, a form of Revisionist Zionism which differed in rejecting Jabotinsky's support of the international boycott of German goods. The German State Zionists were led by Georg Kareski, a dubious financier of high political ambition, who as head of the Jewish nationalist Jüdische Volkspartei had chaired the executive of the Berlin community in the late 1920s. Although the State Zionists did not join the Reichsvertretung, Kareski in 1937 made a concerted effort to take over its authority, both in concert with Heinrich Stahl, whose anti-Zionist views scarcely coincided with his own, and independently by requesting the Gestapo and Propaganda Ministry to impose his leadership. Kareski, who in an interview published in Goebbels's paper *Der Angriff* in 1935 had embarrassingly expressed acceptance of the situation created by the Nuremberg Laws, now sought the title of "Commissar in Charge of Emigration." In place of the Reichsvertretung, the State Zionists called for a fully centralized authoritarian leadership that would drive forward the process of total emigration. Despite Kareski's Gestapo backing, Baeck was able to withstand the pressure of Nazi officials to coopt him and hold Kareski to a relatively minor position in the Reichsvertretung. The following year the government not only withdrew its support of the State Zionists but dissolved the group, allegedly on account of ongoing relations with the "very strongly anti-German Jabotinsky group" and the suspicion that young emigrants from the movement to Palestine were working for the Haganah. Moreover, the regime, which had closely supervised the Reichsvertretung from the start, was at that point ready to take more invasive measures on its own.[35]

Nazi Policy

Although all records of meetings between Nazi and Reichsvertretung officials were apparently destroyed, it is possible to gain an impression of shifting Nazi policy toward the organized Jewish community from related sources that have survived. As mentioned above, there had been an early but abandoned scheme to impose a governing body upon German Jewry. That project was succeeded by a policy of de facto acceptance of the Reichsvertretung as the representative of German Jewry along with the refusal to grant it any official recognition. The government decided to keep a careful watch over its activities, as it did over those of all of the major Jewish organizations, even monitoring religious services in the synagogues. The changing relationship between Nazi officials and the Reichsvertretung mirrored the increasingly aggressive offensive against German Jewry. At first it was relatively cordial, later ever more abusive, especially after responsibility for Jewish matters was gradually transferred to the SS, specifically to Adolf Eichmann, in the late 1930s.[36]

It was not easy for German Jews to realize that, with the Nazi takeover, their strivings to become more German, which had served as justification in their earlier quest for emancipation and as refutation of antisemitic accusations of Jewish foreignness, were now viewed as detrimental to the interests of the new government. Yet the Nazi regime, which was intent on separating the Jews from German society, regarded negatively every effort at further Jewish assimilation. Hence it spurned the petitions and memoranda of those Jewish organizations that claimed to be the most German while looking with favor upon Zionist objectives. As early as November 1935 it dissolved the Verband nationaldeutscher Juden, which it regarded as an "assimilationist organization," fearing that its ideology "would completely distort the view of simple people regarding the National Socialist racial problem." A few months later it dissolved the right-wing Jewish youth group, the Ring-Bund jüdischer Jugend, which was charged with aping the organizational structure of the Hitler Youth and adopting the Führer principle.[37] In this regard the Sicherheitsdienst (SD) was critical, as well, of the Reichsvertretung, which a 1937 report called "an ever larger reservoir of assimilationist Judaism." Another report from the same year noted that "the main task of the SD consists now, as always, in the complete elimination of assimilationists from Jewish political life in order to bring the Jewish question closer to its conclusive solution."[38]

On the other hand, encouraging organized Jewish separatism was likewise problematic as Jews might come to think of themselves as a recognized minority that could make an international case for the receipt of minority rights. Hence it was necessary to keep the Jewish leadership at odds with itself, using ideological differences within the Jewish community to the SD's own advantage.[39] Early on, the government began to favor the Zionists, who shared its goal of massive Jewish emigration, not just from Germany but also from Europe. It wanted Zionism taught in the Jewish schools and adult education programs and greater Zionist influence in the Reichsvertretung.[40] By 1937, the authorities had settled upon the State Zionists as their favorite Jewish organization. Its youth organization was given the unique privilege of wearing uniforms in order to attract members to "this most radical form of Zionism." Long on the lookout for reliable Jewish agents of Nazi purpose, they attempted to impose Kareski, the most extreme advocate of massive forced Jewish emigration and the leader in whom they placed the most confidence. When that maneuver failed, in part because of a letter in support of the Reichsvertretung sent to Baeck by Sir Herbert Samuel on behalf of the British Council for German Jewry, and once observing niceties on account of foreign policy considerations became less important, the Nazis assumed far more direct control of Jewish affairs, reducing the sphere of independent Jewish decision making ever further.[41] Now they wanted a Jewish executive as united as possible in order to carry out their will expeditiously. Differences of opinion within the Jewish leadership were henceforth deemed "marked proof of the sluggishness of the system of democratic rule and the stark failure of the Jews in the administrative field, even when questions pertaining to their very existence were at stake."[42]

A Commonality of Purpose

At first, some of the Jewish leadership, though apparently not Leo Baeck, had believed that an acceptable form of Jewish life would continue to be possible in the ancestral homeland, and hence emigration was posed as only one option among others. However, getting Jews—and especially the youth—to lands where they could be more secure physically and economically increasingly became a focal point of Reichsvertretung activity as time went on and the situation of German Jewry deteriorated. Thus a convergence emerged between the objectives of the Nazi autocracy and the Jewish democracy. The departure of the émigrés left behind a greatly disproportionate percentage of older people whose needs increasingly strained the resources of the Jewish welfare agencies.[43]

As the Nazis made the Jewish situation less and less bearable with the conscious intent of thereby forcing emigration, the Jewish leadership was caught in a severe bind. It too aimed at increasing emigration but, unlike the Nazi authorities, it felt responsibility for the circumstances of the emigrants after their departure. And that required careful planning. Hence it supported vocational retraining and language courses, and it sought means to transfer funds to assist with absorption. Zionists and non-Zionists alike continued to stress the need for carefully planned emigration even after the Jewish situation grew more perilous. The Jewish leadership also insisted that Nazi measures to impoverish the Jews and thereby spur emigration had the untoward result that countries of refuge therefore regarded them as less desirable immigrants and made it more difficult for them to obtain visas.[44] Both Nazis and Jews were frustrated by the unwillingness of countries outside Germany to accept the Jewish emigrants. For the former this resistance, best evident from the failed Evian refugee conference of 1938, was, on the one hand, welcome indication of how widely their dislike of Jews was shared in the world, but it also stood in the way of their desire to dispose rapidly of Germany's Jewish population.[45] For the Jewish leadership the meager supply of immigration visas required difficult decisions of distribution, which were generally made in favor of the young.[46] As the pressure increased, the Reichsvertretung began actively to organize group emigration, especially but not alone for children and young people, for example chartering a boat that was able to bring 540 refugees to South Africa in 1936, just before the imposition of immigration restrictions there.[47] However, the Jewish leaders resisted pressure to load up so-called *Judenschiffe* to uncertain or insecure destinations. It is estimated that, in all, more than half of the approximately 520,000 Jews living in Germany at the beginning of 1933 were able to leave before the war, a large proportion aided in one way or another by the agencies of the Reichsvertretung.[48]

It was above all the mutual desire of expediting emigration, motivated for the Nazis by their wish to make Germany *judenrein* and for the Jewish leadership by the rapid deterioration of the quality of Jewish life to the point of unbearability, that prompted the creation of the successor organization of the Reichsvertretung, the Reichsvereinigung der Juden in Deutschland, in the months following the November Pogrom in 1938.[49] Although Jewish efforts to create a stronger central organization had been under way months earlier, prompted by a law of March 28, 1938, that erased the legal status of the Jewish communities, a new organization did not officially make its appearance until 1939. In some respects the Reichsvereinigung was continuous with its predecessor: its leadership was basically the same, it carried out similar tasks. But, unlike the Reichsvertretung, it was no longer the Jewish representative to the authorities (though it tried to continue playing that role), but the Jewish arm of the Gestapo (though it tried to maintain its independence as much as it was able).[50] It was the Nazi government which determined that all Jews, by racial definition, were its members and required to support its activities, which, though including education and welfare, were to be focused on emigration. It was now no longer Nazi policy to play upon divisions within the Jewish community but to bring about a unified leadership operating less as a democratic representative body and more as a tool under its direct control. As one Jewish organization after another was folded into the Reichsvereinigung, it became the sole bearer of Jewish authority, the communities reduced to the status of its local subsidiaries, remaining independent only in the area of strictly religious functions. Instead of the division into many communities, the German Jews were now to become a single community of Jews in Germany.[51] In its report of 1939, the Reichsvereinigung referred to its work as the "last phase in the process of dissolving" German Jewry.[52] Tragically, the real turning point did not come with the organizational shift from Reichsvertretung to Reichsvereinigung. It came two years later, in October 1941, when the Nazi position abruptly shifted from forcing emigration to prohibiting it and substituting a systematic program of deportations.[53] During all these vicissitudes, however, the position of highest Jewish leadership remained vested in the same person. From the beginning of the Reichsvertretung in 1933 until his own deportation on January 27, 1943, Leo Baeck stood out as the central figure of Jewish leadership.

Politician and Pastor:
The Role of Rabbi Leo Baeck

That Leo Baeck, a rabbi, should be chosen as president of the Reichs-vertretung in 1933, and hence become the personality representing German Jewry to the Nazi government and to world Jewry, was not obvious to all interested parties. The superior position of laity to rabbinate had deep roots in Germany; rabbis were responsible for their words and actions to local community boards. The instance of Max Gruenewald, who served both as rabbi and secular head of the community of Mannheim was regarded as extraordinary. There were those who believed that lay leadership would be more effective. In particular, the head of the Berlin community, Heinrich Stahl, was highly reluctant to allow a man who was his employee to become the most authoritative figure in German Jewry and, once he was in office, tried to unseat him from the presidency of the Reichs-vertretung whenever the opportunity arose. As Stahl confided in 1933, "Baeck, whom we treasure and honor as a great scholar, is not a person we trust in political matters."[54]

However, from the beginning, Leo Baeck enjoyed remarkably wide support. He had not only gained a first-rate reputation as scholar and theologian but shown ability in top positions of secular Jewish leadership ranging from B'nai B'rith to Centralverein to Keren Hayesod. He was then serving as president of the general German rabbinical association that included religious conservatives as well as liberals. Neither ideological Zionist nor anti-Zionist, neither Orthodox nor Reform, Baeck was perceived as a man of the center both ideologically and religiously. On social issues, he shared German Jewry's bourgeois contempt for godless Bolshevism.[55] Among German Jewish leaders, he was the best known both within Germany and abroad. Moreover, he possessed a dignity in appearance and style that Nazi officials, even toward the end, felt bound to respect.[56]

Though generally regarded as above parties, Baeck was nonetheless viewed by opponents of the Reichsvertretung as belonging to an enemy camp. The Jewish right-wing organizations thought him a Zionist; the extreme State Zionists regarded him as an assimilationist. In fact, Baeck tried to create balance and mediate between the factions. Thus he managed to retain the confidence of all of the leading figures within the Reichsvertretung with the exception of Julius Stahl, who was a persistent thorn in his side. Their mutual distaste for one another had many causes: although they were both Liberal Jews, Stahl was a high-ranking Freemason, Baeck a leader of B'nai B'rith; Baeck moved increasingly toward Zionist solutions, Stahl did not envisage a Jewish future in Palestine; Baeck represented the aristocracy of learning, Stahl—who lacked advanced education—that of wealth.[57] Apparently, there were also deep-seated differences of personality and, on Stahl's part, envy that Baeck had gained the most significant position in German Jewry. Contemptuously, he referred to Baeck as "my chief rabbi" (*mein Oberrabbiner*), an expression Baeck found insufferable.[58]

Although Baeck became the titular head of German Jewry in 1933 and held that position until his deportation, he left most of the day-to-day political and organizational work to the executive director of the Reichsvertretung, Otto Hirsch, a man with political experience as a government official in Württemberg and with deep religious convictions. The two seem to have worked together on political issues in complete harmony. Baeck, however, conceived his particular task as not limited to political leadership. By virtue of his office and his background, he likewise became the collective spiritual leader of German Jewry although he was never officially its "chief rabbi."

If as political leader it was Baeck's task to ameliorate the physical position of German Jewry to the decreasing extent that that was possible, as religious leader it was his increasingly difficult task to shore up Jewish morale as the political and economic situation deteriorated. From time to time he would publish a brief word of encouragement or a longer article in the Jewish press. He wrote of the justice that history cannot efface and that a person's highest duties are those toward God. He also wrote that "all genuine faith is a form of spiritual courage, a courage to contradict the world and what it calls facts and consequences, for the sake of God to say no to many a yes that reigns within it and to set a yes against many a no that the world has adopted."[59] Recurrently, Baeck used the word *Haltung*, by which he meant self-restraint (*Zurückhaltung*), but also holding firm, refusing to concede that historical change could undermine transcendent values. Repeatedly, he also stressed that the Reichsvertretung enabled Jews to remain subjects, rather than merely objects of history.[60] In the course of time, Baeck's role shifted from arousing spiritual resistance to providing spiritual comfort. Yet even a note of consolation could contain a veiled message that set Jewish religious eternity against a German history gone awry or turned to Jewish history for the lesson that something which seemed lost today could reappear in the future, a life seemingly ended could be renewed.[61]

A Shackled Leadership

The beginning of massive deportations to the east in the fall of 1941 created a new situation for the Jewish leadership. No longer was there any commonality of immediate purpose with the Nazi authorities. By the summer of 1942 Jewish schools and adult education, which had come more directly under central control, were closed down. The tasks of Jewish leadership were now those imposed upon it by the Gestapo, plus the few initiatives it could undertake on its own: social welfare, resistance, and mitigating distress.

By 1941 the remaining Jewish population was predominantly elderly and in need. In the summer of 1942, Leo "Israel" Baeck was urging those Jews who still had resources to spare to share them generously as part of a campaign called "Jewish Duty." "Jewish community today more than ever," he wrote in the only Jewish periodical then still permitted, the *Jüdisches Nachrichtenblatt*, "means the community of those who help. Helping, with a full heart, with a full soul, and with all of one's fortune is *Jewish duty*."[62] Baeck also tried to do what he could personally to alleviate individual suffering. To a friend in Buenos Aires he wrote in the fall of 1942, "What is there to tell? The circle has grown smaller and more lonely. I am engaged in day-to-day work in order to help and be useful wherever that is possible, and I am grateful whenever I can be there for someone else."[63]

Baeck and his associates also engaged in delaying and resistance activities. In at least one instance Baeck was able to hold back deportation of a group of Jewish youth preparing themselves for agricultural labor in Israel until relatively late in the war, increasing their chances for survival.[64] In the office of the Reichsvereinigung there was a "black box" which supplied money for young people planning to live illegally in Germany.[65] In October 1940, in response to an early deportation of Jews in southwestern Germany to France, the Reichsvereinigung leadership first attempted (unsuccessfully) to intercede with the authorities, then warned Jews away from their homes not to return that evening, and gave aid and shelter to those who had gone into hiding. Finally, as Dov Kulka relates, the Reichsvereinigung proclaimed a day of fasting, binding for all its leadership, as an act of protest, and issued special prayers and sermons to be read in synagogues the following Sabbath. The Nazi response to this Jewish revolt was to arrest and deport Julius S. Seligsohn, the member of the executive who had issued the materials, to Sachsen-hausen, where he soon perished. The Jewish leaders also attempted to pass information on what was happening to Jews to representatives of the press from neutral countries.[66]

Through his colleague, Otto Hirsch, Baeck established contacts with Robert Bosch, a leading German industrialist, active in the resistance in Stuttgart. In his home he kept abreast of the war situation through maps that he received from a sympathetic ex-officer and kept tucked into his Hebrew Bible concordance under the rubric "war" (milhamah).[67] But, in fact, there was little that Baeck or his associates could do to stop or even significantly delay the deportations. If Baeck remained in his position it was because of the genuine fear that the Gestapo would put someone else in his place who would ruthlessly execute its wishes. In Stettin, it had, in fact, imposed a Jewish commissar.[68]

The life of the Reichsvereinigung leadership became one of ever increasing danger, filled with fear that any of their actions would serve the Gestapo as grounds for their own deportation and death. Otto Hirsch had been arrested without charge as early as February 1941, perhaps because of his interventions with Eichmann to halt the deportations to France, and had perished in the Mauthausen camp in Austria the following June. A similar fate befell others.[69] Stahl, who was all set to leave in 1940, was denied an exit visa by the government, then deported to Theresienstadt in June 1942, where he died the following November.[70]

The anguished question that now confronted the Jewish leadership was whether or not to play a role in the deportations as demanded by the Gestapo. Although they apparently did not know the precise fate that awaited the deportees eastward (and that fate differed depending upon particular destination), they had little doubt that the concentration camps meant a cruel death.[71] Nonetheless, it was the shared view of the leaders that if Jews carried out the roundups they could make the ordeal more bearable than if the SS did it themselves. In October 1941, the Gestapo had made the matter entirely clear to two members of the Reichsvereinigung. One of its officials told them bluntly that if the SA and SS were to carry out the roundups, "we know what that would be like."[72] For all of their differences, Baeck and Stahl were of one opinion on this point. They hoped that by playing a role in the process it would be possible to ease physical and psychological suffering and also perhaps gain delays until the system of deportations, for whatever reason, would break down.[73] Thus fellow Jews, in some cases rabbinical students at the Liberal seminary in Berlin, brought those selected for deportation from their homes to the collection places, in Berlin to the Levet-zow Street Synagogue.[74] In determining the names of the deportees, the Gestapo made use of lists compiled by the Reichsvereinigung.[75] During this period Leo Baeck was not the principal contact person between the Reichsvereinigung and the Gestapo. That un-happy task had fallen to Paul Eppstein, who would later head the Jewish Council in Theresienstadt. Baeck continued to conduct the meetings of the Reichsvereinigung and occasionally participate in talks with Nazi officials, but he had little to do with the ongoing work. Since nearly all rabbis had left Germany, Baeck was now, more than earlier, occupied with rabbinical functions.[76] After his de-portation to Theresienstadt on January 27, 1943, the affairs of the very few Jews legally remaining in Germany were placed in the hands of Jews living in privileged mixed marriages. From here to the end of the war, there was no longer any form of Jewish leader-ship in Germany. What remained was pure subservience.

Notes

My thanks to Avraham Barkai for reading and commenting on the manu-script.

1. Bruno Blau, "Zur Geschichte der Reichsvertretung" (Dec. 1937), Leo Baeck Institute Archives, New York (LBIA), AR221 B30/3.

2. Hugo Hahn, "Die Gründung der Reichsvertretung," in Hans Tramer, ed., *In zwei Welten* (Tel Aviv, 1962), 98; Kurt Jakob Ball-Kaduri, *Das Leben der Juden in Deutschland im Jahre 1933* (Frankfurt am Main, 1963), 137.

3. Otto Dov Kulka, ed., *Deutsches Judentum unter dem Nationalsozialismus,* vol. 1: *Dokumente zur Geschichte der Reichsvertretung der deutschen Juden 1933–1939* (Tübingen, 1997), 37–40, 49; Shaul Esh, "The Establishment of the 'Reichsvereinigung der Juden in Deutschland' and its Main Activ-ities," *Yad Vashem Studies* 7 (1968): 19.

4. Ball-Kaduri, *Das Leben der Juden in Deutschland,* 147

5. Friedrich S. Brodnitz, "Die Reichsvertretung der deutschen Juden," in Tramer, ed., *In zwei Welten,* 107; Kurt Jakob Ball-Kaduri, *Vor der Katas-trophe. Juden in Deutschland 1934–1939* (Tel Aviv, 1967), 37.

6. Hugo Hahn to Leo Baeck, August 30, 1933, and Hahn to Kaul Levy, September 4, 1933, LBIA, AR221 B30/3.

7. Ernst Herzfeld, "Meine letzten Jahre in Deutschland 1933 bis 1938," in Monika Richarz, ed., *Jüdisches Leben in Deutschland. Selbstzeugnisse zur Sozialgeschichte 1918–1945* (Stuttgart, 1982), 305.

8. Blau, "Zur Geschichte der Reichsvertretung," 3–4.

9. Kulka, ed., *Deutsches Judentum,* 48, 51–52; Leonard Baker, *Days of Sorrow and Pain: Leo Baeck and the Berlin Jews* (New York, 1978), 159; Esriel Hild-

esheimer, *Jüdische Selbstverwaltung unter dem NS-Regime* (Tübingen, 1994), 13.

10. Kulka, *Deutsches Judentum*, 117–22.

11. Kulka, *Deutsches Judentum*, 139–41; Klaus J. Herrmann, *Das Dritte Reich und die deutsch-jüdischen Organisationen 1933–1934* (Cologne, 1969), 131. The boycott against German goods, fostered by Jewish organizations in Western Europe and the United States as well as by the World Jewish Congress, placed the German Jews in an uncomfortable situation. The earlier Reichsvertretung had already concluded that it had no choice but to oppose the boycott lest it give the Nazis occasion for further discriminatory measures against them. Its view in this regard was shared across the German-Jewish political spectrum. The collective declaration of the Berlin community and the Reichsvertretung of March 29, 1933, and the Zionist declaration of March 27, 1933, are reprinted in Herrmann, *Das Dritte Reich und die deutsch-jüdischen Organisationen*, 61, 63. Herrmann notes that they followed a meeting that Reichsminister Göring had called with representatives of various Jewish organizations on March 25, apparently to force Jewish expressions of opposition to the boycott. It has also been suggested that these declarations were intended to produce cancellation of the planned boycott of Jewish businesses on April 1, 1933. If so, they were unsuccessful. See Hildesheimer, *Jüdische Selbstverwaltung*, 12; also Klaus Drobisch et al., *Juden unterm Hakenkreuz* (Frankfurt am Main, 1973), 89–90; Max Gruenewald, "The Beginning of the 'Reichsvertretung,' " *Leo Baeck Institute Year Book* (*LBIYB*) 1 (1956): 62.

12. The protest against a defamatory speech by Streicher that was sent to the Jewish press in January 1935 is one example. See Kulka, *Deutsches Judentum*, 189–90.

13. *Israelitisches Familienblatt*, April 6, 1933, 2.

14. Petition of the various institutions of Separatist Orthodoxy to the German chancellor, dated October 4, 1933, printed in Hebrew translation in Yitzhak Arad et al., eds., *Documents of the Holocaust* (Jerusalem, 1978), 60.

15. Bruno Woyda, "Um die künftige Stellung der deutschen Judenheit. Programmatische Richtlinien," *Gemeindeblatt der Jüdischen Gemeinde zu Berlin*, October 1933, 319–22.

16. Koppel S. Pinson, "The Jewish Spirit in Nazi Germany," *Menorah Journal* 24 (1936): 230; Heinrich Stahl, "Jüdische Verantwortung," *Gemeindeblatt der jüdischen Gemeinde zu Berlin*, October, 1933, 317–18.

17. Arad et al., *Documents*, 61.

18. Document dated June 21, 1933, reprinted in Franz Meyer, "Bemerkungen zu den 'Zwei Denkschriften,' " in Tramer, *In zwei Welten*, 120–23.

19. Letter of the Reichsbund to Hitler, April 4, 1933, in Herrmann, *Das Dritte Reich*, 66–67. Although it failed in its approach to the Nazi regime, the Reichsbund did persuade President Hindenberg to gain ex-

emption of World War I veterans for a time from discriminatory legislation.

20. Heinrich Stern, "Deutsches Judentum: stirbt es oder soll es leben?" *Jüdisch-Liberale Zeitung*, September 20, 1933.

21. It is Kulka's point that the name change of both organizations was voluntary, not forced as earlier assumed, and therefore indicative of a heightened sense of Jewish independence. Kulka, *Deutsches Judentum*, 233–34.

22. The statement, dated September 22, 1935, and countersigned by all of the major Jewish communities and national organizations, appeared, inter alia, on the first page of the *C.V.-Zeitung*, September 26, 1935, and is reprinted (without signatures) in Kulka, *Deutsches Judentum*, 236–38. The argument for this statement marking a clear shift to a Zionist orientation is made by Herbert A. Strauss, "Jewish Emigration from Germany: Nazi Policies and Jewish Responses (II)," *LBIYB* 26 (1981): 401–2.

23. Günter Plum, "Deutsche Juden oder Juden in Deutschland," in Wolfgang Benz, ed., *Die Juden in Deutschland 1933–1945* (Munich, 1988), 59.

24. See, for example, the first-page editorial, "Gegen Gruppeninteressen— Für die Gemeinschaft," which appeared in the *Gemeindeblatt der jüdischen Gemeinde zu Berlin*, June 13, 1937.

25. Herzfeld, "Meine letzten Jahre in Deutschland," 303.

26. Abraham Margaliot, "The Dispute over the Leadership of German Jewry (1935–1938)," *Yad Vashem Studies* 10 (1974): 136, 141.

27. Letter of Kurt Goldman from Amsterdam to various addressees, dated in May 1939, cited in Ball-Kaduri, *Vor der Katastrophe*, 254–55.

28. Blau, "Zur Geschichte der Reichsvertretung," Anlage 5.

29. *Jüdische Rundschau*, June 11, 1937, 1. See also Francis R. Nicosia, "The End of Emancipation and the Illusion of Preferential Treatment: German Zionism, 1933–1938," *LBIYB* 36 (1991): 253.

30. Kulka, *Deutsches Judentum*, 78–79; Jacob Boas, "German-Jewish Internal Politics under Hitler, 1933–1938," *LBIYB* 29 (1984): 10–11; Hahn, "Die Gründung der Reichsvertretung," 102. The Zionists bitterly resented what they perceived as the efforts of the Reichsbund to gain a better status in Germany for their own members at the expense of the remainder of German Jewry. *Jüdische Rundschau*, July 3, 1934, 6.

31. *Gemeindeblatt der jüdischen Gemeinde zu Berlin*, November 1933, 355–56; *Israelitisches Familienblatt*, October 18, 1934, 1.

32. *Mitteilungen der Jüdischen Reformgemeinde zu Berlin*, October 15, 1933, 1–2. One of its leaders, Bruno Woyda, a Reform Jew and member of the Berlin Community Executive, nearly broke up a meeting held in the Liberal Oranienburgerstrasse Synagogue in Berlin to deliberate about the Reichsvertretung when he refused on principle to cover his head. Only when both the audience and the police officials that were present strenuously objected did he agree to make his plea for Berlin's hegemony with head covered. *Israelitisches Familienblatt*, September 7, 1933, 1.

33. Kulka, *Deutsches Judentum*, 63–64, 82–83.

34. Ibid., 65–67, 135, 408 n. 7.
35. Margaliot, "Dispute over the Leadership of German Jewry," 135–36; Hermann, *Das Dritte Reich*, 9–11; Kulka, *Deutsches Judentum*, 400–1; Michael Wildt, ed., *Die Judenpolitik der SD 1935 bis 1938. Eine Dokumentation* (Munich, 1935), 190–91. On Kareski see Herbert S. Levine, "A Jewish Collaborator in Nazi Germany: The Strange Career of Georg Kareski, 1933–37," *Central European History* 8 (1975): 251–81, and Francis R. Nicosia, "Revisionist Zionism in Germany (II): Georg Kareski and the Staatszionistische Organisation, 1933–1938," *LBIYB* 32 (1987): 231–67. In 1987 Rabbi Max Gruenewald related for the first time that the Gestapo had requested him to form a new Reichsvertretung together with Kareski but without Baeck. Gruenewald managed to refuse, pleading that the Jews of Germany had less trust in him than they did in Baeck. *Allgemeine Jüdische Wochenzeitung*, December 25, 1987/January 1, 1988, 12.
36. Ball-Kaduri, *Das Leben der Juden in Deutschland*, 146–47; Hildesheimer, *Jüdische Selbstverwaltung*, 11, 37.
37. Wildt, *Die Judenpolitik der SD*, 113, 145.
38. Ibid., 122, 148–49.
39. Ibid., 66–69.
40. Ibid., 113, 149, 162; Boas, "German-Jewish Internal Politics," 20.
41. Wildt, *Die Judenpolitik der SD*, 113, 122, 147–48; "Bericht über Schwierigkeiten der Reichsvertretung," August 6, 1937, LBIA, ARA 1579/4851.
42. SD memorandum dated early September 1938, cited in Otto D. Kulka, "The Reichsvereinigung and the Fate of the German Jews, 1938/1939–1943," in Arnold Paucker, ed., *The Jews in Nazi Germany* (Tübingen, 1986), 357.
43. Kulka, *Deutsches Judentum*, 241, 459.
44. Abraham Margaliot, "Emigration—Planung und Wirklichkeit," in Paucker, *Jews in Nazi Germany*, 312.
45. Susanne Heim, " 'Deutschland muss ein Land ohne Zukunft sein.' Die Zwangsemigration der Juden 1933 bis 1938," in Eberhard Jungfer et al., eds., *Arbeitsmigration und Flucht* (Berlin 1993), 65; Arthur Prinz, "The Role of the Gestapo in Obstructing and Promoting Jewish Emigration," *Yad Vashem Studies* 3 (1958): 205–18.
46. Leo Baeck, "In Memory of Two of Our Dead," *LBIYB* 1 (1956): 53; Strauss, "Jewish Emigration from Germany," 400.
47. Paul Sauer, "Otto Hirsch (1885–1941): Director of the Reichsvertretung," *LBIYB* 32 (1987): 363, 366.
48. Margaliot, "Emigration—Planung und Wirklichkeit," 303, 313. Some who left were later trapped by the Nazis in other European countries.
49. Hildesheimer argues that the extant documents do not allow determination of the source of the initiative that brought about the Reichsvereinigung. What is clear is that both sides had an interest in a more effective central organization as long as emigration remained the common objective. See Hildesheimer, *Jüdische Selbstverwaltung*, 80
50. Kurt Alexander, "Die Reichsvertretung der deutschen Juden," in Eva

G. Reichmann, ed., *Festschrift zum 80. Geburtstag von Rabbiner Leo Baeck am 23. Mai 1953* (London, 1953), 86–87.

51. Declaration of Reichsvereinigung printed in *Jüdisches Nachrichtenblatt,* July 11, 1939, 1.

52. "Arbeitsbericht der Reichsvereinigung der Juden in Deutschland für das Jahr 1939," LBIA, AR221 B30/3.

53. The army high command had favored an end to Jewish emigration to Western Europe as early as the outbreak of the war because it was feared that departing Jews would assist the war effort in France and Britain. Max Nussbaum, "Life in Wartime Germany," *Contemporary Jewish Record* 3 (1940): 580. Even after the October 1941 prohibition and until Pearl Harbor on December 7, the Reichsvereinigung succeeded in getting a few hundred more Jews out of Germany to or via neutral countries. Hans Erich Fabian, "Die letzte Etappe," in Reichmann, *Festschrift zum 80. Geburtstag von Rabbiner Leo Baeck,* 88–89.

54. Ernst Loewenberg, "Mein Leben in Deutschland vor und nach dem 30. Januar 1933," in Richarz, *Jüdisches Leben in Deutschland,* 246; Margaliot, "Dispute Over the Leadership of German Jewry," 145; Hahn, "Die Gründung der Reichsvertretung," 102.

55. Drobisch et al., *Juden unterm Hakenkreuz,* 88–89.

56. "Bericht über die Schwierigkeiten der Reichsvertretung," 3. When the Nazis required all Jews to turn in their radios on Yom Kippur in 1939, Baeck waited until the end of the holiday. His action in this instance, as well as his refusal to violate the Sabbath when summoned by the Gestapo, did not provoke punishment. See Baker, *Days of Sorrow and Pain,* 216.

57. Gert Lippman, *A Link in the Chain: Biographical Notes* (Sydney, 1990), 43.

58. Interview with Hildegard Henschel, conducted February 5, 1957, LBIA, ARA 1579/4851; Kurt Jacob Ball-Kaduri, "Leo Baeck and Contemporary History. A Riddle in Leo Baeck's Life," *Yad Vashem Studies* 6 (1967): 127 n13.

59. "Recht und Pflicht!" *C.V.-Zeitung,* March 2, 1933, 71; "Tag des Mutes," *C.V. Zeitung,* September 20, 1933, Supplement One, 1.

60. "Das Judentum in der Gegenwart," *Der Morgen* 9 (1933): 237–40; "Zurückhaltung," *C.V.-Zeitung,* February 1, 1934, 1; "Der Verlauf der Tagung," *Jüdisch Allgemeine Zeitung,* March 27, 1936.

61. "Trostwort der Reichsvertretung zum 'Schabbat des Trostes' " (August 6, 1935) and "Die Reichsvertretung zu Rosch Haschana" (September 30, 1938) in Kulka, *Deutsches Judentum,* 225–27, 429–30. See also John V. H. Dippel, *Bound Upon a Wheel of Fire* (New York, 1996), 122, 146–47, 188.

62. *Jüdisches Nachrichtenblatt,* June 12, 1942, LBIA Microfilm 456 (emphasis in original); Hildesheimer, *Jüdische Selbstverwaltung,* 143–44. However, by this time, everyone was required to contribute to Jewish charitable campaigns, which were closely supervised by the Gestapo. See Avraham Barkai, *From Boycott to Annihilation: The Economic Struggle of German Jews, 1933–1943* (Hanover and London, 1989), 173.

63. Leo Baeck to Rodolfo Löb, November 18, 1942, LBIA, ARA 1579/4851.
64. Related to the author by a survivor of the group, Werner Coppel, who heard about it in Berlin immediately after the war. See also Philip Friedman, "Aspects of the Jewish Communal Crisis in the Period of the Nazi Regime in Germany, Austria and Czechoslovakia," in Joseph L. Blau et al., eds., *Essays in Jewish Life and Thought Presented to Salo Wittmayer Baron* (New York, 1959), 208–9; Esh, "Establishment of the Reichsvereinigung," 33.
65. Esh, "Establishment of the Reichsvereinigung," 37. The late Shaul Esh claimed that the "black box" was of "no real value" but did not indicate why he was of that opinion.
66. Kulka, "Reichsvereinigung and the Fate of the German Jews," 359–60.
67. Baker, *Days of Sorrow and Pain*, 249–50; Avraham Barkai, "Von Berlin nach Theresienstadt. Zur politischen Biographie von Leo Baeck 1933–1945" (forthcoming); Jacob Jacobson, "Bruchstücke 1939–1945," in Richarz, *Jüdisches Leben in Deutschland*, 407.
68. Ball-Kaduri, "Vor der Katastrophe," 255–56.
69. Max Plaut, "Die Juden in Deutschland von 1939 bis 1941," 14, LBIA, ARA 1579/4851; Sauer, "Otto Hirsch," 366–67.
70. Shortly before his intended departure, the Berlin community rabbis, with the notable exception of Leo Baeck, had presented Stahl with the honorary title of *morenu*. On Stahl, see Hermann Simon, *Heinrich Stahl (13. April 1868—4. November 1942* (Berlin, 1993). In a bitter letter, written to his family outside Germany on June 10, 1942, two days before his deportation, Stahl made the devastating but uncorroborated charge that when Eichmann ordered his evacuation, this action "was not opposed to the thinking of 'my friends' in the leadership of the Reichsvereinigung." The letter first appeared, in the orginal German and in English translation, in Lippman, *Link in the Chain*, 49–54.
71. Plaut, "Die Juden in Deutschland," 16.
72. Cited in Hildesheimer, *Jüdische Selbstverwaltung*, 216.
73. Siegmund Weltlinger, *Hast Du es schon vergessen? Erlebnis Bericht aus der Zeit der Verfolgung* (Frankfurt am Main, 1954), 22; Moritz Henschel, "Die letzten Jahre der Jüdischen Gemeinde Berlin," 3, LBIA, ARA 1579/4851; Fabian, "Die letzte Etappe," 87, speaks of creating a "buffer" between the Gestapo and its victims.
74. Weltlinger, *Hast Du es schon vergessen?*, 24–25; Baker, *Days of Sorrow and Pain*, 273.
75. Jacobson, "Bruchstücke," 402–3; Wolfgang Benz, *Der Holocaust* (Munich, 1995), 84–85. Hildesheimer, in *Jüdische Selbstverwaltung*, 219, however, holds that the actual deportation lists were prepared by the Gestapo itself.
76. Hildesheimer, *Jüdische Selbstverwaltung*, 123–26; H. G. Adler, *Der verwaltete Mensch* (Tübingen, 1974), 19; Interview with Hildegard Henschel, 1.

PART III

Religious Reform in Europe

Should and Can an "Antiquated" Religion Become Modern?: The Jewish Reform Movement in Germany as Seen by Jews and Christians

Friedrich Wilhelm Carové was a friend of the Jews. Already in 1818, as a student at the University of Heidelberg, he had proposed a successful resolution to admit Jewish students to the local fraternity.[1] In succeeding decades, he continued to be an advocate of Jewish emancipation and, unlike most educated Christians in Germany, read widely in contemporary Jewish literature. He was well aware that for most German Jews by the 1840s their religion was no longer the traditional faith that had been their heritage from the days of the ghetto: to various degrees the Jews had sought to adapt Judaism to the modern world into which they had increasingly integrated since the middle of the eighteenth century.

However, despite all of his political liberalism with regard to civil rights for the Jews, Carové regarded the modernization of their religion as entirely illegitimate. In the year 1845 he published a collection of his essays on Jews and Judaism which reflected his view, as a Hegelian, that Judaism represented only a stage in the development of Western religion, one that had been superseded long ago by Christianity and by modern philosophy. To be sure, he could acknowledge the continuance of Judaism as a fossil or a mummy, as a relic from an earlier age. But to accept the notion that Judaism might be more than a previous stage of universal development, that it was itself capable of progress, was both philosophically contradictory to Hegelianism and politically repugnant.

In Carové's view, the movement for religious reform in Judaism could not be genuine. It stood in the way of its ordained disappearance in the course of historical progress. Judaism should have been fully absorbed into the *Weltgeist*, leaving no significant residue. It could not turn this process upside down by trying to absorb universalism into its own structure of belief without thereby ceasing to be Judaism. Judaism represented a stage of extreme ethnocentrism in the development of religion, which had progressed beyond it to universalism. Judaism—and for that matter Catholicism—was inherently incapable of internal development. In his own angry words:

> It is downright improper and reprehensible to make the attempt to preserve a religion, which from the beginning was based on privilege and is thoroughly infected with the arrogance of privilege, as is Judaism, by using the pretense of development in order to rob it of most of its essential substance and then to clothe the remaining skeleton with a magnificent garment of humanity and divine universality— one that was woven by foreign hands.
>
> Mosaism and also Catholicism, are—whatever one may say— antiquated forms which . . . still possesses a transitory and local justification, but to which one can no longer attribute any world-historical or lasting significance.[2]

In Carové's view, then, the values that characterize modernity— humanity and universality—could not be integrated into Judaism, no matter how hard the Jews tried to do it. He believed, as did cultured Christians generally in the nineteenth century, that modernity and Judaism were simply incompatible.

Needless to say, that was not the view of the Jews themselves. In Germany, the first indication of a broader tolerance of the Jews in the eighteenth century had resulted in a reconceptualization of Judaism that not only harmonized Judaism with the values of the *Aufklärung*, but made it appear that Judaism was the most complete expression of those values. Moses Mendelssohn, the philosopher and the first prominent enlightened German Jew, was, in practice, strictly observant. He held the orthodox belief that the Torah, the Pentateuch, had been given to Moses at Sinai and that its commandments were wholly incumbent upon Jews in every generation. He did not believe that Judaism, in its essentials, was subject to historical change and development; as a man of the Enlightenment, he held that fundamental truths were eternal and that, in principle, they were accessible to reason in every age. But Mendelssohn gave Judaism an emphasis that was not characteristic before his time. He proposed that, not only was Judaism compatible with the new tolerance and universalistic worldview espoused by the *Aufklärung*, but that its inclusive perspective was inherent within Judaism from ancient times.

Mendelssohn was at pains to point out that, unlike Christianity, Judaism did not hold that salvation was dependent upon the acceptance of a particular revelation. Had not the ancient rabbis already noted that the righteous of all nations had a share in the world to come? Thus, if the overcoming of narrow religious particularism was a demand of modernization, Judaism had met that demand long ago. Moreover, Mendelssohn emphasized that Judaism contained no superrational dogmas. Again, in this regard, it was different from traditional Christianity, which insisted on the acceptance on faith of clearly defined articles of belief outside the realm of common sense. Judaism, by contrast, made no such demands. Its God was not conceived as a Trinity but only as the one Creator and Sustainer of the world, a concept which, Mendelssohn believed, could be established by unaided human reason. Thus, if rationalism be added to tolerance as characteristic of a modern worldview, Judaism here also did not require modernization. It was inherently modern.[3]

Mendelssohn's argument, however, was not widely persuasive. For Gentiles it utterly contradicted the view of Judaism that Christianity had taught through the ages. For centuries, Christians had regarded Judaism as a religion which distinguished sharply between Jews and non-Jews, treating the latter as little better than idolators while holding firmly to the belief that the Jews alone were the people chosen by God. Far from being rational, Judaism was rife with superstitious beliefs and practices. For Christians to have accepted Mendelssohn's interpretation of Judaism as universalistic and rationalistic would have meant not merely some small alteration of conception but a revolution in thinking. It would have meant accepting the idea that Christianity was not an advance over Judaism but only an alternative way of serving God. Even Gotthold Ephraim Lessing, the most generous of *Aufklärung* writers and the close friend of Mendelssohn, could accept Mendelssohn only as a person, a virtuous and tolerant man who happened to have been born a Jew. He was unable to accept his friend's view of Judaism. For Lessing, Judaism was not, and could not become, a modern religion without ceasing to be Judaism. As later for Hegel, so it was for Lessing simply a stage in a universal process of religious development that led beyond it to Christianity.

Unlike the Christians, Mendelssohn's fellow Jews did not have difficulty accepting his *Aufklärung*-inspired interpretation of the Jewish faith as essentially natural religion, contained within the bounds of reason and non-exclusive in its promise of salvation. What was problematic in Mendelssohn's view for an increasing number of Jews, especially in Germany, was that Judaism in practice did not fully reflect Mendelssohn's conception. If Judaism was truly rational and universal in outlook, then why did the prayers include references to angels, to the hope for return to the Holy Land, to the supernatural advent of a messiah, to the rebuilding of the ancient Temple, and to the reinstitution of the sacrificial service? And if Judaism already embodied the values of modernity, why was its aesthetics so out of keeping with contemporary sensibility? The synagogues were devoid of harmonious singing and musical instruments; the prayers were in Hebrew and Aramaic, languages that many male Jews and almost all female Jews were unable to understand. There were no proper sermons to bring edification to the worshipers. Judaism might be modern in its fundamental values, but in its externals it was foreign to the culture of modernity.

Thus the Reform movement was initially a practical effort to modernize not the principles of Judaism but its public manifestations. The initial efforts at religious reform in Germany during the first decades of the nineteenth century—in Westphalia, in Berlin, and in Hamburg—were all directed at modernizing Jewish practice.[4] Although the Reformers continued to hold with Mendelssohn that Judaism had nothing to learn spiritually from Christianity, they had to admit that the church service was better able to address the modern religious consciousness than was the morally and aesthetically unattractive service of the synagogue. Initially, the Reformers made few changes in the prayers themselves. They sought, rather, to modernize the environment and forms of the service and thus make it more appealing in its new cultural context. They instituted decorum where previously there had been disorder, transforming the synagogue into a sanctuary where mundane concerns were left behind. They introduced edifying sermons, with young Jewish preachers modeling themselves on the most outstanding Christian theologians. And they brought the organ into the worship service, not only to enhance the aesthetics of the service, but also to regulate the cadence of the singing. Parts of the service were now read and sung in German, especially so that the women, mostly absent from traditional Jewish worship, could participate more easily. Thus the early Reform movement sought to take the religion which Mendelssohn had declared to be modern in content, but whose religious practices were admittedly antiquated, and make it modern in form as well.

These changes were not, however, understood by the Reformers as an imitation of Christianity. They believed them to be the belated adoption of modern European values that Christianity had already embodied, but which Judaism, on account of its former isolation in the ghetto, had not previously encountered. Thus Leopold Zunz, in the introduction to sermons he delivered at the reformed services in Berlin, could write in 1823 that the idea of the "Israelite-German synagogue" was a "reconciliation between the genuine religion of the Orient and the genuine culture of the Occident."⁵ Judaism simply needed to be clothed in the garb of Western culture. Its more acculturated adherents had gained a level of European *Bildung* which their religious practice should now be made to reflect.

The spirit of this first stage in the Reform movement is well conveyed by the first German Jewish periodical, *Sulamith*, which began to appear in 1806. Its editors readily admitted that the empirical Judaism was not entirely equivalent to Mendelssohn's idealized conception. They instituted a regular column entitled "Gallery of Harmful Abuses, Rude Improprieties and Absurd Ceremonies among the Jews," which attacked and ridiculed such matters as disorderly wedding ceremonies, "excessive ostentation at festivals," and "unnecessary feasting at the birth of a son." As worthy of emulation they noted examples of praiseworthy behavior by rabbis and other Jewish leaders. Both in *Sulamith* and in the Jewish catechisms which now appeared to prepare Jewish students for the new ceremony of confirmation, the emphasis was on "religion" as a broad and common category rather than on Judaism as a separate and specific faith in contrast to Christianity. It was religion in general, rather than any particular manifestation of it, that could unite members of different religious backgrounds. Typical is this suggestion for the religious education of the Jewish child: "By thinking for himself let him learn the sunny nearness of reason, that there is only *one* true religion, just as there is only *one* humanity and one God, and that all religions are only *forms* of this one religion."⁶

Some enlightened Jews went further than the writers in *Sulamith*. Lazarus Bendavid, a Jewish Kantian, had claimed already in 1793 that the truly enlightened among the Jews took a position "equally distant from Judaism and from indifferentism. They are adherents of the genuine natural religion."⁷ For Bendavid, Judaism, on account of its ceremonial law, could not be entirely universalized without ceasing to be Judaism. Kant himself argued similarly: Judaism consisted of laws and rituals whereas true religion was based on morality alone. And therefore, he wrote in 1798: "Pure moral religion means the death of Judaism."⁸ If Jews wanted to be genuinely religious, as a modern philosopher understood religion, they would have to leave Judaism behind, for it was inseparable from its laws, which rendered it necessarily heteronomous, eliminating the moral freedom which Kant regarded as essential to an enlightened faith. Some Jews, among them Moses Mendelssohn's son Abraham, an enthusiastic Kantian, accepted Kant's view of Judaism and thus were able to justify philosophically their conversion to Christianity. For most Jews, however, the Kantian rejection of Judaism was a challenge to show that Judaism was, in fact, a religion of morality. Hence the stress Jews now placed upon moral conduct in their sermons and in catechisms. Although most German Jews in the first half of the nineteenth century did not wholly forsake the ritual laws of Judaism, it was increasingly the moral laws, rather than the ritual ones, that were emphasized in Jewish education.

As Jews integrated economically and culturally into German society, their daily routine came more and more to resemble that of their counterparts in the non-Jewish bourgeoisie. It was indeed the common assumption of the Jewish leadership that as the externals of Judaism became less different from Christianity, as the Jews themselves became more enlightened, Christians would treat Jews with greater respect. Prejudice, they believed, was based on inherent dislike of those whose language and customs seemed foreign. Yet surprising to them, from the very first, adaptation mostly bred animosity. As early as 1807 an anonymous gentile writer in *Sulamith* remarked that hatred toward the Jews only grew with their increased *Aufklärung*. "It seems as if the lordly Christians would really like to keep the Jews in ignorance and begrudge them the light of enlightenment! Facts prove this conjecture since many local citizens have loudly enough expressed themselves against Jewish enlightenment and prefer the dirtiest Orthodox to the cultured man."[9] As we shall see, such preference would in fact frequently be expressed by Christian writers throughout the nineteenth century, not only toward Jews but also toward the Jewish religion.

With the demise of the Enlightenment, Mendelssohn's argument for Judaism's modernity on the basis of its embodiment of Enlightenment ideals lost its force. Within the context of nineteenth-century European thought religious modernity came to mean a critical approach to the historical sources of religion and a religious self-conception that was dynamic rather than static. University-trained Jewish scholars now began to examine their own tradition with the eye of the critical historian. The emergence of a Wissenschaft des Judentums was itself an indicator of Jewish modernization, for it brought the sources of Judaism into the sphere of secular study, subjecting them to criteria external to Judaism itself. Not surprisingly, the most orthodox Jews rejected Wissenschaft des Judentums as undermining the supernatural origins of Bible and Talmud.

More important was the new conception of Judaism as a dynamic entity, which had changed its form during the course of its millenia-long history. Religious reformers like Abraham Geiger, who expounded this view used it to justify reforms on the basis of historical precedent. Moreover, they could argue that, if Judaism had adapted to earlier historical contexts, then it was inherently capable of adapting as well to the modern context in which it currently found itself—as well as to any other which might follow it. It was not tied to any one period of history. Judaism possessed its own history, which was ongoing into the future. Change and adaptation were, therefore, not external to Judaism but inherent in its very essence. Religious reform was not the rejection of Judaism but the revival of a dynamics that may have been dormant during the long centuries of the ghetto but was in no way foreign to it.

To be sure, German Jewish theologians differed on the nature of that development. Samson Raphael Hirsch, the founder of Neo-Orthodoxy, believed that Judaism was a revealed religion whose doctrines and commandments were eternal. But that did not mean Judaism was mired in an earlier stage of history. Rather Judaism took its stance above history, just as appropriate for one age as for another; not lagging behind the modern period but in advance of it. In Hirsch's words: "Then, only then, when the times will have become *appropriate for God*, then will Judaism, as well, be *appropriate for the times*." Only in inessential externals had Judaism changed and would it continue to change in order to adapt to its cultural environment.

Jewish religious reformers went much further. Deeply influenced by Herder and other romantic thinkers, Geiger conceived of Judaism as a historical religion in interaction with its environment. The persecutions of the Middle Ages had left their deleterious imprint upon both Jews and Judaism. In his earliest major essay, published in 1835, he wrote: "Thus the humiliation of former times, which has not fully been removed, has contaminated our faith as well. As much as possible it has crushed the spirit and disfigured the form."[10] For Geiger, modern culture, with its tolerance and critical modes of thought required a new Jewish response. Unreformed Judaism was appropriate for an earlier age; modernity required a new adaptation. Yet because Judaism was inherently dynamic it was possible to modernize it without doing violence to its essence. The problem for Geiger was convincing fellow Jews that modern elements were not foreign grafts upon the tree of Judaism but rather new branches that sprouted organically from the old trunk.

The most radical of the leading religious reformers, Samuel

Holdheim, was among those who did not believe that the old tree was capable of growing into the modern era. For Holdheim modernity represented a revolution from past modes of thought to which Jews could effectively respond only by launching a religious revolution from within their own ranks. As he put it, they were faced with this alternative: "either to be a rabbinic Jew and live outside the times or to live within the times and cease to be a rabbinic Jew. . . . Rabbinic Judaism is the diametric opposite of our time."[11] The Talmud had indeed represented religious progress in its own time, Holdheim believed, adapting biblical Judaism to new circumstances in Roman Palestine and Sassanian Babylonia. But modernity demanded an independence of spirit that the Talmud lacked. Only if Judaism were radically reshaped to fit the modern *Zeitgeist* could it survive in its new intellectual and social environment.

The Reformgemeinde of Berlin, which was established in the 1840s and which soon called Holdheim to its pulpit, embodied this more radical approach to modernization. The greatly abbreviated religious service was conducted almost entirely in German, men were not required to wear hats, and worship was soon held exclusively on Sunday mornings. It retained only those elements in its liturgy that were in keeping with the congregation's "manner of thinking and feeling," which, they admitted, was as much determined by the age in which they lived as by their religion.[12] Their frank subjectivism set this most radical congregation in Germany sharply apart from other nonorthodox Jewish *Religionsgemeinden* that believed traditions, sanctioned by centuries of observance, could not so easily be abolished. Yet it would be an error to assume that the message preached from the pulpit of the *Reformgemeinde* was simply the exhortation to adapt Judaism to the modern age. Interestingly, the little-known sermons of Holdheim's predecessor, Salomon Friedländer, are not devoted to attacks upon Orthodoxy. Rather, they are directed against the notion that Judaism has become obsolete in the modern world. Taking an assertive polemical stand against Christianity, they assert that Israel is the "bearer of the simply determined and only correct doctrine of God," and that its vocation is therefore not yet fulfilled.[13] Thus the Reform movement, even in its most radical guise, did not accept the supersession of Judaism by either Christianity or modernity. Precisely because it was so closely approaching Christianity in form and precisely because its members were so assimilated to German culture it sought the more vigorously to express its difference from Christianity in basic theological content and its mission to play an independent religious role in Germany. Not surprisingly, this combination of assimilation in practice together with continued adherence to the belief that Judaism was a more exalted system of faith put Christians into a quandary. Should they prefer the old Jewish orthodoxy, which they could argue was but a residue of the past, or the new modernized Judaism, which was more similar to Christianity, yet insisted on fiercely maintaining its sense of independence and self-worth?

The evidence indicates that German governments and individual Christian writers and politicians could not make up their minds whether to urge religious reform upon the Jews or to prefer that they remain orthodox and perceptibly different. The Austrian and Bavarian governments followed inconsistent policies, at first favoring religious reform, later putting legal obstacles in its path. Prussia implemented the most extreme anti-reform policy, best illustrated by Friedrich Wilhelm III's edict of 1823 prohibiting even the slightest deviation from accepted custom. The Grand Duchy of Saxe-Weimer took the most heavyhanded pro-reform position, at one point imposing a religious service in the German language upon all Jews, whether they desired it or not.

Various writers provided justifications for each of these contradictory approaches. As early as 1781, the statesman Christian Wilhelm Dohm had argued in favor of the Jews' "civil improvement" partly because greater political integration would induce Jews to reform Judaism. It would encourage them to abandon what Dohm called their "anxious observance of ceremonies and trivialities" and revert to "the freer and nobler ancient Mosaic constitution."[14] Other writers similarly linked advance in the Jews' civil status with religious reform, either as its anticipated result, as in the case of Dohm, or, more frequently, as a precondition for civil equality. The antisemitic writer Friedrich Wilhelm Ghillany absolutely insisted that Germany must demand of enlightened Jews "a reformed Jewish confession," centered upon "Love your neighbor as yourself" and forsaking the messianic hope, dietary laws, and circumcision.[15] Not surprisingly, such writings led many Jews to believe that non-Jews sincerely wanted them to undertake a program of reform—not only of their occupational distribution, their educational system, and their manners, but also of their religion.

However, once they began the process of reform, Jews found that in the eyes of many Christians they now constituted an even greater threat to Germany. For the Prussian *Regierungsrath* Karl Streckfuss reformed Judaism was the equivalent of deism, and, as such, against the conservative political interests of the state. Had deism, after all, not been the faith of the French Revolution? Friedrich Wilhelm III of Prussia possessed the same concerns and they were expressed, as well, by Prince Johann of Saxony before the second assembly of the constitutional estates.

Yet it was not only fear of the Jews spreading deism and sectarianism, also to Christians, that provoked external opposition to Reform. Perhaps the most widespread reason for Christian rejection of Jewish religious reform was that it would make Jews less likely to convert. Those Christians who favored reform believed that it would be only a station on the way to baptism. But it soon began to appear that the Jews' trajectory would take them from Judaism into secularism instead of from Judaism into the church. Hence, Jewish religious reform was highly undesirable. This position was clearly stated by Bonaventura Mayer, a professor of oriental languages in Bavaria. At the very beginning of a book he published in 1842 he invited the Jewish people "to firmly uphold the holy law of their ancestors and wherever any may have strayed from it, to return to it once more." For that, he believed, was the only way a Jew "could approach the goal of all humanity, the acceptance of the truth of the Gospels."[16]

But was the Orthodox Jew really a more likely candidate for conversion than a reformed one? One prominent Christian intellectual, who had himself converted from Judaism, believed not. Friedrich Julius Stahl, a professor of law in Berlin, was the most prominent exponent of the Christian state and had little regard for religious liberalism of any variety. But in his analysis of the effect of Reform he differed from Mayer. Stahl wrote: "From the standpoint of Christian awareness one would surely regard Reform Judaism as something incomparably worse than the old genuine [!] Judaism. But one would be very unjust to put obstacles in its path in order to further attachment to the old Judaism. For it is the bridge to Christian morality and therefore, in the end, to Christianity. And therefore it should receive complete freedom."[17] Only as a bridge that led beyond itself could Reform Judaism be viewed positively.

But what of the assertions of the Reformers that a modern Judaism would not only be able to maintain itself in the modern world apart from Christianity but even become an independent, progressive, and significant element within European culture? To such claims the onetime editor of the conservative *Kreuzzeitung*, Hermann Wagener, replied in language similar to that of Carové, that "the doctrine of the historical development of a spirit that always retains its identity, with which these moderates seek to put Judaism into shape, is, in fact, foreign to Judaism, borrowed from philosophy, and, rightly understood, can be applied among the religions only to

Christianity, because Christianity alone bears a living, always identical spirit within it."[18]

Jews were not surprised that the Orthodox Christian party should be opposed to the idea that the Jewish faith was still very much alive and capable of internal development. What astonished and deeply disappointed them was that liberal Christians took a similar position. Thus Abraham Geiger complained bitterly in 1862 that the *Protestantische Kirchenzeitung*, a journal of the liberal trend in Protestantism, should have especially and repeatedly attacked those Jews who considered their faith most integrally a part of the modern world: "If they show themselves not to be rigid, mentally lazy or antiquated, if rather they develop a sprightly vitality, if they give evidence of a spiritual force and on that basis substantiate demands—then the opponent must seem doubly dangerous."[19] For liberal Christians progress was a virtue in Christianity; it was either inconceivable or objectionable in Judaism.

The most extreme anti-Reform position among Christians in Germany appears among declared antisemites during the last decades of the nineteenth century. By then Jewish Orthodoxy had dwindled to a small minority of German Jewry. Most Jews had become liberals both in religion and in politics. Like few other Germans they had sought to uphold the principles of the *Aufklärung* against narrow forms of romanticism. In fact, it was just that clinging to the principles of an earlier age that now enabled Adolf Stöcker, Court Preacher in Berlin, to make an ingenious argument. Not only was Jewish Orthodoxy necessarily antiquated on account of its inherent inability to undergo development, but Reform Judaism had proven to be similarly rigid. The difference was simply that Orthodoxy had failed to adapt to modernity at all while Reform Judaism had indeed adapted, but only once: to the reigning philosophy at the time of the Jews' emergence from the ghetto in the late eighteenth century. It was today therefore as much a fossil as was Orthodoxy, while Christianity alone had shown itself capable of sustained development. In Stöcker's words: "[Reform Judaism] is neither Judaism nor Christianity, but a wretched remnant of the Age of Enlightenment, whose ideas did not at all originate on Jewish soil, but during a shabby age of the Christian church, and which the church itself has outgrown."[20] However, what really disturbed Stöcker and other antisemites was that the Reformers saw Judaism as possessing a future as well as a past. Although they might be willing to share the present, Stöcker's supporters believed that the future belonged exclusively to Christianity. Stöcker's advice to Jews was that Israel "repudiate the conceit that Judaism will be the religion of the future, when it is so completely the religion of the past."[21]

As one reads through what various Christian writers in nineteenth-century Germany have had to say about the Reform movement in Judaism one wonders again and again whether there was not some prominent Christian writer who viewed the reform of Judaism in positive terms, as Reform Jews themselves saw it: as a revival and successful modernization of an ancient faith. I must admit, to my regret, that I have not found anywhere, even among the most liberal of leading Christian theologians in Germany, the expression of a sense of common purpose with a modernizing Judaism, of a feeling that the Reform movement in Judaism was engaged in a task similar to their own within Christianity. It was only Orthodox Protestant writers who lumped the two together, liberal Judaism and liberal Protestantism, in order to condemn both of them at once. The conservative exponent of philosophical pessimism Eduard von Hartmann made this comparison: "[Reform Judaism] in the same way embodies the dissolution of Judaism as liberal Protestantism does that of Christianity. . . . Reform Judaism is therefore surely no longer to be called Judaism any more than liberal Protestantism is to be called Christianity."[22]

A genuine religious pluralism between Christians and Jews did not develop in Germany. In the course of the nineteenth century, German Jews gained legal and political equality, but the Jewish religion was never regarded as the equivalent of Christianity. Only the Jews themselves believed that Judaism was capable of genuine and independent development in the modern world. Christians did not agree. Thus for the liberal Protestant theologian Adolf Harnack, delivering his famous inaugural address as rector in Berlin in 1901, there was no need to expand the university's theological faculty to encompass general history of religion because, as he put it with regard to Christianity: "Whoever does not know this religion knows no religion, and whoever knows it, along with its history, knows them all."[23]

Should and can an "antiquated" religion become modern? For most German Jews at the beginning of the twentieth century this question had already been answered positively by preceding generations. But for Christian Germany nothing had changed. Reform Judaism was not genuine and genuine Judaism should not and could not become modern. Scholars of the Nazi period often seek to understand why antisemitism spread so disastrously in Germany of the twentieth century. In addition to all other reasons they have adduced, they might also consider the unwillingness in the nineteenth century to recognize the vitality of more than a single faith within the ambit of religious modernity. The recognition that the Germans all along refused to grant to the Jewish religion, the Nazis took away from the Jews themselves.

Notes

1. Shlomo Avineri, "A Note on Hegel's Views on Jewish Emancipation," *Jewish Social Studies* 25 (1963): 148–51.
2. F. W. Carové, *Ueber Emanzipation der Juden, Philosophie des Judenthums und Jüdische Reformprojekte zu Berlin und Frankfurt a. M.* (Siegen und Wiesbaden, 1845), 160.
3. On Mendelssohn see Alexander Altmann, *Moses Mendelssohn: A Biographical Study* (Tuscaloosa, Ala., 1973); Michael A. Meyer, *The Origins of the Modern Jew: Jewish Identity and European Culture in Germany, 1749–1824* (Detroit, 1967), 11–56.
4. For a detailed description see Michael A. Meyer, *Response to Modernity: A History of the Reform Movement in Judaism* (New York and Oxford, 1988).
5. *Predigton. Gehalten in der neuen Israelitischen Synagoge zu Berlin* (Berlin, 1823), vii, note.
6. *Sulamith, eine Zeitschrift zur Beförderung der Kultur und Humanität unter den Israeliten* 3:1 (1810): 348.
7. *Etwas zur Charackteristick der Juden* (Leipzig, 1793), 51.
8. "Der Streit der Facultäten," in *Sämmtliche Werke* 10 (Leipzig, 1838): 308.
9. *Sulamith*, 1:2 (1807): 149.
10. "Das Judenthum unserer Zeit und die Bestrebungen in ihm," *Wissenschaftliche Zeitschrift für jüdische Theologie* 1 (1835): 8.
11. *Das Ceremonialgesetz im Messiasreich* (Schwerin, 1845), 122–23.
12. *Zweiter Bericht der Genossenschaft für Reform im Judenthum* (Berlin, 1846), 9.
13. *Predigten, gehalten im Tempel der Genossenschaft für Reform im Judenthume zu Berlin* (Leipzig, 1847), 18.
14. *Ueber die bürgerliche Verbesserung der Juden*, 1 (Berlin und Stettin, 1781), 143–44.
15. *Die Judenfrage* (Nürnberg, 1843), 46–47.
16. *Die Juden unserer Zeit* (Regensburg, 1842), v–vi.
17. *Der christliche Staat und sein Verhältniß zu Deismus und Judenthum* (Berlin, 1847), 55.
18. *Das Judenthum und der Staat* (Berlin, 1857), 37–38.
19. "Die protestantische Kirchenzeitung und der Fortschritt im Judenthume," *Jüdische Zeitschrift für Wissenschaft und Leben* 2 (1863): 81.

20. *Das moderne Judenthum in Deutschland, besonders in Berlin. Zwei Reden in der christlich-socialen Arbeiterpartei* (Berlin, 1880), 5–6.
21. Ibid., 18.
22. *Das religiöse Bewußtsein der Menschheit im Stufengang seiner Entwickelung* (Berlin, 1882), 537–38.
23. *Die Aufgabe der theologischen Facultäten und die allgemeine Religionsgeschichte* (Giessen, 1901), 11.

CHAPTER 14

"How Awesome Is This Place!": The Reconceptualization of the Synagogue in Nineteenth-Century Germany

When, in 1822, the Jewish community of Alt-Ofen in Hungary completed the construction of a beautiful new synagogue, it called upon its learned and renowned rabbi, Moses Münz (ca. 1750–1831), to deliver an appropriate dedicatory sermon in the Hebrew language. He began by praising their efforts: they had erected a splendid building, "magnificent and elegant with all manner of adornment." And he continued, "I will express to you my feeling of how great is the fulfillment of this commandment in the sight of God. You have done well in that you have magnified the glory of this commandment for it is a very great one indeed to build a house of prayer."[1]

Moses Münz was known as a rabbi who was heedful of the demands of the modern age. He had delivered appropriate addresses on political occasions and in 1811 even allowed Jewish soldiers to eat legumes on Passover. Yet when his colleague, Aaron Chorin, gave approval to the religious reforms that had been instituted in Berlin beginning in 1815, Münz rebuked him severely. Likewise, in his understanding of the nature of the synagogue, he remained attached to the traditional view—as becomes apparent from an analysis of his dedicatory sermon.

Münz defines the synagogue as a *bet tefilah*, a house of prayer. Public worship is a central commandment of Judaism and the construction of a synagogue is meritorious because it enables such prayer to take place. Erecting a building that is beautiful rather than plain has greater merit because it falls in the category of *hidur mitsvah*, of performing a commandment in the most perfect manner, like the purchase of the largest, most attractive, and unblemished *etrog* (citron) for the holiday of Sukkot.

With the assistance of rabbinic sources, Münz expounds upon the remarkable efficacy of prayer when uttered in a synagogue. Although a prayer can be spoken anywhere, it is more likely to be heard when it arises from the gathered congregation. That is the case, however, only because the service conducted in the synagogue is performed according to the regulations of the *Halakhah*, not because of the magnificence of the building. In giving money for the erection of the synagogue, the contributors have gained merit in the sight of God and may therefore rest assured that the Almighty will reward them for their efforts. He will answer their prayers, bestowing upon them the threefold material blessing of children, life, and sustenance.

Following tradition, Rabbi Münz regards the synagogue as a "small sanctuary" (*mikdash me'at*) that contains the indwelling presence of God. Yet it is only a poor substitute for the ancient Temple in Jerusalem. Indeed, the ultimate purpose of communal prayer is to bring nearer the day when synagogue prayers will make way for the reinstitution of Temple sacrifices: "If outside the land of Israel we will stand in our synagogues in awe and will praise and exalt God with a whole heart, then the desire of the Holy One, Blessed Be He, will be increased to the end that these praises will be uttered in the Holy of Holies of His Temple, that there our supplication will find favor before Him."[2] As a place of Jewish worship, the synagogue thus points beyond itself; through the prayers that are uttered within its walls, it acts as an instrument of the final redemption when Israel will be restored to its land, its ancient institutions established once more.

Five years earlier, in the Bavarian town of Floss, a similar dedication ceremony had taken place. Like Münz, the rabbi of the community, Moses Wittelshöfer, had seen this as an occasion to discuss the role of the synagogue. In fact, he had spoken publicly twice in the Hebrew language in two different traditional genres.[3] His first presentation was a sermon, a *derashah*, of the old talmudic variety. It was a talmudic discourse (a *pilpul*) on rabbinic texts dealing with the building of the ancient desert tabernacle and of the Jerusalem Temple. His task here, as upon other occasions when he spoke to his congregation, was to show his acumen in reconciling conflicting views among rabbinic authorities (*letarets kushiyot*).

Wittelshöfer's second presentation was a moral discourse (*Divre musar*). Drawing upon Ezekiel's vision of the ancient Temple (chapter 43), he cleverly formed moral analogies for the synagogue:

among others, the avoidance of violent disputes over synagogue honors and suppression of the deplorable practice of women peeking down at men folk from the gallery or—even worse—men casting their eyes upward at the women. Like Münz, Wittelshöfer also used the occasion to distinguish clearly between diaspora synagogues and the Jerusalem Temple. Although the former, as places of prayer, did indeed possess a measure of holiness—he too called them a "small sanctuary" following the Rabbis' interpretation of Ezekiel's words—they were not *the* sanctuary, the *mikdash* itself, with its priestly service and its choir of Levites. Having been privileged to build this synagogue, he concludes, so may they be privileged "to see built at the summit of the mountain our Temple, our Glorious House, together with Israel our brothers, speedily and in our days."

What made the dedication in Floss different from that in Alt-Ofen was that the laymen persuaded their rabbi to give a sermon in the German language as well.[4] Wittelshöfer undertook this task quite reluctantly, fearing that he might, as a result, be charged with being one of the modernizers, who in Berlin had since 1815 introduced both sermons and some prayers in the vernacular. But, in fact, his German sermon did not differ greatly in form or in content from his two Hebrew presentations. It was a combination of both genres, partly disquisition, partly moral rebuke. As in the Hebrew *derashah*, here too the burden of his sermon was to formulate questions and resolve apparent contradictions, except that the subject matter now was historical rather than *halakhic*. For example: Why did the Greek term for a place of gathering (*synagogē*) come to be applied exclusively to a Jewish house of prayer? Answer: Because the Maccabees had gathered in the Temple, and Jewish houses of prayer later replaced the Temple. Why did Jews mourn at the dedication of the Second Temple? Answer: Because they recalled the sins that had brought about the destruction of the First. This second historical answer leads Wittelshöfer from *derashah* to *tokhahah*, to moral rebuke. In 1813 a devastating fire had burned the old synagogue to the ground. Surely this tragedy had occurred on account of God's wrath and only remorse and repentance would prevent a similar disaster from occurring to this new building as well. Was not sinfulness always characteristic of the Jews? In this new house of prayer (*Bethaus*), however, they might plead with God to hasten the redemption. Indeed, it was not his oratory that would dedicate the synagogue to God's service, he noted, but the first properly conducted service held within its walls. The building possessed no inherent holiness but only the derivative sanctity that attached to it because the community gathered there to sanctify God and to petition for the re-establishment of the ancient glory.

During the course of the nineteenth century the conception of the synagogue held by Rabbis Münz and Wittelshöfer changed radically and very broadly. Much scholarly attention has been paid to liturgical changes in the prayer service as well as to the issue of the use of an organ and of the vernacular in prayer. Such questions separated the Reform movement and its synagogues sharply from others that rejected these changes and brought forth loud controversies. But if we focus in this essay on the more quiet but nonetheless fundamental shift in Jewish understanding of the very nature of the synagogue and its purpose, we will find that the innovations in this area do not clearly distinguish reformers from traditionalists. Rather, to varying degrees, they separate all those who were touched by the world around them from the older view expressed by Rabbis Münz and Wittelshöfer.

Our principal sources for the new conception are more than thirty sermons which, like those of Rabbis Münz and Wittelshöfer, were delivered at the dedication of new synagogues in Germany and Austria-Hungary during the nineteenth century.[5] Although the rhetoric heard on these occasions was to some extent adapted to the large contingent of Christians that was invariably present, there is no reason to believe that the views expressed by the preachers were other than sincere. Before examining these texts, however, it will be helpful to look at a shift in the Christian understanding of public worship which was taking place just a bit earlier.

Johann Andreas Cramer (1723–88), at first Court Preacher in Copenhagen and later a professor in Kiel, was regarded as an enlightened clergyman, well versed in the literary culture of his day. Religiously, however, he remained a supernaturalist who believed in the objective efficacy of prayer. In the latter regard, he remained loyal to the tenets of the Reformation. Like Rabbi Münz, the Christian preacher Cramer held that prayer was a service that the worshiper owed to God. Around the middle of the eighteenth century he spoke of the "duty of prayer" (*Pflicht des Gebetes*) and told his listeners that God would withhold His benevolence from those who failed to engage in public worship. They would, he said, suffer His "righteous and holy disfavor." According to Cramer, the church is a sacred place because that is where ritual acts, like baptism and communion, are performed and because it is there that the Christian pleads for God's mercy.[6]

However, during the last half of the eighteenth century the

views of Cramer and like-minded contemporaries were coming under severe attack—and not only from philosophical radicals. Perhaps the most influential critique of the traditional conception of worship came in a "General Observation" at the end of Immanuel Kant's *Religion within the Limits of Reason Alone* (1793). In the strongest terms the Königsberg philosopher here rejected the notion of petitional prayer. Such prayer, he argued, was no better than "a superstitious illusion (a fetish-making)." Proper worship, he held, was something quite different: the person's "work upon himself (for the quickening of his disposition by means of the *idea of God*)." It was not request but the resolution to improve moral conduct. Only such conduct, not prayer per se, could be pleasing to God. Thus, as Kant saw it, prayer was not itself a commandment or a duty but simply a valuable, not indispensable instrument to deepen moral commitment. It was, in fact, a conversation carried on within the worshiper himself while being ostensibly an address to God. The church, for Kant, was thus not a place where prayer and ritual were offered to God in His service but where reciting prayers and listening to the preacher were "to set in more active motion the moral motivating forces of each individual through a public ceremony."[7] The churchgoing experience was meaningful only if it changed the person, if the congregant left the church morally renewed. Piety, once an end in itself, has here become the servant of virtue. Clearly, this was a critique applicable to church and synagogue alike.

The influence of this subjective conception of prayer and its consequences for the church are apparent in the sermons of the best-known German preacher of the early nineteenth century, Friedrich Schleiermacher. Like Kant, Schleiermacher rejected the notion that God might be influenced by prayer. It is rather we who are changed:

We should cease vehemently requesting the possession of earthly goods or wishing for the prevention of some evil. We should take courage when God has ordained that we do without and that we bear suffering. We should raise ourselves from the powerlessness into which fear and greed drag human beings and attain the sense and full use of our powers, so that we can behave ourselves under all circumstances as is appropriate for everyone who considers that he lives and acts under the eyes and the protection of the Highest.[8]

Schleiermacher would as soon see formulaic prayer disappear altogether unless it can serve as a means not to gaining personal ends but to instilling devotion, to fortifying our moral decisions, and to strengthening our religious sentiments. The worshiper should leave the church, not having cast his desires before God's throne but transformed with new commitment to doing God's will. Thus going to church becomes more an experience of moral reinvigoration than the performance of a religious duty.

For Schleiermacher, the sermon stood at the center of the religious service since it most effectively inspired proper conduct. Moreover, if it were not too long and if it dealt less with doctrine and more with individual conduct, it was the most effective tool for drawing the alienated *Gebildeten* back to the church. Unlike ritual, it could relate religion to intellectual life and culture.

Kant and Schleiermacher's new conceptions of the function of churchgoing in Christian life were not lost on a Jewish community in German-speaking Europe that was engaged in cultural and political integration. If Cramer shared Münz's and Wittelshöfer's view of the house of worship as primarily a place of prescribed prayers and rituals mediated by individual traditions and grounded ultimately in revelation, the next generation among the Jews to varying degrees adopted the new Christian understanding. It is thus an oversimplification to suggest, as is often done, that modernized Jewish worship, especially among the religious reformers, simply imitated Christianity. Rather it took its cue from the response of Christianity to the Enlightenment's critique of traditional religion, which had already transformed much of the larger faith community. Judaism did not so much copy Christianity as follow in its footsteps.

Let us proceed now to the Jewish sources, which yield three new conceptions of the synagogue: as a house of God (*Gotteshaus*), as a sacred place (*Heiligtum*), and as a place of edification (*Erbauungslokal*).

The designation of the synagogue as house of God is not indigenous to Jewish tradition, where the common terms are house of gathering (*bet keneset*), house of study (*bet midrash*), and house of prayer (*bet tefilah*). Yet it occurs with utmost frequency in the Jewish dedication sermons. Although an early dedicatory address, delivered by Rabbi Samson Wolf Rosenfeld in Markt Uhlfeld in 1819, still lacks the term entirely,[9] it is present in the very first line of the sermon at the dedication of a traditional synagogue in Hildburghausen as early as 1811.[10] The later sermons use it repeatedly and sometimes exclusively, especially those most inclined to religious reform. Although the term *synagogue* is usually not abandoned entirely, it is often used to designate the structure rather than to describe its function: a new "synagogue" is dedicated to being a "house of God."

This shift in usage, more than the other two, lends itself to association with the Jews' political ambitions. *Gotteshaus* is a neutral term, common to both church and synagogue. Its use makes the statement that Christian and Jewish houses of worship are not fundamentally different: they are both places dedicated to the one and only God. The language here is the counterpart of the synagogue architecture of the 1830s and 1840s, which in large measure drew upon the style of the Roman basilica as a form that was thought common to church and synagogue structures.[11] Its use created a kind of aesthetic unity between the two faiths. The desire not to stress the Jewishness of the house of God was also apparent in the lack (or at least non-prominence) of Jewish symbols on the outside of many of the synagogues of the period. The exterior appearance would simply indicate a house of God, while only the interior revealed it as a synagogue.

In the dedicatory sermons the synagogue has become the *"israelitisches Gotteshaus,"* differing from its Christian counterpart not in genus, only in species. The radical reformer Rabbi Samuel Holdheim even suggested a threefold categorization of increasing specificity along with diminishing significance. With regard to the new temple of the Berlin Reformgemeinde he said in 1854: "Our dedication is directed first to a house of God, then to a *Jewish* house of God, and finally to the house of God of the first Jewish *Reform Congregation.*"[12] The relatively conservative Leopold Schott even sought to justify its usage from the books of Genesis and Joshua, although, of course, in none of the biblical instances does the Hebrew term *bet el* refer to a synagogue.[13]

The word *Tempel* also occurs in the dedicatory sermons in order to distinguish the new structures from the older ones. In Kirchheimbolanden, for example, the rabbi spoke of the "new temple" (*neue Tempel*) that is now to replace "the old house of prayer" (*das alte Gebethaus*).[14] Yet *Gotteshaus* is used more frequently than *Tempel.* The reason for this lies in the multiple connotations of the latter term. On the one hand, like *Gotteshaus, Tempel* is also a designation common to both Jewish and Christian houses of worship, especially Protestant ones, and especially but not exclusively, in a French-influenced environment.[15] But after the establishment of the independent Reform Temple in Hamburg in 1818, it became a word that had a specific meaning representing a certain type of ritual. Moreover, to call a synagogue a temple meant to recall the ancient Temple in Jerusalem, and that was problematic in two respects. First, it could be interpreted—as the more radical reformers did interpret it—to mean that the new house of worship was a permanent replacement for the ancient site of sacrificial service. Thus to call a Jewish house of worship a temple was to make a theological statement that was best avoided in a Jewish community of diverse views on this subject. Second, *Tempel* was a word that could remind one of the Oriental heritage of the Jews rather than their desired denominational status among religious groups in Germany. Hence the connotations of the word would serve to separate rather than unite. The community leadership in Cassel, for example, did not want their new synagogue to be reminiscent of the ancient Temple since, as they argued, although Christianity too originated in the Orient, churches were not, on that account, expected to reflect their ancient history.[16] Built and understood as *Gotteshäuser*, new synagogues would not suffer from any of these complications.

This concern about Orientalism diminished, of course, after the middle of the century, when the Moorish style of synagogue architecture became dominant in Europe and America. Now the historical link with the East was allowed tangible symbolic expression. In 1858, when the capstone of the new synagogue in the Leopoldstadt in Vienna was laid in place, the preacher Adolf Jellinek announced with pride that it had been dug out of "Zion's holy and divinely consecrated soil" and that "here on Austrian soil it will become the cornerstone, indeed the most important stone, in this building."[17]

Although the term *Heiligtum* occurs with less frequency than either *Gotteshaus* or *Tempel*, the conception of the synagogue as inherently a sacred place is fundamental to almost all of the sermons of dedication.[18] The biblical text that is cited most frequently in the sermons (found in some form in about half of them) is Jacob's expression of worshipful amazement after beholding in his dream a ladder connecting heaven and earth: *"Ma nora ha-makom ha-zeh, en zeh ki im bet elohim ve-zeh sha'ar ha-shamayim"* [How awesome is this place! This is none other than the abode of God, and that is the gateway to heaven] (Gen. 28:17). This text had been applied to the ancient sanctuary of Jerusalem, since, according to the medieval commentator Rashi, the place of Jacob's dream was to become the site for the Temple. But now it was regularly applied to newly built synagogues, not necessarily because the preachers saw them as replacements for the Temple, but because their conception of the synagogue's aura was fully in keeping with the tenor of Jacob's words. In Nuremberg, the verse was inscribed on the main façade of the synagogue, in Stuttgart high up on an interior wall. "Only angels ascending and descending the ladder of heaven must encounter us here, so that the edifice may sustain its heavenly power over us," said Rabbi Holdheim dedicating a synagogue in Goldberg.[19] It was as if the synagogue had attained a kind of mana from on high, an intrinsic force that made itself manifest to those who crossed into its territory. One preacher even saw the building itself as a kind of Jacob's ladder, mediating between heaven and earth.[20]

It is not surprising that the Christian preacher Cramer in discussing the "wonderful merits of Christian houses of God," had likewise cited—even repeatedly—the verse from Genesis, but not in connection with the ancient Temple.[21] For him that Temple, as described in the New Testament, was a place where potential holiness had been desecrated by the profane activities of moneychangers. In light of this Christian conception, it is plausible that Jews, in applying Jacob's words to their synagogues, were also addressing the damaging claim that, from ancient times, they had failed properly to separate the holy from the profane.

The entry into a synagogue was now seen as a step from the realm of the secular into that of the sacred. "At the door of this house lies the border between earthly striving and the most sacred pursuits of everyone who enters," preached Abraham Jacob Cohn in Derenburg. And he called out the verse from Moses' theophany at the Burning Bush: "Remove your sandals from your feet, for the place on which you stand is holy ground."[22] So too Isaac Noah Mannheimer, dedicating the Seitenstettengasse synagogue in Vienna in 1826 made a sharp separation between the sacred and the profane: "In the house of God we have escaped the world and its influence; we are removed from them."[23] Thus the synagogue becomes a "sanctuary" in a double sense: a place of holiness separate from the secular world and a place of refuge from it. Perhaps the most memorable line in this regard is from an anonymous preacher in Königsberg in 1815, who must just recently have read Friedrich Schiller. He opened his remarks by declaiming: *"Neu erbauet stehet der Tempel Gottes, und wir betreten mit Inbrunst, mit Dank, mit religiösen Gefühlen, Heiliger dein Heiligthum."* [Newly built stands the temple of God and with fervor, with thanksgiving, with religious feeling, we enter, O Sacred One, Your sanctuary.][24]

This spatial distinction between holy and profane was associated in Judaism with the ancient Temple, generally not with the synagogue. For millenia the Jewish distinction had been temporal, not spatial, especially between the Sabbath and the rest of the week. In reintroducing spatial sanctity, the preachers were not simply following the cultural code of contemporary Christianity, they were returning to the paradigm of ancient Judaism and, consciously or not, describing their new houses of worship more on the model of the Temple than on that of diaspora houses of prayer. Hence the lack of reluctance to apply biblical passages referring explicitly to the ancient Temple to a newly constructed synagogue: "God is in His holy temple; let all the earth keep silent before Him," said the preacher Sigmund Gelbhaus in Nordhausen, citing Habakkuk 2:20.[25] *Kodesh ladonay* (holy to God) was inscribed on the exterior of the Reform-gemeinde's new building,[26] dedicated in 1854. Gotthold Salomon, the Hamburg Tempel preacher went the furthest when he concluded in 1844 that the new building was to be a *bet tefilah*, a *bet midrash*, and a *bet mikdash*! He saw it not as a *"gathering* house" (*bet keneset*) but, like the ancient Temple, as a *"sacred* house."[27]

With the Temple as model, the dedication ceremony itself became an act of sanctification. It not merely dedicated the new synagogue to the service of God but, in what was conceived by some as a ritual act, drew it across the boundary from the profane to the sacred. "I dedicate you to be a house for the veneration of God, a sacred place of virtue," said Salomon Seligmann Herxheimer in Westerburg, addressing the building.[28] And Mannheimer concluded his address with the words: "So enter now, O God, into your sanctuary."[29]

Once properly dedicated, the synagogue was deemed by some of the preachers, especially the more radical reformers, to possess the innate capacity of transforming the individual who went there to pray. Rabbi Samuel Adler noted that the old synagogue in Alzey was not worthy of the Almighty because it had been unable to raise the spirits of the worshipers to the required degree.[30] The new temple in Hamburg, Gotthold Salomon hoped, would be a house of God that sanctified and made blissful.[31] Samuel Holdheim, in one of his dedicatory addresses, saw sanctification rather as a reciprocal process that transpired between worshiper and building: "The human being has deep longings for a place to which, in consecrated hours of pious enthusiasm, he may communicate [the contents of] his inner sanctuary. The sight of such a place casts the effulgent rays of his pious enthusiasm back upon him. A lively interaction reigns between the consecrated room outside himself and the sanctuary within."[32]

In a synagogue that was intrinsically holy there could be no room for the secular, which would necessarily desecrate it. The dedication of a new synagogue therefore presented more than one preacher with the opportunity of denouncing inappropriate practices that had crept into the service and polluted the atmosphere. A holy place demands reverence, and reverence in the German religious context meant decorum and concerted, not dissonant, worship. In the words of Benedict Hause in Oberaula: "Where the heart is full of devotion, there the lips move *quietly*, there the prayer rises *silently* to heaven like the scent of incense, there no loud *shouting* (*Schreien*) is heard at all."[33]

Not surprisingly, the dedication of new structures could serve as the occasion for instituting synagogue ordinances regulating the behavior of the worshipers. Such *Synagogenordnungen* were issued by traditional, no less than by reform-minded communities and invariably stressed the sanctity of the synagogue. Visitors to the synagogue of the neo-Orthodox *Israelitische Religionsgemeinschaft*, for example, were exhorted that, "mindful of the holiness of the place, they behave in a respectful and dignified manner."[34]

The third fundamental change in the conception of the synagogue is characterized here by the term *Erbauungslokal*. Athough this designation, which was first used in official documents in reference to the Reform temple in Hamburg, does not occur regularly in the literature, the idea that it represents is abundantly present. Of course, synagogues had always been places where, in addition to prescribed prayer, rabbis and preachers conveyed religious messages to the worshipers. But these had been, in the manner of Rabbi Wittelshöfer's addresses, either highly intellectualistic in character or, especially when delivered by popular preachers (*magidim*), intended to urge repentance or to entertain by clever textual interpretation. Here there was a new purpose: to edify, that is to inspire, to change the internal structure of the worshipers, so that they would leave the synagogue in a different frame of mind or heart than when they entered it. As early as 1823, the traditional vice-rabbi of Frankfurt an der Oder, H. M. Baschwitz, proclaimed: "The providence of the wholly beneficent Father has graciously allowed us to build a temple in order to venerate Him and, removed from all distractions, here to edify ourselves."[35] To a high degree such *Erbauung* became the purpose of prayers and sermons, and even of the synagogue building itself.

It is here that the influence of Schleiermacher and his contemporaries is most apparent. Prayer, he had held, is not intended to change God's will but to alter the disposition of the worshiper. This conception of prayer, at best secondary in earlier Judaism, appears prominently in the dedicatory sermons. In 1819 Rabbi Rosenfeld still notes that regular prayer is one of the 248 positive commandments that are obligatory for all male Jews and that God hears and responds to petitions if they are sincere and just. Worship is a service that the Jew owes to God. But he also believes that prayer is "the mightiest support of pious and virtuous conduct,"[36] a position Kant would heartily have endorsed. Later sermons rarely mention prayer as an obligation, nor do they dwell upon its efficacy. Rather it is the *act* of prayer or the time spent in devotion (*Andacht*) which directly alters the subjective state of the individual, imparting a sense of bliss.[37] In other words, the reward of worship is contained within itself. "The holy consequences of prayer upon our entire being," said the preacher in Derenburg, "are as unending as the goodness of the Eternal."[38] Another dedicator saw the result of worship as edification of the spirit, ennoblement of the heart, and awakening the spirit to virtue and true morality.[39] Prayer is not a quest for tangible reward, noted a third. Rather the congregation prays: "Strengthen our hearts so that we may venerate You and follow Your holy will."[40] It is not surprising that the later dedications did not follow in the footsteps of Rabbi Münz, who had cited the talmudic passage: "Prayer is greater than good deeds."[41] For them good deeds were of the essence and prayer only their instrument.

Even more than prayer, it was the German sermon that was believed capable of changing the inner state of the worshiper. It would edify, inspire, and motivate. The new Jewish sermon, heavily patterned on the Christian model, generally did little teaching, though it quoted texts; nor did it rebuke worshipers in the manner of the old *tokhaḥah*. Rather it sought to awaken the individual conscience to the improvement of moral conduct. The sermons would address women as well as men, those uneducated in Hebrew along with those who knew the language. Indeed, the newer synagogues increased the percentage of seats in the women's section because women began to come more frequently, especially to hear the preachers.[42] Like the Christian sermons to which Schleiermacher had referred, the new Jewish ones were also aimed at the *Gebildeten*, the cultured among the worshipers who, following their Christian counterparts, were absenting themselves from the synagogue.

Not only prayers and preachers, however, were instruments of *Erbauung* in the synagogue; the structure of the building itself was intended to serve the same purpose. God could be worshiped anywhere, noted the rabbi in Giessen, but few could raise their spirits without external stimulation. The old synagogue had failed in this task, the beautiful new one, with its aesthetic appeal to the cultured tastes (*gebildete Augen*) of the congregation, would succeed.[43] But it was not only a matter of aesthetics, for in the eyes of at least one preacher the physical characteristics of the synagogue were themselves the transmitters of religious and moral messages. They were the external representation of internal qualities. Thus the community of Kirchheimbolanden in the Rhineland had built a temple that was orderly, roomy, brightly lit, and spotlessly clean. These characteristics were believed to affect the sentiments of the worshiper who entered its space. They would awaken devotion and have "the most powerful influence upon our inner edification, leading us to God, in whose honor such a temple is built; only symmetry, orderliness, and an appropriate style are capable of raising us up to the Creator of all nature for whom symmetry, orderliness, and wise arrangement are the very spirit of His creation."[44]

Thus inspired, the worshiper went forth a changed person, not because a duty had been performed or a specific lesson learned, but because he or she had participated in a comprehensive subjective experience that included the liturgy, the music, the sermon, and even the building itself—all of them instruments for transforming the inner state of the worshiper. When they departed from the synagogue, the worshipers would carry their inner transformation along with them as they left the sacred precincts of God's house and reentered the secular world. Perhaps Isaac Noah Mannheimer summed it all up best in 1826: "God enters the house that pious, childlike sentiment has prepared for Him. And now that house becomes a temple of God and from that temple the person derives the aid that supports and sustains him. Emerging from the temple of God, blessing enters into all the circumstances of life. From the temple of God the wise man gains his insight, he who stands in awe of God derives his strength, and the pious person obtains his hope."[45]

Notes

1. Moshe Münz, *Devir ha-bayit: derashah mefo'eret al devar ḥanukat bet tefilah . . .* (Vienna, 1822), 3.
2. Ibid., 24.
3. Moshe ben Avraham [Wittelshöfer], *Derashah ve-divre musar le-ḥanukat bet ha-keneset ha-ḥadashah po k"k Floss shabat kodesh seder ki tetse 5577* (Sulzbach, n.d.).
4. Idem, *Rede am Tage der Einweihung der neuerbauten Synagoge bei der jüdischen Gemeinde zu Floß am 22ten August 1817* (Sulzbach, 1818). M. Katten presents a brief discussion of this sermon in "Eine Synagogeneinweihung in Bayern 1817," *Bayerische Israelitische Gemeindezeitung* 11 (1935): 288–89, but Katten had not seen the Hebrew texts.
5. These thirty-two sermons are, in alphabetical order: Samuel Adler, *Worte der Weihe, gesprochen zur Einweihung der neuen Synagoge in Alzey am 28. Tischri 5615 (20. Oct. 1854.)* (Alzey, n.d.); anon., *Rede und Gebet zur Einweihungsfeier der Synagoge und zur Einsegnung der freiwilligen Krieger der israelitischen Gemeinde zu Königsberg gehalten am 19ten April 1815* (n.p., n.d.); Hirsch Aub, *Rede bey der Einweihungs-Feyer der Synagoge*

in München, am 21. April 1826 (Munich, 1826); H. M. Baschwitz, *Einwei-hungs-Rede vorgetragen bei Gelegenheit der Synagogen-Weihe zu Frankfurth a. d. O. den 4ten September 1823* (n.p., n.d.); Levi Bodenheimer, *Predigt, zur Einweihungs-Feier der Neuen Synagoge zu Crefeld am 17. Juni 1853* (Krefeld, 1853); Felix Coblenz, *Predigt zur Einweihung der neuen Synagoge in Bielefeld am 20. September 1905* (n.p., n.d.); M. Cohen, "Rede bei der Einweihung des neuen israelitischen Tempels zu Kirchheimbolanden im Rheinkreise; gehalten am 3ten September 1836," *Die Synagoge* 1 (1837): 89–104; Abraham Jacob Cohn, *Des Gotteshauses hohe Bedeutung, Predigt, gehalten zur Einweihung der neuerbaueten Synagoge zu Derenburg am 17. November 1837* (Nordhausen, 1838); David Einhorn, *Predigt bei der Einweihungsfeier der Synagoge zu Kleinlangheim, den 31ten August 1838* (n.p., n.d.); Zacharias Frankel, *Rede bei der Grundsteinlegung der neuen Synagoge zu Dresden den 21. Juni 1838 (28. Siwan 5598)* (Dresden, n.d.); Naphtali Frankfurter and Gotthold Salomon, *Die letzte und die erste Predigt, beim Scheiden aus dem alten Tempel, und bei der Einweihung des neuerbaueten Gotteshauses* (Hamburg, 1844); Sigmund Gelbhaus, *Rede gehalten bei der Einweihung der renovirten und vergrößerten Synagoge zu Nordhausen am 17. August 1888 (10. Elul 5648)* (Nordhausen, n.d.); Aaron Grünbaum, *Das Erbtheil der Väter. Predigt, gehalten am Säkularfeste der Synagoge zu Ansbach am 9. September 1846* (Ansbach, 1846); Benedict Hause, *Predigt bei der Einweihung der neuen Synagoge in Oberaula, am 15ten September 1837* (Hersfeld, 1837); Salmon Seligmann Herxheimer, *Rede bei der Weihe des neuen Gotteshauses der israelitischen Gemeinde zu Westerburg, am 20sten Juni 1823* (Herborn, 1823); Joseph Mich. Hirsch, *Einige Worte bey der Einweihung des Israelitischen Bethauses am 30. August 1811 zu Hildburghausen* (n.d., n.p.); Samuel Holdheim, *Der Segen des Gotteshauses und der Gottesdienst in der Wahrheit. Zwei Predigten, gehalten in der israelitischen Gemeinde zu Goldberg* (Schwerin, 1845); idem, *Predigt bei der am 2. April stattgefundenen Einweihung des Gotteshauses der Genossenschaft für Reform im Judenthum* (Berlin, 1846); idem, *Die Einweihung des neuerbauten Gotteshauses der jüdischen Reformgemeinde zu Berlin. Predigt, gehalten am 10. September 1854* (Berlin, 1854); Israel Jacobson, [*Rede bei der Einweihung des Jacobs-Tempels in Seesen, 1810*], *Sulamith* 3, no. 1 (1810): 303–17; Adolph Jellinek, *Rede zur Einweihung des israel. Tempels in Iglau, am 9. September 1863 (25. Elul 5623)* (Vienna, 1863); idem, *Zwei Reden zur Schlußsteinlegung und zur Einweihung des neuen israelitischen Tempels in der Leopoldstadt am 18. May und 15. Juni 1858* (Vienna, 1858); Joseph Kahn, *Die Feier der Einweihung der neuen Synagoge zu Trier am 9.-10. September 1859—10.-11. Ellul 5619* (Trier, 1860); Eduard Kley, "Predigt zur Einweihung des neuen Gotteshauses in Parchim, den 29. August 1823," *Bibliothek jüdischer Kanzelredner* 1 (1885): 75–82; Dr. Levi, *Synagogenweihe in Gießen am 31. Mai 1867. Abschiedsrede in der alten Synagoge, Weihegebete und Predigt in der neuen* (Gießen, 1867); Moritz Levin, *Die Berechtigung des Gotteshauses. Weiherede gehalten bei der Einweihung der neuen Synagoge zu Nürnberg am 8. September 1874* (Nuremberg, 1874); Abraham Levy

Loewenstamm, *Reden bei der am 19ten August 1836 stattgehabten Einweihung der neuen Synagoge zu Emden* (Emden, 1837); Joseph Maier, *Die Synagoge. Drei Reden zum Abschiede aus der alten und zur Einweihung der neuen Synagoge in Stuttgart* (Stuttgart, 1861); Isaak Noa Mannheimer, "Zur Einweihung des neuen israelitischen Bethauses in Wien am 9. April 1826," in *Gottesdienstliche Vorträge, gehalten im israelitischen Bethause in Wien,* 1 (Vienna, 1867), 1–12; Samson Wolf Rosenfeld, *Die Israelitische Tempelhalle, oder die neue Synagoge in Mkt. Uhlfeld* (n.p., 1819); Leopold Schott, "Die beste Benützung des Gotteshauses. Eine Synagogen-Einweihungsrede (1868)," *Bibliothek jüdischer Kanzelredner* 2 (1872): 294–98; Adolf Schwarz, *Predigt gehalten bei der Einweihung der neuen Synagoge in der Residenzstadt Karlsruhe am 12. Mai 1875* (Karlsruhe, 1875). These sermons can be found in the libraries of the Hebrew Union College-Jewish Institute of Religion in Cincinnati and of the Leo Baeck Institute in New York.

6. Johann Andreas Cramer, *Sammlung einiger Predigten,* 1 (Copenhagen, 1755), 1–30; 7 (Copenhagen, 1758), 329–416.

7. Immanuel Kant, *Religion within the Limits of Reason Alone,* trans. Theodore M. Greene and Hoyt H. Hudson (New York, 1960), 183, 185.

8. F. Schleiermacher, *Predigten* (Berlin, 1806), 32–33.

9. Rosenfeld was unsure, however, whether to use "synagogue" or "temple" and therefore employed both terms alike in his title and text.

10. Hirsch, 1811.

11. Harold Hammer-Schenk, *Synagogen in Deutschland. Geschichte einer Baugattung im 19. und 20. Jahrhundert (1780–1933)* (Hamburg, 1981), 1:105–10.

12. Holdheim, 1854, 10–11.

13. Schott, 1868, 295.

14. Cohen, 1836, 89.

15. Thus Cramer uses the term repeatedly in his sermons along with *Gotteshaus.*

16. Hammer-Schenk, 1:97–98.

17. Jellinek, 1858, 4.

18. This idea is not wholly foreign to Jewish tradition, which ascribes sanctity (*kedushah*) to synagogues and prohibits levity within their walls. But the principal legal texts do not speak of the synagogue as a place that is awesome (*nora*). Moreover, they specifically allow certain activities and actions that in the bourgeois world of nineteenth-century Central Europe would have been considered disruptive of the sanctity of a house of God. For example, the worshiper was permitted to spit on the floor, provided that he immediately wiped the spittle away with his feet. A person could take a shortcut through the synagogue if it was built across a previously existing road. Sleeping, eating, and drinking in the synagogue were permitted under certain conditions. The texts note that a house of study possesses a larger measure of sanctity than a synagogue. A synagogue may be turned into a house of study, but not

vice versa. (See *Shulḥan arukh, hilkhot bet ha-keneset* and the relevant passages in earlier codes of Jewish law.)

19. Holdheim, 1845, 10.
20. Cohen, 1836, 92.
21. Cramer, 1:17–21.
22. Cohn, 1838, 15; cf. Schwarz, 1875, 5.
23. Mannheimer, 1826, 8.
24. *Rede und Gebet*, 1815, 3.
25. Gelbhaus, 1888, 11; cf. Samuel Adler, 1854, 10.
26. *Allgemeine Zeitung des Judenthums* 18 (1854): 495.
27. Salomon, 1844, 24.
28. Herxheimer, 1823, 23.
29. Mannheimer, 1826, 12.
30. Adler, 1854, 9.
31. Salomon, 1844, 6.
32. Holdheim, 1845, 9.
33. Hause, 1837, 16. Interestingly, Münz and Witelshöfer also mentioned in their dedicatory sermons the need for better decorum in their new synagogues.
34. *Synagogen-Ordnung für die Synagoge der Israelitischen Religionsgesellschaft in Frankfürt a. M.* (Frankfurt a. M., 1874), 3.
35. Baschwitz, 1823, 7.
36. Rosenfeld, 1819, 62, 64.
37. Gelbhaus, 1888, 11.
38. Cohn, 1838, 12.
39. Cohen, 1836, 96.
40. Loewenstamm, 1836, 31.
41. Münz, 8.
42. The Dresden synagogue, completed in 1840, had 300 seats for men and 200 for women. The synagogue that had been built in Sülz in 1774 had 300 seats for men and only 100 for women. See Hammer-Schenk, 1:32, 133.
43. Levi, 1867, 13.
44. Cohen, 1836, 96. Cf. Maier, 1861, 15: ". . . erheben uns diese Kuppeln zu den Betrachtungen, die uns zum Bewußtsein unserer hohen Bestimmung . . . bringen; kommt bei dem Anblick des Ebenmaßes und der Uebereinstimmung dieses Gebäudes Ebenmaß und Uebereinstimmung in unser Leben . . . wirkt der Anblick der Reinheit und Würde seiner Formen auf die darin anbetende Gemeinde, daß ihr Leben rein und würdig sich gestalte, und sie sich durch schöne Werke der Gottes- und Menschenliebe auszeichne und hervorthue, wie dieses Haus hervorragt von den übrigen Gebäuden."
45. Mannheimer, 1826, 1–2.

CHAPTER 15

Liberal Judaism and Zionism in Germany

It is customary in German-Jewish historiography to speak of the opposition between Zionists and Liberal Jews, the former represented
by the Zionistische Vereinigung für Deutschland (German Zionist
Association), the latter by the Centralverein deutscher Staatsbürger
jüdischen Glaubens (Central Association of German Citizens of the
Jewish Faith). Indeed, the Centralverein was the most significant
non-Zionist, and sometimes anti-Zionist, organization of German
Jewry, and its members tended to be both political liberals and non-
Orthodox Jews. Yet its basic goal was the quest for harmonization
between good German citizenship and a certain *Stammesbewusstsein*
(awareness of lineage). It did not posit an alternative religious interpretation of Jewish tradition and destiny. On religious matters the
Centralverein, like its foe the Zionistische Vereinigung, remained
neutral. Their differences were political and cultural.

Yet it was on the grounds of religion that Zionism could be
and was opposed, not pragmatically but dogmatically, by both Orthodox and Liberal Jews. When the latter did so they were speaking
not as political liberals but as part of the Reform movement, which,
in order to differentiate itself from its radical wing, by the late nineteenth century had taken on the designation "Liberal." It was these
Liberals who presented the most formidable intellectual, if not political, counterforce to German Zionism. The theoretical struggle between the two in Germany has received far less attention than the
practical conflicts between Zionists and their political opponents,
the liberal political factions they vied with for control of the German
communities, and the Centralverein. My purpose therefore will be

to look at the representatives of Liberal Judaism as a religious philosophy, examine their religious justifications for varying attitudes
to Zionism, and at the same time investigate the changing Zionist
attitude toward Liberal Judaism. I shall begin with the Second Reich,
focus on the Weimar period, and conclude with some comments
about the Hitler years.

The opposition to international Zionism in Germany began with
rabbis. In June of 1897 two Liberals, Heinemann Vogelstein of Stettin
and Sigmund Maybaum of Berlin, expressed their opposition to the
First Zionist Congress. A few weeks later, the Executive Committee
of the Rabbiner-Verband in Deutschland (the general rabbinical association that included Conservatives as well as Liberals) issued a
formal protest, which was endorsed the following year by a nearly
unanimous voice vote of its plenum.[1] As far as we know, no German
rabbi present at that meeting voted against the resolution. Only two,
the Liberal Leo Baeck and the Conservative Saul Kaatz, chose to
abstain.[2]

In the years that followed, religious Liberals, with few exceptions, remained adamant in their opposition to the new movement.
Some of their arguments had little to do with religion: Zionism was
a danger to Jewish political status in Germany, a spur to antisemitism.[3] But especially among the rabbis, other contentions appear as
well, whose main purpose is to declare the Jewish illegitimacy of
Zionism—not because it was "forcing the messianic end" (the reason Orthodox opponents often castigated it), but because it was a
misunderstanding of Jewish history and destiny.

Among the Liberals the chief spokesmen for the religious critique of Zionism were Rabbis Heinemann Vogelstein of Stettin and
Felix Goldmann of Oppeln (and later Leipzig). Of the two, Vogelstein was older and less compromising, Goldmann more profound and less dogmatic. Though organizationally a leader of
Liberal Judaism, Vogelstein was not an original thinker. His generation within the Reform movement had received the heritage of Abraham Geiger and his contemporaries intact and added little to it
themselves. Vogelstein's reaction to Zionism was therefore basically
an attempt to point out where the new movement contradicted the
accepted heritage. He put it very directly: Judaism means the religion of the Prophets of Israel understood as faith in a universal,
moral God and the Jewish mission to bring its tiding to humanity.
Since Zionism undermined that faith, especially among the young,
it constituted a serious danger to the future of Judaism no less than
to the political future of German Jews.[4]

Goldmann, who considered himself a non-Zionist rather than an anti-Zionist, drove to the heart of the matter: Zionism represented a fundamentally different and contradictory understanding of Jewishness. It held that one could be an atheist and at the same time a perfectly good Jew. The Zionists could afford to be neutral and even indifferent to religion, but Liberal Judaism could not adopt that position. While there were indeed Jews who called themselves Liberal and cared little about religion, Goldmann saw them on that account as Jewishly inadequate. Their Jewishness was simply an *Abwehrjudentum* (Judaism defined in terms of defense), and, despite Zionist claims, that was not what Liberal Judaism was all about. Assimilated Jews were indeed the norm, but they stood outside both camps, the common prey of Liberals no less than Zionists. Like the Zionists, Goldmann's goal was to win them over to a more content-rich Jewishness. But that basic content had to be religion, not nationhood, for, as he argued, only Judaism as a religion was historically authentic. And because Judaism, unlike Jewish nationalism, was eternal and not temporal, it alone could assure Jewish survival.[5]

For the most part, Liberal rabbis and laity in Germany continued to see Liberal Judaism and Zionism as fundamentally contradictory. Theoretical nuances were generally lost in the midst of vigorously fought community elections and persistent outcroppings of antisemitism that kept anxieties at a high pitch. Increasingly, Liberal Jews sensed that the Zionists were successfully alienating some of their own offspring, "dripping the Zionist poison into the souls of the children," as one of them put it. In 1912, lay leaders of Liberal Judaism were instrumental in forming an Antizionistisches Komitee (Anti-Zionist Committee),[6] and most of them continued throughout the Weimar period to regard the practical fight against Zionism as a basic imperative of their Liberalism.[7] However, by the early Weimar years, the Liberal rabbinate was neither consistently nor unambiguously anti-Zionist.

In 1918 even Goldmann acknowledged that Jewish nationalism was unobjectionable, provided only that it would recognize the primacy of Judaism as a religion.[8] Religious Jews could legitimately be members of the Zionist organization, according to Goldmann, as long as they did not share the prevalent national view that religion was a dispensable manifestation of Jewishness—as long as they continued to consider religion its essence. Rabbi Caesar Seligmann went further. Although he never joined the ranks of the Zionists and, like Goldmann, continued to insist upon the primacy of religion, Seligmann paid early tribute to its beneficent effect in restoring Jewish self-consciousness to alienated Jews, and by 1918 he could regard their roles as complementary. Both were striving to preserve Judaism, "we through preservation of the Jewish religion, they through preservation of the community."⁹ In Martin Buber, a Zionist and a non-Orthodox believer, Seligmann found points of contact with Liberal Judaism.¹⁰

Although Hermann Cohen did not associate himself organizationally with Liberal Judaism, he was widely regarded as its most respected spokesman. His position on Zionism was similar to that of the more moderate among the Liberal rabbis and laity. Like them he could not conceive of a Jewishness that did not have ethical monotheism as its essence and did not strive for a universal messianic fulfillment. But like them also, he realized that the religious definition was not exhaustive. Judaism, he held in 1916, was not, as the Zionists believed, a nation, but it was a "nationality." As such, and not as a religion alone, it could coexist within the German state. That, of course, did not make Cohen a Zionist. On the contrary, like the rabbis mentioned above, he continued to see Liberal Judaism and Zionism as struggling against one another for the minds and hearts of German Jewry.¹¹

Yet even in the first decade of the century a few intrepid souls had set out to combine the two. The case of Rabbi Emil Cohn is for the most part well known.¹² On account of his Zionism, it is generally noted, he lost his job as a Liberal rabbi in the Berlin Jewish community in 1907, the governing body being unwilling to tolerate his views. However, the Cohn affair was not quite so simple. Cohn had not suddenly become a Zionist. He was a graduate of the Liberal seminary in Berlin, the Lehranstalt für die Wissenschaft des Judentums (Educational Institute for the Scientific Study of Judaism), where he had been the cofounder of a Zionist student society that was quickly suppressed by the administration. Nonetheless, the Berlin Jewish community had hired him, albeit with the proviso that he keep his views out of the pulpit and classroom. Although Cohn did not entirely abide by his promise, it was only when complaint was made against him by the director of a prominent *Gymnasium* that the community board felt compelled to take action.¹³ Moreover, his Zionism did not prevent Cohn from thereafter getting a rabbinical position in Kiel, where no conditions were made about keeping his views private. In fact, while he was the rabbi in Kiel, he delivered an unpublished lecture to the Königsberg Zionist Association on religiosity and Judaism in which he combined Liberal religious views with Zionist ones. He called for a full-scale reformation of Judaism that would bring it religious renewal by "cleansing it of foreign rubble and the withered foliage of . . . suffocating forms." But that renewal, he argued, required genuine religious experience (*Erlebnis*), which was possible only through a historical sense of peoplehood. Zionism was essential if Judaism were to regain its fluidity and religious creativity.[14] Cohn went on to obtain pulpits in Essen, Bonn,[15] and finally again in Berlin, though by that time his religious views had become distinctly conservative and he no longer wholeheartedly affirmed Zionism.[16]

The first German Liberal rabbi to remain true to both Liberalism and Zionism was Max Joseph, the rabbi of Stolp in Pomerania. Like Cohn, he was a graduate of the Liberal Lehranstalt in Berlin, but during the period before political Zionism. Joseph gained public attention with a pro-Zionist work that he published in 1908 entitled *Das Judentum am Scheidewege* (Judaism at the Crossroads).[17] Eschewing both the political and cultural arguments for Zionism, Joseph took a new tack: the Jewish religion will not survive without Jewish nationalism. Or as he put it, "Judaism will either be Zionist or it will not be at all." Joseph went on to show that the Jewish religion, as it developed historically, was inextricably intertwined with national elements without which it could not hope to survive. They appeared both in concepts such as ethical monotheism and practices such as celebration of the holidays. Even the mission of Israel idea, so cherished by Liberal Judaism, he believed, must arouse "a sense of national exultation." The Zionism that is necessary for Jewish religious survival, is not essentially secular in Joseph's view—though that was regularly claimed by his Liberal colleagues. Quite the contrary, it fostered moral idealism, and from there the path was short to religious enthusiasm. In Joseph's words: "The great struggle for the rebirth of the people, which stirs the soul to its depths, is one in which a Jew can scarcely participate without being seized by religious sentiments."[18] Joseph's program entailed the abandonment of what he considered the anti-national course of Liberal Judaism. His own religious Liberalism was especially evident in his approach to the Bible, to which he applied the radical Higher Criticism of his day. But Joseph addressed his book to Liberal Jews almost as if he were not one of them. He did not try to speak as an insider within both traditions, and he did not rise to a position of prominence in Liberal Judaism.[19] In contrast to its counterpart in the United States, German Liberal Jewry failed to produce religious figures like Stephen Wise, Max and James Heller, and Abba Hillel Silver, who were prominent both in their rabbinical roles and in the leadership of organized Zionism.[20]

*　*　*

The early failure to establish a shared identity must also be explained in terms of Zionist attitudes toward Liberal Judaism. For the Zionist leadership in Germany, Liberalism represented the ideological enemy as well as the political enemy in community elections. The enthusiasm that Zionism drew from its adherents, especially the young, was in no small measure dependent upon a sense of generational revolt against the bourgeois establishment, whose ideology was Liberalism. Zionist tactics were less restrained than those of their opponents and their polemics were peppered with sarcasm. They attacked the *sancta* of Liberal Judaism—religious reform, the mission idea—with utmost irreverence. They were unwilling to acknowledge it as a serious form of Jewish identity, except—in an occasional grudging admission—for a very few, mostly the rabbis. They stereotyped it as nothing more than assimilationism, repeatedly showing through beneath a thin layer of Jewish religion. They aroused anxiety by claiming they had won over the youth, that they represented true progress while Liberal Judaism stood for the past. They even claimed their opponents had no right to the term *liberalism*, for true liberalism referred only to the general political movement that had led to emancipation in Germany. The religious Liberals' self-designation was therefore nothing but a smoke screen for a Judaism of convenience, a way station on the road to Christianity. In short, from the Zionist side too, Liberal Judaism and Jewish nationalism were initially seen as incompatible.[21]

Despite a declared policy of religious neutrality, German Zionists often allied themselves politically with the Orthodox, justifying the alliance—seen as cynical by the Liberals—by their claim that Orthodoxy was better able to preserve Jewish distinctiveness. They opposed liturgical reforms that removed national elements from the prayerbook.[22]

In the same period that the Anti-Zionist Committee engaged in its propaganda on the eve of the First World War, the Zionist movement was likewise undergoing a radicalization that set it further apart from the Liberals.[23] Still, the Zionists could not resist noting that among the younger religious leadership of the Liberals a turn to Zionism was increasingly apparent.[24] Following the war, they evolved a new strategy with regard to Liberal Judaism: they would try to use those religious leaders that were sympathetic to Zionism for their own purposes. In 1918 the chief Zionist propagandist in Germany, Alfred Klee, turned to Rabbi Max Joseph, asking him to distribute some Zionist literature and seeking his assistance in enlisting other sympathetic rabbis for active participation in the Zionist cause. For his part, Joseph was not so sure that the ploy would work. "My dear doctor," he replied, "*Golus* [exile] does not make one manly, and the Prussian rabbi is doubly in *Golus*. He trembles quicker than the leaf on a tree. But," he added, "the younger generation of rabbis seems to be somewhat braver."[25]

During the Weimar period that "younger generation" was increasingly occupying rabbinical positions of prominence. Although most were not outspoken Zionists, they were considerably more friendly to the movement than their elders. A number of them were now teaching at the Lehranstalt (during the Weimar years once again raised to the rank of *Hochschule* [college]) in Berlin. Could these men be persuaded to express themselves on Zionism in a manner that would be helpful to the movement? In the mid-1920s, German Zionism changed its course with regard to religious Liberalism. No longer did it see the religious Liberals as the enemy. Now at least some of them became potential recruits for the cause.

A rapprochement between Zionists and Liberals had been in the making as early as 1920 when both groups joined in support of the Palestine Foundation Fund, the Keren Hayesod. Even Rabbi Felix Goldmann signed the declaration, principally, as he wrote in justification, because it was not political and because "building up the land of Israel is an eternal religious obligation that no one can cavalierly remove from the store of our religious commandments."[26] Goldmann also explicitly dissociated himself from Max Naumann's Verband nationaldeutscher Juden (League of German Nationalist Jews), formed in 1921, which regarded Jewish pro-Palestine activity as virtual treason. The views of that group, he suggested, rested on a misunderstanding of the Jewish religion.[27] It is not unlikely that the Verband, many of whose members were also associated with the radical Reform Congregation in Berlin, may have removed from Liberal circles some of the more extreme anti-Zionists.

From the Liberal side the rapprochement proceeded with the unanimous adoption of a neutrality resolution on the subject of Zionism by the Vereinigung der Liberalen Rabbiner Deutschlands (Association of Liberal Rabbis in Germany) in 1927—fully eight years before a similar position was adopted by the parallel organization in America, the Central Conference of American Rabbis.[28] However, the Liberal laity did not go along. Meeting six weeks later, the governing body of the Vereinigung für das liberale Judentum in Deutschland (Association for Liberal Judaism in Germany) unanimously adopted a resolution stating that since religion was the foundation and essence of Judaism, it altogether rejected the idea that it develops out of Jewish nationalism.[29] The split between Liberal rabbis and Liberal laity, which as early as 1912 had manifested itself bitterly on the question of ritual religious obligation, now became increasingly apparent on the issue of Zionism as well.[30]

The German Zionists, for their part, were quick to exploit this split in Liberal Judaism. In October of 1927 the governing body of the Zionistische Vereinigung decided on a new policy, which the protocol of their meeting formulated as follows:

> Liberal Association: The crisis currently existing within its ranks demands the sharpest attack against the Association. It is our task to influence and win over the younger generation of rabbis and to harness for our propaganda (for example, lectures on "Zionism and Liberalism") individual organized Liberals who are also Zionists. The intellectual analysis must present the opposition between Zionism and Liberalism in such a way as to urge attack upon the anti-national reforming tendency, but to allow that the Jewish conception, borne by a national Jewish way of thinking, which is based on the idea of [religious] development, has its place within the Zionist movement.[31]

Shortly thereafter, the German Zionist Central Committee affirmed the new strategy even more specifically. No longer would opponents simply be branded assimilationists. Instead, it called for "penetration of the historical development of liberalism and, together with all necessary critique, an acknowledgment of the lines of connection between it and us ([recognition of] changes within Liberalism)."[32]

This new Zionist line of the mid–1920s had already been put into effect even before the official bodies gave it sanction. In the June 23, 1925, issue of the Zionist paper, the *Jüdische Rundschau*, Zionist activist Hans Kohn had published an article entitled "Liberal Judaism" in which he argued that Zionism and Liberal Judaism were similar in their eclecticism and in their view of Judaism as an ongoing spiritual process. He was careful to distinguish between the "old" and the "new" Liberalism, the former associated with assimilationism, the latter a worthy partner for the Zionists. He even went so far as to acknowledge that Liberal Judaism was of "major significance in our history" because it had broken down the rigidity produced by the preceding centuries of ghetto life. Citing Abraham Geiger's view of an organically developing Jewish tradition, Kohn added: "In this respect we stand on the shoulders of this early Liberal Judaism." But Kohn's rapprochement was limited to a common understanding of Jewish religious history; it did not extend to the future. Here he thought Liberal Judaism lacked a sense of direction, and he did not suggest common goals.[33]

The following year an unprecedented event gave the Zionists

further cause for reflection. In the summer of 1926 Liberal Jews from various European countries and the United States gathered in London to form the World Union for Progressive Judaism. Almost thirty years after the Zionists, Liberal Jews had finally succeeded in creating their own international organization. Henceforth it was no longer possible to accuse them of fearing antisemitic charges about "international Jewry." Nor could their movement be regarded as somnolent.[34] Moreover, the London meeting had refrained from taking any stance with regard to Zionism. Thus when the first official conference of the World Union was scheduled for Berlin in 1928, the German Zionists saw this new challenge as a providential opportunity. They would try to win the delegates over to Zionism.

In anticipation of the conference, Robert Weltsch, editor of the *Jüdische Rundschau*, invited a number of leading Liberal Jews to express their views on the relation between Liberal Judaism and Zionism. Their replies, together with essays by prominent Zionists, then appeared in a special double issue of the paper that was distributed at the conference. Shortly thereafter, they were gathered into a pamphlet for wider circulation together with a foreword by Kurt Blumenfeld, the president of the German Zionist Association.[35] On the front page of the special issue Weltsch declared that there could be no antagonism between Liberalism as a religious worldview and Zionism, and he added his own appreciation for the work of both Hermann Cohen and Claude Montefiore, the leader of English Liberal Jewry and president of the World Union. "The opposition between religious Liberalism and Jewish nationalism has no internal basis," he concluded. However, remembering that there were also Zionists who were religiously Orthodox, he hastily added, that, of course, the *Jüdische Rundschau* did not therefore identify itself with religious Liberalism. Politically its stance remained neutral.[36]

The most important spiritual and intellectual leaders of Liberal Judaism responded to the Zionist invitation with brief, balanced statements. Leo Baeck, who enjoyed the widest respect of all the Liberal rabbis, was neither a Zionist nor an anti-Zionist. But in his advocacy of a more serious, inner-directed Liberal Judaism, he set himself clearly apart from the assimilationist tendency that Zionists had so long condemned.[37] Self-criticism was also the tone of Ismar Elbogen's response. Flexibility, the historian and one of the chief organizers of the Berlin conference noted, was of the essence of Liberalism, and the present demanded a shift from national adaptation toward a return to Jewish roots and toward building bridges to the mass of the Jewish people. Max Wiener used the occasion to make a theological point: Because Liberal Jews recognized a human component in revelation, they—more than the Orthodox—needed to acknowledge the important religious role of the national spirit as a source for the ongoing process of interpretation and reinterpretation of God's will.[38]

Less well-known Liberal rabbis were more explicitly Zionist. Malwin Warschauer was a rabbi of the Berlin community who, like the men just mentioned, also taught at the *Hochschule*. His contribution was unique in offering an internal critique of the Zionist attitude toward Liberal Judaism. Unlike Weltsch and the other Zionist participants, whose smooth words were largely motivated by tactical considerations, who never suggested that Zionism had hitherto erred in its attitude to religious Liberalism, and who certainly did not identify themselves as Liberal Jews, Warschauer chastised his fellow Zionists for failing to recognize that Liberal Judaism contained indispensable religious values and qualities that represented "the most profound and noble aspects of our national spirit." Warschauer called for an alliance of the liberal and national ideas to bring about religious revival. Max Elk, who would later found the first school in Palestine that drew upon Liberal Judaism, the Leo Baeck School in Haifa, even shared the controversial Zionist assumption that Jewish life in the diaspora would always remain deficient. Only in the Jews' own land could the Liberal Jewish idea reach fruition. When the national movement would physically establish its "old-new land," Elk maintained, Liberal Judaism would be its soul.

The conference itself did not raise the Zionist issue, choosing to concentrate on strictly religious matters instead.[39] However, in the following years the drift toward Zionism among German Liberal Jews continued. Although there was still opposition to Jewish nationalism among some Liberal lay leaders—and especially within the circle of the Berlin Reform Congregation—well into the Hitler years,[40] the broadened Jewish Agency after 1928 provided another basis for cooperation alongside the Keren Hayesod. During the Nazi period even Heinrich Stern, the lay head of organized Liberal Judaism in Germany, who had long been an avowed opponent of Zionism, attested that the two movements had grown much closer.[41] The youngest generation of Liberal rabbis, men like Joachim Prinz[42] and Max Nussbaum, were clearly committed to Zionism from the beginning of their careers. Some older men, like Paul Lazarus, became converts in the early 1930s.[43]

As more and more German Jews immigrated to Palestine, Liberal Judaism looked increasingly toward its self-perpetuation there.[44] Caesar Seligmann even suggested that forming a Liberal version of Mizrahi, the Orthodox Zionist organization, might be the best way to achieve that end.[45] In the mid-1930s German Liberal rabbis established congregations in Haifa, Tel Aviv, and Jerusalem.[46] On a visit to Palestine in 1934, shortly before making *aliyah*, the once anti-Zionist Liberal rabbi Max Dienemann wrote in his diary: "The remarkable thing about Palestine is that here one works for the future while in Europe today one lives only for each day and for the liquidation of the past."[47] Liberal Judaism in Germany had come a long way: from the virulent opposition to Zionism in Heinemann Vogelstein's generation, through various forms of acknowledgment and rapprochement, finally to the realization—forced upon it by history—that, without Zion, a Jewish future was not possible.

Notes

1. *Allgemeine Zeitung des Judentums* 61 (1897): 277, 338; *Verhandlungen und Beschlüsse der Generalversammlung des Rabbiner-Verbandes in Deutschland zu Berlin am 1. und 2. Juni 1898* (Berlin, 1898), 30–32. It is not evident from these protocols that Rabbi Selig Gronemann of Hannover voted against the declaration, as maintained in the article in *Encyclopedia Judaica*, s.v. "Protestrabbiner." At the meeting he said explicitly that he was not opposed to it as such. When the declaration had been issued a year before, it had pleased him and he had considered it a "manly deed." However, he now favored a new, more moderately phrased resolution rather than merely an endorsement of the old one.

2. Kurt Wilhelm, "Der zionistische Rabbiner," in *In zwei Welten: Siegfried Moses zum fünfundsiebzigsten Geburtstag* (Tel Aviv, 1962), 55–56.

3. See, for example, the principally non-religious arguments by the son of Abraham Geiger, Ludwig Geiger, in his "Zionismus und Deutschtum," *Die Stimme der Wahrheit* 1 (1905): 165–69, and in Werner Sombert, *Judentaufen* (Munich, 1912), 44–48. Because of his lineage, his editorship of the *Allgemeine Zeitung des Judentums*, and his active role in the Berlin community, combined with his extreme views explicitly favoring virtually complete assimilation, Geiger served the Zionists as a convenient symbol for their stereotype of Liberal Judaism. On Geiger's anti-Zionism, see Yehuda Eloni, *Zionismus in Deutschland. Von den Anfängen bis 1914* (Gerlingen, 1987), 194–200.

4. Heinemann Vogelstein, *Der Zionismus, eine Gefahr für die gedeihliche Entwickelung des Judentums* (Berlin, 1906). That the diaspora was providential, and hence meant by God to be permanent, continued to be the dominant position of German Liberal Judaism. See, for example, Max Dienemann, *Galuth* (Berlin, 1929).

5. Felix Goldmann, *Zionismus oder Liberalismus, Atheismus oder Religion*

(Frankfurt a. M., 1911. Originally appearing as a series of articles in *Liberales Judentum* in 1911, in pamphlet form it was widely distributed, even handed out at large public meetings. *Liberales Judentum* 3 (1911): 263.

6. It is not true, however, as has been repeatedly claimed, that the Vereinigung für das liberale Judentum in Deutschland (Association for Liberal Judaism in Germany) and the Antizionistisches Komitee shared the same address, although on one occasion a meeting of the committee was held in the former's office. Moreover, unlike the Centralverein, the committee did not seek the open participation of Liberal rabbis. No rabbis signed their declarations. See the material on the committee in the Leo Wolff Collection in the archives of the Leo Baeck Institute, New York. The reference to poison appears in the protocol for May 2, 1914. The committee's second pamphlet, *Der Zionismus, Seine Theorien, Aussichten und Wirkungen* (Berlin, n.d.) noted that it was based on the writings not only of the Liberal rabbis Vogelstein and Goldmann but also of the Orthodox rabbi Raphael Breuer and the Conservative Moritz Guedemann.

7. Erwin Seligmann, ed., *Caesar Seligmann Erinnerungen* (Frankfurt a/M, 1975), 159–60.

8. Felix Goldmann, *Warum sind und bleiben wir Juden?* (Leipzig, 1918), 24; idem, *Das liberale Judentum* (Berlin, 1919), 11. Despite his increasing appreciation for Zionist activities, Goldmann continued to view Liberal Judaism and Zionism as two fundamentally opposed conceptions of Jewish existence that were engaged in a contest for the souls of young Jews. See his *Der Jude im deutschen Kulturkreise: Ein Beitrag zum Wesen des Nationalismus* (Berlin, 1930).

9. *Liberales Judentum* 1 (1908–9): 7–8; 10 (1918): 3.

10. Caesar Seligmann, *Geschichte der jüdischen Reformbewegung* (Frankfurt a. M., 1922), 31–33. Seligmann's final position on Zionism before the Holocaust was still more appreciative: "The Jewish national self-consciousness, which revived in Zionism with unparalleled force, was a curative bath in which the Jewish soul of the bloodless masses regained its health." Caesar Seligmann, "Religiös-Liberales Judentum, Rückschau und Ausblick" (mimeo) (n.p., 1938), 16. On Seligmann's role within Liberal Judaism see Michael A. Meyer, "Caesar Seligmann and the Development of Liberal Judaism in Germany at the Beginning of the Twentieth Century," *Hebrew Union College Annual* 40–41 (1969–70): 529–54.

11. Hermann Cohen, *Jüdische Schriften*, 3 vols. (Berlin, 1924), 2:319–40.

12. The most recent treatment is in Eloni, *Zionismus in Deutschland*, 475–83, 508–15.

13. The director of the Mommsen Gymnasium gave the notes from his conversation with Emil Cohn to four Jewish teachers who taught there—and who must have felt threatened that Cohn's position (Jewish identification takes precedence over German) would cast suspicion on

their own views. They, in turn, reported the matter to the governing body of the community.

14. Emil Cohn, "Religiosität und Judentum. Vortrag gehalten am 20. März 1909 in der Königsberger Zionistischen Vereinigung" (mimeo.), in my possession.

15. In Bonn, where he was elected unanimously, Cohn did agree not to make public speeches on Zionism in the immediate area. See Eloni, *Zionismus in Deutschland*, 515.

16. The new religious conservatism is evident in his *Judentum: Ein Auruf an die Zeit* (Munich, 1923). Here Cohn, describing himself as filled with remorse, forsakes both religious Liberalism and Zionism. He now criticizes Liberal Judaism for insufficient attention to religious forms and Zionism for having become a substitute religion. Franz Rosenzweig wrote a review of Cohn's book in *Der Jude* (8 [1923]: 237–40) that was highly critical of Cohn's preachy tone and assumed self-importance but sympathetic to some of his views.

17. Max Joseph, *Das Judentum am Scheidewege. Ein Wort zur Schicksalsfrage an die Starken und Edlen des jüdischen Volkes* (Berlin, 1908). The title was obviously influenced by the collection of Ahad Ha-Am's essays, which had appeared in German translation bearing the title *Am Scheidewege* (Berlin, 1904).

18. Ibid., 90.

19. Joseph's book received no attention in the general press. In Jewish periodicals he was assailed for his critique of Liberal Judaism by Liberal rabbis and for his biblical criticism by traditional ones. Joseph responded to his critics in *Ist das alles? Eine Antwort an die Kritiker und Nichtkritiker meines Buches* (Berlin, 1910). The volume was issued by the publishing house of the Zionist newspaper *Jüdische Rundschau*. As far as I can determine, not until 1926 did an article appear in which both Liberalism and Zionism are affirmed equally. The October 26 issue of the *Jüdische Rundschau* for that year contains a piece by a recently deceased Hans Norden (apparently not a rabbi) entitled "Liberalismus und Zionismus." Norden notes that he had long believed the two were irreconcilable polar opposites and that he had to choose one or the other. At length he had come to the conclusion that they could exist together not only intellectually but also emotionally. He concluded: "Also and above all in feeling, in my sense of closest connection in terms of destiny and race (*Stamm*), I affirm both poles, Liberalism and Zionism." Hans Norden may have been a relative of Joseph Norden, the Liberal rabbi in Elberfeld. The latter made reference to the article in his *Grundlagen und Ziele des religiös-liberalen Judentums*, 2nd ed. (Berlin, 1926), 27n. Joseph Norden's own position, expressed in this pamphlet, was to assign Liberalism and Zionism to two separate realms and then argue that they did not conflict. The former, being an interpretation of the Jewish religion, had Orthodoxy as its opponent; the latter was strictly political. Neither should regard itself as possessing sufficient

Jewish content or seek to impinge upon the realm of the other. Rabbi Norden's toleration for Zionism in principle did not, however, make him a Zionist, since Zionism, he believed, in fact did impinge on the religious realm, for example by pressing Judaism wholly into a national framework.

20. A similar point is made by Wilhelm, "Der zionistische Rabbiner," 70, with regard to German rabbis in general in contrast to rabbis elsewhere in Europe.

21. See especially Heinrich Sachse [Loewe], Dr. Vogelsteins Propaganda für den Zionismus (Berlin, 1906). The publisher was the Jüdische Rundschau; the title to be taken ironically. See also Arthur Ruppin, The Jews of To-Day (London, 1913), 154, and idem, Soziologie der Juden, 2 vols. (Berlin, 1931), 2:187, 189.

22. Jehuda Reinharz, ed., Dokumente zur Geschichte des deutschen Zionismus 1882–1933 (Tübingen, 1981), 83.

23. Marjorie Lamberti, "From Coexistence to Conflict: Zionism and the Jewish Community in Germany, 1897–1914," Leo Baeck Institute Year Book 27 (1982): 84–86; idem, "The Centralverein and the Anti-Zionists: Setting the Record Straight," Leo Baeck Institute Year Book 33 (1988): 127–28; Jehuda Reinharz, "Advocacy and History: The Case of the Centralverein and the Zionists," Leo Baeck Institute Year Book 33 (1988): 121.

24. As early as 1906 Heinemann Vogelstein had remarked that there were "several instances" of anti-Zionist communities appointing Zionist rabbis and teachers who openly espoused their own views and that Zionism was especially prevalent among rabbinical students. Der Zionismus: Eine Gefahr, 10–12; also Sachse, Dr. Vogelsteins Propaganda, 7.

25. Max Joseph to Alfred Klee, May 28, 1918, Alfred Klee Collection, Central Zionist Archives, Jerusalem, A142/58/3. The individuals Joseph was apparently supposed to approach were the biblical scholar and rabbi Sigmund Jampel in Schwedt on the Oder, Rabbi Abraham Schlesinger, a graduate of the Breslau Seminary, and a Rabbi Bernstein, who may be the Hungarian Jewish historian, Béla Bernstein, a graduate of the Neologue seminary in Budapest who held various rabbinical positions in Hungary. Joseph hoped that Klee would help him publish another pro-Zionist work, then in preparation. But nothing seems to have come either of Joseph's propaganda efforts or of his projected volume.

26. Felix Goldmann, Eine ewige religiöse Pflicht: Warum ich den Keren-Hayesod-Aufruf unterschrieb (Berlin, 1922), 5. The piece first appeared in the April 16, 1922, issue of the Jüdische Zeitung of Leipzig, where Goldmann was then serving as rabbi, and was later reprinted as a pamphlet by the Keren Hayesod. A copy is under Goldmann's name in the Central Zionist Archives.

27. Felix Goldmann, Warum sind und bleiben wir Juden? 2nd ed. (Berlin, 1924), 28–29. Cf. Reinharz, Dokumente, 319.

28. The text of the resolution was as follows: "The Association of Liberal Rabbis in Germany declares that the basic character of Judaism is reli-

gious and must remain so. It decisively rejects every attempt to interpret Judaism as an exclusively national structure. It leaves to the personal sense of responsibility of each individual what position to take in relation to Zionism. It hopes that the settlement of Palestine will proceed in a spirit that will assure a revival of Jewish religiosity." *Jüdische Rundschau,* April 1, 1927.

29. Hermann Vogelstein, *Report on Liberal Judaism in Germany to the World Union for Progressive Judaism Conference* (Berlin, 1928), 1–2. However, the "Guidelines of a Program for Liberal Judaism," adopted by the Liberal lay organization (with reservation as to its binding character) in 1912, did not specifically negate Zionism.

30. Seligmann, *Caesar Seligmann Errinerungen,* 159–60.

31. Reinharz, *Dokumente,* 392.

32. Ibid., 398.

33. Hans Kohn, "Liberales Judentum," *Jüdische Rundschau,* June 23, 1925. The article was reprinted in *Zionistische Politik,* ed. Hans Kohn and Robert Weltsch (Mährisch-Ostrau, Czechoslovakia, 1927), 84–96. An otherwise critical editorial in the *Jüdische Rundschau,* February 10, 1925, entitled "Die Lehren der Wahlen," had noted: "Religious Liberalism does not stand in opposition to Zionism or to the Jewish national idea. A large portion of prominent Zionists, in respect of religion, have been Liberal."

34. Robert Weltsch, "Zur liberalen Weltkonferenz," in Kohn and Weltsch, *Zionistische Politik,* 97–106.

35. *Jüdische Rundschau,* August 17, 1928; *Die jüdische Religion und ihre Träger. Beiträge zur Frage des jüdischen Liberalismus und Nationalismus* (Berlin, 1928). The pamphlet also contained a report on the conference by a rather critical Zionist observer who nonetheless remarked on the "Jewish energy" displayed there, an energy he could only call "national." The participants in the symposium, in the order in which their essays appeared in the pamphlet, were Leo Baeck (Berlin), Ismar Elbogen (Berlin), Robert Weltsch (Berlin), Malwin Warschauer (Berlin), Felix Weltsch (Prague), Max Wiener (Berlin), Max Elk (Stettin), Max Grünwald (Mannheim), Maurice L. Perlzweig (London), Max Joseph (Stolp), Ignaz Ziegler (Carlsbad), David Baumgardt (Berlin), Ernst Simon (Jerusalem), and Martin Buber (Heppenheim).

36. Still, Weltsch's wooing of the Liberals did not sit well with the Mizrahi in Germany. At a meeting of the Zionist governing body shortly thereafter, Oscar Wolfsberg, head of the Orthodox Zionists, strenuously objected to what he regarded as a wasteful expression of sympathy. Kurt Blumenfeld was thereupon forced to defend the new policy of trying to win over the Liberals. Reinharz, *Dokumente,* 408–11.

37. Baeck's piece was printed in large type on the front page of the special issue of the *Jüdische Rundschau.* Still before the rise of Nazism, Baeck had said in a speech on behalf of the Keren Hayesod, delivered in Königsberg: "Perhaps your children or grandchildren will have need for the

Land of Israel in order to find shelter there from the anger of the oppressor." Cited by Ernst Simon, "Mashehu al Leo Baeck ha-bilti
yadua," Central Zionist Archives, A198/1, kindly called to my attention
by Esther Herlitz.

38. Two years earlier, in a speech at the organizing conference of the World
Union in London, Max Wiener had expressed a similar view when he
concluded his remarks by saying to his fellow Liberal Jews: "If, therefore, tradition does not mean for us that unqualified authority which it
consititutes for Conservatism, then we must all be guided by a strong
conscious life in common with the the Jewish world community and its
destiny, by work on the great tasks of preserving and gathering our
people, and certainly not least, by concern for the new home in the old
ancestral land." *International Conference of Liberal Jews* (London, 1926),
38. However, when Wiener was later requested to do active Zionist propaganda, he responded that, as a rabbi, he would not get involved in
party disputes. Rather he believed that he best served the cause of "a
genuinely Jewish program," Jewish education, and the work for Palestine by freely and individually expressing himself on the issues. Wiener
thus continued to follow Baeck's lead in avoiding open partisanship.
Max Wiener to Alfred Klee, November 14, 1930, Klee Collection, Central
Zionist Archives.

39. Curiously, the German Liberals were suspected of Zionism among at
least some American Reform Jews. On March 10, 1928, a leading Reform
layman from Pittsburgh, A. Leo Weil, wrote to the secretary of the
World Union for Progressive Judaism (WUPJ), Lily H. Montagu, that he
considered it possible "our German members wanted to have this meeting in Berlin so that they could obtain a large enough attendance of
delegates affiliated with Zionism to commit our organization to that
movement. . . . You will recall that Dr. [Stephen S.] Wise, at our London
conference, made an effort in that direction, and it would not surprise
me at all if a similar movement was being carefully planned and prepared for by Zionists in Germany." WUPJ Collection, 16/1, American
Jewish Archives, Cincinnati.

40. Max Dienemann, *Liberales Judentum* (Berlin, 1935), 19.

41. Heinrich Stern, *Ernst Machen! Ein Wort an die religiös-liberalen Juden* (Berlin, 1935), 11.

42. In *Wir Juden* (Berlin, 1934), Joachim Prinz argued that the triumph of
nationalism over political liberalism should now drive the Jews to the
only possible solution of the Jewish question: the acceptance of their
own status as a nation. And the Jews could not develop culturally and
religiously as a nation except by mass migration to Palestine. Prinz also
preached Zionism from Berlin pulpits, apparently without backlash.
The reprimand [*Massregelung*] he received for a brief sermon delivered
in 1935 seems to have been not on account of its Zionism but because
he challenged the established practice of moving rabbis around from
one synagogue to another, preventing the establishment of lasting ties

between rabbi and congregants. See *Jüdische Rundschau*, May 28, 1935, 3, 8. Prinz continued to serve as rabbi in Berlin until his emigration in 1937. It is therefore necessary to correct Eloni, *Zionismus in Deutschland*, 204, n. 98.

43. *Paul Lazarus Gedenkbuch. Beiträge zur Würdigung der letzten Rabbinergeneration in Deutschland* (Jerusalem, 1961), 19–20.

44. Max Dienemann, "Das Gesicht des religiösen Liberalismus in Palästina," *Der Morgen* 12 (1936): 157–63.

45. Seligmann, "Religiös-Liberales Judentum," 22.

46. See the reports on their work by Max Elk (Haifa) and Kurt Wilhelm (Jerusalem) in ibid., 23–33.

47. *Max Dienemann: Ein Gedenkbuch* (London, 1946), 51.

CHAPTER 16

Gemeinschaft within *Gemeinde*: Religious Ferment in Weimar Liberal Judaism

> Form a *Gemeinschaft* that is rooted in the past, come to terms with the present, and build for the future. Then will the Jewish *Gemeinde* spring back to life and the house of God become its focus.
>
> LEVY ROSENBLATT[1]

Gemeinde

The "New Synagogue" on Oranienburger Strasse in Berlin, dedicated in 1866, was an immense and marvelous structure. Its size and opulence paid visual tribute to the rapidly growing and upwardly mobile Jewish community in the Prussian capital. It would long serve Berlin Jewry as a source of private satisfaction and public pride. The Berlin Liberal rabbi Joseph Aub had composed a new three-volume prayerbook especially for its worship; the talented synagogue composer Louis Lewandowski wrote new compositions for its cantor and choir. To enter the new synagogue was to experience a sense of awe and aesthetic appreciation. One regular worshiper recalled how "the large, richly atmospheric interior, the illuminated high windows, the mighty organ, the trained choir . . . left an indelible impression."[2] The synagogues built later in the century and up until World War I, both in Berlin and in other German cities, were similarly conceived in that they too were monuments of magnificence to demonstrate Jewish emancipation and affluence. Men entered them wearing a top hat, entirely appropriate attire for a setting that had become distinctly formal and in which decorum was the most perceptible hallmark.[3]

Invariably and increasingly, however, the synagogues became monuments in a stricter sense. The three thousand seats of the New Synagogue (eighteen hundred for men and twelve hundred for women) were filled only for the holidays; for the most part, they remained empty. The parvenu excitement that attended the 1866 dedication could not sustain itself against the gains made by secularization. By the Weimar period even Jews who had remained in the countryside were at best selective in their religious observance and hardly scrupulous about refraining from work on the Sabbath. In larger cities such as Hamburg, Frankfurt, Berlin, and Breslau, the majority of Jews did not attend synagogue at all, even on the High Holy Days; in Hamburg the percentage of women who did not attend reached 74 by the late 1920s.[4] In that same commercial city, although there were remarkably few who officially left the community during the Weimar years,[5] barely 40 percent of the members belonged to a religious association (*Kultusverband*), and from 1925 to 1933, one quarter of all Jews getting married chose a non-Jew for a spouse.[6]

For the most part, Jewish life in the larger communities no longer focused on the synagogues. Political struggles among Liberals, Zionists, and Orthodox absorbed both energies and funds; ideological animosities frustrated cooperative religious endeavors.[7] The relationship between the individual and the community was defined in terms of advocacy of a political program, mostly dichotomized between Zionist and anti-Zionist. Adherence to a religious association was designated by the essentially impersonal and external term "membership" (*Angehörigkeit*).[8] Inside the synagogue the worshiper became part of an "audience," which either liked or disliked what was offered it, sometimes responding to a particularly fine sermon with applause.[9] Indeed, the rare occasions when synagogues were filled included performances of oratorios and concerts, such as that given in the New Synagogue in 1930, which featured a piece by Bach played on the violin by Albert Einstein.[10]

All of the eleven community synagogues in Berlin in the year 1927 (six of them Orthodox) were centrally administered through a single office in the Oranienburger Strasse. Although there were also local boards for each synagogue, significant decisions affecting religious life were made by the elected representatives of the organized community, the *Gemeinde*, as a whole. Community rabbis were not consistently associated with a single synagogue but preached in various locations within either the Liberal or Orthodox sector. Some did try to exercise a pastoral role by visiting the sick, holding regular counseling hours, and inviting laypeople to their homes on Friday evenings and holidays. But as Rabbi Alfred Jospe once said from the pulpit of the Levetzowstrasse Synagogue in Berlin, where he preached once or twice a month in the 1930s: "I'm supposed to be a shepherd of souls [i.e., a pastor], but I hardly know a single soul here."[11] Since rabbis were responsible to the central leadership of the community for every word and deed, they were constrained to articulate consensus views in all matters political and religious.[12]

The mechanical and impersonal character of Jewish religious life within the Gemeinde of the large city during the Weimar period is well illustrated by the annual effort in Berlin to accommodate the "three-day-a-year Jews." Since only a minority of the more than fifty thousand adult worshipers could fit into the eleven community synagogues, it was necessary, in the mid-1920s, to rent more than forty halls for the High Holy Day season. A "Festgottesdienst-Kommission" was given the task of finding and preparing dozens of cantors, choir directors and members of choirs, organists, and—most difficult of all—shofar blowers. Since there were not enough rabbis to go around, rabbinical students from the Breslau seminary and the Berlin Hochschule were engaged to give the sermons. Robes and birettas were distributed to the officiants. The liturgy itself was identical in the auxiliary services with what it was in the Orthodox or Liberal synagogues and, with few exceptions, it was read and sung in Hebrew. Although some halls were used repeatedly, new ones had to be rented as the population shifted westward. A special bureau dealt with the rental of seats; poorer community members, though they were all accommodated, could not hope for a place in one of the synagogues and had to make do with attending services in a *Betsaal*. These prayer halls included some of the largest public spaces in Berlin, with seats for as many as two thousand worshipers; among them were such well-known buildings as the Mozartsaal and even the Philharmonie.[13] Thus, attendance at High Holy Day services for most Berlin Jews meant going to a secular hall, probably a very large one; listening to the sermon of an unfamiliar rabbi or rabbinical student; and hearing a liturgy with which they were little acquainted, enacted by the officiants almost entirely in a language they did not understand. Their fellow worshipers, except by coincidence, were strangers with whom they had no relationship. As men and women invariably sat separately, families could not participate together. Only the familiar melodies still resonated and provided some continuity from year to year.[14]

Thus the collective image of Weimar Jewish religious life in the large cities, especially among Liberal Jews, is one of grand synagogues built a generation or more earlier and of a bureaucracy serving the minimal religious needs of an essentially secular and therefore religiously indifferent Jewry. Content with this status quo, however impersonal, Weimar Jews paid token tribute to their religion by an annual tax payment and the symbolic act of attending a worship service once or twice a year. But mostly they just did not want to be bothered. In its general outlines and for most Weimar urban Jews, this image is accurate. But it is not the whole story. To a remarkable and as yet not fully appreciated extent, the status quo in the Gemeinde aroused contemporary discontent from those active within the seemingly most indifferent sector, that of Jewish religious Liberalism. It was a discontent that rested upon new modes of thinking and manifested itself in various ways: in critique, in proposal, and in extraordinary innovation.

Gemeinschaft

As early as 1887, the sociologist Ferdinand Tönnies had sharply distinguished between *Gemeinschaft* (community) and *Gesellschaft* (association), finding the latter, with its substitution of institutional ties for organic ones, to be characteristic of modern times and the former to be the irrecoverable model of preindustrial ages. By the Weimar period, Gemeinschaft had ceased to be merely an analytical category and had become a social ideal, especially for young people and those on the left of the political spectrum. Among Jews it had become a favorite concept in the thinking of the young socialist Gustav Landauer, while those who declared themselves to be religious found it especially in the writings of Martin Buber. Unlike Tönnies, Buber believed that Gemeinschaft need not be assigned to the past, that it could be revived, albeit in somewhat different form, even in an age when the instrumental relationships of Gesellschaft were dominant. Unlike Landauer, Buber developed a religious conception of Gemeinschaft, in which the presence of God became an essential element.

Buber began to advocate the creation of a "new Gemeinschaft" at the turn of the century and continued to elaborate the concept as he moved toward the philosophy of interpersonal relationships represented by his book *I and Thou*. Unlike the old Gemeinschaft, based on ties of kinship, the new one would be founded upon elective affinities. Individualism blocked the way back to the natural connectedness of earlier ages, but it did not obviate the possibility of new forms of community. "A great yearning for Gemeinschaft courses through all the souls of soulful people at this life-moment of Western culture," wrote Buber in 1919.[15] The state, even a socialist state, could never fill the role of a community. That was possible only in the intimacy of small groups and only on the basis of religious relationships. Buber believed that the longing for Gemeinschaft was a longing for God and that only where individuals would allow God to exist could they create a true Gemeinschaft. The quest for community was, religiously speaking, a quest for redemption.

Yet Buber was consistently critical of the ability of organized religion to establish community. The religious denomination, he believed, only wants its own God. "Yet God wants to represent to the individual the meaning of the world and the eternal ideal; for the denomination, God is but the source of advantage in the world to come."[16] According to Buber, religious associations, like their secular counterparts, had taken on the degenerate status of statelike machines. He foresaw no salvation from the curse of unmitigated Gesellschaft characterizing church and synagogue. What was required, he argued, was not the reform of existing institutions but a revolution that would take place outside them.[17] To Buber's way of thinking, the Jewish Gemeinde, by its very nature as an organization, would always remain Gesellschaft and hence religiously sterile. Nonetheless, Gemeinschaft thinking did penetrate the organized Jewish community, where it set off a critique of the values represented by the magnificent monuments and liturgical formalities that were the religious legacy of the nineteenth century to the Jews of Weimar.

Among the most articulate critics was that most "establishment" of rabbis, Leo Baeck. In his essay "Community in the Metropolis," Baeck compared small-town Jewry, where the individual's family was a piece of the community and his community a large family, with Jewish life in the city where Jews were "accounted" part of the Gemeinde but did not "experience" it except upon rare occasions. "The *baal habbajis* [the householder]," he wrote, "has become the taxpayer. The personal element has been pushed aside and finally replaced by the statistical."[18] What had emerged was no longer community but mass, the natural element of politics but not of religion. Masses want to be impressed, and that was precisely the effect of the excessively large synagogues that addressed individuals in their mass, not in community. The relations among the individuals, Baeck admitted, had become those of a Gesellschaft, not a Gemeinschaft. Echoing Buber, Baeck noted that young people were looking for religiosity to counter the negative influences of the metropolis; but he offered no suggestions as to what concrete steps the organized Jewish community might take to meet their needs.

There were other critics as well. Jewish Liberals, longtime advocates of individualism, remained wary of collectivism, not only because they were suspicious of socialism but also because it made them think of Zionism. Nonetheless, they had come to realize, at the very least, that something had been lost. For the Liberals, "Gemeinschaft" became an ideal designation for their own understanding of themselves as Jews. It was more embracing than the nineteenth-century self-designation of religious denomination (*Konfession*) yet less than peoplehood. The longtime leader of organized Jewish religious Liberalism in Germany, Heinrich Stern, spoke readily of "communal consciousness" (*Gemeinschaftsbewusstein*) and "communal work" (*Gemeinschaftsarbeit*).[19] In 1927 the Liberals held a conference, "Gemeinschaft und Individuum," where Rabbi Max Dienemann of Offenbach admitted that the individualism of the earlier age had given way to a stronger sense of engagement, especially as a result of the collective experience of the war years. What needed to be done was to reconcile Gemeinschaft with the free will of individuals. Such Gemeinschaft could be spiritual rather than racial or national. In fact, the sense of belonging to a *Geistesgemeinschaft*, a spiritual community, might work to counter the threat of loss through mixed marriage.[20]

It was also increasingly felt that the existing synagogue, rather than furthering a sense of community, tended to be destructive of it. Here, for example, is one layperson's description of the contemporary worship experience:

> As magnificent as our large community synagogues are in many respects, and although much that is beautiful is offered in the services there, they fail to produce any real living effect. It is not the fault of the functionaries but is due to the fact that the Gemeinden in truth are not Gemeinden, not Gemeinschaften. One arrives, one listens to the service more or less passively, one departs. No one knows anyone else; no one plays any active role in the service, either in shaping it or in carrying it out. So, deep down, one remains unmoved.[21]

A leader of the Berlin Liberal movement asks rhetorically: "Hasn't our worship . . . today become theater? We no longer create worship, we the community!"[22]

The critique extended beyond the synagogue to the rabbinate. The rabbis, whom everyone called "Doctor" whether or not they had the title, were tied to pulpit and lectern when, as one writer in Buber's periodical *Der Jude* complained, the need was for religious leaders of the entire people, not obedient pulpiteers. Unfortunately, the rabbi had become the chief religious employee (*erster Kultusbeamte*)—dependent rather than independent, at the edge of the community rather than in its midst.[23]

Among the critics were also women. They too called for Gemeinschaft within the Liberal synagogue, but they had their special agenda as well. In the 1920s, women were beginning to play a larger role in Christian denominations, even as candidates for preaching positions in the Evangelical Church. In Jewish communities, too, a process of enfranchisement was beginning, as in one city after another women were given a vote in community elections and the right to hold office.[24] But their position in the synagogue remained unchanged. In German Liberal synagogues there were no barriers in front of the women's sections, and women sang in mixed choirs. In some synagogues women also sat on the same floor as the men; but they invariably sat separate. That was true even for services held in the main building of the religiously radical *Reformgemeinde*, and it was true as well for the oldest Reform institution, the Hamburg Temple.[25] Women could participate in neither the service that preceded their weddings nor the memorial services held in their homes after the death of a close relative. The confirmation of girls could not take place within a regular religious service but was relegated to a "celebration" (*Feier*) conducted entirely in German without Torah reading or prayerbook. Apparently in response to increasing dissatisfaction with the status quo, the *Jüdisch-liberale Zeitung*, in its issue of November 5, 1926, presented a symposium entitled "The Woman in the House of God," which consisted of ten statements regarding the role of women in the synagogue, seven of them by women. Not only did the participants, almost without exception, call for expanded activity by women in community and synagogue governance, but most insisted on enhanced participation inside the sanctuary as well. Of the seven women, four specifically raised the possibility of women rabbis. Their feminine talents, two of them argued, would be especially useful in the area of pastoral work.[26]

The growing desire to include women within the community leadership was paralleled by efforts to embrace young people. The latter, it was realized, as participants in Weimar youth culture, had a particularly lively sense of Gemeinschaft. But attempts to instill a sense of responsibility toward the existing community were of little avail.[27] Some non-Orthodox Jewish young people were indeed religious, but at the same time alienated from organized Judaism. "One could almost venture the paradox," wrote the journalist and rabbi's son Friedrich Thieberger, "that our generation is too deeply religious to reach the surface of religious life."[28] Recognizing the gap, Jewish communities tried to provide young people with their own ambience for Jewish worship. Special services were instituted not only for children but also for older youth who were encouraged to take over governance of the *Jugendgemeinde* and officiation at the services. Recognizing that the cultivation of their own *Gemeinschaftsbewusstsein*, their own consciousness of community, was the condition for the younger generation's participation in religious life, a leader of the Liberal Jewish youth movement urged the communal celebration of Friday evenings and holidays together in small homo-geneous groups.[29]

Questions also began to arise about the grandiose synagogue as a model for future construction. Even before the Weimar period the style of synagogues was beginning to change. The emphasis upon the street façade lessened; the outward focus gradually gave way to an internal one. The synagogues built in Essen (1913) and Augsburg (1917) were still immense, but they differed from their immediate predecessors in featuring courtyards and vestibules. The apparent intent was to make the synagogue more of what it had been traditionally—a center of social interchange—rather than, on the Christian model, solely a sacred space for divine worship.[30]

After the war, the Breslau synagogue architect Alfred Grotte set the tone for a very different sacral architecture when he wrote in 1922:

> To be sure, the synagogue is a space dedicated to prayer and therefore to God. But it lacks that sanctity which, for example, a Catholic church possesses on account of its housing a relic and the Host.[31] It is rather a place of being together (*Zusammenseins*) for the community praying to God, whose preacher is not a consecrated priest and which therefore is a space that knows no barrier between clergy and laity. Hence it is justifiable in place of the presumptuous designation "house of God" to choose the much more appropriate "house of prayer," a concept that came into existence long ago and under simi-lar circumstances within Protestantism.[32]

Grotte also believed that in a considerably poorer postwar Ger-many, simple, functional structures would be more appropriate than the grand ones of an imperial age.

Not surprisingly, the language of Gemeinschaft now also en-ters the discourse of Jewish synagogue architecture. Another archi-tect, Max Eisler, sharply reverses the direction of architectural purpose when he writes in 1926: "The Jewish temple of today wants to gather the faithful together, surrounding and encasing their silent Gemeinschaft, not directing attention to itself, but helping to focus their devotion inward."[33]

For economic reasons very few synagogues were actually built during the Weimar period. One of them was the synagogue in Plauen, completed in 1930. In part due to financial constraints, this new building, which was also architecturally the first truly modern synagogue in Germany, became a combination of sanctuary and community center. Here, as one writer noted, *Kult* and *Kultur* were united under one roof so that religion was organically reunited with the rest of Jewish life.[34]

In Berlin the only new structure to be built during the Weimar period was the Liberal synagogue on Prinzregentenstrasse, dedicated in 1930. Like its predecessors, it was large (2,300 seats), though almost a third smaller than the New Synagogue. What made it different was that it was the first and only community synagogue in Berlin where men and women sat together. The Liberals had only attained this concession with great difficulty and by a single vote in the assembly of community representatives. Strong opposition had emerged, especially within the Zionist Jüdische Volkspartei, which claimed that the proposal was divisive.[35] The new synagogue was novel in two other respects as well. First, its seating was partially in the round, rather than in the usual rectangular pattern. Although the stated purpose of the arrangement was to make the pulpit—where liturgy was enacted and sermons given—focal in the structure, it must also have enhanced the sense of community, since worshipers in the spacious balcony could look to each side and see one another's faces. Second, the ark could be separated from the auditorium by lowering an iron curtain, thus allowing the same space to be used for secular Jewish purpose as well.[36]

The last major synagogue to be completed before the rise of Hitler was the new Hamburg Temple, which, in addition to the main sanctuary, contained school rooms, a Gabriel Riesser Social Hall with adjoining kitchen, and a smaller prayer room. The intentions expressed in the year of its dedication in 1931 clearly indicate how fundamentally the model of the synagogue had changed. Its architect, Felix Ascher, defined the purpose of a contemporary Jewish house of worship as "the real gathering place (Sammelstätte) for modern Jews."[37] Its chief cantor, Leon Kornitzer, noted that for too long the congregation's music had neglected the worshipers in favor of the choir; with the new sanctuary, the time had come to introduce more community singing based on traditional Jewish motifs.[38] And the synagogue's rabbi, Bruno Italiener, called particular attention to the role of the second sanctuary within the structure, the "Kleine Tempel," which was intended for daily services: "By creating such a space, the Temple Association, despite the relatively large number of its adherents, returns in its work of inner construction to the principle of the small community which, as is well known, was for centuries the true nucleus for building up Judaism. The outer closer connectedness creates the condition for an inner connectedness, the external Gemeinschaft bridges the way toward a Gemeinschaft of the soul, toward the creation of a new community resting upon common feelings."[39]

But was such a Gemeinschaft really possible in any synagogue that was part of an organized religious community? Could Gemeinschaft theory, anchored in a romanticism that rejected religious discipline, be made the foundation of a faith that stressed the regular performance of religious duties? In the mid-1920s the intellectual periodical of the Liberal Weimar Jews, *Der Morgen,* published a number of articles that addressed this issue. The authors readily admitted that "religiosity," a concept much stressed by Buber and distinguished by him from "religion,"[40] could not serve as the basis for religious Gemeinschaft within the framework of any normative Judaism. It rested on religious experience (*Erlebnis*), while Judaism rested on religious life (*Leben*).[41] Experience could not create a "practicing" (*ausübende*) religious community. That was possible only, in the words of Rabbi Emil Schorsch, on the "unshakable basis of a religious sense of duty that remains independent of whims and romantic moods."[42] Yet the authors also recognized that a sense of Gemeinschaft had become a prerequisite if Liberal Jews were to be attracted to regular prayer, the religious duty most stressed by Jewish religious Liberalism. Eventually, during the Nazi years, one German rabbi, Ignaz Maybaum, would translate Gemeinschaft into the Hebrew word *chevrah* and, following Buber, understand the concept to mean a sacred community before God. But he went beyond Buber in insisting that the chevrah needed to be more than that. It needed regularly to become a *Gebetsgemeinschaft,* a community of prayer in which everyone was a full participant, not merely a "pious listener" (*andächtiger Zuhörer*); and then, when the Torah was taken from the ark, the worshipers needed to transform themselves into a *Lesegemeinschaft,* a reading community studying the text.[43] Yet all these ideas, articulated by the rabbinical leadership, did not prompt the official organs of the Jewish community to reform Liberal services in a way that would bring them nearer the stated goals. It required an initiative emanating from outside the elected lay establishment and the rabbinate to create just such a chevrah (what today is often called *chavurah*) within the skeptical, if not actually hostile Gemeinde of Berlin.

Gemeinschaft within Gemeinde

On Sabbath eve, November 30, 1923, a group of Berlin Jews gathered in the small synagogue of the Baruch Auerbach orphanage located at Schönhauser Allee 162 in the northern section of the city. There they conducted a religious service not authorized by community officials or initiated by any rabbi. The founders and participants were laypeople concerned about the failure of Liberal Judaism to provide the possibility for religious Gemeinschaft. Instead of arguing their case before the recognized organs of the community, they had decided to undertake their own bold experiment.

The moving spirit behind the venture was Hermann Falkenberg (1869–1936), a Jewish educator and Liberal activist who served first as a teacher at the girls and boys middle school of the Berlin community, later as senior instructor at the teachers seminary. Not only was Falkenberg its principal initiator, he was also its chief advocate and supporter.[44] Working closely with Falkenberg was another educator, Professor Josua Falk Friedländer (1871–1942), who taught modern languages, Latin, and Jewish religion in the general schools in Berlin and served on the educational commission of the Berlin Jewish community. Friedländer had studied at Jews' College in London, which was directed by his uncle, Michael Friedländer; and he used his knowledge in arranging the Sabbath liturgy for the new group.[45] The third main figure was Jonas Plaut (1880–1948), like the other two a pedagogue and also director of the orphanage that lent its synagogue to the group.[46]

These Liberal laymen and the others who joined them strongly felt that the service in the "organ synagogues" had become sterile. Having assumed a particular form in the second half of the nineteenth century, it became rigid and development ceased. The liturgy and ambience thereafter remained as fixed as they were in the Orthodox synagogues, unresponsive to shifts in religious thought and feeling. In the words of one member of the group, he too a teacher: "The days may finally be over when people believed that all you needed to do was set up an organ in the synagogue, organize a mixed choir, leave out some prayers, and—presto—you had a Liberal service."[47] On the other hand, they felt that the Reformgemeinde in Berlin, with its radically abbreviated and almost wholly German service, lacked historical roots. They preferred to look to the work of Abraham Geiger, the champion of historical Judaism, who toward the end of his life had served briefly in Berlin. They wanted to restart the process of religious development that had died with Geiger by incorporating the complementary influences of two more recent thinkers. Hermann Cohen's rationalism, indispensable for the way of thinking of modern city people, and Franz Rosenzweig's recognition of the power of faith were thought to be equally essential.[48] The group hoped to win the three-day-a-year Jews back to regular participation in prayer.

The services in the orphanage synagogue, which could hold about two hundred worshipers, differed fundamentally from those in the official Liberal synagogues. Worship on Friday evenings always began fifteen minutes to half an hour after businesses closed. People attending services were expected to arrive before they began and remain until they concluded, and they were expected to attend regularly. Although the major rubrics of the liturgy were retained, repetitions, such as of the *kaddish*, were consistently avoided. In contrast to the practice of the Reformgemeinde, Hebrew was retained for basic prayers, though there were more prayers recited in German than in the standard Liberal synagogues. The passages from the Torah were first read in German and then chanted in Hebrew. Each service was built around a particular religious theme with songs, sermons, original prayers, and special readings all reflecting it so that the service in its totality left the worshiper with a well-defined message. Each Sabbath offered a combination of traditional and novel elements.

But the most radical and remarkable characteristic of these services was their attempt to create a Gemeinschaft within the Gemeinde by focusing more on the worshipers than the liturgy. Those who came to the services were to be full participants, never simply listeners—at the center, not on the periphery. From the very beginning, women sat together with men.[49] Although there was a cantorially educated businessman, a young organist, and a small children's choir to lead the music, everyone was encouraged and expected to sing the hymns and responses together. Anything musical in the nature of a performance was scrupulously excluded. The cantor was to see himself as *sheliach tsibur*, the representative of the worshipers; the prayer was to be once more like the old simple *davnen*.[50] Especially in the first years, laypeople conducted the liturgy. Teachers, lawyers, doctors, and students delivered sermonettes, eight to fifteen minutes in length, until some dissatisfaction arose with their uneven quality. In order to increase participation, the full traditional number of seven men was called up to the reading of the Torah and—in sharp contrast to the Liberal community synagogues—those called up, especially boys celebrating their Bar Mitzvah, were trained and encouraged to read from the scroll themselves. The prophetic selection (*haftarah*) was always read by a layperson. As many congregants as possible were given other tasks, such as opening and closing the ark. Family occasions were noted publicly as part of the service.

The orphanage was located in that part of the city some called the "fortress" of Orthodoxy, where the Gemeinde had cared only for the religious needs of traditionalists. It was populated mainly by the poorer elements of Berlin Jewry, "simple, modest people who have to struggle hard for their living."[51] Its members, who had to pay dues (twelve marks per year in 1928) in addition to their community taxes, were principally from the middle and lower middle class. At first, they received no support from the organs of the community and no cooperation from most of the community rabbis. However, financial assistance did come from Liberal organizations and finally from the community as well.

Rabbinical leadership was also soon forthcoming. In 1925, Rabbi Martin Salomonski (1881–1944) moved to the capital, but as a teacher of Judaism, not a community rabbi. He was therefore free to become the regular rabbi of the new synagogue on Sabbaths and holidays. Salomonski, who was also a novelist, poet, synagogue composer, and founder of Jewish old age homes, became associated with the "Liberal Synagogue of the North," as it was soon called, in a more intimate way than community rabbis with the synagogues that they served.[52] In 1928, however, he became a community rabbi, leaving the group to rely once more primarily on lay preachers from its own midst, but also on rabbinical students from the Liberal seminary in Berlin and visiting rabbis from Berlin and other cities.[53]

For a time, the congregation made do by adapting the prayerbook used in the New Synagogue, but after four years it printed its own liturgy for the Friday night service.[54] Opening right to left, the little booklet edited by Friedländer began not with a choir selection but with congregational singing (Gemeindegesang). Later, the congregation was expected to join in all of the major responses. Theologically, the highly abbreviated liturgy remained quite conservative, retaining, in Hebrew and German, the faith both in a personal Redeemer and in resurrection. Appended were musical notes for the Hebrew responses and German hymns.

Although the congregation began with Friday evening worship in order to attract those Jews who worked the next day, it soon added services for Saturday morning (less well attended than those on Friday evening, which regularly filled the two hundred or so seats in the synagogue) and for all of the major Jewish holidays. On the High Holy Days the synagogue, not surprisingly, could scarcely hold even half of those who wanted to attend. On the Day of Atonement short introductions explained the special prayers for the day before they were recited. For 1925, we have the impressions of a Professor Leopold Wolff, who came to the Yom Kippur service as a skeptic and left with great enthusiasm. Wolff reported seeing "very many young people and couples" as well as "an imposing circle of older people" among whom he found some wearing both hats and traditional prayer robes (Käppchen und Kittel). As the day progressed, the devotion increased. Wolff concluded: "You must believe me when I say that this Day of Reconciliation reconciled me with Judaism because I again begin to hope."[55]

The congregation made a determined effort to revive active celebration of other holidays and to reinstitute customs neglected by the Liberals. During the weeklong holiday of Sukkot, evening and morning services were conducted in the common *sukkah;* and girls were confirmed during a regular holiday service. For Passover, the congregation conducted a communal *seder* on the second night and, in time for the holiday in 1929, produced its own Haggadah. The latter, edited by Falkenberg, was specifically directed to those Jews who had given up conducting a seder, those who "have preserved the memory of the seder evening in their hearts but to whom the traditional form no longer speaks or who are no longer able to awaken in their children the seder evening of their own youth."[56] The Haggadah itself differs from its traditional model in two noteworthy respects. First, it distinctly universalizes the message of freedom by extending it to all who are still enslaved and by including the midrash wherein God castigates the children of Israel for rejoicing while the Egyptians are drowning in the Red Sea. And second, it twice incorporates passages from Stefan Zweig's dramatic poem *Jeremias,* thus lending the volume an aura of contemporaneity.[57]

Recognizing the difficulty of attracting worshipers on weekdays, the congregation focused on observances and celebrations that would not interfere with work times. In 1926, it introduced *selichot,* the service composed of penitential prayers that takes place on a Saturday night shortly before the High Holy Days. It also developed a similar preparatory service (*Einstimmungsgottesdienst*) for the Saturday afternoon preceding Passover, concluding it with the *havdalah* ceremony separating the Sabbath from the rest of the week. These were innovations wholly uncharacteristic of German Liberal Judaism.[58]

Beginning with the High Holy Days in 1927, the group also held youth services, which likewise differed from the rule. Not only were the eves included, but also, to a much greater degree than was customary, the young people, using a specially adapted liturgy, led the service in Hebrew and German and presented the scriptural readings. A year later the number of those participating had doubled and monthly youth services on Friday evenings were introduced as well.[59]

The group wanted to see itself as a *kehillah* (best translated as "congregation," the American term usually inappropriate for Germany, but fitting in this instance), as working to restore the intimacy of the small circle that had once characterized Jewish communities but which the immense Berlin Gemeinde could not itself offer. The group was determined to "build religious life from the bottom up." In the fall of 1925, the congregation published the first issue of a periodical intended to elaborate its point of view, report on its activities, and present subjects of general Jewish religious interest. Not surprisingly, it was called *Die Gemeinschaft*,[60] since from the beginning the group had set itself apart from the synagogues of the Gemeinde as a self-conscious religious community where each "warmed the other with his fire."[61] One writer made the clear distinction: the Gemeinde represents Gesellschaft, the little synagogue in the north of Berlin Gemeinschaft. Some people, wary of too much personal involvement, would always prefer the former, the mass, but others would seek out the latter.[62]

The Liberal Synagogue of the North did not confine its activity to conducting worship services. Aside from the Reformgemeinde, it was the only religious organization in Berlin to hold regular "community evenings" (*Gemeindeabende*) at which topics of Jewish interest were discussed and social ties among the members were deepened. There were also Hebrew lessons and concerts associated with Jewish holidays. In 1926, *Die Gemeinschaft* carried an article arguing that religious commitment in Judaism implied social action, a connection rarely made in German Jewry, however characteristic it had become of Reform Judaism in America.[63] Governance was through a board that included women as well as men. Membership grew only gradually, rising from 101 to 138 in the first two years and then to about two hundred by 1928. But the congregation's influence was felt more widely, so that its leaders could claim they were the nucleus of a new movement, an avant-garde within Jewish religious Liberalism. Four years after the establishment of the synagogue community in the north, a similar venture was undertaken in 1927 in the southwest of Berlin, in the Cecilienschule in Wilmersdorf, where 350 people attended the first service. Here too, as in the north, regular attendance at services and other functions was made a duty of membership. The Wilmersdorf venture lasted for only three years, however, before being merged into the community's new Prinzregentenstrasse Synagogue, which then absorbed elements from it predecessor. In November 1928 two more synagogue communities of the new type were dedicated, one in the West End (also in a school auditorium) and one in the east.[64] Whereas in the West End the results were disappointing, in the east they surpassed expectations, which had been quite modest given the overwhelmingly conservative character of the lower-middle-class Jewry that lived in that part of Berlin. In the early 1930s, other experimental services on the model of the North were undertaken with varying degrees of success in Tempelhof-Oberspree, in the northeast and Reinickendorf/Wedding. The prayer pamphlet for Friday evenings was also used in some synagogues outside Berlin, and *Die Gemienschaft* reached a readership beyond the congregations.[65]

But the young movement was not to succeed as an independent entity. The Depression led to suspension of *Die Gemeinschaft* in 1930, and only one more double issue appeared in 1933, the year of the tenth anniversary.[66] In that same year Hermann Falkenberg wrote a retrospective of the movement. He concluded with these words, which he underlined for emphasis: "The year in which the Liberal Synagogue of the North is marking its tenth anniversary has not become a year of jubilation, for it cannot drive away the concern that perhaps the collective work of the Liberal Synagogue in Berlin is endangered, and therewith the blossoming buds of a living religious Judaism."[67] Nazi Germany would produce its own sense of forced Gemeinschaft among Jews, one hardly anticipated by those who sought, for a time, to create it voluntarily within the Gemeinde.

Notes

1. *Die Gemeinschaft. Hefte für die religiöse Erstarkung des Judentums* 12 (May 20, 1928): 14.
2. Georg Salzberger, "Erinerungen an Berlin," in *Gegenwart im Rückblick. Festgabe für die Jüdische Gemeinde zu Berlin 25 Jahre nach dem Neubeginn,* ed. Herbert A. Strauss and Kurt R. Grossmann (Heidelberg, 1970), 249.
3. See the recollections of Emil Schorsch in *Jüdisches Leben in Deutschland. Selbstzeugnisse zur Sozialgeschichte 1918–1945,* ed. Monika Richarz (Stuttgart, 1982), 187, and note this description by James J. Walters-Warschaurer of his father, Rabbi Malwin Warschaurer, conducting a service at the New Synagogue in Berlin: "For many who attended my father's services, it created an unforgettable impression when he slowly ascended the steps leading to the ark of the Torah where he stopped below the eternal light and bowed his head before the ark and then proceeded slowly to mount the pulpit. When the last sound of the organ had died away, an eager congregation waited to listen to him in complete silence" (*Leo Baeck Institute Year Book* [*LBIYB*] 26 [1981]: 199).
4. Jacob Borut, "Religious Life among the Village Jews in the Western Parts of Weimar Germany" (in Hebrew), in *Yehudei Weimar: Hevra bemashber ha-moderni'ut, 1918–1933,* ed. Oded Heilbronner (Jerusalem, 1994), 90–107. In 1929 it was estimated that in Berlin at least fifty thousand adults did not go to services at all; the majority of the eighty thou-

sand who did go attended only on the High Holy Days. See *Jüdisch-liberale Zeitung* [*JLZ*], February 22, 1929.

5. "It was still the case that society expected everyone to belong to a religion. Where there were churches there also had to be synagogues lest the Jewish community be branded Communist. In many instances this meant doing no more than forwarding the community tax, apart from which the taxpayers simply desired to be left in peace" (recollections of Schorsch in Richarz, *Jüdisches Leben*, 184).

6. Ina S. Lorenz, "Die jüdische Gemeinde Hamburg 1860–1943," in *Die Juden in Hamburg 1590 bis 1990*, ed. Arno Herzig (Hamburg, 1991), 86–90; Georg Salzberger, "Die jüdisch-christliche Mischehe," *Der Morgen* 5 (1920): 18–30. The only rabbis who would officiate at a mixed marriage ceremony were those who served the radical *Reformgemeinde* in Berlin.

7. In Danzig a *Gemeindeverein*, established after the war on a neutral basis, was briefly successful in holding well-attended, community-wide Hanukkah and Purim celebrations. But before long politicization (along with other factors) led to its dissolution. See Samuel Echt, *Die Geschichte der Juden in Danzig* (Leer, 1972), 103.

8. For example, Ina Lorenz, *Die Juden in Hamburg zur Zeit der Weimarer Republik. Eine Dokumentation* (Hamburg, 1987), 1:584–85.

9. Alfred Jospe, "A Profession in Transition: The German Rabbinate, 1910–1939," *LBIYB* 19 (1974): 52.

10. H. G. Sellenthin, *Geschichte der Juden in Berlin und des Gebäudes Fasanenstrasse 79/80* (Berlin, 1959), 67. Most of the items on the program, however, were cantorial music.

11. *Im jüdischen Leben. Erinnerungen des Berliner Rabbiners Malwin Warschauer* (Berlin, 1995), 10–11; Jospe, "Profession in Transition," 52.

12. Alexander Altmann, "The German Rabbi: 1910–1939," *LBIYB* 19 (1974): 33.

13. Salzberger, "Erinnerung an Berlin," 249.

14. *JLZ*, September 2 and 9, 1927.

15. Martin Buber, *Worte an die Zeit*, part 2, *Gemeinschaft* (Munich, 1919), 17.

16. Paul R. Flohr and Bernard Susser, "Alte und neue Gemeinschaft: An Unpublished Buber Manuscript," *Association for Jewish Studies Review* 1 (1976): 51.

17. For Buber's views on *Gemeinschaft*, see, inter alia, Paul Mendes-Flohr, *From Mysticism to Dialogue: Martin Buber's Transformation of German Social Thought* (Detroit, 1989), and Michael Löwy, *Jewish Libertarian Thought in Central Europe: A Study in Elective Affinity* (Stanford, 1988), 48–55. More broadly on "Gemeinschaft" in relation to "Gemeinde," see Michael Brenner, *The Renaissance of Jewish Culture in Weimar Germany* (New Haven, 1996), 36–65.

18. Leo Baeck, "Gemeinde in der Grossstadt" (1929) in his *Wege im Judentum* (Berlin, 1933), 294.

19. "Wie wecken wir das religiöse Interesse?" *JLZ*, February 12, 1926.

20. *JLZ,* October 28, 1927. See also, in the same issue, the lecture by Erich Bayer of Breslau, "Der Kultus, die Gemeinschaft und das Individuum."

21. George Goetz, "'Die Gemeinschaft,' " *JLZ,* October 29, 1926.

22. Ernst Heinrich Seligsohn, "Der 'Laie,' " *Die Gemeinschaft* 3 (March 25, 1926): 10. Seligsohn wanted the rabbi to assume a position within the congregation as *primus inter pares,* not above it, and for worshipers to have the opportunity to address each other since "if everyone knows of everyone else that he has something to say to him here in the house of God, then the community grows together. Indeed, only then does it become a community."

23. F. L. Bernstein, "Der Rabbiner und die Gemeinde," *Der Jude* 2 (1917/18): 491–93.

24. In Berlin the Liberals secured political equality for women in 1924. In Hamburg women acquired it in the Temple Association the same year, but in the general community the right to hold communal office was delayed until 1930.

25. Even in the new Hamburg Temple building, completed in 1931, women still sat in women's galleries. However, in contrast to traditional synagogues, the specifications called for as many seats for them as for the men. See Harold Hammer-Schenk, *Synagogen in Deutschland. Geschichte einer Baugattung im 19. und 20. Jahrhundert (1780–1933)* (Hamburg, 1981), 1:536.

26. The ten participants were Rabbi Hermann Vogelstein, Else Dormitzer, Hedwig Reiss, Henriette May, Moritz Galliner, Minna Schwarz, Paula Ollendorf, Emil Blumenau, Bianka Hamburger, and Martha Coblenz.

27. Salzberger, "Die jüdisch-christliche Mischehe," 30.

28. "Lebensform und religiöse Form," *Der Jude* 8 (1924): 58.

29. Max Vogelstein, "Wir und die andern," in *Zur religiösen Erneuerung des Judentums* (n.p. [Arbeitsgemeinschaft jüdisch-liberaler Jugendvereine Deutschlands], n.d.), 23. The *Jugendgottesdienst,* which apparently goes back well before Weimar, was, however, only a partial success in the Orthodox and Liberal synagogues that instituted it. See *Die Gemeinschaft* 13/14 (August 8, 1928): 14. For the High Holy Days the Berlin Community organized thirteen youth services, some in the auditoriums of synagogues, for children from the ages of eight to fourteen. These services, of course, had no more sense of community than did their adult counterparts. See *Gemeindeblatt der Jüdischen Gemeinde zu Berlin* 14 (1924): 210.

30. Hammer-Schenk, *Synagogen in Deutschland,* 1:506.

31. This contrasts sharply with the view Jews themselves widely held of the synagogue during the nineteenth century. See Michael A. Meyer, " 'How Awesome Is This Place!' The Reconceptualization of the Synagogue in Nineteenth Century Germany," chapter 14 in this volume.

32. "Der Synagogentypus der Nachkriegszeit," *C.V.-Zeitung* 1 (1922): 133; cited in part also in Hammer-Schenk, *Synagogen in Deutschland,* 1:507.

33. "Vom neuen Geist der jüdischen Baukunst," *Menorah* 4 (1926): 521. Eisler also wanted to move the reader's lectern back to the center of the synagogue, its traditional location.

34. Max Eisler, "Neue Synagogen," *Menorah* 8 (1930): 544. Similarly, the Munich architect Fritz Landauer argued the need to bring the organizational life of the Jewish community back into contact with its religious life in a single structure that would serve as a "Gemeindezentrum." See "Jüdische Kultbau von heute," *C.V.-Zeitung* 10 (1931): 342.

35. *JLZ*, February 22, 1929. Rabbinical opinion on this subject, even among Liberal rabbis, was divided. Three rabbis favored mixed seating: Louis Blumenthal, Julius Galliner, and Max Weyl; three were opposed: Juda Bergmann, Julius Lewkowitz, and Malwin Warschauer. Max Weiner and Leo Baeck took intermediate positions. Baeck favored a synagogue that had sections for those who wanted to sit together and for those who wanted to sit separately. The Orthodox rabbis were unanimously opposed. Still in 1935 the Liberal rabbi of Frankfurt an der Oder expressed the view that allowing men and women to sit together was distinctly Christian and allowing women to become religious leaders characteristically pagan. See Ignaz Maybaum, *Parteibefreites Judentum. Lehrende Führung und priesterliche Gemeinschaft* (Berlin, 1935), 55–56.

36. Hammer-Schenk, *Synagogen in Deutschland*, 1:516–17.

37. Lorenz, *Die Juden in Hamburg*, 1:691. Of interest also is Ascher's statement six years later comparing the new structure with its predecessor: "If the old temple in the Poolstrasse was a place exclusively devoted to worship, the new structure in its multifaceted configuration has become a place for the nurture of Jewish community life in its wider sense and constitutes the focus of our Temple community's religious, cultural and intellectual life" ("Der neue Tempel," in *Festschrift zum hundertzwanzigjährigen Bestehen des Israelitischen Tempels in Hamburg 1817–1937*, ed. Bruno Italiener [Hamburg, 1937], 45).

38. Lorenz, *Die Juden in Hamburg*, 1:690.

39. Ibid., 1:694. In referring to the social hall, Italiener noted both Christian and the well-known American Jewish precedents.

40. Martin Buber, *Vom Geist der Religion* (Leipzig, 1916), 50–52.

41. Felix Goldmann, "Religiöse Not," *Der Morgen* 2 (1926): 399.

42. "Jüdische Frömmigkeit in der deutschen Landgemeinde," *Der Morgen* 6 (1930): 49.

43. Maybaum, *Parteibefreites Judentum*, 4, 41, 44.

44. *JLZ*, November 20, 1929; Ernst G. Lowenthal, *Juden in Preussen. Ein biographisches Verzeichnis* (Berlin, 1981), 60. *Wegweiser durch das jüdische Berlin. Geschichte und Gegenwart* (Berlin, 1987), 194, gives the year of his birth as 1869. So closely was the group associated with him that the institution was sometimes called the Hermann-Falkenberg-Synagogue.

45. E. G. Lowenthal, *Bewährung im Untergang. Ein Gedenkbuch*, 2nd ed. (Stuttgart, 1966), 51–53; *Die Gemeinschaft* 21/22 (November 24, 1933): 33. He died in Theresienstadt.

46. Lowenthal, *Juden in Preussen*, 181. Like Friedländer and Falkenberg, Plaut was one of the lay preachers. He was able to leave Germany in 1939. Rabbi W. Gunther Plaut, who celebrated his Bar Mitzvah in the synagogue, is his son.

47. *Die Gemeinschaft* 12 (May 20, 1928): 14. The author is Levy Rosenblatt (1888–1944) who, like Friedländer, taught in the Berlin school system. On Rosenblatt, see Lowenthal, *Bewährung im Untergang,* 141.

48. Hermann Falkenberg, "Bericht über die 10 jährige Tätigkeit der Liberalen Synagoge Berlin" (mimeographed; n.p., n.d., but almost certainly Berlin, 1933).

49. Of the High Holy Day services it was reported that women declared, "Here for the first time a genuine holiday sentiment (*Jaumtauwstimmung*) had seized them since they had heard the word of God while sitting by the side of husband and child" (*Die Gemeinschaft* 2 [December 11, 1925]: 8).

50. Heinrich Stern, "Einige Gedanken und Anregungen zum Gottesdienst," *Die Gemeinschaft* 21/22 (November 24, 1933): 19.

51. Jonas Plaut, "Ein Jahrfünft Liberale Synagoge Norden," *Die Gemeinschaft* 13/14 (August 18, 1928): 10.

52. Lowenthal, *Bewährung im Untergang,* 142–45. Salomonski died in or on the way to Auschwitz.

53. On August 17, 1928, the synagogue held a festive service on the occasion of the World Union for Progressive Judaism conference in Berlin. The speaker, who addressed the group in English, was Julian Morgenstern, president of the Hebrew Union College in Cincinnati.

54. Entitled *Das Freitagabend-Gebet,* it appeared as issue no. 10 of *Die Gemeinschaft* (December 18, 1927).

55. *JLZ,* November 6, 1925. Wolff may have been an anthropologist.

56. *Die Gemeinschaft* 19/20 (April 11, 1930): 20.

57. *Haggada für die Sederabende.* It appeared as no. 16/17 of *Die Gemeinschaft* (Pesach, 1929). Like the earlier Liberal Haggadah by Caeser Seligmann (*Hagada. Liturgie für die häusliche Feier der Sederabende* [Frankfurt am Main, 1913]), on which it was partly based, it omits the call for vengeance (*shefoch chamatcha*) but, in contrast to it, does include the Ten Plagues. The following year Falkenberg gave a course for men and women in the Fasanenstrasse synagogue on how to conduct a seder using his Haggadah (*JLZ,* April 2, 1930).

58. Hermann Falkenberg, " 'Erew' oder Die Stunde des Bereitmachens," *Festgabe für Claude G. Montefiore* (Berlin, 1928), 30–34.

59. *Die Gemeinschaft* 12 (May 20, 1928): 13, and *Die Gemeinschaft* 15 (December 7, 1928): 12; Falkenberg, "Bericht," 9. There was apparently also an unspecified number of groups of non-Orthodox young people, probably in their twenties, who at this time were privately conducting totally independent, "secret" worship services, probably in private homes. The origins of these groups were almost certainly in the Jewish youth movement, which had taught them that certain acts assumed significance only when they are done together. Their conscious intent was to transfer the idea of *Lebensgemeinschaft* to the religious realm—not so much to reform the liturgy as to transform its human context. Deeply under the influence of Buber, they rejected edification as the goal of worship and

substituted for it nothing less than "the dialogue of the individual and the Gemeinschaft with God." Such prayer, one of their number held, was always a nonrepeatable, intrinsically valid act. It could not be borne by a collectivity numbering in the thousands but only by "a community that knows itself and has grown together" (eine sich kennende, eine zusammengewachsene Gemeinschaft). The groups had no choir; their prayer leaders and preachers were themselves part of the Gemeinschaft. Those who gave the sermons did not in fact preach but instead articulated feelings the worship experience had aroused in them; or they taught a passage from a classical Jewish text. Some groups used only Hebrew in the service; others included German. They were more radical than the Gemeinde Liberals in that they did not repeat prayers, but they also rediscovered some that the Liberals had thrown out. One such group, it was reported, built its own *sukkah* in the countryside. See Ernst Heinrich Seligsohn, "Gottesdienst der Jugend," *JLZ*, November 25, 1927. Regrettably, I have not been able to find further sources on this interesting phenomenon and therefore cannot judge its extent or duration.

60. The issues generally appeared in advance of Jewish holidays and initially focused on them. Later issues were devoted to community institutions or religious questions. Three issues were dedicated to exemplary figures: Abraham Geiger, Moses Mendelssohn, and Franz Rosenzweig. Altogether twenty-two numbers (some of them double issues) appeared between September 19, 1925, and November 24, 1933. Today it is exceedingly rare. I was able to use a microfilm copy made from the holdings of the Leo Baeck Institute in New York and supplement it with the group's Haggadah in the Hebrew Union College Library in Cincinnati. However, I have not been able to obtain issue no. 18 and part of issue no. 21/22.

61. George Goetz, "Die 'Gemeinschaft,' " *JLZ*, October 29, 1926.

62. [Benno] Gottschalk, "Gemeindeabende," *Die Gemeinschaft* 13/14 (August 18, 1928): 21.

63. The article, "Soziale Pflichten" (*Die Gemeinschaft* 3 [March 25, 1926]: 7–8) dealt with poverty in the Prenzlauer Berg neighborhood in which the synagogue was located and called upon the northern branch of the Liberal Association to instill the conviction "that social work means the fulfillment of religious duty, that social sentiment and social action are the foundations of true Judaism. The obligation of the Liberal associations is not fulfilled by arousing religious feelings through worship. It is just as necessary to sharpen the social conscience, for only out of the union of both does true religious Judaism arise." The author who signed only as B. F. was undoubtedly Bertha Falkenberg, Hermann's activist wife, who was third on the list of Liberal candidates for the Berlin Jewish representative assembly in 1930. See *JLZ*, November 27, 1930. On this subject see also Walter Krojanker, "Judentum und Wirtschaft," *JLZ*, January 14, 1927, where reference is made to the social

consciousness of the Jewish Religious Union in England and of circles within international Protestantism.

64. Each of these three synagogues had two women on its governing board of eleven or twelve directors.

65. One source refers to it as "the periodical read by so many" (*JLZ*, November 20, 1929). Still, the very large figure of three thousand copies per issue that is given in the *Jüdisches Jahrbuch für Gross-Berlin* ([1928], 149), seems unlikely.

66. It contained contributions not only by the leaders of the group but also by Rabbis Leo Baeck, Benno Gottschalk, and Hermann Sanger; by Professor Ismar Elbogen of the Hochschule für die Wissenschaft des Judentums; and by Heinrich Stern, the leading lay figure among the Liberals.

67. Falkenberg, "Bericht," 16. However, Rabbi W. Gunther Plaut, in a letter to me dated September 30, 1995, recalled that services were still being held in the Auerbach Synagogue as late as the summer of 1937. For a recently published recollection of the "Hermann-Falkenberg-Synagogen," see Nathan Peter Levinson, *Ein Ort ist, mit wem du bist. Lebensstationen eines Rabbiners* (Berlin, 1996), 37.

CHAPTER 17

The German Model of Religious Reform and Russian Jewry

Historians of the religious reform movement in modern Jewry have been notably neglectful of Eastern Europe. They have projected a historical image which takes definitive shape in Germany, is more faintly reproduced in other Western European countries, and is later refocused somewhat differently in America. It is scarcely visible at all in Russia except in those instances where German-speaking Jews ventured eastward. When Simon Bernfeld first published his history of the Reform movement in 1900, the Russian Empire was absent from its pages. Only when he reissued the volume in 1923, with an added chapter on "recent currents," did Bernfeld see fit to devote a few very tendentious and undocumented paragraphs to the religious reform proposals of Y. L. Gordon, Moses Lilienblum, and Peretz Smolenskin.[1] David Philipson, on the penultimate page of his standard work on the Reform movement, written in 1907, simply noted in brief that "even in Russia, supposedly the land of orthodoxy par excellence, have there been and are there individual writers, like Leon Gordon, M. L. Lilienblum, R. A. Brodes [sic] and others, who have given voice to views similar to those whereof the reform movement is the recognized exponent."[2] The second edition of Philipson's work, in 1930, did not even include this much. Philipson believed that since he found no organized effort to break away from the rabbinical interpretation of Judaism within Russian Jewry, it did not belong within his purview.

If indeed modern Jewish religious reform is so narrowly defined as to include only substantive change in the prayers and the complete supersession of rabbinic Judaism, then only an occasional echo of it is to be found in the East. However, a broader definition, embracing other endeavors, intellectual and practical, to harmonize Jewish tradition with modes of thought and expression which characterized European culture since the eighteenth century, yields considerable material for analysis.

Although some scholars have drawn attention to new religious ideas and practical reforms comparable to those in the West, they have done so either within the context of general history, while dealing with related subjects, or in specific studies of an individual or an institution.[3] Jewish religious reform in Eastern Europe of the nineteenth century as a subject in its own right remains virtually unexplored. What needs to be done initially is to locate those religious phenomena in Eastern Europe which represent a modernizing religious reform. The second step is to determine the origins of these tendencies both in the context of Eastern European Jewry's political and intellectual milieu, and in relation to the model of such religious reform presented by German Jewry. One must also endeavor to assess the relative significance of this particular Jewish religious confrontation with modernity in terms of its breadth and depth of impact. Finally, since after considerable discussion, agitation, and experimentation, this impact—where it was felt most strongly—resulted eventually in secularist, rather than revised religious forms of thought and behavior, the causes for this failure of religious reform must be determined in reference to all of the relevant factors affecting the material and spiritual situation of Russian Jewry.

This essay claims to be nothing more than a first venture, seeking to map out the territory, to draw certain comparisons between Germany and Russia, and to offer some thoughts regarding the specific nature and scope of Jewish religious reform in Eastern Europe. Much more will have to be done to broaden the evidence, to test and refine the interpretation.

Our point of departure will be German Jewry. Even as the Russian Haskalah was to a large extent inspired from the West, often mediated via Galicia, so too did religious reform in Eastern Europe receive its impetus from a Jewish community that served it as the model of religious modernity. Yet the course of Jewish intellectual development in German Jewry was clearly different from Russia. In Germany the same energies that produced the "Berlin Haskalah" of the late eighteenth century soon flowed into a movement of religious, especially liturgical, reform, as cultural integration quickly ceased to be a disputed issue and as both non-Jews and the Jews themselves rapidly came to define Jewish identity predominantly in religious terms. By the 1840s, there were few Jews anywhere in the

German states who remained closed to German culture. Champions of religious orthodoxy were almost as rooted in modern European civilization as were less observant Jews. The issues that divided them were matters of religious belief and practice.

In Eastern Europe the conflict between Hasidim and Mitnagdim, with its roots in the latter half of the eighteenth century, continued to dominate the scene, though the mutual enmity waned. The newly emergent intellectual element, the Haskalah, was not in its essence a religious movement but an effort to attain broader cultural horizons, to create a secular Jewish literature, and to modernize and rationalize Jewish education. It drew upon the eighteenth-century example of the Jewish philosopher and man of German letters, Moses Mendelssohn, not upon the nineteenth-century German religious reformers. Religious reform was at times part of the Haskalah program, but it was not its essence. The contemporary German model—which included varying degrees of theological, aesthetic, political, and legal revision—was therefore limited in its appeal. It was not wholly applicable to the context and strivings of Russian Jewry. Yet religious reform was not an insignificant or side issue. Could German Jewry, after all, be taken as a model of westernization without reflecting on how it has subsequently dealt with religious modernization?

In considering religious reform in Russia, we shall therefore note and attempt to explain its similarities with the German model and its divergences from it. We shall focus our attention first on the "German" synagogues in Russia, then on the Max Lilienthal episode, on the role of the rabbinate, and finally on the writings of three men, who though they were known primarily as Maskilim, put forward an interesting variety of proposals for religious reform.

Synagogue reform in Eastern Europe was not modeled on the German Reform movement; it was associated with German Jewry as a whole. The Hamburg Temple, with its modified prayerbook and its worship service conducted partly in the vernacular, did not serve as an example, nor did the liturgical reforms which were penetrating more gradually into other German Jewish communities.[4] What became exemplary of modern religious expression for those East European Jews most exposed to the currents of Western culture was the formal ambience of the synagogue service which, with variations, had become standard in the central synagogues of many German communities by the middle of the nineteenth century. Reformers in Eastern Europe drew on those elements which had become the common reform of German Judaism, applying no less to the service conducted in the Hamburg community synagogue under the supervision of Hakham Isaac Bernays than to the separatist temple of that city. Little wonder that the East European congregations which introduced reforms were not thought of as reforming but simply as re-creating a German synagogue in the Russian Empire.

Toward the middle of the nineteenth century, "German" prayer services were established in a number of Russian cities: in Odessa, Warsaw, Riga, and Vilna.[5] The distinguishing elements common to these congregations were principally aesthetic. The service was conducted in an orderly, decorous manner. A cantor and a choir of boys presented the musical portions of the service, introducing uniformity of cadence. Disruptive elements were removed from the synagogue, rendering its atmosphere more worshipful, but also less informal and relaxed. The Western-style sermon represented the greatest innovation. On the German model,[6] it was a moral discourse intended to edify, inspire, and instruct. It differed both from the learned Talmudic discourses delivered upon occasion by East European rabbis and from the entertaining, often ingenious biblical interpretations of the popular Magidim. This new type of sermon, borrowed by German Jewish preachers from their Christian counterparts and adapted to Jewish values and symbols, was usually delivered in the German language (the modern tongue closest to Yiddish), though there are also Hebrew examples, and during the second half of the century Russian and Polish began to take the place of German.

The initiators of these congregations and their spiritual leaders often came from abroad. In Odessa, the modern synagogue, established in 1841, was known as the "Broder Shul" because its members were mostly immigrants from Galicia. These three hundred or so families represented a well-to-do mercantile element, possessing international connections, and heir to the Galician Haskalah. In 1847 they dedicated a lovely new sanctuary where attendance numbered in the hundreds. The music was said to rival that of the Viennese cantor, Solomon Sulzer, and to be "both edifying and appealing."[7] In the unique setting of Odessa, where the Galicians aristocratically dominated community affairs, the Brody synagogue came to serve as a model for the larger community house of worship, which in the course of time adopted some of its reforms. In 1860 the Odessa community imported as its official rabbi Dr. Simon Schwabacher from Württemberg, who for nearly twenty years had served congregations in Austria, Germany, and Galicia. He immediately introduced weddings within the community synagogue rather than in its courtyard. But as a rule he attended services in the Brody synagogue where he gave regular German sermons and presided over confirmations. When Schwabacher came under attack, it was not so much for his modernity, as for his lack of facility in Russian.[8]

In Warsaw the "German Jewish congregation," consisting of some 300 families, invited Abraham Goldschmidt, who had first given a sermon there in 1838, to be its regular preacher. Goldschmidt was born into an enlightened family in Posen, studied in Breslau and later in Berlin, where he received a doctorate. During his studies in the West, he had made it a point to hear the sermons of the best-known German preachers. In fact his German roots were sufficiently deep that he felt increasingly less at home within the ever more fervently Polish enlightened stratum of Warsaw Jewry, leaving there to accept a pulpit in Leipzig in 1858.[9] Later this congregation became exceptional in the Russian Empire by making ideological omissions in the prayerbook and reciting a portion of the liturgy in the vernacular.[10]

Jews in the Baltic states possessed a particularly strong German attachment. Courland and Livonia had originally belonged to the Teutonic Order before being annexed by Russia, and they preserved their German cultural heritage. The Christian population was predominantly Protestant and jealously guarded its special privileges against incursions from the central government in St. Petersburg.[11] The Jews here were likewise more Germanic than their coreligionists elsewhere in the Czarist Empire. A portion of them dressed in the German fashion, spoke the German language, and engaged in secular study.[12] In their case the German cultural orientation was not limited to a circle of wealthy immigrants or Maskilim that set itself apart from the general community. In 1837 the official leadership of the Jewish community of Riga, which was engaged in seeking permanent residence rights in the city itself, sought to strengthen its political position and at the same time to provide for its educational and spiritual needs through the establishment of a modern school and the introduction of regular sermons in the synagogue. Unable to find anyone properly qualified for the position of head teacher and preacher within the Russian "fatherland," they turned to the German rabbi Ludwig Philippson, editor of the *Allgemeine Zeitung des Judentums*, with the request to suggest someone "who would enable us to experience the sounds of our native tongue, and who is, moreover, sufficiently familiar with the intellectual movement of the Jews in Germany—in other words, a German." Only such a man, they believed, could speak to their hearts. The candidate was to combine thorough Jewish learning with scientific education (*wissenschaftliche Bildung*), to be genuinely pious and not disinclined to the ceremonial components of religion. They did not seek a rabbi, since the community already possessed someone who functioned in a Jewish judicial capacity.[13]

Max Lilienthal[14] was the candidate chosen for the Riga position. Born in Munich, Lilienthal had received a doctorate from the university there in 1837. He was twenty-three years of age when in 1839 he traveled to Russia to assume his position. On the way he stopped to consult with a number of Jewish religious leaders in Germany. Apparently he was especially impressed by Philippson, whose model he sought to follow and whose portrait adorned his wall in Riga.[15]

In his capacity as preacher, Lilienthal introduced two major innovations. The first was a German sermon delivered every third sabbath, on holidays and on special occasions. Yet even in this most Germanic portion of the Russian Empire, Lilienthal's inspirational, flowery messages were appreciated by only a portion of his listeners, while his pure German language left some unable to comprehend his words. In a letter to his brother[16] he noted that those who came sought either entertainment or an opportunity for criticism, but unlike a German congregation, they did not seek edification. Used to the style of the Magidim or of the halakhic discourse, they did not easily adjust to so unfamiliar a form. It appears that Lilienthal also wore clerical garb such as had been adopted by modern rabbis all along the religious spectrum in Germany. However, once he began to introduce sermons that were more similar to the familiar *derush*, Lilienthal was able to reach larger numbers and even local Polish Jews would attend. Rabbinic citations from Talmud and Midrash appeared in his sermons, though it was always a particular biblical text that was chosen for special attention. Although during his brief tenure in Riga, Lilienthal did not introduce any substantive changes into the liturgy, and thus maintained the good will of the traditional rabbi, his sermons reflected the political reorientation which was more characteristic of German Jewry than of Russian. Palestine was for him "the spiritual fatherland of the divine faith of all human beings" while the wish expressed at Passover to celebrate the holiday the following year in Jerusalem was interpreted to refer to that city's heavenly counterpart.[17]

Lilienthal's second major innovation in Riga was the confirmation ceremony for girls, which was held in the synagogue on the Feast of Weeks in 1840. Twenty-three young ladies, who had completed a course of religious instruction in the fundamentals of the Jewish faith, were publicly asked questions from the catechism composed by the German Reform rabbi Solomon Herxheimer four years earlier. Then both parents were called upon to bless their daughters.[18]

When Lilienthal left Riga to work for the government in St. Petersburg, the Riga community, in 1843, again appointed a university-educated Bavarian, Abraham Neumann, to take his place and in 1854 to assume the rabbinical office as well. In the course of time the community developed a decorous service led by a musically trained cantor and choir. But the liturgy and customs of the synagogue remained traditional.[19]

In neighboring Courland the pattern was similar, though somewhat delayed. Lilienthal delivered a German sermon in Mitau for a special occasion in 1840,[20] but the service seems to have remained unchanged until Solomon Pucher, one of the early graduates of the Vilna Rabbinical Seminary, became the official rabbi of the community in 1859. Though born in Poland and without university education, Pucher was acquainted with the work of the "new Jewish theologians" in Germany, including Ludwig Philippson and Samuel Hirsch. He introduced German sermons and, like Lilienthal twenty years earlier in Riga, a confirmation ceremony for girls. But despite his best efforts during a tenure of more than thirty years, Pucher's attempts to institute further reforms met with insuperable opposition. While a good many among the five thousand souls in his community were "rationalists," Pucher explained in a tract against Christian missionaries published in 1867, Mitau Jewry was more susceptible to the charge of religious excess than religious insufficiency. He went on to paint a picture of virtually universal sabbath and holiday observance and of Jewish homes where almost without exception dietary laws were observed with "primitive stringency."[21]

The separatist congregation of the Vilna Maskilim was as conservative as the other "German" synagogues even though its members were severe critics of majority religious attitudes in Lithuanian Jewry. The details of its origins are not entirely clear and our principal contemporary source,[22] apparently for personal reasons, is unsympathetic to the enterprise. However, it seems that some time during the early 1840s a group of young Maskilim, who felt ostracized and alienated from the general community, established a Sabbath prayer service in the home of a traditional but tolerant Jew whose sons were part of the circle. The participants gathered there from all over the city, not only in order to pray together but also for the opportunity to discuss the events of the day and to provide one another moral support in their enlightenment endeavors. Through their communal worship they were able to give ritual form to their own interpretation of Jewish identity as open to the modern world.

It seems to have been this desire for collective religious expression among the like-minded, rather than criticism of the existing service, which brought them together. The group was originally called the "Berlin prayer circle" (*minyan berliner*) because—typically for the Russian Maskilim of the time—its members' Jewish orientation was modeled on that of the earlier Mendelssohnian Haskalah, but probably also because the service bore a resemblance to that of German synagogues.

A second stage in the development of this group occurred in 1847 when it decided to rent a small third-floor apartment which would serve exclusively as its synagogue, now given the name "Tohorat Hakodesh."[23] The main room, which had seats for fifty men and twenty women, was very simply furnished. The liturgy was traditional to the point of retaining the holiday *piyutim*. What set this synagogue apart was the decorum, the choir of ten boys, the use of cards indicating the sequence of those to be called to the Torah instead of a public sale of these honors, the location of the reader's desk (*bimah*) next to the ark, and the institution of a regular edifying sermon. However, unlike the similar services recently established in other cities, the sermon here was not delivered in German but most likely in Hebrew.[24] Only when a special dedication service was held for local government officials did the censor of Jewish books, Wolf Tungendhold, give an address in German. The regular preacher was the Haskalah Hebrew poet Abraham Dov Ber Lebensohn (Adam Ha-Kohen), who spoke once a month, on every sabbath preceding the New Moon.[25]

Shortly thereafter another modernized synagogue was established in Vilna within the building of the newly founded rabbinical seminary. The congregation here consisted of the students, their counselors, and their teachers. The prayers were recited in unison, each participant having been provided with a uniform prayerbook that included a German translation. One of the students conducted these daily services with careful attention to the proper pronunciation of the Hebrew. On sabbaths there was a choir of twenty-five students which sang according to musical notes. Following the sabbath morning services, a student or one of the teachers presented a modern sermon either in German or in Hebrew. At times the sermon was in the nature of a moral exhortation, at times more an interpretation of biblical and rabbinic texts aimed at their simple and direct meaning (*peshat*).[26]

In 1863 Lebensohn, who taught Hebrew and Aramaic at the seminary, edited a collection of twenty-two sermons for sabbaths, holidays, and special occasions, which were to serve the students as models of the homiletic art.[27] Fourteen of them—some exceedingly long—were written in Hebrew by Lebensohn and by two other teachers, Judah Shereshevsky and Hayim Katzenellenbogen. The remaining eight were translations by members of the seminary faculty of sermons delivered originally in Germany. It is worthy of note not only that as late as 1863 homiletical models were still sought abroad but that the three preachers chosen represented the spectrum of Jewish religious orientation in Germany. Three of the German sermons were originally delivered by the outstanding preacher Solomon Plessner, a Neo-Orthodox rabbi and outspoken opponent of the Reform movement; two by Ludwig Philippson, the moderate reformer who because of his editorship of the *Allgemeine Zeitung des Judentums* may have been better known in Eastern Europe than any other modern German rabbi; and three by Gotthold Salomon, preacher at the Hamburg Temple, famous not only for his homiletical skill but also as a member of the radical wing of the Reform movement.[28] Clearly, in his selection, the editor sought to make no distinction among the various factions in German Judaism. Nor was there any reason to do so. Points at issue between reformers and traditionalists in Germany were rarely reflected in their sermons. In rejecting the traditional Jewish *derush* for the edifying religious and moral discourse, they were wholly alike.

The much discussed and variously interpreted Max Lilienthal episode[29] provides us with an opportunity to examine both how nineteenth-century German Judaism appeared to the Russian government, to Russian traditional Jews and to Russian Maskilim, as well as how Russian Jewry looked to a reformist German rabbi in the 1840s.

     After spending only two years in Riga, Lilienthal was called upon by the Russian Minister of Education, Serge Uvarov, to act as the government's emissary to the Russian Jewish communities, to advocate and eventually to implement a broad program of reform focusing especially upon education. During the course of five years, he worked out proposals for the government in St. Petersburg, traveled about the Pale of Settlement, and participated in a government-sponsored conference that resulted in the establishment of the Crown school system. Personal circumstances and political disillusion regarding the good will of the Czar persuaded Lilienthal to discontinue his Russian work in 1845 and to settle in America. However, his tenure as plenipotentiary to the Russian Jews created an interesting confrontation between East and West.

     Count Uvarov, who headed the Ministry of Education from 1833 to 1849, was a brilliant man of complex personality who combined an early attachment to free thought with a willingness to subvert all principles in order to stay within the good graces of his master Nicholas I. He had spent time in Germany, admired Goethe, and preferred to write in German and French rather than in Russian.[30] To Lilienthal—and for that matter to the Russian Maskilim—he appeared to be a "humane human being" who had the welfare of the Jews at heart.[31] He told Lilienthal: "I am a friend of your people; believe me if we had such Jews as I met in the different capitals of Germany, we would treat them with the utmost distinction, but our Jews are entirely different from those in other countries."[32] Uvarov thus wanted to reshape Russian Jewry on the German model, though his ultimate purpose—like that of the Czar, but more subtle—was clearly to open their eyes to the truth of Christianity. In 1841 Uvarov wrote to Ludwig Philippson telling him that he envisaged an educational reform of the Jews in the spirit of Mendelssohn and that the deplorable moral and intellectual state of Russian Jewry could be raised only through an impetus arising from within Judaism itself.[33] In permitting Lilienthal to ask Philippson and other German Jewish leaders—including Isaac Marcus Jost, Abraham Geiger, and Isaac Noah Mannheimer—to come to Russia themselves or to recommend candidates to fill the projected educational and rabbinical positions, Uvarov was apparently seeking to import the necessary leaven from abroad. Some of the Russian Maskilim were sympathetic to such an endeavor, believing that effective modernization could come only from German rabbis.[34] Lilienthal himself thought that such an influx was essential if Russian Jewry was to advance as quickly as possible from the pre-Mendelssohnian to the post-Mendelssohnian age.[35] No less than 142 candidates expressed in writing their willingness to go to Russia. They were not necessarily associated with the German movement for religious reform. The Russian Ministry of Education, through Russian diplomats in the West, was aware that German states had not always looked favorably upon Jewish religious reform. On the one hand Jewish "neologism," as one of them called it, could be regarded as a closer approach to Christianity, but on the other it was also a politically dangerous step in the direction of atheism.[36] For the time being, the matter of the candidates' religious philosophy was left open, and there never proved to be a necessity for resolving it. Eventually the Russian government dropped Uvarov's scheme altogether. With very few exceptions, it was determined instead to use whatever talent was locally available in Russia. Rejecting specifically German patterns, the government chose to model the Crown schools on their Russian counterparts.[37] The leaven for reform would instead by supplied from within: by the clear prospect of punishments in case of noncompliance and the vague hope of political gains in the event of cooperation.

In propagating its program, the Russian authorities dangled before Jewish eyes the prospect of a reduction in political and economic disabilities.[38] Russian Maskilim, like Isaac Ber Levinsohn, noted that in Western Europe rulers began to lighten the Jewish yoke and Christians to write on their behalf once Jews became more open to the world around them.[39] Benjamin Mandelstamm held that their differentiating Jewish garments not only insulated Jews from modern culture but also militated against emancipation by setting them apart to no purpose.[40] Lilienthal himself suggested to Uvarov that Russia should adopt the French pattern in which Jews received emancipation at a time when most of them were still closed to the non-Jewish world, with cultural integration following only thereafter. But Uvarov held up to Lilienthal the German model instead: the Jews must take the initiative and thus try to win the favor of the Czar. In other words, as in Germany, Jews would have to earn emancipation step by step. It all sounded very familiar to Lilienthal who relates in his memoirs: "I understood that the old game was to be played here, too."[41] The difference was, of course, that one of the players in this game had no intention of playing fair. While in Germany, too, conversionist motives were abundantly present in considerations of the Jewish question, liberal opinion was at intervals sufficiently significant to allow for real political advances. Hopes for a similar development in Russia under the rigid and oppressive autocracy of Nicholas I appear in retrospect to be delusions born of desperation.[42] Lilienthal only later came to realize that "the imperial seducer" intended only to sow a path of frustration: enlightenment, alienation from Jewish tradition, followed by deprivation of all tangible rewards in the absence of baptism.[43]

During his travels in the Russian Pale, Lilienthal came into contact with the entire spectrum of Russian Jewry: Hasidim, Mitnagdim, Maskilim. Of particular interest is his relationship with the traditional factions. While, to be sure, Lilienthal was a religious and educational reformer who hoped to launch a broad reformation of Russian Jewry, he was deeply impressed by the intensity of Jewish religious life, the sabbath atmosphere that reigned in Vilna, the religious personalities of Rabbi Yitzhak of Volozhin and of the Stadt-Magid of Vilna.[44] Almost like the assimilated German Jews who about the time of World War I enthused over their discovery of the undiminished vitality of Jews in Eastern Europe, Lilienthal responded to his encounters with a certain veneration which set him apart from the more radical Maskilim. The latter, who saw the traditionalists only as their enemies, possessed little sympathy for this outsider's romantic nostalgia. To be sure, Lilienthal's effort to establish good relations with the traditionalists was also good politics, but his memoirs, based on his travel diary, reveal an unfeigned envy of what he termed their "inward happiness."[45] Their mode of study had virtues of which German Wissenschaft des Judentums was bereft:

> We study the rabbinic literature because we wish to dig out the scientific treasures hidden and unexplained in these literary pyramids of old; because we intend to use the results of our investigation either for the consolidation of orthodoxy, or the construction of reform, or to add our share to the immense stores that science is gathering from everywhere. They study with their heart, with sincere love and respect for religion; we study with our mind, coolly dissecting the most tender fibers of religious life. While they feel blissfully happy we speculate with deadly indifference.[46]

Lilienthal not only recognized the Russian Jews' apprehensions regarding the intent of the Czar, promising in his open letter, *Magid Yeshuah*, to stand with them against any infringement of Torah or Talmud,[47] he also sought to allay their fears that enlightenment by its very nature would lead to wholesale apostasy such as they heard had occurred in Germany. He tried to reassure them that the "old blunders" would not be committed again.[48] But the presumed ill effects of the Western Jewish enlightenment troubled Russian Maskilim no less than traditionalists.[49] Even they related to the Western model with ambivalence. Especially given the greater pressure in Russia, some of them were not entirely certain a fully integrated Russian Jewry could retain its Jewish identity.

In Russia, as in the West, successful religious modernization depended upon the transformation of the rabbinate. Religious reforms in Germany were instituted at first by laymen, generally in opposition to local rabbinical authorities. In the second decade of the nineteenth century it was unusual to find a man like Menahem Mendel Steinhardt, one of the rabbinical members of the Westphalian Jewish consistory, who was willing to argue for moderate reforms both in ritual law and synagogue customs.[50] Yet by the 1830s a new type of rabbi was emerging in Germany who combined secular education with Jewish learning, who favored a program of reform ranging from purely formal and conservative to substantial and radical, and who sought to embody the role of moral exemplar, preacher, and enlightened educator, which David Caro of Posen had set forth in his *Berit Emet* in 1820. As German Jewry came to define itself increasingly in purely religious terms, spiritual leadership fell almost exclusively upon this new rabbinate, with its conflicting views on religious reform but its basic agreement regarding the value of cultural integration. Whether inclined to neo-orthodoxy or to reform, to hastening the process of modernization or to moderating it, the German rabbi soon became the specialist in Judaism, whose task it was to transmit the religious heritage to Jews increasingly distant from tradition and lacking extensive Jewish knowledge.[51]

The Russian rabbinate did not follow the same pattern. Russian Jewish religious leadership in the first half of the nineteenth century remained in varying degrees opposed both to secular education and to religious change. The proponents of reform in Eastern Europe thus continued for a much longer time to be laymen who found it necessary to combat the rabbis as the principal obstacles to their endeavors. But these laymen—the Maskilim—were likewise different from their German counterparts. Their Jewish consciousness remained intense and their Jewish knowledge profound for a longer period of time. Whereas in Germany the Hebrew language as an instrument of enlightenment had for all practical purposes given way to German by the second decade of the nineteenth century, in Russia it continued to play this role—along with Yiddish—for another three generations. The East European Maskilim were not ready to center Jewish life wholly on religion and therefore to focus it upon rabbinical leadership. While they did favor a rabbinate less hostile to secular knowledge and more willing to perceive Jewish tradition as flexible, they did not envisage modern Russian rabbis exercising the broad role of Jewish leadership assumed by their colleagues in Germany. Although some Maskilim favored the importation of rabbis from Germany,[52] Mordecai Aaron Guenzburg—one of the most respected among them—was not at all sure that what Russian Jewry needed was "doctors," as he somewhat contemptuously called the German rabbis. To be a rabbi in Russia, he believed, had to mean in the first instance not sermonics but profound knowledge of Torah, in particular the ability "to trace passages in the *Shulhan Arukh* back to their root and their principle in the Talmud."[53] Among all groups in Eastern Europe the rabbinate remained associated with traditional legal functions, which it continued to perform to a far greater extent than was true in the West. Those who sought to reform the rabbinate in Eastern Europe preferred to hold up the example of the rabbinate in ancient times when Jewish religious leadership was characterized by broad intellectual horizons and by halakhic innovation based on responsiveness to time and place.

In contrast to Germany, an effective modern rabbinate did not develop in Russia. The principal cause for this failure seems to have been the heavy hand of the Russian government. Not only did it repeatedly arouse suspicion and resentment by conversionist efforts and oppressive measures, it blatantly interfered in the selection of Jewish religious leadership. In 1835 it outlined the institution soon to be known as the Crown rabbinate, consisting of rabbinically trained Jews knowing Russian, who were henceforth the only rabbis recognized as such by the government. Their duties, in fact, often included little more than the performance of certain clerical tasks such as the registration of births and deaths. With few exceptions these men did not enjoy the respect of the communities in which they served. Public opinion differentiated between them and the genuine rabbis, chosen informally for their knowledge and piety, but enjoying no official status vis-à-vis the government. Only here and there were Crown rabbis able to exercise real leadership. Because they had to be reelected every three years, these men usually preferred to avoid antagonizing any influential segment of the community. The projects for religious reform which some of them harbored often remained unarticulated for reasons of economic self-concern.[54]

In 1847 two modern rabbinical seminaries, intended to train candidates for the Crown rabbinate, were established in Vilna and in Zhitomir. They lasted for twenty-six vicissitudinous years before finally being transformed into teachers' colleges in 1873.[55] When the Vilna seminary reached its tenth anniversary in 1857, it issued a Hebrew description of the school and statement of its goals by one of the senior students, Jacob Gurland, as well as a German speech in honor of the occasion by another student, Solomon Pucher. The rabbinic ideal that we find represented here reflects awareness both of the German model and of the particular situation of the Jews in Russia. As in Germany, the rabbi is to possess a high level of both secular and Jewish education. Repeatedly, this theme is formulated in characteristic Haskalah dualities: religion and knowledge (*dat im da'at*), secular wisdom with Jewish law (*hokhmah gam torah*), and the like.[56] For Pucher, gaining modern culture (*Bildung*) implies westernization: "to reconcile Russian Jewry once again with life, to snatch its body from Asiatic disfigurement, to check the enslaving oppression of superstition." The school, he believes, must be "a reflection of our Western, cultured brothers."[57]

What will make the new Russian rabbi different from his German counterpart is his task. For Gurland, he must above all be a mediator between the Jewish community and the government, able to communicate in the language of the country and thus to protect the interests of his fellow Jews.[58] Though the actual term does not appear, the rabbinical role he emphasizes the most might well be called by the traditional name *shetadlanut*, intercession between the Jewish community and the authorities upon whom its welfare depends. It is of course likely that Gurland stresses this role because he believes traditional Jews skeptical of the seminary can most easily appreciate its value. Yet there is no reason to doubt that the Jewish supporters of the seminary hoped its graduates would be able to speak for the Jewish community in political matters with an official authority not enjoyed by individual Maskilim and with a persuasiveness which traditional rabbis, lacking the requisite linguistic and cultural tools, were unable to muster.

The apologists for the Vilna seminary argued that instruction in the institution would deprive secular culture of its erosive force by integrating it with Jewish tradition. As Pucher envisaged it, the seminary was to channel the stream of modern culture into the existing riverbed, taking care that its rushing waters should not damage the tender plant of religion. Yet, likewise using a horticultural image, he pictured the new rabbis playing the role of religious reformers, "with sore hands tearing out the weeds and misshapen plants from the vineyard of the Lord."[59] The graduates clearly had hopes of bringing religious reform, albeit moderate, to Russian Jewry.

In fact, the seminaries proved unable to fulfill their projected goals for rabbinical training. They were beset by mistrust—if not outright opposition—on the part of traditional Jews, government interference, and a poorly motivated student body. The teaching of secular disciplines mostly by Christian teachers created a heightened awareness of separation between Jewish and general subjects rather than their integration. Few students completed the rabbinical program[60] and of these only a very small percentage enjoyed widespread authority.[61] Instead of bridging the gap between Crown rabbis and the rabbis accepted as such by the masses, the seminaries only exacerbated the divisions. As one modern Jew in St. Petersburg put it: "Our old rabbis are obsolete and our new ones are not rabbis."[62] As late as the 1870s Russian Jewry had been unable to produce a broadly cultured yet religiously respected rabbinate. The German model in this instance struck few roots in Russia.

If under Nicholas I, Jewish enlightenment and religious reform were hampered by an oppressive and coercive government policy, with the relatively more liberal reign of Alexander II fresh hopes were aroused for a comprehensive modernization of Russian Jewry linked to political gains. For more than a decade, beginning in the late 1850s, new suggestions for reform, including specifically religious elements, were put forward for consideration. While they differ in emphasis and with regard to particular points, they bear common characteristics which serve not only to unite them but generally to set them apart from Jewish religious reforms in Germany. We shall limit our analysis to three writers: Joachim Hayim Tarnopol (1810–1900), Leon Mandelstamm (1819–89), and Moses Leib Lilienblum (1843–1910).[63]

Tarnopol, a wealthy Odessa merchant, together with Osip Rabinovich edited the short-lived first Russian Jewish periodical *Rassvet* (1860–61).[64] About 1858 he composed a proposal for the "moderate and progressive reform" of Russian Jewry. It was published a decade later in Russian and three years after that was reworked into a French version.[65] To a greater extent than the other Russian writers, Tarnopol looks to the German Jewish experience, drawing, he tells us explicitly, upon the writings of Ludwig Philippson, which have "so much contributed to the regeneration of our people not only in Germany but in all of Europe."[66] He wants Russian rabbis to be versed both in the ancient texts and in the modern Wissenschaft des Judentums, and he believes that a proper rabbinical seminary in Russia would have to seek its teachers of Jewish theology, history, and literature in Germany. Yet he recognizes that Germany has also produced a radical reform which he regards as destructive because it sowed communal discord and created widespread repugnance to the desired progress.

Although Tarnopol stresses the moderation of his own reform program, which he claims will be based on both the Written and the Oral Law,[67] he constructs it upon a principle characteristic especially of radical German reform from the early nineteenth century onward.[68] Tarnopol insists that the observance of external forms may sometimes aid in the development of moral principles and cardinal virtues, but such observance is always to be regarded only as a means, never as the essence of the faith. He believes that it is among the chief tasks of the modern rabbi to separate the instrumental from the essential in Judaism, thereby helping to reconcile tradition with contemporary reality.

More than other Russian advocates of religious reform, Tarnopol focuses his attention upon the synagogue. For him—as for much of German Jewry—the worship service takes on increased significance as other forms of Jewish religious observance become less common among the enlightened youth. The synagogue must therefore be made more capable of attracting the new generation, which has received a modern education. "Our youth," he writes, "desires to be edified in a temple possessing the most imposing dignity and the most suitable forms."[69] However, Tarnopol suggests no more than the very limited program of reforms which, as we have seen, were already introduced in some congregations: decorum, choir, sermon, plus perhaps the confirmation ceremony and the abolition of certain holiday *piyutim*.[70] He believes that once these innovations have gained a wider acceptance, Judaism in Russia will become both viable and respectable.

Leon Mandelstamm, the first Jew to study in a Russian university, was until 1857 Lilienthal's successor in St. Petersburg, charged with supervising Jewish education.[71] Afterward he settled for a number of years in Germany, where he had earlier done additional university study. Hardly a radical thinker, Mandelstamm vigorously defended the Mosaic origins of the Pentateuch against the current of modern biblical criticism that began with Spinoza.[72] In 1860, or very shortly thereafter, he published in Berlin a volume entitled *Thalmudische Studien*, which included a section devoted specifically to religious reform.[73] In contrast to Tarnopol, Mandelstamm is not concerned with aesthetic considerations, such as the atmosphere of the synagogue. He chooses instead to focus on matters of substance: the text of the Kol Nidre, the blessing of the New Moon, the wearing of a beard, angelology, and the post-biblical expansion of the dietary laws. In each instance a historical explanation is given followed by proposals for reform. Of particular interest is the attention he devotes to Jewish women, whose exceptional status in Jewish law he regards as no longer appropriate. He suggests both to teach them Torah and to subject them to those religious obligations relating to the festivals which the Halakhah requires only of men.

Mandelstamm finds that in ancient times Jewish law developed in accordance with historical circumstance. He tells his readers that Abraham recognized the necessity of reform and that Moses was "a reformer." But most especially it was the Talmud which reformed Jewish law to harmonize it with contemporary reality and to lighten some of the burdens imposed by the Torah. And he believes it has not lost its value as an instrument of reform: "Talmud in hand [!], we can still for a long time do full justice to the valid demands of the new age."[74] Mandelstamm thus projected the image of a classical Judaism which evolved and adapted to contemporary conditions, which only in later times of persecution ceased to develop. He called for a "learned reform" based on the spirit underlying individual laws and taking into consideration minority views

preserved in the Talmud. No doubt influenced by the German reformers, he put forward a theoretical model very similar to theirs.

Like Mandelstamm, Moses Leib Lilienblum also found in the
Talmud a precedent for contemporary religious reform.[75] In a series
of essays in the Hebrew periodical *Ha-Melits* beginning in 1868, this
man of extraordinary intellectual integrity called on the Russian rabbinate to take halakhic initiatives in order to reestablish the link between religion and life which had existed in Talmudic times. For
Lilienblum, however, the course of German Judaism served less as
exemplar than as warning: if the Russian rabbis would not act
speedily to bridge the ever widening gap between the law and contemporary reality they would lose their authority, as had the traditional rabbis in Germany. Unchecked individualism would reign
supreme in Russian Judaism as it did already in the West.[76]

Among Russian advocates of religious change, Lilienblum's
concerns are the furthest removed from those of German synagogue
reform. For him, the worship service is entirely of secondary significance. Prayer itself, he reminds his readers, is not an explicit biblical command and private prayer is no less acceptable than public.
The German Jews' emphasis on the synagogue service is for Lilienblum simply an imitation of the gentiles. Prayer was ordained in
place of the Temple sacrifices, and the latter, he notes, were not
greatly esteemed by Israel's prophets. Lilienblum was convinced
that once a Jew had lost the inner motivation for prayer, synagogue
reform would merely substitute an aesthetic experience for a religious one. In his eyes the synagogue was not the symbol and center
of Jewish life, as it was for Tarnopol and for Jews in the West, and
therefore synagogue reform, he tells us bluntly, is simply "not
worth talking about."[77]

What does matter to Lilienblum is the task of easing the burden of Jewish law and custom in order to maintain a common
ground between traditional and enlightened Jews, to prevent the
fragmentation which has afflicted Jewry in the West. Initially, he
sought only to adjust those practices which became current since
the *Shulhan Aruch*, which have no clear Talmudic basis, and which
unnecessarily set Jews apart from non-Jews or were drawn from
mystical conceptions. However, Lilienblum rapidly came to challenge the authority of earlier authorities as well: first the *Shulhan
Aruch*, which he hoped to displace by a new code of Jewish law, and
then the Talmud itself, declaring, as had the German reformers, that
even in its halakhic elements it was essentially a human product
subject to revision by later generations. The Talmud remained authoritative for Lilienblum only as a model of religious adaptation,

not as a sacred text. It "was created according to [the demands of] place and time, founded principally upon the spirit of reform."[78]

For a while Lilienblum hung on to his belief in the revealed character of the Written Law, claiming that in this respect his views differed from those of German reformers like Samuel Holdheim.[79] However, within a few years his exposure to biblical criticism, mediated to him especially by the Galician thinker, Abraham Krochmal, made even this last pillar of revelation collapse. In the West idealistic religious philosophy, absorbed during the period of its prominence into Jewish thought as well as Christian, enabled liberal Judaism to withstand the blows of historical criticism. But in Russia, where Orthodox Christianity did not achieve a synthesis of religion with modern philosophy or science, the period of reform coincided with the popularity of an antimetaphysical positivism which left no room for a religious faith whose authoritative texts had been shown to be the product of historical evolution.[80] Lilienblum became an outsider to religious Judaism both in belief and in practice. For a time he still argued for reforms in those areas, such as marriage and divorce, which affected all Jews regardless of their religious views or degree of observance. But he gave up hope of giving impetus to a new synthesis which would unite religion with life.[81]

If we now cast our glance back upon all three writers, certain common elements are apparent. Each of them sought a reform based on both the Written and Oral law. Each hoped to revive a stagnant halakhic creativity, none to bypass the Halakhah for a simple biblicism or a mere assessment of the demands of the Zeitgeist. In this respect they resembled the conservative wing of religious reform in Germany. However, unlike the German reformers, none of the three attempted a reinterpretation of Jewish theology. They confined themselves to advocating changes in the synagogue service or in ritual law by reference to historical precedent and practical necessity. Lilienblum had stressed that Judaism was a religion of deeds, not of beliefs. Nor did any of the three advocate even a single substantial change in the liturgy or the recitation of any portion of the prayers in the vernacular. The issues which so much troubled German reformers—the failure of the younger generation to understand Hebrew, the ethnocentrism of certain prayers, the hope for return to Zion—these did not trouble the Russians. For all three, Jewish religion and nationality were necessarily bound to one another and it was not the task of religious reform to rend them asunder. Though they possessed hopes that, as Tarnopol put it, inner regeneration would bring about external emancipation,[82] in a multinational empire with no concept of citizenship they did not assume that Russification demanded transforming Judaism into a religious denomination.[83]

Yet the political aspirations which these advocates of religious reform did possess were soon to be shattered, and with them the foundation upon which much of their program was based. An unremittingly hostile environment is not conducive to the gradualism represented by religious reform. With hopes disappointed in the last years of Alexander II, and with the resurgence of oppression and persecution under Alexander III, religious reform in Russia was divested of rationale, lost much of its significance, and became relegated to those more decorous congregations whose numbers had somewhat increased when privileged Jews were permitted to settle in cities of the interior. Most of Russian Jewry now either remained within the bastion of orthodoxy or sought its salvation through secular means: emigration, socialism, or Jewish nationalism. In Jewish socialist ideology there remained little room for any religious expression; in Jewish nationalism loyalty to the people became the dominant value. As Lilienblum put it in the wake of the pogroms of 1881: "All of us are holy—atheists no less than believers are becoming martyrs."[84] Having turned to Zionism, Lilienblum came into possession of a new standard for judging religious observance: "the national spirit." Like Ahad Ha'Am, and unlike most of German Jewry, he now saw little value in those observances which might make viable a Jewish life integrated within modern non-Jewish society. He chose to emphasize instead only such religious elements as he believed to be most deeply rooted in the spirit of the Jewish nation and therefore able, as he had put it earlier, to set the Jews apart as "a people which dwells alone."[85]

The combination of German stimulus and felt need for reform thus proved insufficient to launch a statistically significant modernizing religious movement on the Western model. The unbridgeable intellectual gap between traditionalists and Maskilim, the failure to create an effective modern rabbinate, but most of all the newly hostile political atmosphere made Jewish religious reform in Russia ultimately episodic and peripheral, a possibility only very incompletely realized. In the last years of the century, a portion of Russian Jewish orthodoxy did increasingly accommodate itself to the surrounding world, but it did not do so within the context of a conscious movement for religious rapprochement. Only in the relatively more hospitable intellectual and political climate of the West could organized religious reform flourish broadly and attain dominance within the Jewish community.

Notes

Research for this study was made possible by a fellowship from the American Council of Learned Societies. I wish to express my thanks to Professor Michael Stanislawski for his critical reading of the manuscript and helpful comments.

1. Simon Bernfeld, *Toldot ha-reformatsyon ha-datit be-yisrael* (Warsaw, 1923), 244–48.
2. David Philipson, *The Reform Movement in Judaism* (New York, 1907), 563.
3. These works will be cited below in connection with the subjects that they treat.
4. Exceptional is the opinion expressed privately by Isaac Ber Levinsohn in 1842. He sees no objection to changing the liturgy "for the better," pointing out that liturgical differences already exist and that innovations have been made even in recent centuries. He finds that the German reformers went too far in introducing ideological changes, but they certainly had the right to abbreviate the service. See David Ber Nathanson, *Sefer zikhronot* (Warsaw, 1875), 68–69, and Raphael Mahler, *Divre yeme yisrael*, VI (Tel Aviv, 1976), 277–78.
5. According to *Der Orient* 6 (1845): 322–23, a decorous service with choir was also introduced into the "German" congregation in Cracow during the last days of that city's status as an independent republic.
6. See Alexander Altmann, "The New Style of Preaching in Nineteenth-Century German Jewry," *Studies in Nineteenth-Century Jewish Intellectual History*, ed. A. Altmann (Cambridge, Mass., 1964), 65–116.
7. *Allgemeine Zeitung des Judentums (AZJ)* 6 (1842): 264–66; Nathanson, 67; Osip Rabinovich, "The New Jewish Synagogue in Odessa" (1847, in Russian) *Sochineniia*, III (Odessa, 1888), 373–80 (my thanks to Judith Zabarenko for help with the Russian); Joachim Tarnopol, *Notices historiques et caractéristiques sur les israélites d'Odessa* (Odessa, 1855), 64–65, 104–5. There was sentiment in favor of electing Max Lilienthal to be the rabbi and preacher of this congregation after he delivered a sermon there during his travels in 1842. See Isaac Marcus Jost, *Geschichte der Israeliten*, X:2 (Berlin, 1847), 331; Menashe Morgulis, *Dor ha-haskalah be-rusyah* (Vilna, 1910), 45.
8. Moses Reichsberg, *Pene Aryeh* (Odessa, 1889). At the beginning of the twentieth century, the Brody synagogue possessed an organ. So did the synagogue of the Odessa Jewish Clerks' Society, which for a time also worshipped with a female choir (*Jewish Encyclopedia*, s.v. "Odessa"). Jewish religious development and conflict in Odessa is discussed in detail by Steven Zipperstein, "The Jewish Community of Odessa from 1794–1871: Social Characteristics and Cultural Development" (UCLA doctoral dissertation, 1980), 107–27, 184–203.
9. *Gedenkblätter zur Erinnerung an Rabbiner Dr. A.M. Goldschmidt* (Leipzig, 1889); *AZJ* 2 (1838): 209; 4 (1840): 90, 102.
10. S. Briman, "The Reform Controversy in Hebrew Literature" (Hebrew), *He-Avar* 1 (1952): 129.

11. Nicholas V. Riasanovsky, *Nicholas I and Official Nationality in Russia, 1825–1855* (Berkeley and Los Angeles, 1959), 144, 232–33; Philipson, 139.

12. *The Occident* 5 (1847–48): 253.

13. *AZJ* 1 (1837): 410–14; Anton Buchholtz, *Geschichte der Juden in Riga* (Riga, 1899), 112–13. According to Jost (op. cit., 307), Jewish newspapers from the West, though admitted into Russia only in limited quantities, made their way to various regions and instructed the Russian Jews regarding changes in the German synagogue.

14. On Lilienthal's activity in Riga see Philipson, 15–19, 137–49, 220–43.

15. A. Berliner, ed., *Aus dem schriftlichen Nachlasse der Brüder Jolles aus Lemberg* (Berlin, 1909), 45–46.

16. Philipson, 148.

17. M. E. Lilienthal, *Predigten in der Synagoge zu Riga* (Riga, 1841), esp. 5, 9, 89, 157.

18. Ibid., 29–45. For those of his congregants who desired it, Lilienthal also conducted the wedding ceremony in the German manner, including a wedding sermon and the expression of oral consent to the marriage by both the bride and groom (*AZJ* 4 [1840]: 339).

19. Adolf Ehrlich, *Entwickelungsgeschichte der israelitischen Gemeindeschule zu Riga* (St. Petersburg, 1894), 14–15, 19, 21. In 1863 Neumann took over the rabbinate of St. Petersburg.

20. M. E. Lilienthal, *Rede am Dankfeste für die von Seiner Kaiserlichen Majestät den . . . Ebräischen Colonisten-Familien erwiesenen Wohlthaten* (Riga, 1840); Philipson, 250–57.

21. S. Pucher, *Offenes Sendschreiben an die kurländischen Herren Synodalen* (Offprint from the *Baltische Monatsschrift*, September 1867), 217–40; *AZJ* 42 (1878): 490; A. Shochat, *Mosad ha-rabanut mi-ta'am be-rusyah* (Haifa, 1975), 52.

22. Benjamin Mandelstamm, *Ḥazon la-mo'ed* (Vienna, 1877), 2:6–90. See also the unpublished letters cited and the analysis presented in Emanuel Etkes, "Compulsory Enlightenment as a Crossroads in the History of the Haskalah Movement in Russia" (Hebrew), *Zion* 43 (1978): 307–9.

23. The name was chosen by Lebensohn, apparently from a prayer of Hezekiah in 2 Chronicles 30:18–19: "The good Lord will provide atonement for everyone who sets his mind on worshiping God, the Lord God of his fathers, even if he is not purified for the sanctuary" (New Jewish Publication Society translation). The verse would be appropriate for a congregation of less than wholly observant Maskilim.

24. I see no reason to assume with Etkes that the sermons were delivered in "Germanized Yiddish." The printed sermons of Lebensohn are in Hebrew, and we know that he preached in Hebrew at the synagogue of the Vilna rabbinical seminary.

25. Adam Ha-Kohen Lebensohn, *Kinat sofrim* (Vilna, 1847), 48. This synagogue continued on into the twentieth century. By 1903 its members were finally able to construct their own building, a temple in the Moorish style which seated 300 men and 200 women. See *Ha-Tsefirah* 30:2 (1903): no. 220.

26. Jacob Gurland, *Kevod ha-bayit* (Vilna, 1858), 66–68.

27. *Kovets derushim* (Vilna, 1863).

28. The Hebrew collection does not make specific reference to the German sources. I have succeeded in tracing down all but one of the eight. They are to be found in Salomon Plessner, *Belehrungen und Erbauungen in religiösen Vorträgen* 1 (Berlin, 1836), 195–210, and 2 (Berlin, 1836–37), 81–100, 297–316; Ludwig Philippson, *Siloah* (Leipzig, 1845), 136–46, 147–56; Gotthold Salomon, *Mose, ein heiliges Lebensgemählde* (Hamburg, 1835), 94–106; idem, *Eliah* (Hamburg, 1840), 250–63.

29. The most recent treatments are Etkes, 280–99, and Michael Stanislawski, *Tsar Nicholas I and the Jews: The Transformation of Jewish Society in Russia, 1825–1855* (Philadelphia, 1983).

30. Riasanovsky, 70–71, 170–71.

31. *AZJ* 6 (1842): 603; B. Mandelstamm, 47.

32. Philipson, 194.

33. Julius Hessen, "Die russische Regierung und die westeuropäischen Juden," *Monatsschrift für Geschichte und Wissenschaft des Judentums* 57 (1913): 267–68.

34. E.g., in the call issued by a group of Maskilim in 1840 (Nathanson, 55); also B. Mandelstamm, 40. For a contrary view: Hessen, 499n.

35. *AZJ* 6 (1842): 604.

36. Hessen, 494–95. When the Minister of Education discovered in 1851 that the students at the Vilna rabbinical seminary had made extraordinary advances in secular education, it was decided to lower the level of non-Jewish studies and to insist on complete religious observance. See Yehuda Slutsky, "The Rabbinical Seminary in Vilna" (Hebrew), *He-Avar* 7 (1960): 34.

37. Philipson, 39–40. Stanislawski notes that the decision not to import Jewish personnel from abroad (or any foreigners from the West) followed from Nicholas's xenophobia in the wake of the revolutions of 1848.

38. In his letter to Moses Montefiore, which had been approved by Uvarov, Lilienthal wrote that the government intended to improve the political status of the Jews (Hessen, 497–98). See Philipson, 194, 247.

39. Isaac Ber Levinsohn, *Bet yehudah* (Vilna, 1839), 363–64.

40. B. Mandelstamm, 45.

41. Philipson, 196–97.

42. The Czar had adopted the slogan coined by Uvarov: "orthodoxy, autocracy, nationality." As outsiders religiously and ethnically in a regime which stressed conformity, the Jews could hardly possess realistic expectations of making significant economic and political advances while still retaining a significant separate identity.

43. *Asmonean* 10 (1854): 101; *Jewish Times*, January 28, 1870, 3–4.

44. Philipson, 167, 269–82, 341–53.

45. Ibid., 287.

46. Ibid., 288.

47. Published in Vilna, 1842, 11.

48. Philipson, 297–98.

49. For example Levinsohn, 361.

50. See his *Divre Igeret* (Rödelheim, 1812).

51. On the rabbinate in Germany see Ismar Schorsch, "Emancipation and the Crisis of Religious Authority: The Emergence of the Modern Rabbinate," in *Revolution and Evolution: 1848 in German-Jewish History,* ed. W. E. Mosse el al. (Tübingen, 1981), 205–47.

52. Nathanson, 55.

53. Mordecai Aaron Guenzburg, *Ha-moriyah* (Warsaw, 1878), 43–48.

54. *Ha-Shahar* 6 (1875): 82–83; *AZJ* 42 (1878): 489. On the Crown rabbinate in general see the above cited volume by Shochat.

55. On the Vilna seminary see the above cited article by Slutsky.

56. See especially the Hebrew poetry at the beginning of the Gurland volume.

57. S. Pucher, *Betrachtung über die Decadenfeier in der Rabbinerschule und eine Rede bei derselben Gelegenheit* (Vilna, 1858), 19, 21.

58. Gurland, 9–13.

59. Pucher, *Betrachtung,* 7–11, 21–22.

60. The Warsaw rabbinical seminary, established by an order of Alexander I in 1825, was even less successful in this respect. Not one of its students had become a rabbi by 1840. For a defense of this institution on other grounds see *AZJ* 4 (1840): 330–36.

61. One of the few graduates, in addition to Pucher himself, who did make a name for himself as a champion of Jewish causes and as an outstanding preacher and educator was Solomon Minor. He served as rabbi first in Minsk and then in Moscow.

62. "F. G.," in *AZJ* 42 (1878): 485.

63. To be sure, there are others as well, especially Judah Leib Gordon (1830–92); but I regard these three as quite representative. Gordon himself urged support of Lilienblum's proposals. See *Igrot Yehudah Lev Gordon* (Vilna, 1894), 1:148. An early attempt to claim that the spiritual leaders of each generation were authorized to modify laws and customs in accordance with the contemporary reality was made by Menashe of Ilya in his *Alfe Menashe* (Vilna, 1822). However, he was forced to water down the argument when threatened with the burning of his book in the synagogue yard. See Simon Dubnow, *History of the Jews in Russia and Poland* (Philadelphia, 1918), 2:115–16. A sampling of views on religious reform by Haskalah writers is to be found in Yehuda Slutsky, *Tenuat ha-haskalah be-yahadut rusyah* (Jerusalem, 1977), 92–95. For an exposition of the polemics between reformers and traditionalists, see Gideon Kazenelson, *Ha-milhamah ha-sifrutit ben ha-haredim ve-ha-maskilim* (Tel Aviv, 1954). He points out that Gordon differed from Lilienblum in concentrating on a satirical treatment of the contemporary Jewish religious leadership rather than on the precedents for reform in Jewish tradition. Kazenelson deals also with the religious reform proposals of Samuel Joseph Fuenn, editor of *Ha-Karmel,* and Alexander Zederbaum, editor of *Ha-Melits.*

64. On him see Alexander Orbach, *New Voices of Russian Jewry* (Leiden, 1980), 28–31.
65. I have used the French text: *Réflexions sur l'état religieux, politique et social des israélites russes. Essai sur une reforme modérée et progressive, dans le domaine du judaisme en Russie* (Odessa, 1871).
66. Ibid., 25.
67. See also his views in *Ha-Magid* 4 (1860): 178–79, 184; Zipperstein, 239–43.
68. See, for example, *Sulamith* 1:1 (1806): 332–35.
69. Tarnopol, *Réflexions*, 22.
70. In his earlier book Tarnopol had rejected the views of those who desired synagogue music wholly in the modern fashion. He believed the melancholy chant should be retained because it is learned in childhood and is redolent with the sacred historical memories of the Jewish people. Even though the chant might offend the ears of non-Jews, it speaks to the heart of the Jew. See Tarnopol, *Notices*, 106–9.
71. On an interesting aspect of Mandelstamm's educational work for the Russian government, see Michael Stanislawski, "The Tsarist Mishneh Torah: A Study in the Cultural Politics of the Russian Haskalah," *Proceedings of the American Academy for Jewish Research* 50 (1983): 165–83.
72. See his *Biblische Studien*, 3 vols. (Berlin, [1862]), esp. 2:6, 13, 29.
73. The date of publication (June 21, 1860) is given only for the section entitled "Rabbi Joschua ben Hanania," which was probably issued before "Reform im Judenthum." This section is the first according to its own title page, but the second according to the general title page. Moreover, the individual title pages for the two sections call the work *Horae Thalmudicae* rather than *Thalmudische Schriften*. Perhaps Mandelstamm reissued his two "Talmudic" studies as a single volume after completion of his biblical work, changing the name of the volume to correspond with *Biblische Studien* and rearranging the order of the two sections. The place of publication for both sections is Berlin.
74. Ibid., 47.
75. There are two studies of Lilienblum specifically as a reformer: Ezra Spicehandler, "The Life and Religious Views of Moses Leib Lilienblum" (Hebrew Union College MHL Thesis, 1946), and S. Briman, cited above. See also the chapter in Joseph Klausner, *Historiyah shel ha-sifrut ha-ivrit ha-ḥadashah* (Jerusalem, 1953), 4:190–300, and Kazenelson, 76–93.
76. *Kol kitve Moshe Leib Lilienblum* (Cracow, Odessa, 1910–13), 1:51–52, 100. Alexander Zederbaum, the editor of *Ha-Melits*, was relatively more favorably inclined to German Judaism. See Orbach, 131–45, and on the East European response to organized religious reform see M. A. Meyer, "The Jewish Synods in Germany in the Second Half of the Nineteenth Century" (Hebrew), *Studies in the History of the Jewish People and the Land of Israel* 3 (1974), 109–10.
77. Ibid., 126, 185–86.

78. Ibid., 37–41, 66. This is the viewpoint expressed by Samuel, the hero in Reuben Asher Braudes's unfinished novel, *Ha-dat ve-ha-ḥayim*, which originally appeared in installments in *Ha-Boker Or* from 1876 to 1879. Samuel, for whom Lilienblum served as the model, was especially concerned with burdensome ritual ordinances of recent vintage and contemporary rabbinic decisions which were particularly onerous for the poor. In the most recent two-volume edition (Jerusalem, 1974), see especially 1:137, 147, 227, 279–86, 362–73; 2:247–62.

79. Ibid., 67.

80. Cf. Spicehandler, 47.

81. Moshe Leib Lilienblum, *Ketavim otobiyografiyim*, ed. S. Briman (Jerusalem, 1970), 2:159–60, 166.

82. Tarnopol, *Réflexions*, 15.

83. Of the three, Tarnopol is closest to German Jewry in seeking national rapprochement. Like the more traditional Western Jews, he symbolized and universalized the messianic idea without favoring removal of the hope for return to Zion from the prayerbook (ibid., 139). There were, nonetheless, Maskilim who followed the Western model completely with respect to nationality, reducing Judaism entirely to a religious faith. Examples are given by Slutsky, *Tenuat ha-haskalah*, 103, 105–6, and by Israel Zinberg, *A History of Jewish Literature*, tr. Bernard Martin (Cincinnati, 1978), 12:191.

84. Lilienblum, *Ketavim*, 3:173.

85. *Kol kitve*, 1:127; 3:88.

CHAPTER 18

Jewish Religious Reform
in Germany and Britain

Jewish religious reform began, both in Britain and in Germany, with relative moderation, followed later by a more radical expression by those Jews who regarded the earlier efforts as insufficient. In Germany, the first reform endeavors in Westphalia during the period of French domination, as well as in Berlin and in Hamburg during the second decade of the nineteenth century, although severely condemned by traditionalists, were mild in comparison with the radical ideology and practical reforms instituted by the *Reformgemeinde* in Berlin in the late 1840s. Similarly, in Britain, the reforms of the West London Synagogue in the early 1840s seem moderate indeed in comparison with the thoroughgoing radicalism of the Liberal Judaism that began in London at the beginning of the twentieth century. I shall divide my discussion according to the British developments, dealing first with the rise of Reform Judaism in Britain. I will then turn to Liberal Judaism, the later religious expression within British Jewry. In each instance I will attempt to draw general comparisons with the Reform movement in Germany in a number of relevant areas, including the external political and religious, that is, Christian, context of Jewish religious reform, as well as in the inner context, the Jewish community. I will then deal with ideology, practice, and influence. The first section will also include a brief case-study comparison of the Hamburg Temple and the West London Synagogue.

The Reform Movement in Germany
and the West London Synagogue

The relation between state and religion was quite different in Germany and in Britain. German states assumed responsibility for religious life by regulating the churches and approving their officials. With regard to the Jews, the states had, as early as the eighteenth century, whittled away at the autonomy of the Jewish communities. In the nineteenth century, they pursued contradictory strategies toward the same objective. Some chose to use state authority to further integration and the ultimate absorption of the Jews by encouraging religious reform as a step toward conversion. Others sought to suppress reform in order to make Judaism appear out of step with modernity so that Jews would be more likely to take the leap into Christianity. In both cases, they embarked upon an *Erziehungspolitik*, a politics of education, which was to render the Jews gradually fit for the emancipation that, in Germany, they enjoyed only in part. Although the required "education" was broadly understood to include occupational redistribution and cultural attainments, it was also linked to political pressure for religious reform. Differing attitudes between state governments resulted in the suppression of religious reform in Prussia in 1823 at the same time that the government in independent Hamburg allowed it to exist alongside the established community. In contrast, although men such as Francis Goldsmid were displeased with remaining political disabilities, British Jews in the 1840s enjoyed far more equality than did their coreligionists in the German states. To be sure, one cannot entirely exclude the political motivation in Jewish religious reform in Britain. Morris Joseph, minister of the West London Synagogue, once explicitly said of its founders that they "had to prove that they deserved their liberties, and one of the proofs was their ability to set free their own minds."[1] In Britain, however, where the pressure was far less, where nonconformity was ever more broadly tolerated within Christianity, and where the state did not interfere in internal Jewish affairs, the political factor in Jewish religious reform was far less significant. Yet even with regard to Germany it is a reductionist error to see religious reform as fundamentally, or even exclusively, motivated by political considerations.

The religious milieus in which Jewish religious reform developed in Germany and Britain were important in each instance. For German reformers the Protestant Reformation served as a precedent for thoroughgoing religious change; later, the *Aufklärung* theology of the eighteenth century brought enlightened Protestantism very close to the kind of enlightened Judaism advocated by Moses Mendelssohn—so close that his somewhat wayward disciple David Friedländer believed that its tenets were not at variance with a rationalized Judaism. The more historically conscious and critically oriented currents in nineteenth-century German Protestantism made scholars like David Friedrich Strauss seem to the reformer

Abraham Geiger, for example, models for a critical approach to Judaism. And, of course, the German churches provided examples of decorum, music, religious instruction, and homiletics that greatly influenced the early Reform movement there. By the 1840s the German reformers were seeking to cast off some of the more obvious influences, but the success of reform efforts continued to be influenced—not surprisingly—by trends in Christianity. In southern Germany ultramontane currents for a time suppressed reform in Catholic Bavaria; in Protestant Prussia, later in the century, the increasing failure of the church to address contemporary issues slowed the process of Jewish reform.

In Britain, trends within Christianity played a large role in shaping the ideology of Jewish religious reform and differentiating it from its counterpart in Germany. It is well known that the British reformers in the 1840s, unlike the Orthodox, differentiated sharply between the authority of the Written and the Oral Law. The former, contained in the Pentateuch, was divinely revealed and binding for all time; the latter, contained in the Talmud, was worthy of reverence, but was human in origin. Both bibliocentrism (which its critics called bibliolatry) and criticism of "rabbinism" were widespread among British Christians at the time, especially among evangelicals within the Church of England. One can trace these views most easily in the writings of the missionary Alexander McCaul, who was by no means an enemy of the Jews.[2] (In 1840 he had written an eloquent defense of the Jews against the Damascus Blood Libel of that year.) It was likewise the high regard for the Hebrew Bible among Christians that made it much easier for the first minister of the West London Synagogue, David Woolf Marks, to defend the prophecies for the ultimate ingathering of Israel into its land—a belief that McCaul, from his Christian perspective, fully shared. Among German Jews there was also a trend to give primacy to the Bible over the Talmud, but biblical criticism gained influence in Germany much earlier, undermining fundamentalism except among the Orthodox. Moreover, the influence of historicism in Germany, derived from the universities and affecting Christianity and Judaism alike, drove toward relativization of the Bible's message and eroded the qualitative difference between Scripture and Talmud. Still, the British position was not so different from that of Zacharias Frankel in Germany (or Isaac Mayer Wise in the United States), who sought to preserve the special sanctity of the Bible by disallowing biblical criticism a priori while engaging in historical study of the rabbinic traditions.

No less important than the external political and religious context for understanding Jewish religious reform is the structure of the Jewish community. As Jakob Petuchowski pointed out, there were two models of religious reform: from within and from without.[3] The former became possible for the first time when Israel Jacobson assumed control of the Israelite Consistory of Westphalia during the reign of Napoleon's brother Jerome. Here religious reform, albeit of a different kind, was imposed upon all by a reformist religious leadership. The same occurred later with the promulgation of *Synagogenordnungen*, as in Württemberg. On the other hand, in Berlin in 1815 and in Hamburg in 1818, reform came into existence as an initiative intended only for those disposed to it and without the support of the official community.

In Britain the West London Synagogue was similarly an independent initiative undertaken only after the existing institutions had turned a deaf ear to the reformers' requests. Here, as also initially in Germany, the organized community remained Orthodox and the new institution was marginalized. Indeed, this was easier in Britain, where the centralized structure of a chief rabbinate and Board of Deputies could effectively ostracize the West London Synagogue as a dissenting group outside British Judaism as a whole, whereas in Germany opponents of reform were forced to increase their authority by gathering condemnatory rabbinical opinions from far and wide.

Another relevant point of comparison in regard to community is the relation between Sephardim and Ashkenazim. In Germany, although the first cantor of the Hamburg Temple was named David Meldola, the Reform movement was basically an Ashkenazi affair. Sephardi Jewry, for German Reform, was not an element of its social composition but rather its internal Jewish model. The reformers in Berlin and Hamburg used the Sephardi pronunciation and Sephardi rituals (such as lifting up the Torah *before* reading it), and they incorporated elements of the Sephardi liturgy into their prayerbooks. Ashkenazi Jews suddenly became Sephardi in their practice because Sephardim were thought to be examples of a more open-minded Jewry. However, in Britain Sephardim joined Ashkenazim in creating the West London Synagogue of British Jews, which was intended, in part, to bridge the gap between the two groups, enabling families with close business and social ties to worship together. The Sephardim also brought with them a *Marrano* background, which may help to explain British Reform Judaism's inclination to give higher theological status to the biblical over the talmudic text, a tendency which Chacham Nieto had already vigorously combated in the seventeenth century.

What most clearly separated the ideology of the German reformers from those in Britain is that the Germans very soon came to the conception of a progressive Judaism, which had evolved from biblical to rabbinic to contemporary, and which would continue to evolve in the future. This conception, much influenced by contemporary continental thought, is, as far as I can determine, wholly absent from the writings of David Woolf Marks. For him, religious reform was rather a return to the pristine Judaism of the Bible. He did not perceive the Talmud to be an advance from the Bible and he saw his own reform project as completed with the inauguration of the synagogue. German Reform developed a theology based upon critical historical evaluation of the classical sources, which corresponded to efforts then being made by Christian scholars in Germany but lacking in the British milieu. The leading German reformer, Abraham Geiger, could claim in 1844 that "a *wissenschaftliche Theologie* is totally unknown" in Britain, where only practical and edifying doctrines could gain respect. There, in his view, Judaism must become either a rigid traditionalism, barely affected by contemporary realities, or a group of dissenters like the West London Syngagoue, which merely served the practical needs of its members and did not even attempt to penetrate the depths of critical scholarship. Geiger excused this superficiality by referring to the relative newness and heterogeneity of British Jewry and its intellectual focus on textual refutation of Christian missionaries, who were more active in Britain than in Germany.[4]

And yet there are elements common to both countries which require further attention, for example, the use of subjective criteria to evaluate worship; some use of evidence for liturgical change in the past, adduced by German Wissenschaft des Judentums, as precedent for change in the present; and reference to the contemporary zeitgeist as a motive for reform. A hitherto unremarked similarity lies in the advocacy of women's equality in the synagogue. In fact, here Marks was in the vanguard in including in the liturgy an original Hebrew and English "Prayer for a Woman on Attending Divine Service, after Child-Birth" and arguing in his consecration discourse that, in opposition to "eastern customs totally at variance with the habits and dispositions of enlightened people," women should participate "in the full discharge of every moral and religious obligation."[5]

In terms of practice, the West London Synagogue differed from the German reformers by being, on the one hand, more conservative in retaining the texts calling for the restoration of Israel and, on the other, more radical in eliminating celebration of second days of Holy Days and blessings without biblical foundation. But in other respects there were no great differences. Decorum, vernacular sermons, and confirmation ceremonies were common to both. With the exception of the contemporary *Reformgemeinde* of Berlin, Hebrew was the language of prayer in both countries. By 1859 the West London Synagogue had an organ, almost a decade before such an instrument could be installed by the Liberals in a community synagogue in Berlin.

Influence, too, certainly existed, though it appears to have been strictly unidirectional. Regular reports in the *Jewish Chronicle* indicate that the British reformers (and their opponents) were well aware of events in Germany and that some saw the religious ferment there in the 1840s as desirable for British Judaism, even if its more radical manifestations were severely criticized.[6] Texts by both Goldsmid and Marks indicate similar awareness, as does the fact that the British reformers first sought their minister in Germany. In 1836 there had even been a petition by members of the London Sephardi synagogue to sanction "such alterations and modifications as were in the line of changes introduced in the reform Synagogue in Hamburg and in other places."[7] A generation later, when the editor of the *Jewish Chronicle*, Abraham Benisch, wrote a historical overview of Judaism in 1874, his brief treatment of the modern period was remarkably Germanocentric, following Heinrich Graetz in citing the life of Moses Mendelssohn as its beginning.[8] Finally, as has often been noted, the Reform congregations established in Manchester and Bradford were composed mostly of German-Jewish immigrants and were both clearly influenced by the German movement.

That said, the major institution of Reform Judaism in Britain, the West London Synagogue, must be seen primarily as a response to the particular British situation, both practically (for example, the founders' desire to have a synagogue close to their places of residence) and intellectually (for example, rejection of rabbinic commandments as divine), rather than as an attempt at imitation. Indeed, it was Benisch who took pride in the differing character of British Jewry when he wrote:

> Of all the nations of Europe the British is the most practical, and its Jewish section undoubtedly partakes of this characteristic. . . . May Germans indulge in philosophical disquisitions and hair-splitting distinctions at the enunciation of these ideas [the re-establishment of the ancient Sanhedrin, which Benisch was proposing as the only institution authorized to make major reforms] and Frenchmen in smiles and witticisms, it becomes the grave Englishman to ponder on the situa-

tion and weigh it, reject these ideas if found wanting; but take them up in earnest if deserving support.[9]

Departing briefly from thematic comparison to consider a comparison of dynamics, I would call attention to some striking similarities between the course of events in Hamburg after 1818 and in London after 1840. In each place the existing community lacked effective leadership; in Hamburg there were three elderly *dayyanim* (rabbinical judges) with no influence on the younger generation; in London, there existed a vacancy for the position of the Sephardi *Chacham* and an eighty-year-old Ashkenazi chief rabbi, Solomon Hirschell, a virtual recluse who never mastered the English language. Alienation from the synagogue had occurred in both places for various reasons, allowing the reformers to claim, with some justification, that they alone could address the religious needs of the younger generation. In each instance the Orthodox responded with condemnations, backed up, in Hamburg, by representations to the government. When both groups failed to stifle the new institutions, they each resorted to appointing new leaders of their own: Isaac Bernays in the first case, Nathan Marcus Adler in the second. Both men were college-educated and far better able to fight the reformers on their own turf. Both instituted regular vernacular sermons and brought about decorum, taking much of the wind out of the reformers' sails. Both were hired on the understanding that they would not issue new bans against the reformers, yet both found ways to express their opposition.

German and British Liberal Judaism

In the latter half of the nineteenth century, Liberal Judaism gained, at least nominally, the adherence of the overwhelming majority of German Jews. The more radical *Reformgemeinde* in Berlin occupied a unique position, existing officially within the community but also possessing its own independent religious institutions. At the other end of the religious spectrum, strict neo-Orthodox Jews formed their own, wholly separate, *Austrittsgemeinden* in various cities, but these fringe groups were relatively small. In the inclusive *Einheitsgemeinden*, Liberals almost always prevailed in community elections. In Britain, by contrast, Reform Judaism remained a peripheral stream at the edge of British Jewry. The reasons for this contrast are multiple, but perhaps the most significant of them are contextual and structural. In Germany, where some states, including Prussia, refused to give official recognition to Judaism, and where ambivalence reigned with regard to support for Orthodoxy or Reform, neither faction could gain established status. Liberals won because their party expressed ideas judged more in keeping both with the German Jews' desire for political and social acceptance and with the intellectual and aesthetic climate of modernity. In Britain, by contrast, Orthodoxy came to possess establishment status, symbolized by the chief rabbinate. Moreover, it was an Orthodoxy that demanded only vague adherence to its principles and support of its institutions. It did not require observance.[10] For Victorian Jews, nominal adherence to the established Orthodoxy provided the same "respectability" that middle- and upper-class Anglicans sought from their religion. Thus, if in Germany to be Orthodox required justification against the arguments of Liberals, in Britain it was the Reform Jews who had to justify their deviance from an Orthodoxy that was widely deemed the Jewish equivalent of the Church of England. In this respect, British Jewry was more closely related to the Jews of France, who also possessed central institutions in the form of a consistorial structure and a chief rabbinate, and where a similar formally adaptive Orthodoxy made no effective religious demands. Orthodoxy in Britain became yet more firmly established when the United Synagogue was created by an Act of Parliament in 1870, which officially gave control of Ashkenazi ritual to the Chief Rabbi. But there was also an internal reason for the failure of Reform Judaism to expand to any significant extent until the twentieth century: its own failure to respond to changes in the British intellectual environment.

As noted earlier, in Germany biblical criticism had already become a public issue by the 1830s. Although as sensitive a subject among Jews as among Christians, awareness of its ramifications doubtless played a role in the development by German-Jewish thinkers of an evolutionary, progressive theology that regarded the Bible as only one stage (however significant) in the ongoing development of Judaism. Conversely, the absence of biblical criticism as a public issue in Britain in the 1840s made it possible for the West London Synagogue to subscribe without qualms to the revelation of the Pentateuch in its totality. However, biblical criticism came to Britain with a vengeance in subsequent decades, undermining the foundation upon which Reform Judaism, no less than Orthodoxy, had been built. Earlier, criticism had been set aside as a dubious German preoccupation. However, from the 1850s onward it made its presence strongly felt in Britain, resulting in major controversies and in actions against its proponents ranging from condemnation to removal from academic positions to heresy trials. As its advocates tended to be respectable clergymen, the influence was seen as all the more seditious and could less easily be explained away as originating within circles hostile to Christianity. Its leading proponents were, as one scholar pointed out, *"believing* critics."[11] By the 1890s, biblical criticism had been absorbed by most branches of Christianity, as well as by the universities. A second challenge was posed in these same years by Darwinism. It too affected the Bible, in this case with regard to the central conception of the place of humanity within creation. Reform Judaism, as defined by the West London Synagogue, was no more able to deal effectively with either of these challenges than was Orthodoxy.

In 1863, Abraham Benisch attempted to refute Bishop Colenso's objections to the historical character of the Pentateuch, but had to admit, somewhat ambiguously, that "our belief in the authenticity of the Pentateuch, the same as of all other books of the Bible, does not depend exclusively upon the belief, that they were necessarily, such as we possess them, written by the authors to whom they are commonly attributed, but upon our belief that their form and contents are the same as they were in the time of Ezra and his companions and successors."[12] These men, according to Benisch, purged the text of "spurious elements" and then "gave the work the sanction of their authority, considered by the Jews as divine." Not only did Benisch's slight retreat have little impact, it remained for decades an isolated example. Darwinism seems to have provoked virtually no refutation by British Jews at all.[13]

By the end of the nineteenth century, British Reform Judaism not only remained institutionally marginalized but had also failed to exploit its innate advantage of adapting to historical change. British Jews who were intellectually dissatisfied with Orthodoxy possessed no Jewish institution that addressed the major issues of the time. Some were drawn informally to those peripherally Christian or non-denominational movements that were most open to modernity, such as Unitarianism and the Theistic Church, founded in 1871. People began to speak of the "Jewish Unitarian" or the "Unitarian Jew."[14] The last decades of the nineteenth century were in fact the "heyday of Liberal religion" in Britain, which briefly enjoyed remarkable attractive power.[15] Jews, as well as Christians, were among those drawn to it as offering greater harmony with criticism and science than did any available form of Judaism. Unitarianism also stressed social action, which had not been a major theme in British (or German) Jewry, but which had its religious basis no less in the prophetic literature than in the life of Jesus.

Given the profoundly altered intellectual climate and the dissatisfaction of increasing numbers of British Jews, especially among the better off and better educated, with the existing Jewish religious institutions, it is not surprising that a new religious movement should emerge. Unlike Reform Judaism in Britain, Liberal Judaism began with intellectual reflection and only a decade later embarked upon a hesitant process of institutionalization. In 1889, Claude G. Montefiore and Israel Abrahams founded the *Jewish Quarterly Review*, with the intention of publishing articles on contemporary issues as well as critical historical scholarship. In this new journal, unlike the *Monatsschrift für Geschichte und Wissenschaft des Judentums*, the scholarly flagship of German Jewry founded by Zacharias Frankel, articles by biblical critics, including the controversial W. Robertson Smith, could appear. Here, as well, Montefiore, a scion of one of the leading Jewish families, began to advocate a more radical version of Judaism than then existed in Britain. Montefiore, a student of Benjamin Jowett at Oxford and much influenced by him, became the first British Jew to argue systematically for the incorporation of biblical criticism into Judaism. According to him, the two fundamental doctrines of Judaism—theistic belief in God and belief in the moral law—remained unaffected by criticism. Although these ideas were not exclusive to Judaism, the "mission of Israel" to propagate them in unadulterated form within the world set Judaism apart and required the survival of the Jews as a separate entity. Jewish practice and rituals, in Montefiore's view, possessed only instrumental significance.

Montefiore's ideas, and the establishment of Liberal Judaism in Britain in the first decades of the twentieth century, were undoubtedly responses to the particular British environment of that time, just as British Reform Judaism, in its theological components, had been a response to its own intellectual and political milieu. Montefiore represents the orientation that Hugh McLeod has described as characteristic of the churchgoing gentry of the time: "Belief in Truth, and the necessity of discovering what it was, and Duty, and the necessity of following it."[16] Yet it is remarkable how far British Liberal Judaism was dependent upon ideas and practices developed in Germany. The "mission of Israel" concept, broadly enunciated by Moses Mendelssohn, had become a central doctrine of German Jewry across the religious spectrum. Ethical monotheism, as the essence of Judaism, was reiterated endlessly in German-Jewish sermons, especially among the non-Orthodox. The desire to give centrality to faith and morality, while minimizing religious observances, was characteristic of the radical *Reformgemeinde* in Berlin, which had no equivalent in Britain; so too was extensive use of the vernacular in the liturgy.

Montefiore, who had studied in Germany, was conscious of these connections. In the *Jewish Quarterly Review*, he described the first rabbi of the *Reformgemeinde*, Samuel Holdheim, as "a great reformer" and noted: "Without by any means agreeing with all that the Berlin *Reformgemeinde* has done, it is with the movement in which he took so leading a part that I feel the deepest and closest spiritual kinship."[17] As Holdheim in his day had been willing to take radical positions partly in response to the religious radicalism of *Deutschkatholiken* and Protestant *Lichtfreunde*, which enjoyed brief prominence in Germany during the 1840s, so did Montefiore, at the end of the century, advocate a similar radicalism in seeking to address the issues with which the left wing of British Protestantism, but not British Judaism, had come to terms.

Montefiore's dependence on German-Jewish thought extended, however, beyond the *Reformgemeinde*. Unlike the British Reform movement, and like German reformers across the spectrum, he believed in a concept of religious progress through progressive revelation that made the Bible a stage in an ongoing evolutionary process. As Israel Zangwill pointed out, "In England the idolatry of blind Bible-worship has died out among the cultured. . . . The 'Biblical' rock of the Reform Movement is proving a quicksand."[18] Montefiore's Liberal Judaism was largely a response to that British development, but it turned for an answer to the ideology of the German movement.

It is significant that the opening essay in the very first issue of the *Jewish Quarterly Review* was written by the prominent Jewish historian and professor at the conservative Jewish seminary in Breslau, Heinrich Graetz. Entitled "The Significance of Judaism for the Present and Future," it presented a theology that was almost precisely that of Montefiore and would later become the basis of British Liberal Judaism.[19] Like Montefiore, Graetz stressed that the essence of Judaism was ethics and the avoidance of idolatry, that Judaism was inherently rational, and that its rationalism made it "the sole stronghold of free thought in the religious sphere" and endowed it with the ongoing mission of overcoming "erroneous belief." Graetz was even ready to criticize excessive ritualism as "a fungoid growth which overlays [Jewish] ideals." Rituals, he argued, were "the means to an end, and that end is the memory of the past." In a lecture given at the Anglo-Jewish Exhibition in London in 1887, Graetz spoke favorably of the "new method of biblical inquiry . . . that clears up most doubts, and makes commentary superfluous," a method regrettably only "slightly utilized" by Jews.[20] Montefiore was not alone in his certainty that Graetz, though perhaps inconsistent, did not regard the existing text of the Bible as Mosaic.[21] It is therefore not surprising that Israel Zangwill, in criticizing the views of both men, should group Montefiore and Graetz together as expressing similar views.[22]

Graetz had a far higher regard for Britain and for the potential of British Jewry than Abraham Geiger had had earlier in the century. Although this may have been due in part to the religious stagnation of German Jewry, which preceded the appearance of a new generation of major Jewish thinkers at the end of the nineteenth century, it must also have been influenced by the rise of antisemitism in Germany in these years. Whatever the reason, Israel Abrahams was convinced that Graetz believed the future of Judaism lay with the English-speaking Jews.[23] Indeed, during his visit, Graetz proposed that British Jewry was best qualified to establish a "Jewish academy" which would combine research with laying down guidelines for the Jewish future. In the antisemitic atmosphere of Germany such an academy would be regarded as "a piece of Jewish impertinence," but in Britain it could prosper.

The conservative Liberal[24] Jews of Germany and the radical Liberal Jews of Britain (who had created an independent movement within British Jewry by 1909) came together collectively for the first time in 1926 at the founding conference of the World Union for Progressive Judaism, held that year in London. The interchange at this meeting clearly reflects the similarities and differences between the movements at that time. A striking point of ideological similarity was that each movement was decidedly anti-Zionist, believing Zionism to be a retreat from the mission of Israel. But for the German Liberals, living in an antisemitic atmosphere, anti-Zionism was a much more central concern and they felt compelled to counter Zionist arguments effectively lest they nurture *Judenhass*. For many Liberals in Germany, lamented the Liberal leader Heinrich Stern, their liberalism consisted exclusively of fighting Zionism.[25] In Britain, with its more benign atmosphere and its responsibility for the Balfour Declaration, Zionism was less troubling an issue in 1926, just as the traditional prayers for the restoration of Zion had not troubled the founders of the West London Synagogue in the way that they did their German counterparts. Even though Montefiore, like his coworker Lily Montagu, was opposed to Zionism, he was pleased that one of the ministers at the Liberal synagogue at that time, Maurice Perlzweig, was a fervent Zionist.[26] In Germany, the prominent Liberal rabbis remained cool or lukewarm toward Zionism until the Nazi period.[27] In neither Germany nor Britain, however, did anti-Zionism set the Liberals apart from their Orthodox co-religionists.

A significant point of difference between German and British Liberal Jews related to social justice. Both groups frequently defined their faith as "Prophetic Judaism," but it was the British Liberals, like their American counterparts, who took the practical implications more seriously.[28] In part this was due to the influence of Lily Montagu, who devoted much of her life to working with the poor. But it was undoubtedly also a reflection of different religious environments. By the 1890s the Anglican clergy had expanded its social concerns, whereas the German clergy steered clear of social issues. Still, in this regard British Liberal Judaism was far behind American Reform Judaism, which had been profoundly influenced by leading thinkers of the Protestant Social Gospel.

The attitude to Christianity was yet another point of difference. Montefiore was the leading Jewish champion of Christian-Jewish rapprochement in his day, stressing repeatedly that Jews needed to view the New Testament more sympathetically. This view stood in sharp contrast to that of the German-Jewish thinker Leo Baeck, who viewed Christianity, especially in its Lutheran manifestation, as the Romantic antithesis of a rational Judaism. No doubt Montefiore's attitude was a reflection of the greater Christian friendliness toward Judaism that he had himself first encountered in Oxford. In Britain it became possible for Christian religious bodies to join with their Jewish counterparts in the discussion of social and economic questions from a religious point of view.[29] Such interaction in Germany occurred only among individual intellectuals, not on the level of organized religion.

Since Liberal Judaism in Germany operated within the *Einheitsgemeinde*, it was also obliged to take a more conservative stance on ritual matters, lest the Orthodox within the community be driven into one of the *Austrittsgemeinden*. Moreover, coalitions of Orthodox Jews and Zionists were sometimes able to block Liberal proposals, as happened in Berlin with regard to the institution of late Friday evening and Sunday morning services.[30] With only one exception (and that not until 1930), men and women sat separately at Liberal services, and when the veteran preacher Lily Montagu came to Berlin for the World Union for Progressive Judaism convention in 1928, only the independent *Reformgemeinde* invited her to speak from its pulpit. Only in Germany was the bar mitzvah ceremony retained for boys while only girls underwent confirmation. In German Liberal Judaism the service remained almost entirely in

Hebrew, whereas British Liberals made do with less than half the liturgy in Hebrew and also composed new English prayers of their own. Male worshipers in Germany wore hats; most of their counterparts in Britain, except for the ministers, did not. Lay participation in conducting services, including that of women, was common among British Liberals, but not in Germany. Viewed as a whole, German Liberal Judaism was, in matters of liturgy and ritual, closer to British Reform than it was to British Liberalism.

The religious differences would become more apparent to British Jewry when German Jews, fleeing from Nazism, came to Britain by the tens of thousands during the late 1930s. Not always well treated by their British counterparts, they at first felt more at home with each other.[31] In London they formed their own German-speaking Liberal congregation at Belsize Square in 1939,[32] but the non-Orthodox among them also joined the existing Liberal and Reform congregations, and about twelve of their former rabbis were soon called to pulpits in various parts of Britain.[33] The German Jews in Britain persisted in their love for the Jewish traditions of their native land, favoring the music of Sulzer and Lewandowski and the liturgical customs with which they had been brought up, and sometimes influencing the religious life of the congregations they joined in the direction of more ceremonial, thoughtful, and decorous worship. The Leo Baeck College, opened in London in 1956, was named after the symbolic figure of German Jewry and had a faculty that was in large measure composed of German-Jewish refugees; it succeeded in bringing together in a single rabbinical seminary the divided progressive movements of British Jewry.[34] Thus, in this last stage of their relationship, the German Jews exercised their influence more directly upon their British co-religionists, just as the German-Jewish diaspora influenced Jewish host communities wherever the refugees scattered.

Notes

1. "The Jubilee of Political Emancipation" (Protocol of a Commemorative Dinner under the Auspices of the Jewish Historical Society of England, held on 30 November 1908), *Transactions of the Jewish Historical Society of England* 6 (1912): 102.
2. Alexander McCaul, *The Old Paths; or a Comparison of the Principles and Doctrines of Modern Judaism with the Religion of Moses and the Prophets*

(London, 1837), 237–40; David Feldman, *Englishmen and Jews. Social Relations and Political Culture, 1840–1914* (New Haven, 1994), 55–65.

3. Jakob J. Petuchowski, *Prayerbook Reform in Europe: The Liturgy of European Liberal and Reform Judaism* (New York, 1968), 31–83.

4. Abraham Geiger, "Nachrichten," *Wissenschaftliche Zeitschrift für jüdische Theologie* 5 (1844): 450–51.

5. David Woolf Marks, *Forms of Prayer* (London, 5601 [1841]), 3:105; Rev. D. W. Marks, *Discourse Delivered in the West London Synagogue of British Jews on the Day of Its Consecration* (London, 5602 [1842]), 19.

6. For example, the *Jewish Chronicle* reported on the rabbinical conferences held in Germany in the mid-1840s, clearly evidencing sympathy for the moderate position of German-speaking reformers like Zacharias Frankel and Hirsch Fassel. See *Jewish Chronicle*, 21 August 1846, 197–98; 16 October 1846, 1–2. See also David Cesarani, *The Jewish Chronicle and Anglo-Jewry, 1841–1991* (Cambridge, 1994), 3–29.

7. Cited in Moses Gaster, *History of the Ancient Synagogue of the Spanish and Portuguese Jews* (London, 1901), 171.

8. A. Benisch, *Judaism Surveyed* (London, 1874), 105. An editorial in the *Jewish Chronicle* for 25 April 1873 calls attention to the multiple "intimate associations between the Jews of England and the Jews of Germany," noting, inter alia, that "perhaps seventy of every hundred Jews of middle age had German grandfathers" and that "we owe many of our Anglo-Jewish clergy and literati to Germany."

9. Benisch, *Judaism Surveyed*, 132.

10. Interestingly, it was a group of German immigrants to Britain which, in 1886, established a congregation in a northern suburb of London that required a higher standard of observance from its members. It was clearly modeled on the Frankfurt separatist community. V. D. Lipman, *Social History of the Jews in England, 1850–1950* (London, 1954), 94.

11. Gerald Parsons, "Biblical Criticism in Victorian Britain: From Controversy to Acceptance," in Parsons, ed., *Religion in Victorian Britain* (Manchester, 1988), 1:250; see also Josef L. Altholz, "The Warfare of Conscience with Theology," in ibid., 4:163–64.

12. A. Benisch, *Bishop Colenso's Objections to the Historical Character of the Pentateuch and the Book of Joshua Critically Examined* (London, 1863), ix–x; Feldman, 124.

13. The only refutation of which I am aware was written for the *Jewish Chronicle* by its editor, Michael Henry, in 1871. See Cesarani, 59. But neither am I aware of full treatments by German-Jewish thinkers. In the United States, Darwinism became an unavoidable and persisting issue for Reform rabbis. Kaufmann Kohler addressed it favorably in 1874. See my *Response to Modernity: A History of the Reform Movement in Judaism* (New York, 1988), 274–75.

14. C. G. Montefiore, "Some Notes on the Effect of Biblical Criticism upon the Jewish Religion," *Jewish Quarterly Review* 4 (1892), 293–406.

15. Hugh McLeod, *Class and Religion in the Late Victorian City* (London, 1974), 249–50.

16. Ibid., 151.
17. *Jewish Quarterly Review* 1 (1889), 272, 278. Montefiore must also have been responsible for the appearance of an article by Immanuel H. Ritter, current rabbi of the *Reformgemeinde*, entitled "Samuel Holdheim: The Jewish Reformer," in ibid., 202–15. The connection is also noted in Edward Kessler, *An English Jew: The Life and Writings of Claude Montefiore* (London, 1989), 87. Yet in a later article entitled "Liberal Judaism in England: Its Difficulties and Its Duties," *Jewish Quarterly Review* 12 (1900): 618–50, Montefiore makes no specific reference to German models.
18. Israel Zangwill, "English Judaism: A Criticism and a Classification," in *Jewish Quarterly Review* 1 (1889): 398–99. He also wrote of British Christianity that many of the Christian bulwarks had been swept away by "a scientific Renaissance, in which the evolution doctrine has been only one of a host of dissolvent influences . . . but Judaism stands, so Jews assert, untouched. The breath of new knowledge has passed through English Judaism, the wind has passed with its pollen dust; but has impregnated nothing. Even the Reform movement was more a natural and very trivial branching-out from the compulsion of inner forces, than a result of any new external influences" (*Jewish Quarterly Review* 1 [1889]: 379).
19. *Jewish Quarterly Review* 1 (1889): 4–13; *Jewish Quarterly Review* 2 (1890): 257–69, reprinted in Heinrich Graetz, *The Structure of Jewish History and Other Essays,* ed. Ismar Schorsch (New York, 1975), 275–302.
20. Graetz, *Structure of Jewish History,* 259–74.
21. *Jewish Quarterly Review* 4 (1892): 300. In *Jewish Quarterly Review* 2 (1890): 267, Graetz wrote that the part of Leviticus dealing with sacrifices "shows itself externally as well as internally to be a foreign element." L. M. Simmons reported that Graetz spoke to him of the Pentateuch as a composite work. Simmons, "The Breslau School and Judaism," *Jewish Quarterly Review* 4 (1892): 398. But see also Graetz's critique of standard biblical criticism in the *Jewish Chronicle,* 5 August 1887, 9.
22. *Jewish Quarterly Review* 1 (1889): 399.
23. *Jewish Quarterly Review* 4 (1892): 192.
24. In Germany "Reform" had come to mean the radical *Reformgemeinde*.
25. Heinrich Stern, "Die Entwicklung des deutschen liberalen Judentums," in *International Conference of Liberal Jews* (London, 1926), 44–45.
26. C. G. Montefiore, "Liberal Judaism in England," in *International Conference of Liberal Jews,* 64.
27. For the attitudes of German Liberal rabbis to Zionism in this period see my "Liberal Judaism and Zionism in Germany," in Shmuel Almog et al, eds., *Zionism and Religion* (Hanover and London, 1998), 93–106.
28. *Second Conference of the World Union for Progressive Judaism* (London, 1930), 157–58.
29. Montefiore, "Liberal Judaism in England," 65.
30. *First Bulletin of the World Union for Progressive Judaism,* December 1929, 13.

31. Geoffrey Alderman, "Anglo-Jewry and Jewish Refugees," *AJR Information*, June 1987, 3. Cecil Roth reports the witticism that the British were prepared to return the colonies to Germany if Germany would return Golders Green to England (October 1962).

32. Marion Berghahn, *German-Jewish Refugees in England* (London, 1984), 167–69, 234. In Birmingham Liberal Jews went to the Orthodox synagogue because they were more at ease with a service mainly in Hebrew than one mostly in English. See Zoë Josephs, *Survivors: Jewish Refugees in Birmingham, 1933–1945* (Warley, West Midlands), 1988, 174–75.

33. Gerhard Graf, "The Influence of German Rabbis on British Reform Judaism," in Dow Marmur, ed., *Reform Judaism: Essays on Reform Judaism in Britain* (Oxford, 1973), 156–57. The influx helps to explain the growth of both Reform and Liberal Judaism in England during the 1930s. Comparing figures for 1929 and 1938, the number of weddings conducted in Reform synagogues increased from 31 to 71; in Liberal synagogues from 8 to 64. See Lipman, 218.

34. Albert H. Friedlander, "The German Influence on Progressive Judaism in Great Britain," in Werner E. Mosse et al., eds., *Second Chance: Two Centuries of German-Speaking Jews in the United Kingdom* (Tübingen, 1991) (Schriftenreihe wissenschaftlicher Abhandlungen des Leo Baeck Instituts 48), 425–35.

PART IV

American
Jewry

CHAPTER 19

German-Jewish Identity in Nineteenth-Century America

One of Simon Dubnow's principal contributions to Jewish historiography was his conception of shifting hegemonic centers, each for a time exercising a dominant influence on Jewries in other parts of the world. Such centers spiritually strengthened those younger or weaker Jewish communities that were dependent on them. Yet in the course of time and for a variety of historical reasons, some of these initially peripheral settlements themselves made successful bids for hegemony. Thus, according to Dubnow, Spanish Jews gained independence from the Oriental Gaonate in the tenth century, and five hundred years later the mantle of leadership fell upon the German-Polish Jews. In the twentieth century, Dubnow looked toward a joint hegemony shared by Jews in the European-American Diaspora and in the Land of Israel.[1]

Whatever the shortcomings of Dubnow's grand scheme, when applied to the entire course of Jewish history the notion of an inchoate Jewry looking to an established, intellectually productive one for inspiration and guidance, then gradually—or fitfully—breaking away to assert its own primacy is suggestive for specific instances. It can, for example, be usefully applied to the relation of the American-Jewish community to its German-Jewish origins during the nineteenth century.[2] From the beginning of large-scale Jewish immigration from Germany to the United States in the 1830s until the demographic submergence of German Jewry in America beneath the flood tide of East European immigrants at the end of the century, there was a discernible tension between forces making for preservation of the German-Jewish heritage as represented by Jews still in

Germany, and those that pressed in the direction of greater spiritual independence. While German Jewry could and did serve as a model of modernization, especially in matters of religion, acculturation in the United States worked mostly in the opposite direction: toward an assertion of independence from the German matrix. Although for a period of time German Judaism was venerated almost without qualification, by the last decades of the nineteenth century its hegemony was under severe attack even by those German Jews in America who owed it the most. The purpose of this essay is to trace this conflict of forces as it appeared in the realms of culture and religion and to explain the eventual disavowal of German Judaism as a model for American Jewry.

Unlike its European antecedents, American Jewry did not undergo a multidimensional process of modernization. Only about 2,000 Jews were living in the British colonies when the colonists successfully gained their independence. The United States enshrined in its constitution the political equality for members of all religious groups for which European Jews were still struggling, in part by giving evidence of their modernity. Moreover, American Jewry was not forced into a narrow economic structure, nor did it possess the comprehensive corporate structure of its European counterparts or an authoritative rabbinate of the old style. From the start, American Jews were integrated into the general socio-political life to a degree that was only partially achieved in Central Europe even after a long process of modernization. Only in the spheres of culture and religion can one speak meaningfully of a process of Jewish modernization as opposed simply to the universal processes whereby all immigrants adapted to American life.

Between 1825 and 1875 the Jewish population in the United States grew from about 15,000 to about 250,000. The vast majority of the immigrants in that period came from Germany, initially from the villages and small towns in Bavaria and other southern states, later also from northern Germany. They emigrated because of legislative restrictions limiting Jewish marriages and choice of occupation, but their main motive was economic self-improvement. Few came at any time solely because of the attraction of American political ideals. Those who could stay usually remained. Particularly in the first half of the nineteenth century, the German-Jewish immigrants were mostly young, male, and poor, ill-educated Jewishly, and with little if any secular culture. Modernized German Jews began to come to America only in the 1850s and then again after the Civil War. All but a few intellectuals spurned emigration at any time. Many of the early migrants moved to small towns in the

American South and Midwest, peddling inexpensive items and maintaining in America those rural patterns of life with which they had been familiar in Germany.[3] The rapid urbanization of Jews in Germany only after midcentury was paralleled by the German-Jewish experience in America.

Most of the early German immigrants had little time for matters either Jewish or German. They struggled to make a living and to improve their economic lot wherever possible. Their occupational situation required their gaining a basic knowledge of the English language, considerable freedom from ritual constraints, and full devotion to the great American enterprise of "making money." But while Americanization was the key to economic success, it was also pursued out of a sense of gratitude for what the new land offered. Supporting oneself in America was not easy, and some succumbed to the hardship, but there were no artificial barriers to advancement for those who combined skill or intelligence with hard work. In their initial drive to establish themselves economically, the early immigrants rarely looked back upon Germany with any nostalgia. They had never really identified as Germans either politically or culturally. Most spoke and wrote only Judeo-German (Yiddish), not the German of Moses Mendelssohn, and were unacquainted with the classics of German literature. Germany primarily represented for them the restrictiveness which they had been pressed to flee; positively, the old country meant little more than the landscape of their childhood.

Leaving Bavaria or Württemberg also meant leaving behind the pervasive religious atmosphere of its Jewish communities. Judaism in America was represented by the well-established Sephardim whose congregations those German Jews interested in religion initially joined, in preference to transplanting their own rite. Although there were considerable numbers of German Jews in America already in the eighteenth century, the first successful Ashkenazi congregations were not established until the 1820s.[4] And even after the foundation of German synagogues, the trend to association with the more Americanized, prestigious, and dignified Sephardi congregations continued in some German-Jewish circles well into the nineteenth century. It is noteworthy that one of the principal Americanizers of German Jewry in the United States, Isaac Leeser, though himself born in Westphalia, served a Sephardi congregation, Mikveh Israel in Philadelphia. Yet the Ashkenazi members were often treated as pariahs by the Sephardim and regarded with some contempt by more German-conscious Jews. Rabbi David Einhorn used to call them "Portugiesen aus Schnotzebach."[5] As long as the German Jews were neither themselves Americanized nor brought with them any significant modern cultural baggage from Germany, the Sephardi elite presented the best example of what a modern American Jewry should be like. But as German Jews appeared in the United States in ever greater numbers, as those who came had increasingly undergone modernization in Germany, and as the earlier immigrants from Germany found more time for culture and religion, a specific German-Jewish identity in America began to emerge.

As early as 1807, a member of the Bleichröder family, then resident in New York, had written that Jewish immigrants in America were considerably more cultured than those who were born in the country.[6] Although this purported correlation between newness to the American scene and a higher cultural level may not have held in the succeeding decades, it was generally still true in the 1850s. As larger numbers of acculturated German Jews came to the United States, the process of Americanization slowed considerably. Germany ceased to be merely a land of origins and its Judaism no longer seemed inappropriate to the American context. For more than a generation after midcentury, American Jews of German origin looked across the ocean for direction and inspiration.

The more favorable attitude of American Jews to things German was influenced by the rising respect accorded German culture in the United States. Jews constituted only a small portion of the 5.5 million Germans in America according to the census of 1850. By the 1860s it was widely felt that Germany had much to offer America and even that the mission of its emigrants was to conquer the New World for German values.[7] While not all cities became as Germanized as Milwaukee, Cincinnati, or St. Louis, the German immigrants sought minimally to preserve certain elements of their old life in the New World. The most obvious attribute of their cultural origins was the German language. Immigrant churches in America fostered the mother tongue, as did a variety of social, fraternal, and philanthropic societies. German-language newspapers flourished. Thus, while earlier Yiddish-speaking Jews had no support in the American context for retaining their language—and as a result Americanized very rapidly—German-speaking Jews were part of a larger language group which encouraged their endeavors to preserve the German heritage.[8]

Still in the 1840s Jewish parents usually did not attempt to teach their children German. When Rabbi Max Lilienthal served in New York during that period, he was forced against his will to give confirmation instruction in English.[9] In the next two decades, however, a considerable proportion of the Jewish immigrants made determined efforts to pass on the German language—and hence German culture—to their children. In 1856, on a visit to Easton, Pennsylvania, Isaac Leeser complained that there, as elsewhere, parents in the Jewish school insisted on having German as the vehicle of instruction. Three years later Rabbi Bernhard Felsenthal of Chicago estimated that 90 percent of the present Jewish generation in America either knew only German or knew it better than English. Despite assimilatory pressures, German Jewry in America had considerable success in maintaining the German language. As late as 1874, the *Deutschamerikanisches Conversationslexicon* pointed out that German predominated in the majority of some 400 Jewish communities in the United States. And even a decade later, Rabbi Isaac Mayer Wise noted that in a number of congregations English-speaking children still had to learn their catechism in German, and the German language was taught in the Sabbath schools "as if were part of Judaism."[10]

While English usually had to be used in business, German was retained in the sanctuary of the home as the language of the family. Women immigrants especially continued to read and speak mostly German. To a high degree it became the language of the synagogue. Congregational records were kept in German, in one case—Rodeph Shalom of Philadelphia—after they had been written in English for a number of years.[11] More important, and for a longer period of time, German served as the language of sermons and portions of the liturgy. Orthodox congregations no less than Reform ones wanted preachers who could deliver religious discourses of the type that were familiar to them from Germany. But for some Reform leaders the use of German in the synagogue was not merely a concession to familiar structures and expressions, not simply a passing phase in the process of Americanization. Felsenthal noted that the younger generation should learn German because the German people were still the leading cultural influence in the world "and we bow our heads in reverence before its spirit . . . we American-German Jews." The German tongue, it seems, was thought essential for modern spirituality even in America. Germany, said Rabbi David Einhorn, was the "land of thinkers, presently the foremost land of culture and, above all, the land of Mendelssohn, the birthplace of Jewish Reform. . . . Now if you remove the German spirit—or what amounts to the same thing, the German language—you have torn away the native soil and the lovely flower must wither." Without the German language, Einhorn believed, the Reform movement was nothing but a shiny veneer. It was a mannequin without heart or soul; neither proud temples nor magnificent chorales could breathe any life into it. Hanns Reissner was right when he claimed that for the first generation of Jewish immigrants to America and beyond, German became nothing less than a "sacred language."[12]

The retention of the German language was facilitated by the usually favorable relations between Jewish and Gentile immigrants. The Christians who took the initiative to leave Germany were less likely to have harbored anti-Jewish prejudices than those who remained, and once they arrived most of them readily accepted the American value of social equality. When Jews with German professional training reached America, having fled German discrimination, they were, ironically, hailed as representatives of superior German university training. With few exceptions, Gentiles welcomed Jews into German cultural societies whose counterparts in Germany would have most likely excluded them. In San Francisco in 1852, a Jew headed a cultural and social club that included the most distinguished Germans of the city. German Jews could feel like insiders in these groups while they still remained outsiders in America.[13]

Educated Americans gave considerable attention to German-Jewish writers, encouraging Jews to take pride in their former compatriots. Emerson, a great fancier of German literature, had also read Moses Mendelssohn; Heine was repeatedly translated into English by Americans, his poetry and essays frequently discussed. American periodicals mentioned the popular German-Jewish novelist Berthold Auerbach more often than any German author except Goethe; and for a time Auerbach was possibly more widely known in America than any German writer.[14] Jews and non-Jews came together in celebration of their common cultural heritage. Thus it occurred that German Jews in America continued the modernization process begun in Germany within an imported German context, thereby paradoxically slowing down their assimilation to modern America.

Even Jews who had not attained a formal education while still in the old country sought to make up for it once they had established themselves economically in America. They created their own literary societies and listened to lectures in German on diverse topics. In Philadelphia, a Gabriel Riesser Society was in existence for many years.[15] Religious leaders established German-language Jewish newspapers and German sections in those which were published in English. Isaac Mayer Wise's popular *Die Deborah* endured for nearly half a century, from 1855 to 1902. A new Jewish intellectual journal, *Der Zeitgeist,* was established in Milwaukee as late as 1880.

German Jews in America broadened the framework of organized Jewish life, which for the Sephardim had been centered strictly upon the synagogue. They formed a panoply of independent fraternal and charitable associations, perhaps patterned in part upon such long-standing German-Jewish models as the *Gesellschaft der Freunde* and the *hevrot* of the German communities. Yet the manner of raising funds—dinners, charity balls, lotteries, and the like—was strictly American.[16] The most significant early association founded by German Jews in America was B'nai B'rith, which originated in New York in 1843 and was apparently modeled upon Freemasonry. By 1851 there were eleven B'nai B'rith lodges, all but two conducting their transactions in German. Unlike the synagogue, which in the 1850s was already dividing traditionalists from reformers, and which left out those German Jews who had become wholly indifferent to religion, B'nai B'rith could include all German Jews within a framework which was secular without being secularist. Indeed, it has been suggested that B'nai B'rith in America initially served the function of a "secular synagogue."[17] As such, it enshrined and perpetuated the culture and mores of German Jewry. Like the German-language synagogue, B'nai B'rith thus served as a brake upon assimilation by creating a unique amalgam of peculiar Jewish symbolism and transplanted German values. Yet the German element does not seem to have lasted as long in B'nai B'rith as it did in the synagogue. By 1855, the order had already changed its official language from German to English.

One of the reasons that German Jews looked to their old homeland for inspiration was that they had not yet produced in America the equivalent of a Heine or a Riesser. In the nineteenth century, Jews in America remained outside the cultural establishment to a greater degree than in Germany. Despite discrimination, a number of Jews in the old country had gained professorial chairs by the 1880s. There were notable Jewish philosophers, writers, poets, artists. But here in America, lamented an anonymous writer in a German-Jewish periodical, Jews "have contributed nothing either in art or in science." They had failed to produce men of the political stature of an Eduard Lasker or the literary merit of a Berthold Auerbach because the German spirit had insufficiently penetrated American Jewry, which, alas, was too much concerned with outer show and too little with inner content.[18] For this writer, and for others, Germany signified the life of the spirit while America meant chasing after the almighty dollar.

As American Jews admired their German brethren for contributing so richly to general culture, so too they esteemed their work as modern scholars of Judaism and bearers of Jewish religion and culture. Abraham Geiger's *Jüdische Zeitschrift für Wissenschaft und Leben* had its readers and contributors in America as did Ludwig Philippson's *Allgemeine Zeitung des Judentums*, the more traditional *Israelitische Wochenschrift*, and Samson Raphael Hirsch's neo-Orthodox *Jeschurun*. American rabbis praised and depended upon the work of Leopold Zunz and his fellow workers in the vineyard of Wissenschaft des Judentums. By comparison, American-Jewish culture remained weak and immature. In 1878 Bernhard Felsenthal protested that American Jewry could not yet be expected to produce significant scholarship on its own. A few years earlier, in 1866, he had written that American rabbis could only be trained in Germany, preferably in Berlin, where they could study with Zunz, Steinschneider, and other teachers at the Ephraim'sche Lehranstalt.[19] In the 1870s, the Hochschule für die Wissenschaft des Judentums drew students from America, including Felix Adler, who shortly thereafter left the Jewish fold to found the Ethical Culture movement, and Emil G. Hirsch, who became a prominent Reform rabbi in Chicago. A decade later, Bernard Drachman, subsequently a teacher at the Jewish Theological Seminary in New York, and Morris Jastrow, who became a professor of Semitics at the University of Pennsylvania, were the first American-born Jews to study at the Breslau Jüdisch-Theologisches Seminar.

For the sake of the younger generation, which was not fully at home in the German language, American Jews began translating into English major works of German-Jewish thought and scholarship. Among the most active translators were the most Americanizing of the Jewish leaders in the United States, Isaac Leeser and Isaac Mayer Wise. Leeser, who also did English translations of the Hebrew Bible and prayerbook, produced an English version of Mendelssohn's *Jerusalem* in 1852. In rapid succession, Wise contributed to the *Asmonean* English excerpts from the writings of Zunz, Geiger, Frankel, Rapoport, Luzzatto, Krochmal, Holdheim, Jost, and Graetz. Others produced similar gleanings for English-language Jewish periodicals. In 1865, Geiger's *Judaism and Its History* appeared in New York, and all three works published by the predecessor to the present Jewish Publication Society during its three-year existence from 1872 to 1875 were translations from the German. The first major project of the society's later successor in name and task was a slightly abridged translation of Graetz's multivolumed history, which appeared between 1891 and 1898.[20] In terms of Jewish culture and scholarship, up to the last decades of the century American Jews appreciatively accepted the hegemony of German Jewry.

German Judaism served as the model in the sphere of religion almost to the same degree as in the sphere of culture. American-Jewish leadership was not closed to specifically American influence, but until it gathered strength, until it recognized that American Jewry was destined to overshadow its nineteenth-century German source, it ascribed religious authority to the German thinkers who had sought to create postghetto Jewish ideologies and to the innovations which had modernized the German synagogue. This was especially true for the reformers, but not for them alone. The traditionalist Isaac Leeser, for example, greatly admired the Berlin rabbi Michael Sachs, whose position on the religious spectrum he represented in America, and both he and those who shared his religious views have been regarded as American exponents of Zacharias Frankel's positive-historical Judaism.[21] When American Jews sought to adapt their religious institutions to the modern world, they looked to the German example as a guide. The extent to which their religious leaders minimized or maximized the German connection seems to have depended largely on how deep their own German experience had been. Neither Leeser nor Wise had German university training or much direct acquaintance with the intellectual ferment in German Jewry during the first half of the century. Most of those who were especially tied to Germany—like Rabbis David Einhorn, Samuel Adler, and Samuel Hirsch—had both. Upon arrival they set out to make American Judaism a true copy of the German original. Only gradually did they begin to claim that the copy possessed a lovelier form and a rosier future than the model upon which it was fashioned.

Much has been written about the first efforts at religious reform in the United States which took place in Charleston, South Carolina, beginning in 1824. It seems evident that those members of Beth Elohim, a Sephardi congregation, who sought to introduce decorum, an English sermon, a few prayers in the English language, and somewhat later an organ, were motivated by specifically American influences, especially by Protestantism in the city. Yet even at the beginning they expressed their awareness of religious reform in Holland and Germany. And when Gustav Poznanski, who had lived in Bremen and Hamburg, became preacher and reader of the congregation in 1836, he brought with him the spirit of the Hamburg Reform temple, which had embodied Sephardi elements in its pronunciation of Hebrew, in the melodies used for the liturgy, and in the formulation of certain prayers. Some of the English hymns, published by the congregation in 1842, were adapted from the Hamburg temple's *Gesangbuch,* and the memorial service on the Day of Atonement was taken from its prayerbook. A little later Beth Elohim introduced the confirmation ceremony, based on the ritual formulated by Rabbi Leopold Stein of Frankfurt.[22]

For modernizing Ashkenazi Jewish congregations in America, the Hamburg temple ritual served as the chief model. A native of Hamburg living in Baltimore helped to found the first specifically Reform congregation in America, Har Sinai, in 1842. He was commissioned to present to the members a description of the temple's prayerbook, which had just appeared in a revised edition amidst great controversy. It was thereupon adopted and apparently used until David Einhorn introduced his own prayerbook in 1856.[23]

Temple Emanu-El of New York, which held its first service in 1845, did not begin its rapid process of reforms until more than a decade later. Yet from the beginning its choir sang chorales from Munich and Vienna while members listened to sermons in German, at first by Ludwig Merzbacher from Fürth and later by Samuel Adler. Not until 1868 did the congregation elect a second professional preacher whose task was to address the congregation in English. Without doubt the introduction of reforms did reflect, as Leon Jick has argued, the upward social mobility of the congregation. But it is worth noting that David Einhorn attributed the slow progress of Reform at Temple Emanu-El to the disproportionate influence of the small "aristocratic Portuguese element" in the congregation, that element which was the most established in American society. Moreover, the reforms which were eventually introduced were nearly all precedented in Germany, the leadership was well aware of German examples, and despite increasing wealth, the ambience of Temple Emanu-El and similar congregations in New York and elsewhere remained more German than American for decades.[24] If Reform was motivated solely by the desire for rapid Americanization, its Germanic character remains inexplicable.

Increasingly the German congregations in America were led by men who had been influenced by the modern rabbinate in Germany. In Baltimore and Cincinnati there were former students of Leopold Stein, in New York, men who had been instructed as children by Samuel Adler and David Einhorn. Not surprisingly, the wealthier German synagogues in America soon sought to obtain leading figures from Germany as their rabbis. Abraham Geiger twice refused offers; Leopold Zunz, a contributor to the first German-language American-Jewish periodical, *Israels Herold*, was considering a position in New York as early as 1833. Others did come, at first mostly less well-known individuals (except Max Lilienthal), and then more prominent names after midcentury. German speakers continued to dominate the American rabbinate as late as 1872, when an editorial in the *New York Herald* took note of how few men were capable of delivering sermons in English.[25]

The outstanding Germanizer among nineteenth-century rabbis in America was David Einhorn, who, beginning in 1855, successively occupied pulpits in Baltimore, Philadelphia, and New York. His influence through his prayerbook *Olat Tamid*, his intellectual journal *Sinai*, and the perpetuation of his ideas by his similarly inclined sons-in-law Emil G. Hirsch and Kaufmann Kohler was ultimately more decisive for Reform Judaism in America than the less radical ideas of Isaac Mayer Wise. While Wise, the proponent of Americanization, was by far the more popular and practically effective leader, it was Einhorn's philosophy that dominated the Reform movement in America from the 1870s until the 1930s. In an article he published in *Sinai* in 1859, Einhorn wrote: "German research and knowledge constitute the source of the Jewish Reform idea, and *German* Jewry possesses the mission to gain life and currency for this idea upon American soil." Without it, American Jews might well give up their ceremonial laws and their old customs, but they would do so out of accommodation, not within a principled system that affirmed a modernized Judaism even as it rejected outdated forms. Only German Jews, nurtured on German-Jewish religious thought, could have any conception of Judaism's historical development or its universal character. At least for the present, Einhorn believed the Reform idea still required the German umbilical cord; it was too young in America, too much in ferment to divest itself of its original German shell. Only after the German-Jewish heritage would be fully absorbed could American Jewry seek to be more independent, to substitute the English language for the German, and to embark on its own course. In all but one important respect Einhorn was very American: he spoke out from the pulpit on controversial issues such as slavery, a venture rarely if ever undertaken by rabbis in Germany in the nineteenth century.[26] Although Einhorn's devotion to the spiritual heritage of the German nation remained undiminished to his final sermon in 1879, his respect for Jewish thinkers in Germany, especially for those who called themselves "Reformers," had begun to decline precipitously a decade earlier. By the 1870s it was not only the Americanizers but Einhorn and other Germanists among the radical Reformers who were seriously questioning whether Philippson, Geiger, and other German Reformers could still serve as guides for the Jewish religion in America. A revolt was under way, and even Einhorn became a part of it.

As the radical Reformers' views on German Jewry soured, they drew nearer to those of that most enthusiastically American among the American-Jewish Reformers, Isaac Mayer Wise. Bereft of all nostalgia for Europe, Wise did not identify himself actively as a German Jew or encourage others to do so. He consistently took pride in his coreligionists' capacity to acculturate rapidly in America, leaving behind foreign attachments while clinging all the more fervently to their inherited identity as Jews. Modernization, in Wise's writing, was associated with America, not Germany. In the United States Jews faced new challenges which Wise believed they had not encountered abroad. Forced to respond to a throng of propagandizing missionaries and to raucous atheists, the "thoughtless ceremonial Jew" was transformed into the "thinking and enlightened Israelite."

As early as the 1850s, American Jewry had already shown its mettle. In 1855, the Cleveland Conference brought together a handful of moderate Reformers and traditionalists to affirm their belief in the divine origin of the Bible and in the Talmud as its authoritative expositor. Wise, who was a participant, immediately insisted that this conference had done more than the German rabbinical assemblies of the 1840s and the current meetings in Giessen and Wiesbaden. It had defined principles, not just dealt with specific practices. Moreover, the American meeting had done more good than "the dry historical investigations of [Zacharias] Frankel's school. The latter, however much we appreciate their scientific labor, entirely neglect the wants of the time; writing the biographies of the old Talmudists, they forget the questions of the day and the disunion and disharmony that tears the congregations asunder." As synagogues became more German in the early 1860s, Wise struggled against the trend. Sarcastically he wrote: "The Alexandrine Hebrews had a Greek ritual, the Babylonians adopted the Chaldean, and the American Israelites, in the midst of an English speaking community, should be German? They call that reform, we call it retrogression." Yet in those years, even Wise was forced to preach in German in his Cincinnati congregation at least every other week.[27]

For Wise, Europe represented above all oppression. He felt no loyalty whatever to the Austrian Empire of his origins.[28] In America Jews preached upon occasion from Christian pulpits; in 1860 Rabbi Morris Raphall had opened a session of Congress with a prayer. The equivalent in Germany would be hard to imagine. What contemporary German culture offered, Wise held in the 1870s, was not religious idealism but such enemies of religion as materialism and Darwinism. America, by contrast, had given the Jews liberty. Here they were free to participate in its great and manifest destiny; here, Jewish religious values could find a fertile soil. The Jewish leadership in Germany, Wise believed, had failed to appreciate the virtues either of America or of its Jewry. Men like Ludwig Philippson used every occasion to put it in its place. They could not grasp "the significance of American Jewry for all Israel."[29]

Wise's assessment of the critical attitude shared by the Jewish leadership in Germany was no exaggeration. Ludwig Philippson expected that the men he recommended for American pulpits and teaching positions would continue to write appreciative letters. When they did not, he accused some of "gross ingratitude" and claimed that others were "purposely seeking to estrange Jews there completely from German Judaism." According to Philippson, American Jewry could lay no claim to significant religious creativity. Its entire religious development was "either brought along or imported from Germany." To argue otherwise was an "absurd presumption." It was the daughter raising herself above her mother to whom she owed everything; it was the self-flattery of insisting "we savages are after all better men."[30]

Zacharias Frankel's position was not as possessive or as crudely stated, but in its own way it was even more devastating. In an article in his *Monatsschrift*, Frankel related a few facts about the Jewish settlement in America, but then noted—still in 1863—that American Jewry really had no right to claim that it possessed a history at all. Frankel held in common with his colleague, Heinrich Graetz, that Jewish history in its proper sense consists of endurance in the face of suffering on the one hand and of spiritual creativity on the other. But American Jewry had never had to struggle for its survival and it had not yet produced a significant religious or scientific literature. Thus American Jews would simply have to recognize that they had yet to enter Jewish history. Not surprisingly, when Graetz published volume eleven of his *Geschichte der Juden* in 1870, he devoted only a solitary sentence and a half to the Jews of America. Even in the later English edition Graetz included no more than a single paragraph on the subject.[31]

One of the most favorably disposed toward American Judaism within the German-Jewish religious leadership was Abraham Geiger. This inclination was especially marked at the end of Geiger's life, after he had taught American students at the *Hochschule* in Berlin. Geiger encouraged his friend, David Einhorn, in the difficult task of transplanting the German spirit to the tumultuous American environment, submitted material to his periodical *Sinai*, and directed Kaufmann Kohler to the United States as the land of promise for progressive Judaism. While Geiger believed that American Jewry still lacked maturity, he could appreciate its hopeful freshness and even admit that perhaps German Jews were like the biblical Reubenites who reached their patrimony first, aided their brethren, but did not themselves settle in the promised land.[32] It was only when the American rabbis dared to challenge his wisdom that Geiger became defensive, or rather a bit aggressive.

In preparation for the Leipzig Synod held in the summer of 1869, Geiger had composed a list of theses on liturgy and marriage laws which he wanted that assembly to consider.[33] Later the same year, eleven American Reform rabbis gathered in Philadelphia in order to deal collectively with religious issues and especially with questions of marriage law.[34] The participants included all the major American Reformers, ranging from the most radical to relative moderates like Wise and Moses Mielziner. One of them, Kaufmann Kohler, had just arrived from Germany and had been present at the Leipzig Synod.[35] The Philadelphia deliberations were conducted in German, and references were made to Leipzig and to Geiger's theses. A series of resolutions, ranging from the theological to the practical, was adopted and speedily became known in America and in Europe. On a number of points the resolutions deviated from Geiger's theses, to his very great displeasure. In the tone of a father castigating his wayward sons, the veteran German Reformer now chastised the Philadelphia gathering for straying from the proper path. The conference "must give up all petty jealousy toward the old homeland," he wrote in his *Zeitschrift*. "It should rather recognize spiritual depth as it is nurtured in Germany and participate in it, utilizing without conceit the greater freedom in practical matters given them by their circumstances."[36] With all his sympathy for American Jewry, Geiger could not yet reconcile himself to German Jewry being located on the periphery rather than at the center of religious modernization, or to his views being ignored or contradicted by his colleagues in America. Perhaps he also recognized that the Philadelphia Conference, for all its German character, was an assertion of intellectual independence.

Even more striking than Geiger's parental expression of rejection was the overreaction to it by his spiritual son, David Einhorn. In an article in the *Jewish Times,* Einhorn accused Geiger of believing that the Torah was only to be found *me'ever layam* (beyond the ocean), of taking the position *im aini kan mi kan* (if I am not here, who is), and in effect holding the Philadelphia rabbis to account for not declaring *"in Geiger Alles, ausser ihm Nichts!"* (roughly: Geiger knows it all). Aside from the psychodynamic tension of the situation there were of course general and specific points of significant difference between the two men. Einhorn leveled the most substantive general charge against Geiger when in the same article he called him, not favorably, a repentant, a *ba'al teshuvah*.[37] Geiger, as well as others of the early Reform leaders in Germany, had made their peace with the exigencies of united Jewish communities embracing liberal as well as conservative elements. Unlike Samuel Holdheim who, as Jakob Petuchowski has shown, was in some respects more of an antecedent for Einhorn than was Geiger,[38] other Reformers in Germany had not stuck by their principles; the movement had succumbed to concession and compromise. Hence, it could no longer claim to be on the leading edge of religious development. In America, with its religious voluntarism and lack of communal constraints, religious reform was freer to take its destined course. And in fact, just as the Reform movement in Germany was becoming more conservative, its offspring in America was becoming ever more radical in theory and practice. Ironically, Wise was now closer in spirit to German Reform than was Einhorn.

The most significant single difference between Geiger and the American Reform rabbis concerned the position of women, an issue determined by the disparity of cultural values between the two countries. The Philadelphia Conference had voted to allow a bride to respond to the wedding formula recited by her husband by uttering the same words given only a change of gender. This institution of reciprocal vows, combined with an exchange of rings, did not find favor in Geiger's eyes. While he was willing to recognize the wife's equality with her husband, he insisted that the two would always occupy a different position in society, that the husband would "always remain master of the house" and would have the determinative say. The husband should, therefore, speak for both while "the chaste bride, who has already more whispered than audibly spoken her 'yes' should not have to speak and act publicly, but rather attend the words of her husband with a soulful look as she eagerly stretches out her finger so that the ring can be placed upon it. For the future as well," Geiger concludes, "the husband will be the one who gives, the wife the one who receives."[39] For all of his Germanism, Einhorn was by now sufficiently Americanized to brand such talk the worst romanticism. Though he claimed that women's equality was a prophetic, and hence not originally an American notion, Einhorn lived in an environment where women—for all the disabilities they still suffered—were treated more as equals than in Germany. The Jewish traveler I. J. Benjamin had been struck and offended by the Women's Rights movement which he encountered in the United States in 1860.[40] While in nineteenth-century Germany even Liberal congregations seated men and women separately, in America the "family pew" had spread to nearly all the larger synagogues, including very conservative ones; and one looks in vain in nineteenth-century Germany for an equivalent of the American Rebecca Gratz, founder of the modern Jewish Sunday school.

During the 1870s and 1880s, even in those circles which had heretofore been most worshipful of their German antecedents, there now arose a chorus of criticism for Germany and German Jewry, together with praise for America and its Jews. The case of Rabbi Bernhard Felsenthal of Chicago is illustrative. No one except perhaps Einhorn had been more fervent a devotee of German culture and more attached to German Jewry than Felsenthal, who had written in 1866: "With regard to the assertion that we should emancipate ourselves from German Jewry and proclaim our independence, we say: Alas, for us if we were now to free ourselves from German Judaism and its influences! As in the Middle Ages the sun of Jewish scholarship shone loftily and marvellously in Spain . . . that sun now stands in the German heavens and from there sends its beneficent light to all Jews and Jewish communities among the modern cultured nations. Germany has replaced Sefarad."[41] Felsenthal argued that, without the influence of German Jewry, American Judaism would "either sink into an ossified orthodoxy or into nihilistic, raw and presumptuous bar-room wisdom." Both would be of a strictly American variety. Orthodoxy would more likely be a kind of hysterical Methodism, a benightedly strict Calvinist puritanism, or an ostentatious High Church display than a Torah-true Judaism in accord with Talmud and poskim. For the nihilists, Thomas Paine would serve as the model.[42] In short, Felsenthal believed that American Jewry—across the religious spectrum—still required a subservient relationship to German Judaism lest it assimilate the worst characteristics of American religion and philosophy.

In succeeding decades, however, Felsenthal's views changed almost completely. He came to believe that America had as much idealism as Germany, and without the attendant sickly romanticism. He even went so far as to claim that the American environment had been a blessing for Judaism; it had not had to suffer governmental interference because of the American separation between church and state, and thus had been able to develop freely on its own. In fact, Americanization represented the real test of Jewish modernity. Could it survive in an open cultural context without state authority for community taxation as was the case in Germany? It was a challenge which American Jewry had met very well. In "idealistic" Germany, Felsenthal now writes with sarcasm, Jews did not make the same sacrifices to establish Jewish institutions that were being made in America. Moreover, American Judaism was more tolerant of diverse religious expressions. In contrast to the situation in Germany, American Jewry held no elections of a centralized *Gemeinde* which could factionalize the communities. Each of the three branches recognized the right of the others to practice Judaism differently.[43] Perhaps it is no mere coincidence that as Felsenthal was becoming more of an American, he was also becoming a fervent Zionist. Although Zionism during the 1880s was just as much a minority viewpoint in the United States as it was in Germany, to Felsenthal the pluralistic American milieu must have seemed more capable of tolerating a Jewish national movement than the more conformist political atmosphere of Germany.

During the 1880s it became much more difficult for American Jews to speak favorably of the German state. While some had welcomed Prussia's liberalism in the 1860s and celebrated its victory over France in 1871, Germany was now seen as a land whose purported spirituality had failed to curb a vicious outbreak of antisemitism. Rabbi Jacob Voorsanger of San Francisco protested that the language of the German antisemite Adolf Stöcker had no place in the American synagogue.[44] As for the Jews of Germany, by American-Jewish lights they had not risen sufficiently to the occasion. Adolf Moses, the rabbi of Mobile, Alabama, severely castigated the philosopher Hermann Cohen, when, in response to the antisemitism of Heinrich von Treitschke, he expressed the hope that Judaism would eventually dissolve into German Protestantism and that the Jews would one day lose the physical characteristics that set them apart. However profound Cohen's philosophy, his supine response showed that an attack on his Jewishness could turn an otherwise clear mind to confusion. American Jews, said this radical Reformer, were proud of their racial characteristics and did not intend to give up their separate religious identity for the sake of national unity.[45]

From the perspective of German Jews in America, the lessons to be learned from the Jews of Germany were now mostly negative ones. For the radical Reformers, German Judaism had settled into stagnation, into a "murky swamp," as Kaufmann Kohler put it. The living spirit of Judaism had fled Germany, he believed, the "prophetic spirit that once called forth Reform has been exhausted." Although the founding fathers had failed in their own land, what they had sought to build could be created in America. While some of the Germanizing American rabbis continued to look askance at Isaac Mayer Wise's organizational efforts, sooner or later they had to recognize his accomplishments: a Union of American Hebrew Congregations in 1873 and the first successful American seminary, the

Hebrew Union College, which he founded in 1875. Eleven years later, Conservative Jews in America also established their own theological seminary. It remained now only to assert the new hegemony. Adolf Moses put it with typical American hyperbole in 1882: "From America salvation will go forth, in this land (and not in Germany) will the religion of Israel celebrate its greatest triumphs." Or, as Kaufmann Kohler believed, Judaism in the new world will reinvigorate Judaism in the old. American Jewry had learned from Germany; now it was ready to teach.[46]

If the Philadelphia Conference in 1869 symbolized the rabbinic turn toward independence in religious matters, the successful completion of the *Jewish Encyclopedia* in 1906 marked the coming of age of American-Jewish scholarship. German Jewry had failed to produce a collective monument of equivalent stature. Now its best scholars contributed to an American project whose editorial board was entirely composed of Jews resident in the United States. Although almost all the American writers—who wrote many of the most significant articles—had been trained in Wissenschaft des Judentums abroad, they were pursuing their discipline in America.[47]

It is ironic that just as the mantle of modern Jewish religious and intellectual leadership was passing from Germany to America, German Jews in the United States found themselves inundated by an influx of their brethren from Eastern Europe. It is equally ironic that this influx of East European Jews was largely responsible for sustaining the remnants of a separate German-Jewish identity in America for another generation and more. Still not a part of the American establishment, but for the most part ever more peripherally Jewish, the wealthier New York families now stressed their German ancestry far more than their Oriental heritage.[48] Eager to remain separate from the newcomers, even as they sought to promote their welfare, the *yahudim* segregated themselves both socially and religiously on the basis of their German origins, thus braking somewhat an otherwise accelerating pace of Americanization.[49] For their part, East European Jews in America—whether devoutly Orthodox or secular Yiddishists—possessed their own Old World loyalties. Thus it was not until after the Holocaust that hegemony within the Jewish people would finally pass incontrovertibly to American Jewry, and to the state of Israel.

Notes

1. Simon Dubnow, *Nationalism and History*, ed. Koppel S. Pinson (Philadelphia, 1958), 272, 348.

2. A most valuable tool for the exploration of this subject has been Rudolf Glanz, *The German Jew in America: An Annotated Bibliography* (Cincinnati, 1969).

3. Bertram W. Korn, *Eventful Years and Experiences* (Cincinnati, 1954), 1–26; Bernard D. Weinryb, "The German Jewish Immigrants to America," in Eric E. Hirshler, ed., *Jews from Germany in the United States* (New York, 1955), 113–26; Rudolf Glanz, *Studies in Judaica Americana* (New York, 1970), 188–89, 192; Leon Jick, *The Americanization of the Synagogue, 1820–1870* (Hanover, N.H., 1976), 39, 137, 175.

4. Jick, *Americanization of the Synagogue*, 20–26.

5. *Deutsch-Amerikanische Skizzen für jüdische Auswanderer und Nichtauswanderer* (Leipzig, 1857), 47–50; Emil G. Hirsch, "Hüben and Drüben," *Jewish Reformer*, February 5, 1886, 11; Max J. Kohler, "The German-Jewish Migration to America," *Publications of the American Jewish Historical Society* (New York, 1909), 9, 87–105.

6. *Hame'asef* 8 (1809): 13–14, German supplement.

7. Emil Lehman, *Die deutsche Auswanderung* (Berlin, 1861), 81, 102–3.

8. Glanz, *Studies in Judaica Americana*, 12; Hyman B. Grinstein, *The Rise of the Jewish Community of New York, 1654–1860* (Philadelphia, 1945), 207–9.

9. Glanz, *Studies in Judaica Americana*, 70; *Allgemeine Zeitung des Judenthums* (*AZJ*) 11 (1847): 145.

10. Jacob R. Marcus, *Memoirs of American Jews, 1775–1865*, vol. 2 (Philadelphia, 1955), 87; Bernhard Felsenthal, *Kol Kore Bamidbar: Über jüdische Reform* (Chicago, 1859), 24; Glanz, *Studies in Judaica Americana*, 99, 138–39, 222; Bernhard Felsenthal, *Jüdisches Schulwesen in Amerika* (Chicago, 1866), 10–11; Isaac M. Wise, "Judaism in America," *American Jews' Annual* 1 (1884–85): 44.

11. Jick, *Americanization of the Synagogue*, 21, 222; H. G. Reissner, "The German-American Jews, 1800–1850," *Leo Baeck Institute Year Book* (*LBIYB*) 10 (1965): 93–94.

12. Felsenthal, *Kol Kore Bamidbar*, 24; David Einhorn, *Ausgewählte Predigten und Reden*, ed. Kaufmann Kohler (New York, 1880), 90; Reissner "German-American Jews," 92.

13. Glanz, *Studies in Judaica Americana*, 98–100, 214, 237–39; Reissner, "German-American Jews," 65–68, 94–97; I. J. Benjamin, *Three Years in America, 1859–1862*, vol. 1 (Philadelphia, 1956), 241; Weinryb, "German Jewish Immigrants," 124; Glanz (144–45) also notes some instances of discrimination.

14. Henry A. Pochman, *German Culture in America* (Madison, 1957), 143, 172, 338–39, 346, 684–85.

15. *Die Deborah* 5 (1859–60): 62; Grinstein, *Jewish Community of New York*, 202; Albert M. Friedenberg, "American Jews and the German Revolutionary Movements of 1848–1849," *PAJHS* 17 (1909): 205.

16. Kohler, "German-Jewish Migration to America," 103; Glanz, *Studies in Judaica Americana*, 157.

17. Deborah Dash Moore, *B'nai B'rith and the Challenge of Ethnic Leadership*

(Albany, 1981), 1–34. See also *Deutsch-Amerikanische Skizzen*, 89–108; Reissner, "German-American Jews," 98–100.

18. "Americanisirtes Judenthum," *Der Zeitgeist* 1 (1880): 237.

19. Adolf Kober, "Jewish Religious Life in America as Reflected in the Felsenthal Collection," *PAJHS* 45 (1955–56): 100, 125; Felsenthal, *Jüdisches Schulwesen*, 30–34.

20. Bertram W. Korn, *German-Jewish Intellectual Influence on American Jewish Life, 1824–1972* (Syracuse, 1972), 8, 13, 21.

21. *Occident* 20 (1862): 369; Moshe Davis, *The Emergence of Conservative Judaism* (Philadelphia, 1965). Yet the German influence on those men who founded the Conservative movement in America seems to have been considerably less. For example, as Davis notes (109), they did not have the same commitment to the German language. It is interesting that of the nineteen leaders of the "Historical School" in America whom he singles out for special biographical treatment (329–66), only seven—just slightly more than a third—came from Germany. Four were from Hungary and three were Sephardim. This difference of origins may have been at least one factor in the split between Conservatives and Reformers during the 1880s. It should also be noted that Lance Sussman, in his *Isaac Leeser and the Making of American Judaism* (Detroit, 1995), has been able to argue persuasively that Leeser's Judaism is better defined as an immutable doctrinal Orthodoxy than as a historically conditioned development.

22. Maurice Mayer, "Geschichte des religiosen Umschwunges unter den Israeliten Nordamerikas," *Sinai* 1 (1856): 101–7, 171–81; *Hymns Written for the Service of the Hebrew Congregation Beth Elohim* (Charleston, S.C., 1842); Lou H. Silbermann, *American Impact: Judaism in the United States in the Early Nineteenth Century* (Syracuse, 1964); Jick, *Americanization of the Synagogue*, 12–13, 55–56, 81–86; Bernard Martin, "The Americanization of Reform Judaism," *Journal of Reform Judaism* (Winter 1980): 35–36.

23. Wise, "Judaism in America," 42; Mayer, "Geschichte des religiösen Umschwunges," 198–200.

24. *AZJ* 11 (1847): 22; *Sinai* 4 (1859): 161–69; Mayer, "Geschichte des religiösen Umschwunges," 202–3; *New Era* 4 (1894): 121–32; Grinstein, *Jewish Community of New York*, 353–71; idem, "Reforms at Temple Emanuel of New York," *Historia Judaica (HJ)* 6 (1944): 163–74; Jick, *Americanization of the Synagogue*, 88–96.

25. *Jewish Reformer*, January 29, 1886, 11; Korn, *German-Jewish Intellectual Influences*, 18; Guido Kisch, "Israels Herold: The First Jewish Weekly in New York," *HJ* 2 (1940): 75–76; Morris W. Schappes, *A Documentary History of the Jews in the United States, 1654–1875*, 3rd ed. (New York: Schocken, 1971), 554–57. At Emanu-El, German was maintained until 1879. See Martin, "Americanization of Reform Judaism," 38. Rodeph Shalom of Philadelphia alternated the language of sermons until close to 1894. See Henry S. Morais, *The Jews of Philadelphia* (Philadelphia, 1894), 76. According to Robert Kahn, ("Liberalism as Reflected in Jewish

Preaching in the English Language in the Mid-Nineteenth Century"
[Hebrew Union College DHL dissertation, 1949], 53), only in the late
1860s did the German sermon become the exception.

26. *Sinai* 4 (1859): 161–62; Einhorn, *Ausgewählte Predigten*, 90, 185; Bernhard
N. Cohn, "Early German Preaching in America," *HJ* 15 (1953): 101–2.

27. *Die Deborah* 1 (1855–56): 313; *American Israelite* 2 (1855): 137; 8 (1862):
324.

28. Jacob R. Marcus, *The Americanization of Isaac Mayer Wise* (Cincinnati,
1931), 8–12.

29. *Die Deborah* 2 (1856–57): 340; Joseph Gutmann, "Watchman on an
American Rhine," *American Jewish Archives* 10 (1958): 135–44. David
Einhorn, despite his Germanism, shared some of Wise's messianic
hopefulness regarding America. See Gershon Greenberg, "The Signifi-
cance of America in David Einhorn's Conception of History," *American
Jewish Historical Quarterly* 63 (1973): 160–84.

30. *AZJ* 29 (1865): 405–7; 44 (1880): 435.

31. Zacharias Frankel, "Zur Geschichte der Juden Amerikas," in *Monatsschrift für Geschichte und Wissenschaft des Judenthums* 12 (1863): 366–67;
Heinrich Graetz, *Geschichte der Juden*, vol. 11 (Leipzig, 1870), 231; idem,
History of the Jews, vol. 5 (London, 1892), 749–50. By contrast the earlier
historian, Isaac Marcus Jost, showed a relatively high degree of interest
in American Jewry. Although he too noted that "there cannot yet be a
history of the American Jews" because their communities were still too
atomized, he devoted a special section of sixteen pages to them. He
listed all of the communities and institutions known to him as well as
Jews who had held political offices, and he devoted special attention to
Mordecai Manuel Noah's Ararat project for a Jewish colony on the Ni-
agara River. See Isaac Marcus Jost, *Geschichte der Israeliten*, vol. 10 (Berlin, 1847), 221–36.

32. *Jüdische Zeitschrift für Wissenschaft und Leben* (*JZWL*) 2 (1863): 66–67; 11
(1875): 224–25.

33. *JZWL* 7 (1869): 161–67.

34. *Protokolle der Rabbiner-Conferenz abgehalten zu Philadelphia, 3–6 November
1869* (New York, 1870). An English translation of the proceedings was
published by Sefton D. Temkin as *The New World of Reform* (Bridgeport,
Conn., 1971).

35. Later Kohler noted: "The broadness of view and independence of
thought, which characterized all the deliberations, formed a striking
contrast to what I had heard and witnessed at the Leipzig Synod." See
his *Personal Reminiscences of My Early Life* (Cincinnati, 1918), 12. On the
Leipzig and Augsburg synods, see Michael A. Meyer, "The Jewish Synods in Germany in the Second Half of the Nineteenth Century" (Hebrew), *Studies in the History of the Jewish People and the Land of Israel* 3
(1974): 239–74.

36. *JZWL* 8 (1870): 21–22.

37. *Jewish Times* 2 (1870–71): 107, 187–88.

38. Jakob J. Petuchowski, "Abraham Geiger and Samuel Holdheim: Their Differences in Germany and Repercussions in America," *LBIYB* 22 (1977): 149–59. Petuchowski shows that Einhorn had already been critical of Geiger on a previous occasion.

39. *JZWL* 8 (1970): 12.

40. Benjamin, *Three Years in America*, 1:34.

41. Felsenthal, *Jüdisches Schulwesen in Amerika*, 36–37.

42. Ibid.

43. *Die Deborah*, July 19, 1894, 5–6.

44. *Occident* 20 (1862): 363–66; *Jewish Times* 3 (1871–72): 76; *Der Zeitgeist* 3 (1882): 220.

45. Adolf Moses, *Prof. Dr. Hermann Cohen in Marburg und sein Bekenntniss in der Judenfrage. Eine Reminiszenz und Kritik* (Milwaukee, 1880).

46. *Der Zeitgeist* 1 (1880): 268–69; 3 (1882): 10, 249; *Jewish Reformer*, January 29, 1886, 12.

47. Korn, *German-Jewish Intellectual Influences*, 9–10.

48. Stephen Birmingham, *"Our Crowd": The Great Jewish Families of New York* (New York, 1967), 148–49.

49. Kaufmann Kohler no doubt spoke for many German Jews in America when, as late as 1910, he extolled the German people's deeper sense of history, their science, philosophy, and biblical criticism, while condemning only their tendency toward a racial definition of German identity. See *Tägliches Cincinnatier Volksblatt*, February 23, 1910, 5. The influence of German Judaism reappeared in the twentieth century with the transplantation of Samson Raphael Hirsch's neo-Orthodoxy and the discovery of the German-Jewish thinkers Hermann Cohen, Leo Baeck, Franz Rosenzweig, and Martin Buber. For this twentieth-century German-Jewish influence see Korn, *German-Jewish Influences*, 14–15, and Martin, "Americanization of Reform Judaism," 50–55.

CHAPTER 20

The Refugee Scholars Project
of the Hebrew Union College

In the years 1935 to 1942, the Hebrew Union College in Cincinnati brought to its campus eleven scholars who had become victims of Nazi persecution. For a few of them, the call to HUC literally saved their lives; for others, already outside the German sphere, it made possible a new start in their careers. The formulation and carrying out of this project in its various stages, the difficulties that had to be overcome, and the individual successes and failures constitute a significant chapter in the history of the College even as they shed light on a specific application of the immigration policies of the United States. On the whole, the episode reflects favorably on HUC, while providing additional evidence of the State Department's callous indifference to the plight of refugees from fascist oppression.

With Hitler's rise to power in 1933, Jewish academicians who had succeeded in gaining university positions during the liberal Weimar period found themselves summarily discharged and hard-pressed to earn a living. Some were able to find new employment in universities outside Germany; others languished in unsuitable occupations. Those whose fields were related to Jewish studies in many instances sought to associate themselves with a specifically Jewish institution either in Germany or abroad. In the fall of 1934, at a joint meeting of faculty and Board of Governors, the Hebrew Union College made its initial commitment to help in solving the problem. It was decided to appropriate $4,000 to bring two German Jewish scholars to the College.[1] This project would be carried out in addition to plans then being formulated to provide full maintenance for five German rabbinical students currently enrolled at the liberal seminary in Berlin.[2] The initial proposal was limited indeed. Two refugee scholars already in the United States, Julius Lewy and Guido Kisch, would be asked to teach at the College for a single semester in the year 1935–36. If funds remained, then Michael Wilensky, currently in Lithuania, would be brought to Cincinnati for a year to catalogue the Hebrew manuscripts.[3] While Kisch, a historian of law, did not join the HUC faculty, becoming instead a visiting faculty member at Stephen Wise's Jewish Institute of Religion, Lewy and Wilensky both came to the College, each to remain in Cincinnati until his death.

Julius Lewy had been professor of Semitic languages and Oriental history at Giessen until he was dismissed in 1933. A temporary teaching position at the Sorbonne in Paris[4] was followed by a call to be visiting professor at Johns Hopkins University in the fall of 1934. But Hopkins offered Lewy no permanent appointment and neither did the Jewish Theological Seminary, where he taught on a grant from the Emergency Committee in Aid of Displaced German Scholars the following spring.[5] For the first semester of the academic year 1935–36, Hopkins was again willing to employ Lewy as a temporary replacement for William Foxwell Albright, but after that his prospects were gloomy indeed. There were few positions in Assyriology in the United States. Columbia did not show an interest in Lewy, and at the Oriental Institute in Chicago Lewy's Judaism and his Zionism both worked to his disadvantage.[6] He needed an additional six months of academic employment in the United States in order to be eligible for a permanent immigration visa. The College initially appointed Lewy for a semester and then, against its original intent, kept on reappointing him, at first on a visiting basis to replace the absent Nelson Glueck, and then permanently. Although as late as 1938, Julian Morgenstern, the HUC president, was still trying to find a place for him in a more suitable institution,[7] Lewy adapted himself to giving courses in Bible as well as Assyriology. His appointment, moreover, laid the foundation for what soon became one of the leading American programs in Semitic studies.

Michael Wilensky had managed to leave Communist Russia for Berlin, along with a group of Jewish intellectuals headed by Hayyim Nahman Bialik, in the year 1921. In Germany he had worked with Bialik in the Dvir Hebrew Publishing House and produced his critical edition of the medieval grammatical work by Jonah ibn Janah, *Sefer ha-Rikmah*. After the Nazi takeover, Wilensky fled to Lithuania, where he was settled in a small town without work and without citizenship when he received his invitation from the College in 1935. Wilensky had been recommended to Morgenstern by a number of scholars though he had had no experience in cataloguing manuscripts. It was intended that he come for only a single year and return upon completion of his task. But from the beginning Wilensky saw it otherwise. He did not believe there would be a return trip.[8] Once in Cincinnati he proceeded with his task slowly and deliberately, making careful and extensive notes on each manuscript. After a year, he fell ill. The College authorities seriously considered returning him to Lithuania, where his wife, a physician, had remained behind. But Mrs. Wilensky wrote Morgenstern emotionally that not only would her husband have no work in Lithuania, but termination of his position would likely bring on a fatal stroke. Ismar Elbogen also wrote to Morgenstern on her behalf. In the end, Wilensky recovered and the College paid for his wife's travel to join her husband in America. He remained at his cataloguing tasks until his retirement in 1943.[9]

Word that the Hebrew Union College was interested in employing displaced Jewish scholars spread rapidly throughout Europe, bringing one application after another to Morgenstern's desk.[10] Some of the men had experience in teaching Jewish subjects, others claimed they could shift from previous academic interests. But their applications were all refused. The College considered the candidacy of Eric Werner, a musicologist who had managed to enter the United States on a visitor's visa in October 1938, only because there had been no one to teach Jewish music after the retirement of Abraham Z. Idelsohn in 1934. Werner was engaged for two years on the recommendation of Rabbi Jonah B. Wise of New York and was thus enabled to receive a nonquota immigration visa. In this instance, too, the appointment eventually became regular and permanent.[11]

Until the fall of 1938, no further action was contemplated. At this early stage the College was interested only in helping somewhat to alleviate the employment problem by giving temporary work to men who could be useful to it for a limited period of time.

Yet there was one highly respected European scholar who enjoyed such standing in the entire Jewish academic community that the College undertook to initiate a scheme for his resettlement in America—although it would derive no direct benefits. Ismar Elbogen had taught since 1902 at the *Lehranstalt* (formerly *Hochschule*) *für die Wissenschaft des Judentums*, the liberal seminary and school for advanced Jewish studies in Berlin. He had been the teacher and counsellor to HUC students studying abroad after their ordination; for a semester he had taught in New York at the Jewish Institute of Religion. In 1937 Elbogen made the decision to leave Germany, having found life there "insupportable." On the initiative of William Rosenau, rabbi in Baltimore and a member of the HUC Board of Governors, a unique plan was formulated whereby Elbogen would come to America as "Research Professor in the fields of Jewish and Hebrew Research." He would be supported by equal grants of $1,000 per year from the Hebrew Union College, the Jewish Institute of Religion, the Jewish Theological Seminary of America, and Dropsie College in Philadelphia. In the name of all four institutions, Morgenstern issued the call to Elbogen in May, 1938. The elderly man arrived in New York a few months later. There, as earlier in Berlin, he continued to work for the rescue of fellow scholars and former students.[12]

As the situation in Nazi Germany grew ever more grim, the Board of Governors of the College decided much more needed to be done. At its meeting of October 20, 1938, upon the recommendation of Rabbi Solomon Freehof of Pittsburgh, it appointed a committee to consider what HUC might do to ameliorate the plight of refugee scholars, possibly providing them with room and board in the College dormitory.[13] In the following weeks, an imaginative project was formulated: the Hebrew Union College would establish a "Jewish College in Exile" on its campus. Apparently modeled on the University in Exile, which was established in 1934 by Alvin Johnson as the graduate faculty of the New School for Social Research in New York,[14] it was initially contemplated to provide for some twenty-five German Jewish scholars of repute during a period of two to three years. They would have the library at their disposal to pursue their studies and be able to perfect their English under the tutelage of the College's students. While at HUC, they would be able to establish contacts and adapt themselves to America.[15]

As a result of what was happening in Europe, Morgenstern envisioned a new role for the College. When added to its existing faculty, these new men would make HUC one of the great centers of Jewish research and scholarship in the world. With the demise of the institutions of higher Jewish learning in Germany, Wissenschaft des Judentums would be transplanted to the soil of Palestine and America. It thus became the task of the Hebrew Union College to help raise up a new generation of Jewish scholars, a responsibility previously left to Europe.[16] Although the appointments were to be temporary, it was intended that the scholars' immigration be permanent. For with the *Kristallnacht* pogrom of November 9–10, 1938, only a few weeks after Freehof's initial proposal, any thought of return was patently absurd. With the outbreak of physical violence, the HUC project took on a new dimension of urgency.

In November, two weeks after *Kristallnacht*, Morgenstern informed Elbogen, now settled in New York, of the project which was planned and asked him to draw up a list of names. Besieged by requests for assistance from abroad, the elder scholar was deeply moved at the news: "מים קרים על נפש עיפה שמועה טובה" (cool water for a weary soul is a hopeful message), he replied. "It is the first act of speedy and ready help after the last pogrom." From the names which Elbogen supplied, Morgenstern eventually chose nine: Alexander Guttman, Franz Landsberger, Albert Lewkowitz, Isaiah Sonne, Eugen Täubler, Max Wiener, Walter Gottschalk, Abraham Heschel, and Franz Rosenthal.[17] Official invitations were sent to each of them on April 6, 1939. Adding the name of Arthur Spanier, who, under special circumstances, had been asked to accept a position somewhat earlier, the College thus made an irreversible commitment to ten men, some with families.

In accordance with the current interpretation of United States immigration law,[18] which provided for the granting of nonquota visas only to scholars who would be paid a minimal salary over a period of at least two years, the initial call was issued to seven men to be research professors at $1,800 per year and two (Heschel and Rosenthal) to be research fellows at $500 per year plus room and board. Along with the official letters, to be presented to the local consul, went a private message which noted that the College would expect the men, if possible, to live in the dormitory, deducting a portion of their salary for maintenance, and that the commitment was for only two or three years until they could make an adjustment to America.[19] As the letters of invitation did not go out until after consultations by mail with the Visa Division of the State Department, the College authorities fully expected that the appointments would qualify. They surely did not anticipate the degree to which they would have to increase their commitment, nor that in some of the cases—despite their best efforts—the rescue attempt would fail.

The problems that the entire project faced with the United States government first became apparent in the case of Arthur Spanier.[20] Along with thousands of other German Jews, the former Hebraica librarian at the Prussian State Library and later teacher at the *Lehranstalt* had been arrested and put into a concentration camp following *Kristallnacht*. He wrote to Elbogen, his former colleague, in New York, that he would be released only on the basis of assured emigration. Elbogen thereupon urged Morgenstern to give him an appointment at the College so that he might be immediately released and admitted outside the quota. Through Elbogen and Rabbi Jonah B. Wise an arrangement was worked out whereby Spanier's sister in New York would pay the difference between the value of her brother's services to the College and the salary of $2,000 he would be offered. She also agreed to be responsible for his support after two years. Elbogen noted that the agreement "fulfills מצוה פדיון שבויים [the commandment to free the captives] and has no risk."[21] The College's appointment of Spanier as instructor of rabbinics, in December, 1938, apparently influenced his release from the concentration camp;[22] but it did not secure him a visa. Unable to discover the reason for the refusal, Morgenstern finally succeeded[23] in arranging an interview with Avra M. Warren, head of the Visa Division of the State Department, for May 20, 1940, in order to discuss the case.

What Morgenstern learned at that conference astonished him greatly, however typical it later proved to be of State Department policy.[24] The Visa Division had ruled that Spanier was primarily a librarian, not regularly a professor at a legitimate institution of higher learning; hence he was ineligible. Moreover—and incredibly—the Berlin consul had accepted as valid the Nazi government's demotion of the Berlin liberal seminary from the status of Hochschule to that of Lehranstalt in 1934. On this basis, as well, it claimed that Spanier did not qualify: the Lehranstalt, as a mere "institute" not of university rank, was clearly inferior academically to the Hebrew Union College, and the immigration law was understood to exclude the grant of a nonquota visa to a scholar coming from an institution of lower status abroad to one of higher status in the United States.[25]

The decision in the Spanier case threw the success of the entire College in Exile project into doubt. It was now anticipated that Guttmann, who was also associated with the Lehranstalt, would be ineligible, as well as Lewkowitz, who had taught at the Breslau seminary, and Sonne, who had taught at seminaries in Florence, Italy, and on the Isle of Rhodes. The cases of Rosenthal and Heschel looked even bleaker as they were young scholars without established academic status. Max Wiener, Morgenstern was told in Washington, would be regarded as a rabbi rather than a professor since he had exercised both functions. Even the remaining invitations, those to men who had taught at recognized German universities, were invalid since the State Department at this stage was no longer willing to admit scholars merely for purposes of research.[26]

Morgenstern returned to Washington three weeks later for a second conference. This time he was joined by Rabbi David Philipson, of Cincinnati, and Rabbi Solomon Freehof, of Pittsburgh. The three College representatives met with Warren and two of his assistants. Their strategy was apparently to persuade the government officials that the project, as initially formulated, was of benefit not only to the College but also to America. The preservation of Wissenschaft des Judentums, they argued, would "redound greatly to the credit of our nation as a center and the fosterer of objective scientific scholarship."[27] They were also trying to counter the anticipated new interpretation of the law which made only those offered permanent teaching appointments eligible for nonquota visas. As Morgenstern could not know how successful any of these men would be in teaching American Reform rabbinical students, he was necessarily reluctant to commit himself to including all of the invitees as regular instructors, nor was he feeling at ease about making a permanent commitment to men whom he and the faculty did not know personally. Indeed, the regular faculty of the College at the time numbered only about a dozen men. He admitted to Warren that their chief service would be that of scientific research. His honesty had the effect of producing a ruling that the project did not qualify for nonquota visas.

Earlier in 1939, at a conference held between representatives of the Departments of State, Labor, and Justice, it had been decided that purely scientific institutions without a student body were not eligible to appoint refugee scholars outside the quota. While the HUC was clearly an instructional institution, the College in Exile was not. Warren concluded, six weeks after the interview, that Hebrew Union College could bring in professors on a nonquota basis only if they were appointed "as regular members of its faculty, primarily to instruct, or to confer the benefit of their knowledge upon, students thereof, and for positions of a continuing, rather than a temporary or intermittent character; provided, of course, such scholars were able to meet the requirements of the law with respect to their past vocational experience."[28] Such a commitment was far beyond that originally intended. But the project was already publicized and funded. Most important, its significance and urgency were daily becoming more apparent.

In order to avoid any further misunderstanding, Morgenstern, joined this time by the Board of Governors chairman, Ralph Mack, arranged for a third conference in Washington. On September 20, 1939, they met first with Assistant Secretary of State George Messersmith[29]—an interview arranged by Rabbi Edward L. Israel, of Baltimore, through Isador Lubin, a Jewish senior official in the Department of Commerce. There followed another session with Warren. This time Morgenstern was given precise instructions under what conditions of appointment the men would be granted nonquota visas.[30] The very next day he issued new official letters of invitation. In each instance the recipient was now asked to become a regular "teaching member of the Faculty" for "an indeterminate period," defined to mean "that it is our intention that this appointment shall be permanent." Once again a private supplementary letter went along as well. It indicated that while the College would make use of the man's services for teaching to the extent that it would be feasible and advantageous to the school, there would not be enough instructional opportunities available to allow a full schedule for each man. The work would still basically be that of research. Morgenstern also sent a letter to the American consul in each man's area of residence. A month later the Board of Governors approved the new terms of appointment.[31]

By the time of the third State Department meeting, one of the scholars on the list had already managed to gain admission to the United States. Franz Landsberger had been professor of the history of art at the University of Breslau before the Nazis removed him in 1933. Thereafter, he had served as director of the Berlin Jewish Museum until it was forced to close. Like Spanier, Landsberger had been placed in the Sachsenhausen concentration camp following *Kristallnacht*, and for him as well Elbogen had made a special appeal to Morgenstern.[32] While in the camp, Landsberger had the good fortune of receiving an invitation from British classicist Gilbert Murray to visit him in Oxford. Though the document was sufficient to effect his release, he could remain in England only for a temporary period. In March 1939, while still in Berlin, he learned that his name was on Morgenstern's list, and he gladly accepted the initial invitation when it reached him in England two months later. Though Landsberger encountered the same difficulties as the other invitees when he presented his letter of appointment to the American consul in London, he was fortunate in receiving the assistance of a Mrs. Thomas W. Lamont, who was able to persuade the consul to tell her the conditions under which Landsberger would be admitted. When informed, Morgenstern wrote to the consul on July 10, 1939, referring to the proffered position as involving teaching responsibilities and the expectation of permanency. His letter succeeded in securing a nonquota visa for Landsberger and his wife, enabling them to arrive in America late in August, just a few days before the outbreak of war.[33]

A second scholar on the list, Max Wiener, avoided the necessity of awaiting approval of the College's appointment by accepting an earlier invitation to become the assistant rabbi of a Reform congregation in Syracuse, New York. Although he did not intend to fill this rabbinical post except for the briefest period, he decided to use the nonquota visa he received for it in the summer of 1939. His intention was to make his way from Syracuse to the College as soon as possible. Shortly after the High Holy Days that year he did indeed come to Cincinnati. But his stay there was not a happy one. Though a profound scholar of Jewish philosophy and intellectual history, Wiener was already fifty-seven years old when he arrived, had difficulty with spoken English, and was asked to teach Mishnah, Talmud, and liturgy rather than philosophy. After two and a half years, the College secured a pulpit for him in Fairmont, West Virginia, which, unfortunately, proved even less satisfying. Max Wiener was the only one of the refugee scholars whom the College decided not to retain.[34]

With the arrival of Landsberger and Wiener, and with the unconditional refusal of a visa to Walter Gottschalk, a Semiticist who was apparently rejected because he had served as a librarian in the Near East Department of the Berlin Municipal Library rather than as a professor in a recognized teaching institution,[35] the list of those still awaited was reduced to seven. Because of their limited academic backgrounds, it was anticipated that the two youngest men, Franz Rosenthal and Abraham Heschel, might have the most difficulty. In fact, because each of them was able to make his way to England, they received visas quite promptly once their second letters of invitation reached the American consul in London.

Though Franz Rosenthal was only twenty-five years old when the College brought him to Cincinnati, he had already gained an enviable reputation as a Semiticist and won a prestigious international prize for his work. From Germany, he had managed to make his way first to Uppsala, Sweden, and then to London. About a month after the second letter of invitation was issued, the London consul received a message from the Secretary of State's office affirming that Rosenthal's as well as Heschel's appointments came within the purview of the nonquota section of the Immigration Act.[36] In the case of Rosenthal it remained only to determine whether his four semesters of teaching at the *Lehranstalt* were sufficient to satisfy the requirement of having previously carried on the vocation of professor at a ranking educational institution. By the end of November, at the discretion of the American consul, Rosenthal was granted his visa. Elbogen's prediction that, once in the United States, the young scholar would get a fellowship within a very short time[37] proved correct as early as 1943, and in 1948 he resigned his position at the College to succeed Giorgio Levi Della Vida in the chair of Arabic at the University of Pennsylvania.

Abraham Heschel had been registered for a regular immigration visa in Frankfurt since June 1938, and he expected that his number would come up in March 1939. But when he was deported as an alien Jew from Germany to Poland in November 1938, the American consul in Warsaw, who received his documents, refused even to look at them for at least nine months. Morgenstern's first invitation, sent to him in Frankfurt, reached Heschel in Warsaw. He was delighted to accept and indicated his intention (a wise one indeed) to try to obtain the American visa in a friendlier country. During the summer of 1939, Heschel was able to get a transit visa to England and eventually, after receiving the revised invitation, to persuade the London consul that his teaching activity at the *Lehranstalt*, in the adult education program of the *Reichsvertretung* (the national Jewish organization in Germany), and in the Warsaw seminary would qualify him for a nonquota immigration visa to the United States. He received the visa in January 1940 and began teaching at the College later that year.[38] Already known for his books on biblical prophecy and on Maimonides when he arrived at HUC, he soon became the most widely known of the group, not only as a scholar but as a leading theologian. After four years in Cincinnati, he accepted an appointment to the Jewish Theological Seminary of America.

The most delicate case for the College was that of Isaiah Sonne. An erudite scholar of medieval and Renaissance Jewish creativity, Sonne had originally been brought to Morgenstern's attention by Professor Jacob Mann of the HUC faculty and by Simon Bernstein, the director of the Palestine Department of the Zionist Organization of America. The latter enabled Sonne to get a tourist entry permit for Palestine, good for several months. The Polish-born Sonne was thus able to leave Italy shortly before he expected to be expelled, along with other foreign Jews. He was given a nonquota visa in Jerusalem on November 15, 1939, not long after he received the College's second letter of invitation. But in his case difficulties then arose from the side of the College. Certain members of the faculty had expressed opposition to seeing Sonne become one of their number, while Morgenstern had serious doubts about his ability to be an effective teacher of American students. Given the specialized area of Sonne's competence, there was, moreover, little possibility of his finding a position elsewhere. "In all probability," Morgenstern wrote candidly to Ralph Mack, "he would constitute a permanent burden on us." A plan was therefore formulated to pay Sonne a stipend for two years in Palestine in lieu of the salary he was promised in Cincinnati. Even Elbogen concurred that Sonne would doubtless be happier in the environment of Jerusalem. Nelson Glueck of the College faculty, who was about to return to his work in Palestine, was given the task of convincing Sonne. The latter, however, would not be persuaded. Before Morgenstern could write a definite letter to him, Sonne was on his way to the United States, fearing that his visa would expire if he delayed unduly.[39] Once he arrived in March 1940, however, the College fulfilled its obligation to him fully while he, in turn, contributed richly to its scholarly reputation.

Although the consuls in London and Jerusalem responded affirmatively and quite soon after the second letters of appointment were issued, in Berlin—where the situation was most desperate— the consulate engaged in frustrating, frightening delay. Alexander Guttmann, a Talmud scholar, had remained in Berlin as the only full-time regular member of the *Lehranstalt* faculty. With the outbreak of war, his situation became far more difficult. Yet the consulate would not act until it had rechecked the status of the *Lehranstalt*, and it was in no hurry to complete that task. Incredibly, it once again turned to "the German authorities" in its attempt, dictated from Washington, to redetermine the matter. By February 1940, there was still no response.[40] Guttmann himself thereupon made an effort to furnish the consul with documents attesting to the *"Hochschule* status" of the *Lehranstalt*, while Morgenstern did his best to bring pressure to bear on Berlin directly as well as via Washington.[41] At length, the *Lehranstalt* was declared an institution of higher learning, and Guttmann received his visa on March 26, 1940, fully six months from the date the second invitations were issued. Once in Cincinnati, he was immediately given a full teaching load since Talmud was the one field in which the College then truly needed instructors. For many years he remained an active member of the faculty in Cincinnati.

The case of Eugen Täubler stands out from the others as the only one in which the recipient of an HUC invitation chose initially to refuse it. A distinguished historian of ancient Rome, Täubler had taught at the universities of Zurich and Heidelberg before the Nazi regime forced him to restrict his scholarly pursuits to the Jewish sphere. Beginning in 1935, he taught at the *Lehranstalt*. In March 1939, Täubler had written to Solomon Zeitlin at Dropsie College and to Henry Slonimsky at the Jewish Institute of Religion in search of an appointment. Each institution had passed the request on to HUC, which included him on its list. To the April invitation Täubler replied that he was unsure whether he would be able to accept the call and that he was continuing his correspondence with Slonimsky. Then nothing further was heard from him in Cincinnati for eight months, though, like the others, he received the second, more desirable invitation in September. Finally, the College learned in January 1941, that he had been refused a nonquota visa. The American consul in Berlin had seen fit to rule that the present faculty of the Hebrew Union College was altogether adequate for the size of its student body and that, in consequence, there was no justification for granting visas to prospective additional personnel.[42] Morgenstern wrote immediately to the Visa Division to investigate the matter, with the result that Täubler was granted a visa for himself and his wife within a month. Once in the United States, he claimed that he had remained behind because he regarded his work there as essential; others thought he had been unable to tear himself away from Germany. Never really desirous of coming to HUC, he was not happy in a rabbinical seminary, though he stayed in Cincinnati until his death in 1953. His wife, Selma Stern-Täubler, a historian in her own right, served for a number of years as archivist of the American Jewish Archives.

Of both Guttmann and Täubler it can be said that the College's invitation clearly saved them from eventual deportation and likely death. In the two cases that remain, Lewkowitz and Spanier, the College failed. Albert Lewkowitz was the sole member of the Breslau Jewish Theological Seminary's faculty to appear on Morgenstern's list.[43] He was a teacher of Jewish philosophy with considerable standing in the field. Both he and Spanier decided to seek temporary asylum in Amsterdam while awaiting the outcome of their efforts to gain visas. Morgenstern addressed communications on their behalf to the American consul in Rotterdam, who had received their files from Germany. Lewkowitz's chances for a visa looked good once the Breslau seminary was recognized by the United States government as an institution of sufficient rank, along with the *Lehranstalt*. But then the Germans bombed Rotterdam and, as a result, the records of his service in Breslau were lost. A new statement from Germany was required,[44] and apparently it was not forthcoming before the United States closed all its consulates in Germany in July 1941. Another Morgenstern conference with Warren that month, this time arranged by Senator Lister Hill of Alabama, produced no result.[45] Lewkowitz's only hope was to get to Spain and there apply for a regular quota visa. This he was unable, or unwilling, to do. He remained in Holland and was eventually placed in the Bergen-Belsen concentration camp. Fortunately, he was among those selected for a prisoner exchange in 1944[46] and thereupon he was permitted entry into Palestine. Arthur Spanier was not even so relatively fortunate. The American consul in Rotterdam declared him definitely and finally ineligible because he had been a librarian rather than a professor. Though Morgenstern then did his best to get Spanier out as a nonpreference alien, he achieved no result.[47] Spanier died in Bergen-Belsen.

Once the chances of successfully bringing over Spanier and Lewkowitz had receded, and with the prospect of Wiener's departure, the decision was made to attempt bringing one more refugee scholar to Cincinnati. Difficulties were not expected since Samuel Atlas, a scholar of Talmud and Jewish philosophy, had been teaching in England since 1934. A call was issued to him in May 1941 on the same terms as the other refugee scholars. Atlas was eager to come to the United States, not only because he had no permanent position in England but also because the war had stranded his wife in Montreal. But Atlas's case fell under a new set of restrictions, recently imposed out of an imagined fear that Nazi spies might enter the United States as immigrants.[48] Visas could now be refused to anyone who had relatives in Axis-occupied countries, and Atlas had a brother in Lithuania and a sister in Estonia. Moreover, procedures for gaining visas had become considerably more complex and cumbersome than heretofore. It seemed that Atlas's case would be held up interminably and might eventually be decided in the negative. Morgenstern therefore wrote a letter to Henry Morgenthau Jr., Secretary of the Treasury, whose parents had been interested in the College. In asking the secretary's intervention for Atlas, the HUC president poured out his dismay at the frustration caused him by the long struggle for the refugee project:

> I regret, however, that I must say that, as a result of negotiations with this [State] Department, and with Mr. Warren personally, extending over a number of years, I have no confidence that my request of Mr. Warren will receive favorable consideration, or that this application for a visa will be granted despite the fact that I know of no reason why it should not be. I have had repeated contacts with the Visa Division during the last two years and a half in connection with the efforts of the Hebrew Union College to bring over a number of Jewish scholars to teaching positions in it. And I am sorry to say I have never been able to accomplish anything whatever with that Department unless it was possible to bring pressure from some person high in the present administration upon the Office of the Visa Division.[49]

Morgenthau, who would later assume an independent role in rescuing Jews,[50] asked Under Secretary of State Sumner Welles to investigate Atlas's case. Within a few days the application was approved. After passing through a gauntlet of U-boats in a convoy of cargo ships, Atlas was able to join the faculty in Cincinnati early in 1942. He was the last of the refugee scholars to arrive.

The entire Hebrew Union College project is perhaps summed up in a letter which Michael Guttmann, the head of the Budapest seminary and father of Alexander Guttmann, wrote to Morgenstern on April 23, 1939. What the college is doing, he wrote in German, "is a deed which has its unique historical value and will remain memorable for all times. It is a noble rescue, not alone of the Jewish teacher, but also of the Jewish teaching."

Notes

I am grateful to the following individuals who orally and in writing responded to my inquiries and supplied me with documents: Samuel Atlas, Alexander Guttmann, Dora Landsberger, Franz Rosenthal, Margit Sonne, Eric Werner, and Theodore Wiener. All written materials have been deposited in the American Jewish Archives in Cincinnati.

1. Board of Governors Minutes (BGM), October 30, 1934.
2. On this subject, and for the history of the Hebrew Union College-Jewish Institute of Religion in general, see *Hebrew Union College-Jewish Institute of Religion at One Hundred Years*, ed. Samuel Karff (Cincinnati, 1975).
3. BGM, May 24, 1935.
4. Lewy's wife, Hildegarde, likewise an Assyriologist, remained behind to salvage as much of their belongings as possible. To elude the Nazi censors, Lewy's instructions to his wife took the form of alleged citations from Akkadian texts he claimed to have found in the Louvre. Not knowing Akkadian and never suspecting the contents of the quotations, the Nazi censors allowed the messages to pass (*Cincinnati Enquirer*, February 15, 1941).
5. HUC president Julian Morgenstern likewise applied to the Emergency Committee for funds to support Lewy's appointment, but he was turned down as at that time there was no thought of providing a permanent position (Edward R. Murrow to Morgenstern, June 14, 1935, File E, Box 1553, American Jewish Archives [AJA]). In addition to the Jewish Theological Seminary, the Emergency Committee made grants to a number of Jewish institutions, including the Hebrew University, the Jewish Institute of Religion, the College of Jewish Studies, the YIVO, and the American Academy for Jewish Research. But the HUC, which absorbed far more refugee scholars than any other Jewish institution except the Hebrew University, was never able to obtain any assistance. On the work of the Emergency Committee, which was supported almost exclusively by prominent Jewish foundations, see Stephen Duggan and Betty Drury, *The Rescue of Science and Learning* (New York, 1948).

6. Morgenstern to Lewy, January 8, 1935, Lewy to Morgenstern, March 11, 1935, Julius Lewy File, Box 3204, AJA.

7. Morgenstern to John A. Wilson at the Oriental Institute, July 26, 1938, ibid.

8. Michael Wilensky File, Box 3204, AJA, especially his letter to Morgenstern of August 13, 1935. See also Ismar Elbogen File, Box 1553, AJA.

9. On Wilensky's life and scholarly work, see N. H. Tur-Sinai's introduction to the second edition of *Sefer ha-Rikmah* (Jerusalem, 1964) and Samuel Atlas in *Studies in Bibliography and Booklore*, December 1955, 51–52.

10. Among those who applied, or whose names were submitted by organizations, were men of scholarly accomplishment, including Fritz Bamberger (philosophy), David Baumgardt (philosophy), Nahum Glatzer (history), Martin Plessner (Semitics), and Joseph Prijs (bibliography and history). The correspondence is mostly in Box 732, AJA.

11. Eric Werner File, Box 3204, AJA; BGM, November 22, 1938.

12. On the Elbogen project, see Elbogen File; Cyrus Adler File, Box 1550; and the correspondence between Elbogen and Adolph Oko, Box 2328, AJA. To Franz Rosenthal he wrote on April 12, 1939: "Uns könnte es gut gehen, wenn die Sorge um die Heimatlosen nicht wäre."

13. BGM, October 20, 1938. The original proposal to work with the Central Conference of American Rabbis and include congregational rabbis as well as scholars seems to have been early abandoned despite the initial intent (*CCAR Yearbook* 49 [1939], 31, 34–35). Only one refugee rabbi, Max Vogelstein, of Coblenz, took up residence in the dormitory.

14. On the University in Exile, see Norman Bentwich, *The Rescue and Achievement of Refugee Scholars* (The Hague, 1953), 48–52; Duggan and Drury, 79–82. In 1960 the HUC-JIR awarded Alvin Johnson an honorary degree.

15. Morgenstern to Elbogen, November 25, 1938, Elbogen File.

16. See Morgenstern's speech to the Thirty-Sixth Council of the Union of American Hebrew Congregations, January 15–19, 1939 (*UAHC Proceedings*, 13:766–68).

17. BGM, April 9, 1939.

18. The relevant passage was Section 4(d) of the Immigration Act of 1924, which exempts from quota restrictions: "An immigrant who continuously for at least two years immediately preceding the time of his application for admission to the United States has been, and who seeks to enter the United States solely for the purpose of, carrying on the vocation of minister of any religious denomination, or professor of a college, academy, seminary, or university; and his wife, and his unmarried children under 18 years of age, if accompanying or following to join him."

19. The official letters and the private letters are contained in the files of each of the men in the AJA.

20. Unfortunately, the Spanier file has been lost, and the case must be reconstructed from other sources.

21. Elbogen file.

22. Margaret Spanier to Morgenstern, December 16, 1938, Morgenstern File, Box 1560, AJA.
23. Probably thanks to the unnamed "influential friend of the College in Washington" to whom Morgenstern had written in April 1939 (BGM, April 19, 1939).
24. A great deal of attention has been devoted to this subject. Some of the basic works are Arthur D. Morse, *While Six Million Died* (New York, 1968); David S. Wyman, *Paper Walls* (Amherst, Mass., 1968); Henry L. Feingold, *The Politics of Rescue* (New Brunswick, N.J., 1970); and Saul S. Friedman, *No Haven for the Oppressed* (Detroit, 1973).
25. BGM, May 25, 1939.
26. Ibid.
27. Morgenstern to Warren, July 2, 1939, summarizing the meeting. This letter and related documents are contained in File 811.111 Colleges, Record Group 59, The National Archives (NA).
28. Warren to Morgenstern, August 11, 1939, on the basis of decisions reached two days earlier. These decisions were in turn based on a report by the legal adviser of the State Department, of August 2, 1939, prompted specifically by the case of Franz Rosenthal. The report referred to a letter by Franklin H. McNutt, of the Ohio Department of Education, attesting to the high standing of the Hebrew Union College and also the "good impression" made by the college representatives at their Visa Department interview. But it concluded that since, according to the "general instruction" of May 9, 1939, only a scholar whose task would be "primarily to confer the benefit of his knowledge upon the students rather than to pursue his own studies" could qualify, only those to whom the college gave regular teaching assignments would be eligible (ibid.).
29. During his earlier service as United States consul in Berlin, Messersmith had urged a liberal policy on granting visas to Jewish refugees (Zosa Szajkowski, "The Consul and the Immigrant," *Jewish Social Studies* 36 [1974], 10). In 1940 he was replaced by the much less sympathetic Breckinridge Long.
30. BGM, October 2, 1939.
31. Ibid., October 19, 1939.
32. Elbogen to Morgenstern, December 8, 1938, Elbogen File.
33. Franz Landsberger File, Box 3204, AJA.
34. Max Wiener File, Box 3204, William Rosenau Correspondence, Box 2330a, AJA.
35. There is no file on Gottschalk in the American Jewish Archives. He was presumably sent the second, revised letter of appointment to Belgium, where he was then residing. Gottschalk's appointment was originally made conditional upon receiving support payments from his cousin, a wealthy attorney in Brussels (BGM, October 19, 1939, January 7, 1940). I have been unable to determine his ultimate fate.
36. The letter of November 9, 1939 (NA) was originally sent to the Ameri-

can consul in Dublin as, for a time, a moratorium had been declared on the granting of additional visas in London.

37. Elbogen to Morgenstern, December 8, 1938, Elbogen File.
38. Abraham Heschel File, Box 3204, AJA.
39. On Sonne see the Isaiah Sonne File, Box 3204, and the Morgenstern File, Box 1351, AJA; also BGM, February 28 and March 20, 1940.
40. Cyrus B. Follmer, American vice-consul, to Alexander Guttmann, February 8, 1940, Michael and Alexander Guttman File, Box 3204, AJA. At the request of the consulate, Leo Baeck had presented a report on the status of the *Lehranstalt* as early as December 1939. However, it was apparently deemed insufficient (Alexander Guttmann to Morgenstern, February 28, 1940, ibid.). Guttmann recollects hearing from Max Wiener that a U.S. consular official in Berlin had said to him: "Why do you want to emigrate? In five years the situation will be the same in America."
41. BGM, February 28, 1940.
42. Ibid., January 22, 1941; Hilfsverein Zedakah to Hebrew Union College, January 6, 1941, Eugen Täubler File, Box 3204, AJA. This was in keeping with State Department policy at that time (cf. Wyman, 173–79).
43. As in the case of Spanier, there is no file extant for Lewkowitz in the AJA.
44. BGM, November 27, 1940.
45. Morgenstern to Carl Pritz, July 23, 1941, Morgenstern File, Box 1354, AJA.
46. Morgenstern to Lt. S. W. Hubbel, USNR, August 3, 1944, Morgenstern Correspondence, uncat., AJA.
47. Morgenstern tried to send a statement supporting Spanier's application as a regular quota immigrant to the consul in Rotterdam via the Visa Division. Three weeks later Warren returned the statement to Morgenstern, because no postage was affixed. The letter was sent again with proper postage, but valuable time was lost (Täubler File).
48. For details see Morse, 300–303; Feingold, 160–61; Wyman, 193–205.
49. Letter of September 26, 1941, Samuel Atlas File, Box 3204, AJA.
50. Morse, 93; Feingold, 297.

CHAPTER 21

American Reform Judaism and Zionism: Early Efforts at Ideological Rapprochement

It is well known that Reform Judaism in the United States remained officially in opposition to the Zionist movement until the 1930s and that only in the following decade did the Central Conference of American Rabbis (CCAR) publicly state that Zionism was "fully within the spirit and purpose of Reform Judaism."[1] The first years of the century are usually seen as a period in which Reform Judaism and Zionism were generally thought to be incompatible and during which the two movements struggled with one another to win over American Jewry.[2] Attention is sometimes called to prominent exceptions: Reform rabbis such as Stephen S. Wise, Judah Leon Magnes, and a few others in the early period, as well as leading personalities, such as Abba Hillel Silver, somewhat later. But relatively little has been written about the influence and ideological positions of the early Zionists within the camp of Reform. Was Zionism within Reform Judaism perhaps more significant even in this early period than has usually been acknowledged? How did Reform rabbis, finding their Zionism condemned by their rabbinical colleagues, and their Reform Judaism berated by their Zionist associates, go about seeking an ideological rapprochement between them? It is my contention that if organized American Reform Judaism was able at a later stage to move from an avowedly anti-Zionist to a pro-Zionist position without a major crisis of identity, this development was possible because the groundwork had already been laid in the first years, when the majority on both sides of the two movements seemed to be mortal enemies.

During the first two decades of the twentieth century not only did most Reform Jews in America believe Reform Judaism and Zionism to be incompatible, Zionists as well believed them to be mutually exclusive. One Zionist publicist wrote: "It is very doubtful whether the Nationalistic reform Jew may rightly be called a reform Jew at all, because the notion, reform, is identical with the notion of assimilation."[3] When Joseph Jasin, a Reform rabbi who served from 1908 to 1910 as the full-time secretary of the Federation of American Zionists, dared to suggest in the Zionist journal, the *Maccabean*, that enemies of Zionism might also be found outside the Reform movement and friends within it, he received a strident, uncompromising reply from the secularist editor, Louis Lipsky. Zionism, according to Lipsky, was unalterably opposed to Reform Judaism and it would be detrimental to the interests of the movement to cease attacking it at every opportunity. Lipsky held out no hope that Reform Judaism might ever become Zionistic, much less that Zionist ideology would one day find room for principles of Reform Judaism. "However," Lipsky noted, "that does not mean that we despair of ever converting Reform *Jews* to our way of thinking." Lipsky believed that religious progress in the Diaspora was impossible without detriment to nationality. As a Reform rabbi, Jasin not surprisingly felt ill at ease among Zionist leaders who were unwilling to grant legitimacy to his dual identity.[4] From the other side, the influence of Conservative Jews in the leadership of the American movement made the liberal Stephen Wise most uncomfortable, for he felt that this "pseudo-orthodoxy," as he called it, denied him the right to call himself a leader of Jewish life and thought.[5] It seemed as if true conversion to Zionism meant forsaking not just the anti-Zionist position of most Reform Jews but Reform Judaism as such. Faced with this dilemma, some Reform Zionists, like Judah Leon Magnes, had increasing difficulty in thinking of themselves as Reform Jews. In one instance a Zionist graduate of the Hebrew Union College refused to continue calling himself a Reform rabbi,[6] while Stephen Wise, though remaining associated with Reform institutions, preferred to use the term "liberal," which was free of the anti-Zionist onus.

Given this mutual agreement regarding the antithetical natures of Reform Judaism and Zionism, it is remarkable to note the extent of support which Zionism enjoyed among leading Reform Jews long before the movement as a whole moved even to a position of neutrality. It is not simply a matter of a few exceptions which prove the rule. In 1907 it was asserted at the CCAR convention that "thousands" of Reform Jews were committed to Zionism,[7] and ten years later a resolution offered by a non-Zionist rabbi pointed out that the congregations which the members of the Conference served were "in all cases divided into Zionist and non-Zionist view-points."[8] Well over a dozen American Reform rabbis were active and explicit supporters of the Zionist movement before 1920.[9] To be sure, they represented only a small percentage of the Central Conference of American Rabbis, but the influence of these men far exceeded their numbers. Of Bernhard Felsenthal, the eldest among them and for many years a rabbi in Chicago, an anti-Zionist opponent wrote in 1897 that he "carries greater weight with Jews of all classes than almost any other man in the country."[10] Gustav Gottheil at the turn of the century was regarded even by those who disagreed with him as the best-known rabbi in America.[11] As senior rabbi of Temple Emanu-El in New York, he was spiritual leader of the richest, largest, and most influential Reform congregation in the United States. For four years, from 1906 to 1910, Judah Leon Magnes served in the same congregation, unabashedly preaching Zionism from its pulpit and serving simultaneously as secretary to the Federation of American Zionists. In 1917 Magnes's senior rabbi at Emanu-El, Joseph Silverman, hitherto an anti-Zionist, likewise declared himself a Zionist, bought a shekel and attended a dinner in honor of Louis Lipsky.[12] Joseph Krauskopf, at the time when he accepted the Basle Platform in that same year, was a past president of the CCAR, as well as rabbi of the most important Reform congregation in Philadelphia. Stephen S. Wise drew thousands to hear his sermons in New York, whether or not he was preaching on Zionism. The Zionist Max Heller of New Orleans was rabbi of the most prominent congregation in the city. He served as president of the CCAR from 1909 to 1911, having been elected to the vice-presidency two years earlier, immediately after his election as honorary vice-president of the Federation of American Zionists; his first election occurred at a convention during which he made a fervent plea for Zionism.[13] Four other members of the CCAR in 1920, who were already Zionists, later became presidents of the Conference.[14] Clearly this growing minority of Reform rabbis was no mere cross section of the CCAR; in large measure they were among its most prominent and promising members.

One Zionist purpose had all along been accepted by nearly all Reform Jews, whether or not they called themselves Zionists. Support of Jewish colonization efforts in Palestine had already been advocated by Isaac Mayer Wise before the turn of the century.[15] When in 1914 Max Heller sent out a letter to fellow Reform rabbis asking them to raise money for the Federation of American Zionists' Emergency Fund in support of the colonies in Palestine, fifty-five agreed and only nine refused.[16] Six years later the CCAR adopted a resolution which declared it the duty of all Jews to contribute to the reconstruction of Palestine.[17]

To a surprising extent Reform Jews also agreed with Zionists in their assessment of antisemitism. Few believed it was about to vanish with the dawning of the twentieth century. But while Zionists made the persistence of antisemitism an argument for their program, leading Reformers who opposed Zionism drew a contradictory conclusion. To Kaufmann Kohler, Zionism in 1903 represented "a retreat before the foe by way of East Africa or Asia."[18] One rabbi termed Zionism "a plan of complete surrender," while another wrote of "the Tribe of Judah, like a whipped cur, crawling back to his old lair in the caves of Judea."[19] Reformers did believe it would eventually be overcome. Few of his colleagues were willing to agree with Max Heller that antisemitism would always and everywhere exist as long as the Jew sought to be different. To Heller's mind, though, the alternatives were clear: submergence or emergence, utter assimilation or national resurrection.[20]

Many Reform Jews who were anti-Zionists felt that the principal threat came from *political* Zionism. But, as Felsenthal pointed out, the difference between supporting individual settlements and favoring a charter from the Sultan, which would guarantee their security, was not so great. Nor would even a Jewish state there present a problem in terms of Reform Judaism. Felsenthal believed it could become a "Jeffersonian democracy." And certainly not all Jews were required to live there. It was for the persecuted Jews of Eastern Europe.[21] The real point of contention in the Reform camp was over the implications of calling Palestine the *sole* homeland of the Jewish people. Rabbi Samuel Schulman of New York, an avowed anti-Zionist, said in 1917 that if the Basle Program would call for a secured home for Jews in Palestine instead of for *the* Jews, he would at once join the Zionist movement.[22] Similarly, Leo Franklin, when he was president of the CCAR, wrote to Louis Lipsky in 1920 that his association could not participate in a Zionist Organization of America convention "whose purpose is to stress the establishment in Palestine of *the* Jewish national home." But he added: "In any movement looking to make Palestine a land not merely of refuge for the downtrodden Jew, but as well a place where a fuller expression may be given to the spiritual genius of the Jew, you may be assured of the full and wholehearted cooperation of the CCAR."[23] For most Reform Jews—especially after the Balfour Declaration—it was the implication that America was not equally a homeland for the Jew, which was the real thorn in the program of political Zionism.

Often the conflict between Reformers and Zionists focused on the question of Jewish self-definition. Are the Jews a religious community or a nation? Yet even such an avowed opponent of Zionism as Kaufmann Kohler recognized that "religion and *Volkstum* in Judaism constitute an indissoluble unity."[24] Their relation was like that of soul and body. What especially bothered him about Zionism was that it tended to neglect the religious element in favor of the national. Reformers outside the Zionist camp as well as within it were suspicious of the militant nationalism which had developed in the late nineteenth century. But this did not necessarily imply for them the rejection of Jewish particularity. For Reform Jews, who declared the universality of the Jewish faith and during this period did not stress ritual observance, it was Jewish ethnic particularity which served as an important brake upon assimilation. While Reform leaders fought Zionists and the Orthodox on one front, they had to take care not to expose themselves to the arguments of the Ethical Culturists who saw no value whatever in the continuation of Jewish identity.[25]

If the conflict with political Zionism called for one kind of solution, the encounter with spiritual Zionism demanded an answer of a different kind. Although some Reform and Conservative Jews found it much easier to be cultural Zionists, the claims of cultural Zionism, unless reinterpreted, were even more threatening to what Reform Judaism believed itself to represent. Reform Judaism was committed to the belief that Jewish spiritual survival and creativity were possible in the Diaspora. To admit that American Jewry required inspiration from a center in Palestine amounted to an admission of failure. It meant that American Jewry, instead of being the leading edge of the Judaism of the future, the focal point of spiritual development, was relegated to the periphery, robbed of its independence. The non-Zionist Julian Morgenstern, for example, was all in favor of Palestinian interests and activities and had no objection to fellow Reform Jews laboring for a Jewish homeland and even an independent Jewish state. But, as he put it, "we believe with perfect faith that Judaism can live and perpetuate itself and expand here in America, entirely without the need of foreign stimuli, whether from Palestine or elsewhere."[26] If the conflict between Reform Judaism and spiritual Zionism was to be resolved, a positive role had to be found for Zionism within the framework of Reform Judaism and likewise a purpose for Reform Judaism within Zionist ideology.

The issue on which debate centered was the doctrine of the mission of Israel. In its original form it held that the Diaspora was a providential act of Divine will, making it possible for Israel to bring its religious and moral message to the nations of the earth. Once that task was accomplished in the near or distant future, Judaism would in fact, if not in name, be the faith of all civilized mankind. Zionist leaders almost invariably ridiculed this notion as arrogant and pretentious. They pointed out that the average American Jew scarcely acted like a missionary for Jewish ideals and that Diaspora Jewry in the modern world had failed to produce outstanding religious thinkers who possessed the respect of both Jews and Gentiles. Moreover, Jewish monotheism was not far removed from the monotheistic faith of most Christians. Reform Jews who were also Zionists had to admit that the mission idea, as commonly formulated, was bound to evoke satire.[27] Yet as far as I am aware, no Zionist Reform rabbi during this period was willing to abandon the mission idea completely. Magnes, to be sure, tended to emphasize its inadequacies, but even he refused to set it entirely aside.[28] Most of the Zionist Reformers sought a reinterpretation or modification of the doctrine.

Bernhard Felsenthal was to my knowledge the first to advocate a new concept of Jewish mission compatible with Zionism, and it was his ideas on the subject, elaborated and sometimes modified by younger men, which eventually won out in Reform Judaism. As early as 1897 Felsenthal held that the mission of Israel could best be served if there were a Jewish center in Palestine. Later he wrote that the Jews who would live in Palestine would be in a far better position to undertake the Jewish task of being a light to the world. They could become a model nation in regard to moral and religious conduct of life, while in the *Golah* there was little or no opportunity to fulfill the prophetic mission. Moreover, in an age of railroads, steamboats, and newspapers, there was no need for Jews to be scattered among the nations in order to propagate the ideals of Judaism. In short, Israel's mission required what Felsenthal called a Jewish *Musterstaat*. Combining Ahad Ha'am with Reform doctrine, he informed the CCAR that "from Israel's own country, as from a center, could go forth and would go forth a rich stream of grand ideas, benefitting adjacent countries in Asia and influencing largely other countries in Europe, in America, and in other parts of the world."[29]

Stephen Wise added an important qualification. He stressed that for the foreseeable future the mission of the Jew in the Diaspora would continue along with the project of creating a spiritual center in Palestine.[30] A cultural center in Zion was, in fact, a project to which few Reform Jews could take exception, provided that it would concentrate on the propagation and elaboration of the religious ideals of Judaism and that it left a significant role for the great bulk of Jewry which would continue to live in the Diaspora.

What did perpetually bother Zionists in both the Reform and Conservative movements was the secularity of the Jewish culture being established in Palestine and the prominence of nonreligious Jews within the leadership of both spiritual and political Zionism. After a bitter debate at its 1917 meeting, the CCAR voted for a resolution which did not even mention Zionism but which condemned "every unreligious or anti-religious interpretation of Judaism and of Israel's mission in the world."[31] Despite their many differences, Kaufmann Kohler and Solomon Schechter agreed that the only valid interpretation of Judaism was a religious one. Schechter put it most strongly in a letter written in 1903: "To me Zionism divorced from the religious idea is a menace."[32] Likewise, the financier Jacob Schiff, a Reform Jew who took religion very seriously, found the unwillingness of the Zionist leadership to take a positive position on Jewish religion the chief stumbling block to his joining its ranks.[33] Among political Zionists the principal villain was usually thought to be Nordau, an outspoken enemy of religion.[34] Among the cultural Zionists, the problem lay with the founder of the movement, Ahad Ha'am. Yet even some anti-Zionist Reform rabbis greatly admired him. Jacob Voorsanger of San Francisco, in a pamphlet rejecting return to Zion, called Ahad Ha'am "our great Odessa master," and praised his recognition of the superficiality of Jewish consciousness in the West. Judah Magnes called Ahad Ha'am from the pulpit "the first harmonious modern Jew" and held him up as a model of the Reform ideal of integrating the Jewish and non-Jewish worlds.[35] Ahad Ha'am presented a challenge; it was imperative for Reform Zionists to come to terms with him.

Within the camp of Reform no one was a more ardent champion of Ahad Ha'am than David Neumark, a member of the faculty of the Hebrew Union College from 1907 until his death in 1924.[36] Neumark's credentials both as a Reform Jew and as a cultural Zionist were impeccable. He had received rabbinical ordination at the Hochschule in Berlin, written a doctoral dissertation on Kant, and he was sufficiently committed to Reform Judaism for Kaufmann Kohler, the bitter opponent of secular Zionism, to employ him to teach philosophy to rabbinical students. At the same time he had been an early associate of Ahad Ha'am, contributing regularly to Hashiloah and participating in the planned "Otzar Hayahadut" project. Even after Neumark moved to Cincinnati, the two men maintained contact. In a more systematic and thoroughgoing fashion than any other

Reform Jew, Neumark determined to break down the barrier between Reform and Zionism and thus to justify his commitment to both. Unlike most of his Reform colleagues, who were mainly concerned with making room for Zionism within Reform Judaism, Neumark set himself the task of interpreting Zionism in such a way as to make a progressive religious conception of Judaism vital to the spiritual and material success of the movement.

Neumark argued that Zionism was indifferent to religion because it misunderstood what the Jewish religion really was. Jewish faith, properly understood, was not acceptance of a set of presuppositions or adherence to all the commandments. It was rather to be understood as a quality of the national character. "Faith is one of the attributes of the soul. It is a spiritual sense, similar to a sense of logic, a sense of beauty, a sense of morality, and the like." Even as the Greeks possessed a genius for beauty and the Romans for law, so Jews possessed a special sense for religion which gives rise to all Jewish creativity. "Our people possesses no capacity or attribute which is not rooted in its faith and its religion." Thus Neumark could conclude that nationalism without religion was wholly foreign to the historical character of Jewish nationality—"our religiosity constitutes our nationality."[37] Decades before Yehezkel Kaufmann, Neumark argued against his fellow Zionists that religion, not nationality, was the motivation for Jewish unity and sacrifice.

As a Reform Jew, Neumark believed that this religious capacity developed over the centuries and would continue to progress, producing new forms of expression, more pure and more spiritual. While modern Jewish nationalism might regard specific elements of Jewish faith and practice as outdated forms of Jewish spiritual expression, it could not eliminate religion entirely without divesting itself of its spiritual essence. "Take from our nation its religious genius and you will thereby nullify its nationality."[38] It followed, though he did not state it explicitly at this point, that while cultural Zionism might set aside Orthodox Judaism, it would have to view positively a progressive conception of Judaism as compatible with and necessary for the development of the Jewish spirit.

For Neumark the "national religion" of Judaism required an independent political framework in order to reach its potential. Jewish religious life in the Diaspora would always remain fragmented. Hence it followed that religious leaders who were serious not only about the preservation of Judaism but also about its further development should become wholehearted supporters of the Zionist movement. But by the same token, Zionism could not succeed unless it developed a positive attitude toward the Jewish religion. Neumark held out little hope that Zionism could win over the Orthodox masses of Eastern Europe. They were too closed to human efforts to bring about redemption. Yet if the Zionist movement was to reach its goals, it had to win over those Jews in the West who recognized the legitimacy of human initiative but whose Jewishness was based on a religious identity.[39] Neumark seemed to be saying to East European Zionists like Ahad Ha'am that their conception of Jewish religion might hold for East European Jews, who were overwhelmingly Orthodox, but not for those in the West. There were also practical reasons for acknowledging the centrality of faith in Jewish nationality. The leaders of Western Jewry were rabbis and officials of religious communities. The failure of the Zionists to win over major Jewish communities in Austria and Germany was due in large measure, Neumark believed, to their inability to recognize that organized Jewish life in the West was built upon religious institutions. Only by paying heed to the indissoluble unity of religion and nationality (without associating itself organizationally with any religious party) could Zionism win over the mass of Western Jewry. Neumark did not suggest that a religious affirmation be made incumbent upon all Zionists—"even the atheists among us can be fully Zionists"—but they should not be allowed to give direction to the movement: "They do not have the right to demand from the nation that for their sake it conceal the religious essence of its nationality. When an individual seeks toleration from the group, one grants it to him; but if he seeks sacrifices, one rebukes him severely."[40] Later he called secular Zionists "spiritual cripples with regard to the essence of the nation's particularity."[41]

The cultural Zionists certainly recognized the centrality of morality in Judaism which has its origin in the Hebrew prophets. But, according to Neumark, the originality of the Prophets did not lie in their notions of social justice but in their linking of human morality with a particular conception of God. "The disagreement between the prophets of Israel and the prophets of the nations of the earth was only this: the prophets of Israel believed in a God free of passions, in a God who is capable of being just and therefore is just in fact."[42] Thus Jewish particularity rests not upon morality but upon religion. Zionists frequently accused Reformers of distorting the Prophets by making them into universalists. Neumark contends that secularizing the Prophets is equally a distortion.

While complaining in his Hebrew articles about the prominent role secular Jews enjoyed in the Zionist leadership, Neumark tried to convince readers in America that they were mistaken about the Zionists. Only a few extremists in the Zionist camp negated the Jewish religion—he held—even as only extremists among Reform Jews were sworn enemies of Jewish nationalism. Each side failed to grasp that religion and nationality in Judaism were intertwined and could not be pulled apart. But fortunately, with the exception of Max Nordau, there were few such extremists in the Zionist leadership. Most of them were religious, even if they did not recognize that fact. When one examined Ahad Ha'am's thought, for example, one found that he was far more religious than he was willing to admit. In fact, his religious views were amazingly harmonious with those of the proponents of Reform Judaism. But not only Ahad Ha'am. Neumark so broadened the category of Reform Jew that it included anyone who was not Orthodox or militantly anti-religious. Thus, since Herzl was not Orthodox and yet—increasingly in the course of his Zionist activity—became observant of Jewish traditions, he too could properly, if paradoxically, be called a Reform Jew. Herzl's disputes with prominent Reform Jews were so bitter and rancorous precisely because they were internal conflicts. Neumark's extraordinary thesis made it impossible to argue that Zionism and Reform Judaism were essentially at odds. If Herzl was a Reform Jew, how could Reform Judaism oppose Zionism? But Neumark did not even stop with Ahad Ha'am and Herzl. He finally comes to the astonishing conclusion: "In fact, all modern Zionists, except perhaps a very few who may not be religious at all, are good Reform Jews. Ahad Ha'am is a good Reform Jew. . . . So are Dr. Klausner, Sokolow, and all Zionists in Europe and America whom I know personally or by their utterances. All are good Reform Jews who want to return to the idea of redemption by using secular means to bring it about."[43]

Perhaps we should attribute it to the perversity of the philosopher in him that Neumark could come to conclusions which seem so patently in opposition to the situation as perceived by the protagonists themselves. But there may nonetheless be some truth to Neumark's assertion, made in 1916, that the conflict was not a "difference in principles" but rather a "noisy and superficial controversy."[44] Certainly in ideological terms the two movements were beginning to intertwine. Perhaps it was less Neumark's intention to describe objectively the true affiliation of Herzl and Ahad Ha'am than to shock his readers into realizing that the polemics of each side much exaggerated the differences. His article, which was even reprinted in the anti-Zionist *American Israelite,* helped to lay the basis for rapprochement.

Of course Ahad Ha'am did not take kindly to being designated a Reform Jew. Although he had originally welcomed Neumark as a rare Western partisan of his side against Herzl, he objected to being termed religious by any definition, Orthodox or Reform. He wrote to Neumark that in his view religion was related to nationality "like flame to ember." The Jewish religion was inconceivable without Jewish nationality, but not vice versa. "Although it is not possible to be a religious Jew without acknowledging the existence of our nationality, it is possible to be a national Jew without acknowledging certain things in which religion requires belief."[45] Yet Ahad Ha'am criticized Max Nordau for not appreciating the national and historical value of the Sabbath, and though often critical of Reform Judaism, did praise Abraham Geiger and his contemporaries for stressing against Christianity "the superiority of the internal elements—religious and moral—which are unique to Judaism." Like the classical Reformers, he wrote of the spiritual uniqueness of Judaism and held aloft the prophetic call for social justice.[46] His insistence upon historical continuity made Zionism seem less of a break with Jewish tradition. Yet the role which religion plays for Neumark, Ahad Ha'am ascribed to morality, which until the modern period had always been dressed in religious garb. Ahad Ha'am believed that Jewish morality had a future, but he doubted whether the same was true of Jewish religion. While the Reformers dreaded the appeal of the Ethical Culture movement founded by Felix Adler, Ahad Ha'am could admire Adler's movement as a model for the formation of societies devoted to moral issues "without any reference to religion."[47] As early as 1892 he had stated his position definitively vis-à-vis the Reform movement: "There are among us 'Reformers' who think it possible for us to remove the husk from religion, the ritual commandments, and to preserve only the kernel, the abstract doctrines. . . . They do not realize that it is the old barrel in its old form which is holy, and all that is in it is sanctified on its account, even if it becomes empty and is refilled with new content from time to time."[48]

Even if Ahad Ha'am's concept of morality could be seen as bordering upon the religious, here was an irreconcilable difference. What for Ahad Ha'am constituted the unit of religious continuity— the barrel (ritual practice)—was for the Reformers dependent on historical circumstance. He sought to refill the old forms with new content, while the Reformers sought to pour the old wine—the eternal ideas of Judaism—into new barrels. In frustration, Neumark could only hope that Ahad Ha'am be given the opportunity to settle in the Land of Israel for there "the religious spirit which is in him will be renewed. . . . He will liberate himself completely from 'natural laws' in matters of religion, ethics, and history: 'Let him who desires to enjoy the divine splendor go and engage in Torah in the Land of Israel.' "[49]

Neumark's attempt to shatter the accepted stereotypes was not isolated. A new conception of the relation between Reform Judaism and Zionism was rapidly gaining ground, especially among those who were associated with both movements, but also among some Reform Jews who did not call themselves Zionists.

The Zionists in Reform ranks increasingly distinguished between "official Reform Judaism" and Reform Judaism as it was in essence. The former was only a "particular school of Reform Judaism"; the latter could easily encompass Zionism.[50] The essence of Reform was not any anti-Zionist doctrine. Its basic principle was religious development, which set it in opposition to Orthodoxy, but not to Zionism.[51] Unlike Orthodoxy, Reform Judaism had shown awareness of the need for Judaism to adjust to changing historical circumstances. But therefore it followed—so thought Felsenthal—that had they lived in the twentieth century instead of in the nineteenth, the founding fathers of the Reform movement would surely have become Zionists. Thus Zionism was not a break with Reform tradition. Indeed it was incumbent upon Reform Judaism to remain loyal to its own principle and to recognize the need for a new stage in its own development. In the nineteenth century the most significant Jewish task in the West was formulating a religious conception of Judaism which would be viable in a modern cultural context; in the twentieth century it was the struggle against assimilation which required a Zionist program.[52] Or as Max Heller put it: "Reform and Zionism are really two consecutive waves of a renaissance movement, the one being a renaissance of Judaism, the other a renaissance of the Jew."[53] When Martin Meyer identified himself as a "Reform Jewish Zionist" in 1917,[54] he was affirming a composite Jewish identity that incorporated both elements without conflict.

In the newly emerging Reform ideology, Reform Judaism and Zionism were not only complementary; they were dependent on one another for their success. Reform Judaism needed Zionism to rouse Jewish consciousness among individuals alienated from all Jewish life. Like Solomon Schechter, the Zionist Reform rabbis believed that Zionism in the Diaspora could serve as a bulwark against assimilation. If Reform was to promote Jewish idealism, it required the more intense Jewishness which only Zionism could provide. Far from destroying Reform Judaism, Zionism in fact served to preserve it.[55]

But the Zionist Reformers also held that Zionism needed Reform Judaism to provide it with a transcendent sense of purpose.

Meyer was convinced that the racial bond could not hold Jews together. Zionism would have to "fall back upon the old thought of Israel's world mission."[56] The mission idea, reinterpreted to include the spiritual center in Palestine, was thus intended to become the common purpose of both movements or, as Stephen Wise understood the relationship: "Liberalism will preserve Judaism and Zionism will preserve the Jew."[57]

The task of rebuilding Palestine was seen as flowing directly from long and frequently enunciated Reform principles of concern for the downtrodden and social idealism. The pioneers were deserving of assistance not alone on general humanitarian grounds but also because they were attempting to build a society grounded on the affirmation of social justice to which Reform Judaism in America had committed itself collectively as early as the Pittsburgh Platform of 1885. Gustav Gottheil went so far as to suggest that the New Yishuv represented a modernizing reform of the Old in the same way that Reform Judaism represented a religious modernization of Orthodoxy.[58]

Most early Reform Zionists—like most American Zionists in general—understood their task to lie in the Diaspora and expressed no overwhelming sense of exile. A notable exception to the rule—aside from Judah Magnes—is Max Heller. As early as 1910 he wrote: "We cannot sing the song of Zion on the soil of the stranger,"[59] and he looked forward to an exodus of Jews from America to Palestine. Against Ahad Ha'am, Heller argued that a national culture could not be built in the Diaspora; the first priority must therefore be to win the land.[60] Speaking at a convention of the CCAR in 1919 he said: "It is because I want to live where I can have a Sabbath that I want to go to Palestine. The person who wants Zionism for the other fellow is insincere."[61] How different this sounds from the "Zionism is good Americanism" line of Louis Brandeis and his supporters in the Zionist Organization of America![62] Yet it was Brandeis's "respectable," philanthropic Zionism, supplemented by a mild dose of Palestine-centered Jewish culture and enhanced with an increasingly favorable attitude to religion, which eventually won out in America.[63] And that was a Zionism easy for even anti-Zionist Reformers sooner or later to accept.

Toward the end of his life Kaufmann Kohler could make a statement which broke radically with his earlier views. Kohler declared in 1919:

Let Palestine, our ancient home, under the protection of the great nations, or under the specific British suzerainty, again become a center of Jewish culture and a safe refuge for the homeless. We shall all welcome it and aid in the promotion of its work. Let the million or more of Jewish citizens dwelling there . . . be empowered and encouraged to build up a commonwealth broad and liberal in spirit to serve as a school for international and interdenominational humanity. We shall all hail the undertaking and pray for its prosperity.[64]

He insisted only that there be also a place and a task for Jews in America. Such an ideology—which became characteristic of the vast majority of Zionists in the United States—was one to which few could take exception. Though the majority of Reform Jews remained ambivalent about Zionism for another two decades, in the long run Bernhard Felsenthal was proven correct in his prediction at the turn of the century: "Alle, Alle werden Zionisten."[65] By 1920 becoming a Zionist was already no harder ideologically for Reformers than for any other Jews in America. The foundation for rapprochement between the two movements had been set into place.

Notes

1. On the subject of Reform Judaism and Zionism in general, see especially: Arthur J. Lelyveld, "The Conference View of the Position of the Jew in the Modern World," *Retrospect and Prospect*, ed., B. W. Korn (New York, 1965), 129–30; David Polish, *Renew Our Days: The Zionist Issue in Reform Judaism* (Jerusalem, 1976); Cyrus Arfa, "Attitudes of the American Reform Rabbinate toward Zionism, 1885–1948," New York University Doctoral Dissertation, 1978; Alfred Gottschalk, "Israel and Reform Judaism," *Forum* 36 (Fall/Winter 1979), 143–60.
2. For the early period see the excellent book by Evyatar Friesel, which has been most helpful in preparing this study: *The Zionist Movement in the United States, 1897–1914* (Hebrew) (Tel Aviv, 1970). See also Naomi Wiener Cohen, "The Reaction of Reform Judaism in America to Political Zionism (1897–1922)," *Publications of the American Jewish Historical Society*, vol. 40, part 4 (June 1951), 361–94; Joseph P. Sternstein, "Reform Judaism and Zionism, 1895–1904," and Herschel Levin, "The Other Side of the Coin," *Herzl Year Book*, vol. 5 (1963), 11–31, 33–56.
3. *American Jewish Chronicle* 1 (September 22–29, 1916), 612; cf. Stephen S. Wise, in *American Hebrew* 94 (December 12, 1913), 188.
4. *Maccabean* 18 (January 1910), 30–32. See also Friesel, *Zionist Movement in U.S.*, 121–22, 146, 276.
5. Wise in *American Hebrew*, 189–90.
6. *Maccabean* 29 (November 1916), 84.
7. *Central Conference of American Rabbis Year Book* (hereafter *CCARY*) 17 (1907), 31.

8. *CCARY* 27 (1917), 133.

9. The names of which I am aware are Bernhard Felsenthal, Gustav Gottheil, Max Heller, James Heller, Jacob Raisin, Max Raisin, Joseph Jasin, Judah Magnes, Martin Meyer, Stephen Wise, Abba Hillel Silver, Joseph Krauskopf, Felix Levy, David Neumark, Barnett Brickner, Michael Solomon. It is likely that there are others as well.

10. *American Israelite*, October 28, 1897.

11. According to the anti-Zionist Jacob Voorsanger, cited in Richard Gottheil, *The Life of Gustav Gottheil* (Williamsport, Penn., 1936), 276.

12. *American Jewish Chronicle* 3 (May 18, 1917), 36; 3 (September 14, 1917), 499.

13. *American Hebrew* 81 (July 19, 1907), 262.

14. Felix Levy (1935–37), James Heller (1941–43), Abba Hillel Silver (1945–47), Barnett Brickner (1954–56).

15. *American Israelite*, October 28, 1897; *Hebrew Union College Journal* 4 (1899), 54.

16. Gary P. Zola, "Reform Judaism's Premier Zionist: Maximilian Heller," Hebrew Union College Archival Research Paper, 28.

17. *CCARY* 30 (1920), 141.

18. Kaufmann Kohler, *Hebrew Union College and Other Addresses* (Cincinnati, 1916), 20.

19. *CCARY* 17 (1907), 235; Jacob Voorsanger, *Zionism* (San Francisco, 1904), 47.

20. *Menorah* 31 (December 1901), 423.

21. *American Hebrew* 64 (January 13, 1899), 389–90.

22. *American Jewish Chronicle* 3 (September 14, 1917), 491.

23. *CCARY* 30 (1920), 183–84.

24. Kaufmann Kohler, *Grundriss einer systematischen Theologie des Judentums* (Leipzig, 1910), 7.

25. *American Hebrew* 80 (January 25, 1907), 311; Benny Kraut, *From Reform Judaism to Ethical Culture* (Cincinnati, 1979), 153–68.

26. *CCARY* 29 (1919), 237.

27. For example, Heller in *Maccabean* 19 (January 1911), 231.

28. Judah L. Magnes, *Zionism and Jewish Religion* (Philadelphia, 1910), 4–5.

29. *American Hebrew* 62 (December 10, 1897), 201; 64 (January 13, 1899), 389; *Maccabean* 5 (March 1903), 131–38; *CCARY* 17 (1907), 33–34.

30. *American Hebrew* 94 (December 12, 1913), 190.

31. *CCARY* 27 (1917), 140–41, 202.

32. Norman Bentwich, *Solomon Schechter* (Philadelphia, 1938), 315; Friesel, *Zionist Movement in U.S.*, 244.

33. Bentwich, *Solomon Schechter*, 321; Friesel, *Zionist Movement in U.S.*, 166; idem, "Jacob H. Schiff Becomes a Zionist," *Studies in Zionism* 5 (Spring 1982), 52–92.

34. For example, *American Israelite*, September 10, 1903.

35. Voorsanger, *Zionism*, 45; *American Hebrew* 80 (January 25, 1907), 311.

36. On him, see Samuel S. Cohon, "Rabbi David Neumark," *Hadoar* 17

(New York, 1937), 332–33, 359–60; Joshua Bloch, "David Neumark," *Sefer Hashanah Lihude Amerika* 5 (New York, 1940), 256–68; Ezra Spicehandler, "Hebrew and Hebrew Literature," *Hebrew Union College— Jewish Institute of Religion at One Hundred Years*, ed., S. E. Karff (Cincinnati, 1976), 457.

37. *Hashiloah* 1 (1906/1907), 366.
38. Ibid.
39. *Jüdische Chronik* 4 (1898), 274–81, 298–303, 331–35.
40. *Hashiloah* 5 (1898/1899), 102–3.
41. *Ahi'asaf* 12 (1904/1905), 31.
42. *Hatoren* 2 (1914/1915), 145.
43. Cited according to the English version which appeared in the *American Jewish Chronicle* 1 (September 22–29, 1916), 635–637, and in the *American Israelite*, October 19, 1916.
44. *American Jewish Chronicle* 637.
45. *Letters of Ahad Ha'am* (Hebrew) (Jerusalem-Berlin, 1923–25), 1:182; 4:148–49; 5:311–12.
46. *At the Crossroads* (Hebrew) (Berlin, 1930), 3:79; 4:38, 47.
47. *Hashiloah* 5 (1898/1899), 9.
48. *At the Crossroads*, 1:139–40.
49. David Neumark, *From a Corner* (Hebrew) (New York, 1917), 96.
50. *American Hebrew* 86 (April 29, 1910), 678; *Maccabean* 20 (March-April 1911), 96.
51. *American Hebrew* 81 (May 24, 1907), 62; 81 (July 12, 1907), 235.
52. Bernhard Felsenthal, "Sind Wir Noch Juden?" *Populär-wissenschaftliche Monatsblätter* 16 (1896), 56; "Jüdische Thesen," *Festschrift zum siebzigsten Geburtstage A. Berliners* (Frankfurt, 1903), 91–92; *Maccabean* 5 (March 1903), 136.
53. *American Hebrew* 81 (July 12, 1907), 248.
54. *Maccabean* 30 (January 1917), 134. I believe this is the first time that the two appellations appear joined together.
55. Ibid., 131–32, 134.
56. *American Hebrew* 81 (September 13, 1907), 467.
57. *American Hebrew* 94 (December 12, 1913), 190.
58. *American Journal of Theology* 6 (1902), 283–84; cf. Max Raisin in *Jewish Exponent* 59 (July 3, 1914), 9.
59. *Maccabean* 18 (February 1910), 47–48.
60. *Maccabean* 30 (August 1917), 315; *American Hebrew* 74 (May 13, 1904), 798.
61. *CCARY* 29 (1919), 300.
62. Louis Brandeis, *Zionism and Patriotism* (New York, 1916), 6; *Brandeis on Zionism* (Washington, D.C., 1942), 36, 84, 142.
63. Ben Halpern, "The Americanization of Zionism, 1880–1930," *American Jewish History* 69, no. 1 (September 1979), 15–33.
64. *CCARY* 29 (1919), 287.
65. Emma Felsenthal, *Bernhard Felsenthal: Teacher in Israel* (New York, 1924), 79.

CHAPTER 22

Abba Hillel Silver as Zionist within the Camp of Reform Judaism

In his adulatory Hebrew biography of Abba Hillel Silver, Isaiah Vinograd wrote: "In Silver's heart the idea took shape to conquer Reform Judaism for the Zionist idea and through it to impose the idea of the [Jewish national] renaissance upon all of America."[1] It was with this purpose in mind that Silver became associated with the Reform movement. If he could conquer the most powerful and resistant citadel of anti-Zionism, all opposition to Silver's fundamental ideology of Zionism would melt away. Vinograd's implication is clear: Silver was always a Zionist at heart; his allegiance to Reform Judaism was, above all, a tactic to serve the Zionist cause.

This view that Silver's loyalties lay fundamentally with Zionism is echoed, though less blatantly, by Marc Lee Raphael in the only full-length biography of Silver in English. "Silver was primarily a Zionist for whom Jewish statehood and Hebrew culture were increasingly the highest values of his career, and for whom the constant use of Hebrew demonstrated the importance he attached to cultural Zionism throughout his life. He was above all else a Zionist, albeit of the American kind." According to Raphael, this distinguishes Silver from men like Stephen S. Wise, James Heller, and Louis Newman, whom he identifies as "Reform rabbis who were Zionists."[2]

The views of Vinograd and Raphael differ sharply from those of other writers on Silver, specifically of men who knew him personally within the Reform movement as well as within Zionist circles. Herbert Weiner called the rabbinate "the central commitment of Abba Hillel Silver's life."[3] David Polish cites this passage in Weiner and adds, perhaps in intended contradiction to Vinograd's view: "Silver believed in the compatibility of Reform and Zionism, not the conquest of Reform by Zionism. For him, Zionism represented a vital addition to Reform, not a substitute."[4] Similarly, his close friend—though not, like him, a confirmed Zionist—Solomon Free- hof claimed of Silver that "the rabbinate was central to his heart and mind," that "Rabbi Silver was the title which he cherished most" and that "wherever he spoke, at whatever great Jewish assemblage, or in the councils of the nations, he spoke as a Rabbi."[5]

There is a measure of truth in each of these opposing views. Surely, Silver was interested in winning over the Jewish religious establishment for Zionism. The most blatant admission of this mo- tive of which I am aware occurs in a letter to fellow Zionist Reform rabbi James G. Heller of Cincinnati. In 1929, Stephen S. Wise had proposed organizing Reform and Conservative Zionist rabbis to for- mulate a united program of liberal religion and Zionism. Heller sup- ported this project and proposed it to Silver, who responded disdainfully: "I believe it is poor tactics to say the least. Our objec- tive should be not to divide the American rabbinate into two sharply distinguished and opposite groups, but in winning control over all existing Rabbinical organizations for Zionist purposes."[6] But Silver also insisted that his achievements as a Zionist were "never separate or apart from my profession as a rabbi. Zionism was always a part of my conception of historic Judaism, and I came to it not as a secular nationalist but as a devout Jew."[7]

Clearly the matter is complex: one of dual loyalties, sometimes in severe conflict with one another. Silver felt not fully at home in a Reform Judaism that was not Zionist but was just as unhappy in a Zionism that espoused secular nationalism. He was, I believe, a deeply religious Zionist, whose religion was, ironically perhaps, Classical Reform Judaism. That Classical Reform Judaism at the be- ginning of Silver's career was dominantly, if not wholly, anti-Zion- ist. He certainly did seek to "Zionize" it, but to do so from the position of his own Reform commitment. Beginning with his stu- dent days at the Hebrew Union College, he was always—in sharp contrast to Stephen S. Wise—a *ben bayit* (one of its own) within the movement. His struggles to make Reform Judaism over in his own image were fought from within, not as one conquers a foreign cita- del but as a dispute among members of the same family. This essay will trace the various stages of that dispute focusing on the crucial arguments and actions in relation to the development of the move- ment and to Silver's rabbinical and Zionist careers.

The Hebrew Union College

When Silver came to Cincinnati in 1911, the Hebrew Union College was still recovering from the dispute between anti-Zionists and Zionists that had contributed to the departure of three faculty members a few years earlier. The Reform theologian Kaufmann Kohler remained president of the institution, but, Silver recalls, students were free to preach their senior sermons on Zionist topics if they chose to do so. There was no ideological indoctrination. Kohler had appointed David Neumark, a close associate of Ahad Ha'Am, as professor of philosophy, and it was under his aegis that a Hebrew-speaking society was organized among the students. Although the Reform movement continued to be dominated by German Jews, candidates for the rabbinate were increasingly coming from the ranks of East European Jewry.

Still, the Jewish atmosphere was quite different from what the young Silver had experienced in Lithuania and New York. Given the traditional character of his parental home, it remains a bit strange that he should have chosen Hebrew Union College over the Jewish Theological Seminary. Silver himself explained it in religious terms: "I and my young friends were reaching out, quite unconsciously, for a more liberal type of Judaism."[8] He recalled that his awareness of Reform Zionists such as Gustav Gottheil, Judah Magnes, and Stephen Wise, played a role in his decision.

Clearly Silver was quite content in Cincinnati, where he founded a student magazine and gave the valedictory address. And the experience transformed him. He emerged after four years as a Classical Reform Jew, fully dedicated to a non-halakhic Judaism that stressed, above all, the message of the Prophets and the ethical mission of Israel.[9]

Silver always remained a loyal alumnus of the Hebrew Union College. He served a term as president of its Alumni Association and as a member of its Board of Governors; he delivered addresses for Founders' Day and Ordination; and he sent his son there for a rabbinical education. In 1925 he received an earned doctoral degree from the college; he was himself a generous donor to its campaigns and helped to raise funds for it in Cleveland. Silver claimed to have sent more students to the college than any other rabbi. During the 1930s a group of students in Cincinnati prided themselves on being his disciples.[10] In 1947 the non-Zionist rabbi Edgar Magnin even proposed that Silver should become president of the Hebrew Union College, a suggestion Silver declined because he thought the college should be led by "a person far less controversial than I am."[11]

Of course, Silver's loyalty to the college was dependent on its maintaining at least a neutral attitude toward Zionism. When he heard that the anti-Zionist rabbi Louis Wolsey questioned a prospective student he had sponsored during his admission interview regarding his Zionism and impressed upon him its incompatibility with Reform Judaism, Silver fired off an angry letter to the registrar stating that if anti-Zionism has become a requisite, "I should like to be informed, so that I may be guided in my relation to the institution in the future." The registrar reassured Silver that, in fact, not only was this student admitted by unanimous vote, but the college had no policy with regard to the Zionism or non-Zionism of its student body.[12]

Silver's relations with Kaufmann Kohler's successor as president of the Hebrew Union College, Julian Morgenstern, had their distinct ups and downs. Morgenstern greatly appreciated and wanted to preserve Silver's loyalty to the college, the more so as the other great Zionist Liberal rabbi, Stephen S. Wise, headed a rival seminary. He offered Silver an honorary degree in 1941, attributing its award to recognition of his recent service as president of the United Palestine Appeal.[13] But he was not a political Zionist. When Silver, as president of the Alumni Association, urged that the association join in sponsoring a National Conference for Palestine to meet with the visiting Chaim Weizmann in 1937, Morgenstern was hesitant and expressed misgivings, especially as the planned conference might affiliate itself with the American Jewish Congress, headed by Wise. "On the other hand," he noted, "we owe the courtesy [to at least be present] to Weitzmann [sic] and doubly so since Weitzmann himself, as the holder of an honorary degree from the Hebrew Union College, is actually an honorary member of our alumni association."[14]

In the early 1940s, however, relations between Morgenstern and Silver became severely strained. Morgenstern not only joined the "non-Zionist" American Council for Judaism but, with limited success, attempted to persuade his faculty to sign on as well. In his opening-day address to the student body in the fall of 1943, he declared Revisionist Zionism "practically identical with Nazist and Fascist theory." (It was reported in the press as referring to Zionism *tout court*.)[15] Silver now turned on Morgenstern, with whom he had even until then maintained cordial relations,[16] and supported Rabbi Joshua Loth Liebman's public protest, justifying his action because he believed the address had hurt the college. Deluged by letters and telegrams of protest, Silver was prepared to go even further than Liebman and bring charges against Morgenstern to the board of the college.[17] Clearly, Silver perceived the statement as most unfortunate and perhaps reacted as strongly as he did because it served to embarrass him in Zionist circles.[18] With Morgenstern's eventual, if lukewarm, conversion to political Zionism following the war and the new presidency of Nelson Glueck, Silver renewed his close association with the college, which lasted to the end of his life.

The Young Star of Reform Judaism

With remarkable rapidity the newly ordained Abba Hillel Silver rose to the top of the Reform movement. After barely two years in Wheeling, West Virginia—at the age of twenty-four—he was elected rabbi of one of the most influential Reform congregations, The Temple, in Cleveland, Ohio. His predecessor there, Moses Gries, was a Classical Reformer in every respect, including a marked coolness toward Zionism. That the congregation should select Silver, whose Zionism was certainly known to them, is the best indication of the reputation the young man had already gained as a most capable religious leader and an extraordinarily talented orator. Still, the connection between Silver and The Temple was not easily made. While he was pressing his candidacy, questions were raised, presumably by leaders of the congregation, regarding his Zionism. In response, Silver wrote a most interesting letter to Gries. Since it represents the first extant elaboration of Silver's personal reconciliation of his Zionist and Reform views and helps us to understand his success in the Reform movement, it seems worthy of extended citation. The crucial sections of the letter read as follows:

> I believe that we are a people possessing spiritual uniqueness, dowered by Providence with a mission to serve mankind through religious leadership. This is primary and fundamental in my concept of Judaism. Else, I would not be in the ministry.
>
> The hope which prompts thousands of faithful Jews today to safe-guard their precious heritage, to intensify their Jewish life and to enrich its content by establishing a spiritual and cultural centre in Palestine cannot but meet with my sympathy and approval. Not that I see in the establishment of such a centre, a solution of all Jewish problems the world over, but that such a centre may be contributory towards a galvanization of Jewish life the world over—and any movement which aims at a deepening of Jewish consciousness and at a strengthening of Jewish spiritual solidarity cannot be foreign to me.
>
> For me the political phase of Zionism has at all times been secondary and incidental and with the emancipation of Russian Jewry, it has become negligible. I cannot grow enthusiastic over the establishment of a little Jewish state in Palestine. Should the nations of the world, however, at the conclusion of this war, favor the granting to

the Jews in Palestine the privilege of political independence—and certain events seem to point in that direction—I cannot see where that
would be detrimental to their own welfare or to the status of the Jews
in America or the world over.

In this I am conscious of no double allegiance. I am in heart and
soul an American; for I see in America the gradual unfolding of those
divine principles of justice and righteousness for which my people
has so bravely lived and suffered. The destiny of American Israel is,
and must forever remain, interlaced with the destiny of America.

And in conclusion, permit me to say, that in my humble opinion Zionism is not the vital problem of American Israel today. I hold
that the significance of Zionism, as a political movement, has been
over-estimated both by its friends and its enemies. The most pressing
and perplexing problem which American Judaism faces is not Zionism—but religious apathy and indifference, frightful ignorance and
lack of organization. Our problems are spiritual, pedagogic, administrative and we must solve them here and *now*.[19]

Silver concluded that if his sentiments militated against "a mutual
sympathy of pulpit and pew," he would prefer that his name be
withdrawn from candidacy.

The letter apparently made Silver acceptable to both Gries and
the board of The Temple. But when Stephen S. Wise visited Cleveland, he was shocked to learn how far the alleged Zionist, who as a
boy in New York had founded the Dr. Herzl Zion Club, was willing
to bend in order to attain the position. Initially, he had heartily con-
gratulated the young rabbi and offered his assistance in all matters.[20]
Now, to his dismay, he had learned that Silver's Zionism had
"passed muster," that it was "so qualified as to be altogether unobjectionable." And he was not beyond a cynical insinuation: "I cannot believe that you have suffered such an impression to go out as
would on any ground lead anyone to imagine that you would abate
your devotion to Zionism in order to secure a pulpit on any extrinsic
ground whatever."[21] In his response, Silver declared any imputation
that he had modified his views to pass muster was "downright calumny and slander." There had been no conditions or tacit agree-
ments. Yet, regrettably, the "nasty rumor" had spread widely. He
assured Wise that he had been for years a disciple of Ahad Ha'Am
and that he had come to Zionism "through my love of Hebrew Culture and Literature and for the mighty promises which it holds as a
'galvanizing force' in Jewish life."[22] He even sent Wise a copy of
his letter to Gries. But it seems unlikely that Wise could have been
persuaded by the Gries letter, which spoke of political Zionism as
"secondary and incidental." As for Silver, he was deeply offended
by Wise's almost unveiled suspicions. Later it was claimed by one

of Wise's disciples that Silver never forgot the incident and never forgave Wise for it.[23]

Some time after Silver's "honeymoon" at The Temple, according to Vinograd, he received an order requiring him to cease giving Zionist sermons and engaging in nationalist activities. Thereupon, he relates, Silver immediately offered his resignation and forced the board to back down.[24] If the incident occurred as described,[25] it indicates not only that Silver, from the start, would not kowtow to the board, but also that in this very early test of wills he was able to make himself once and for all master of The Temple, enjoying a position of unquestioned authority that he maintained easily thereafter throughout his rabbinical career. As would rapidly become apparent, Silver's Zionism was no barrier to his leadership either within his congregation or within the Reform movement.

Among his colleagues in the Reform rabbinate Silver was treated as a prodigy. Already in 1916, only a year after his ordination, he was called upon to address the annual convention of the Central Conference of American Rabbis (CCAR), the first of more than half a dozen sermons, lectures, and addresses that he would be asked to deliver to his assembled colleagues in succeeding years.[26] Unlike Wise, who rarely attended, Silver was usually present at CCAR conventions, even during those years when Zionist activity claimed most of his time.

To a Zionist colleague Silver confided that this attendance on the part of Zionist rabbis was essential to counterbalance the forces arrayed against them.[27] Yet already at this point in his career Silver was reluctant to introduce the divisive topic of Zionism into the deliberations of Reform rabbinical and lay bodies. He feared then, as he did later, that the chief result would be to give the anti-Zionists a platform for their views. They had more to gain by such debates than the Zionists, who could best manage their ascendancy without éclat.[28] In the 1920s he chose instead to work incrementally, inducing the CCAR to cooperate with the Palestine Development Council in the economic rehabilitation of Palestine and the promotion of Jewish settlement there.[29]

No less remarkable than Silver's early prominence among his rabbinical colleagues was his acclaim among the laity. As early as 1923, the now thirty-year-old rabbi was called upon to give the sermon at the Golden Jubilee Convention of the Union of American Hebrew Congregations meeting at Carnegie Hall in New York. During the 1920s and 30s he was inundated with speaking requests at a variety of Reform congregations. Perhaps most surprising are his repeated speaking appearances at Rockdale Avenue Temple in Cincinnati, whose rabbi was the very incarnation of American Reform anti-Zionism, David Philipson.[30]

Silver's early broad acceptance within the Reform movement was due not only to his readiness to avoid harping on Zionism in his invited speeches; it was also attributable to a philosophy of Judaism which had as much or more in common with Reform anti-Zionists as it did with secular Jewish nationalists. Like Morgenstern,[31] Silver preached the advent of an "American Judaism" that would embrace the best elements of its German and East-European antecedents. From the former it would take prophetic idealism, from the latter warmth and mysticism. Like Isaac Mayer Wise, Silver was convinced (and it was not a view he ever gave up!) that, as he put it in 1919, "the golden period of Judaism in Spain will be as nothing compared to the golden period of Jewry in America in the days to come."[32] He was similarly persuaded of the glory of America which, created "by the grace of God," was destined to become "the great proving ground for the hopes of the world . . . the microcosm of which the whole of humanity is the macrocosm."[33] Such optimistic oratory was inspiring and inspiriting to his listeners, especially at a time, following World War I, when antisemitism and isolationism were running rampant. Speaking to the UAHC Jubilee convention in 1923 Silver said not a word about Zionism, certainly not that antisemitism should induce any reconsideration of Isaac Mayer Wise's ebullient hopes for America. His response to the recrudescence of hatred was pure Classical Reform in the tradition of David Einhorn: "We know that the world needs us most when it hates us most and so we shall continue to be the humble servants of the most High."[34]

Silver's Classical Reform Judaism found expression especially and persistently in his advocacy of the mission of Israel. This doctrine, not peculiar to Reform Judaism but fervently adopted by it, had long been a principal argument against Zionism. If Jews were to be a light unto the gentiles, how could they perform that task unless they were scattered among the nations. Zionism, it was argued, represented a withdrawal from the Jews' God-ordained mission. Silver was not the first Zionist in the Reform movement to reconcile the mission idea with Zionism by slightly modifying its doctrinal content. The Classical Reform rabbi of Chicago—and earliest of the Zionist rabbis in the movement—Bernhard Felsenthal had already noted in 1897 that the mission of Israel among the nations could only be strengthened if there were a spiritual center in Palestine, and Stephen Wise had argued similarly that the diaspora mission of the Jew would continue in coordination with the Palestinian center.[35] Silver simply echoed that view more loudly. On the one hand, a nation did not need to be completely scattered to play the role of missionaries—it required a base and source of inspiration. But on the other, the Jewish people without the mission idea was doomed to insignificance. Silver put it most strongly in a sermon that he delivered at The Temple in 1926: "It would be a mistake on the part of the champions of Jewish nationalism to push to the background this inspiring motif of Jewish life. I would not wish my people to become another statelet, another little Montenegro somewhere, merely for the sake of existing as a separate entity there. I wish my people to continue as a light-bringer unto mankind."[36] Silver's defense of the mission concentrated more than that of his predecessors on the doctrine's roots in Prophetic and Pharisaic Judaism, its Jewish legitimacy. The idea became false only when it was deprived of the national foundation that was required to sustain it.[37] Most significantly, only the mission idea would preserve Judaism among Liberal Jews in the United States: "Even the strong appeal which Palestine is making today to many of our people will not prove sufficient to command their loyalty in the days to come."[38]

In these years Silver was not only an advocate of doctrinal Reform Judaism, he became its fervent defender against those who were subjecting it to attack. The major assault, in 1925 and 1926, came from a group of secularist Jews around the *Menorah Journal:* the talented Jewish intellectual Elliot E. Cohen, the advocate of a secular "Hebraism" Horace Kallen, and the editor of the journal Henry Hurwitz. These men mercilessly indicted religious Judaism, the synagogue, and the rabbinate. They particularly reveled in subjecting the cherished mission of Israel to merciless ridicule. Few Reform rabbis were as equipped as Silver to rise to the defense. He possessed bona fides both as a scholar and a Zionist and he could hold his own in any debate. In response to the raging of the "heathen," as Silver dubbed this group, he drew back from Ahad Ha'am and argued that Judaism had survived on account of its religion, not its culture, and only the Jewish religion would preserve it in the future. And that religion would be passionately held by Jews only if they believed in the mission of Israel.[39]

Silver's strong conviction—frequently expressed in the interwar years—that the only true Judaism was religious Judaism was reflected in the decision of his congregation in 1929 to eliminate all secular activities in the temple building, a decision that could hardly have been made without his approval. The purpose of a synagogue, he believed, was to concentrate on religious worship and education.[40] Not surprisingly, Silver also defended the mission idea when Mordecai Kaplan declared it both dangerous and absurd.[41] It was no more absurd than the words of the Prophets, Silver declared, and if it was dangerous as an advocate for Judaism to take on Trinitarian Christianity as well as all forms of social privilege, then, Silver insisted, one should be prepared to live dangerously.[42]

It would be a mistake to conclude, however, that Silver's Zionism in the 1920s had fallen silent. From time to time he spoke on the subject from the pulpit or wrote on it in an article. He stressed the centrality of Palestine in Jewish history and in contemporary Jewish life. Yet what is clear from these expressions is that Silver continued to be, as he had said in the letter to Wise of 1917, a cultural rather than a political Zionist. Although he recognized the need for a refuge for persecuted Jews, Silver would not raise that goal to the status of ideology:

> A people that constructs a life philosophy on suffering is a neurotic people, and I would be humiliated if the only claim which Israel had upon me was the fact of its age-old suffering and martyrdom. It isn't the misery of our people which makes Palestine a burning issue today, nor is it anti-Semitism. . . . It is not the persecuted bodies of my people that need Palestine so much as the persecuted and harassed spirit of the race that needs a refuge and a sanctuary. . . . At no time was the spirit of our race so much in danger by compromising and fawning and cringing as at the present time, and we want a home for this soul of our race where it can live in a congenial environment, where it can create and evolve new and finer spiritual and cultural values with which to bless mankind in the future even as it has blessed mankind in the past.[43]

Silver would return to the Herzlian Zionism of his early youth only when Nazism made that imperative.

The Zionism Battle in the CCAR

When the Committee on Synagogue Music made its report at the convention of the Central Conference of American Rabbis in 1930, it was not expected to cause controversy. But, extraordinarily, Stephen S. Wise was present for the convention and chose to make an issue of what he regarded as a serious omission: the words and music of "Hatikvah" would not appear in the revised hymnal. When it became known to him that "The Star Spangled Banner" would appear, Wise went into a diatribe and forced a recorded vote of the plenum, which—remarkably—resulted in 65 votes in favor and 59 against.[44] The Jewish press responded favorably to this expression of Zionist sympathy, seeing it as a symbol of increasing Jewish unity on the Zionist issue.[45]

Silver was not present at the 1930 convention. However, a few months later, he received an extraordinary letter circulated to the entire CCAR by the chairman of the committee revising the hymnal, Rabbi Louis Wolsey. A confirmed anti-Zionist, Wolsey used the occasion to vent his spleen on the Zionism that was infiltrating the CCAR[46] by subjecting "Hatikvah" to vigorous denigration: it was musically unworthy; "inspired by some Slavic or Spanish drinking song, . . . an undevotional and non-religious poem; . . . completely counter to the theology of the Union Prayer Book; . . . its inclusion definitely commits the American Jew to the singing of two national anthems; . . . [and] many laymen of the Reform synagogue have already stated that they would not permit the new Union Hymnal to be used in their congregations if Hatikwah [sic] is to be included." For these reasons all members of the CCAR were asked to send in their straw votes on the subject to the chairman. Wolsey failed to note that such a mail vote could not overturn the decision of the convention, but his intent was clearly to undermine its representativeness so that it could be overturned the following year. Ten members of the committee signed Wolsey's letter; Rabbis Jacob Singer, Morris Lazaron (then still in his Zionist period), James G. Heller, and Solomon Freehof did not.[47]

When Silver received the letter, he sent off a telegram to the president of the CCAR, Rabbi David Lefkowitz, registering his "vigorous protest" that such a letter could have been sent, declaring it "unwarranted, illegal and a clear challenge to the sovereignty of the convention," and asking him to repudiate it immediately.[48] Yet it is interesting that when Lazaron suggested to Silver that the "Hatikvah" controversy should lead to a more general confrontation in which Zionists and anti-Zionists in the CCAR would finally have it out at the next convention, Silver balked. "It seems that a battle is inevitable," he replied to Lazaron, "and if it must come the Hatikwah [sic] might as well serve for a battle-field as anything else." But then he added that good tactics would require allowing the anti-Zionists to take the offensive. He was convinced that majority control had already passed to the Zionists: "Let the anti-Zionists bring the matter up again, if they want, at the next convention of the Conference. They will be licked again."[49]

Not only were they licked again, they were trounced. In what was likely a stratagem to gain victory on a revote, Wolsey ruled that the conference's will, expressed at the last convention, required that all verses of "Hatikvah" be included in the hymnal. But when this bloated proposal was brought to a vote, it was adopted by a voice vote and the succeeding motion to exclude the five-versed "Hatikvah" lost on a roll call vote 41 to 54. Silver had opposed taking the second vote, desiring both to let the decision of the previous year stand and to avoid division.[50]

But divisions within the CCAR were becoming ever more profound as the Zionist rabbis emerged more clearly as the majority and the remaining anti-Zionists and non-Zionists felt increasingly pressed to the wall. Following the votes on "Hatikvah," the next Zionist-related issue to come before the Conference was one that brought the rabbis into internal Zionist politics. In 1934 Rabbi Samuel Wohl of Cincinnati, the president of the League for Labor Palestine, asked Rabbi Edward Israel to draw up a statement favoring the Labor movement in Palestine that would obtain as many CCAR signatures as possible. Publication of the statement would be timed to coincide with Jabotinsky's visit to the United States and would, by implication, imply a rejection of Revisionism even as it was, in content, an identification with the principles of the Histadrut. Silver signed on as a member of the endorsing committee, along with fellow Zionists in the Reform rabbinate and Hebrew Union College faculty members Jacob Marcus and Nelson Glueck. The statement, which identified the program of the Histadrut with the principles of Prophetic Judaism, secured 241 signatures, at that time over 60 percent of the conference, including men who were not avid Zionists. When the statement was published a few weeks later together with a similar one by Conservative rabbis, Stephen S. Wise wrote a foreword in which he declared the two statements "destined to become historic."[51] Nonetheless, shortly after the statement was circulated, it was viciously attacked by a disciple and close associate of Wise, Rabbi Louis I. Newman, the most prominent Revisionist in the CCAR. Newman had sought in vain to prevent issuance of the statement and then, with almost no success, appealed to rabbis who had signed it to repudiate their signatures. Rabbi Israel, who was active both as an advocate of social justice and as a Zionist, responded that the ideas it expressed seemed appropriate for the CCAR, which had long criticized economic inequality in the United States. Silver, a General Zionist, supported the statement rather than place himself in opposition to a declaration that linked Reform Jewish values, to which he subscribed, with those of the socialist Histadrut.[52]

The famed debate on Zionism at the convention of the CCAR the following year has been seen as "truly a meeting of giants," with the old forces of anti-Zionism, represented by its most articulate spokesman, Rabbi Samuel Schulman of Temple Emanu-El in New York, arrayed against the strongly emergent Zionism within the Reform rabbinate championed by Abba Hillel Silver.[53] Silver himself claimed correctly that "it was at this Conference that the opposition of the Central Conference of American Rabbis to Zionism was finally officially abandoned" and "replaced by a position of benevolent neutrality."[54]

Yet the "debate" itself, which was followed by a discussion that went on long into the night, was full of paradoxes and ironies. It was the third of three discussions scheduled respectively on the subjects of God, Torah, and Israel, with an eye to formulating a revised platform for the Reform movement.[55] Born in 1864 and Silver's elder by almost thirty years, Samuel Schulman was indeed a representative of the "older generation." He was certainly a Classical Reformer, but he was hardly a fervent anti-Zionist. As early as 1918 he had written to Lina Strauss, a prominent Zionist member of his congregation who accused him of undermining Zionists efforts, that although he refused "to recognize Palestine as a homeland for the Jewish people, for the whole Jewish nation," he did recognize "the tremendous importance of what the Allies are doing with respect to the promise of Palestine to the Jews." He was not a Zionist because he was opposed to a secular Jewish nationalism that would render Israel no different from other nations and because he chose to emphasize Jewish religion rather than nationality.[56] By 1935 he had come considerably closer to Zionism. To be sure, he still spoke of the Jewish entity as Keneset Yisrael and firmly rejected Mordecai Kaplan's idea that Judaism was a civilization in which religion was optional for contemporary participants in it. But, in contrast to Silver, he stressed the importance of a return to Jewish "individuality," by which he meant the particularism of Judaism expressed through "the fruitful power of the ceremonial law as a discipline and a hallowing and purifying influence in our lives."[57] In the debate it was Schulman, not Silver, who made settlement in Palestine a trying but necessary challenge specifically for Reform Jews. "Palestine will lead to a new synthesis," he expounded, and therefore "Reform Judaism has the grandest opportunity in its history; it has the opportunity of martyrdom [!]. Let it send half a dozen young men or more to Palestine to bring the message of Progressive Judaism." And he called for a religiously based Zionist commitment: "Let us also feel that Palestine is a field for us. . . . Not to stand aloof is our aim, but recognizing the value of Palestine for hundreds of thousands of our brethren in Israel, let us help increase the settlement and, at the same time, let us bravely uphold the truth that Israel is not a Goy like other Goyim."[58]

Silver's lengthy, carefully balanced oration offered no such inspiration. It was more a historical overview of the subject than a call to Zionist colors. Like Schulman, he argued for the centrality and indispensability of religion in Judaism and its necessity for Jewish survival, at least in the Diaspora.[59] He did not make a case specifically for political or even for cultural Zionism. His opposition was directed against those who attempted "to substitute a part for the whole." They might be the pure religionists (whom he compared with Paul) or the secular nationalists; both presented only a partial view of "the total program of Jewish life," which embraced the religious mandate of mission as well as the national aspirations of the Jewish people.[60]

During the next two years Silver served as a member of the committee that drew up the Columbus Platform, adopted by the CCAR in 1937. As is well known, that platform used the language of Herzl and Ahad Ha'Am in advocating the creation of a Palestine that was a "Jewish homeland" and haven of refuge and also a "center of Jewish culture and spiritual life." As a member of the committee, Silver may have played a role in preventing any less Zionistic language. When its chairman, the Hebrew Union College theologian and cultural Zionist Samuel S. Cohon, suggested that much acrimony could be avoided by omitting the phrase "a Jewish homeland," Silver apparently refused to accede and Cohon accepted the position of the "orthodox Zionists" in the CCAR.[61] Indeed, by 1937, even David Philipson, also a member of the committee, was willing, at least reluctantly, to accept the idea of a homeland in Palestine. Zionist conceptions were making rapid progress among the Reform rabbis, in part—but only in part—due to Silver's efforts. The support of the younger rabbinical generation was there in any case. It was only in the area of Zionist political policy where serious differences among Reform religious and lay leaders remained and where they would soon rise to the surface, resulting in a degree of acrimony that was unprecedented in earlier debates. During these years—the early 1940s—Silver became vice-president and then president of the CCAR at the same time that he was the most prominent and effective champion of an uncompromising insistence on Jewish statehood.

ACJ and AJC

Beginning in the late 1930s, paradoxically, Silver's criticism of nationalist excess became more vocal in response to Nazism even as his Zionism came to focus on a political goal. Speaking to the graduating class at Hebrew Union College in 1936, Silver branded fascism the "new paganism" and deplored the nationalism "which has more or less run riot in the modern world." Yet at the same time, with the increasingly precarious situation of the Jews in Germany and, later, the rest of the European continent, he was forced to turn more vigorously to the political Zionism of his youth, distinguishing it from other forms of national aspiration that clearly contravened Jewish religion and morality. He told the ordinees: "The rabbi should encourage the co-operation of his people in up-building the Jewish Homeland in Palestine . . . , because a Jewish homeland will help to normalize the status of our people in the world, because it will remove the element of desperation—of fighting with our backs to the wall—from our renewed struggle for equality and emancipation . . . , because it will serve as haven for hosts of our people who must now seek new homes in a world where doors are everywhere closing." Only as a last reason for supporting Zionism did Silver list his hope that "this Jewish Homeland may become in the days to come a vast dynamo of creative Jewish cultural and spiritual energies."[62] But even more now, at least to Reform audiences, Silver criticized Jewish spokesmen who offered a Jewish nationalism that substituted for Judaism a nationalism that was "unredeemed by a moral vision and responsibility" or which neglected the spiritual needs of Jews in the diaspora. Jewish nationalism, in Silver's view, had to be distinctly different from the fascist variety; it had to be guided by the prophetic ethics long stressed by Reform Judaism.[63]

It was this unwavering loyalty to Reform ideology that continued to make Silver persona grata within Reform rabbinical and lay circles even as he became ever more visible within world Zionism. In 1943, when he was head of the American Zionist Emergency Council, Silver was elected unanimously to the vice presidency of the CCAR and thereby virtually assured of the presidency two years later.[64] During the years of his CCAR presidency, 1945–47, he also served as president of the Zionist Organization of America. In order to carry out his Zionist and congregational duties along with the CCAR presidency, Silver delegated day-to-day tasks of the office to his vice-president, boyhood friend, and fervent admirer, Rabbi Abraham Feldman—which seems not to have stirred up resentment, although Feldman's candidacy for the vice-presidency had provoked unusual controversy.[65]

It was in 1942, the year before Silver's election to the CCAR vice-presidency, that the last great Zionist controversy within the Reform rabbinate occurred. At issue was a proposal for the CCAR to support the demand that the Jewish population of Palestine be given the privilege of establishing a military force that would fight under its own banner on the side of the Allies. The existence of such a force, all realized, would be a strong argument for Jewish sovereignty following the war. When the resolution passed by a vote of 64 to 38, the American Reform rabbinate had placed itself on the side of maximal Zionist ambitions. It had also seriously alienated about a fifth of the conference, men who now went on to form the American Council for Judaism (ACJ), dedicated to combating "the political emphasis now paramount in the Zionist program."

Silver's attitude to his colleagues who joined the ACJ was uncompromising. Although he did not attack them personally, as did Stephen S. Wise, he refused to sit down with them at a meeting intended to bring reconciliation[66] and did not support Solomon Freehof's attempts at mediation. To Freehof he wrote in regard to Wise's attack on ACJ members Fineshriber and Wolsey: "Rabbis who enter the political arena must be prepared to receive blows even as they give them, and should not turn squeamish when the blows which they receive are resounding ones."[67] Later, as president of the CCAR, Silver suggested that the 1943 resolution of the CCAR, which urged members to seek termination of the ACJ, should now, given its unfortunate and politically pernicious continuance, be understood to imply immediate dissociation from it.[68]

Silver was similarly resolute but more compromising with regard to residual opposition to political Zionism's contemporary aims among the Reform laity. The Union of American Hebrew Congregations had participated in the American Jewish Conference of 1943 and, unlike the American Jewish Committee, not bolted when that conference, influenced decisively by Silver's oratory, passed a resolution calling for the establishment of a Jewish commonwealth. But it did abstain on the crucial vote, claiming the need to seek approval from the UAHC Executive Board. Following the sessions of the conference, prominent laymen within the movement, marshaled by Judge Horace Stern of Philadelphia, put pressure on Rabbi Maurice Eisendrath, the UAHC's newly elected vigorous executive director, to categorically dissent from the Palestine resolution of the Conference, especially as abstention was being widely interpreted as concurrence. Zionists, including Silver, wanted the executive board to ratify it. Fearing public controversy, which could only weaken his efforts to expand the Union, Eisendrath turned to Silver just before the scheduled meeting of the board urging his endorsement of a compromise board resolution that he had worked out together with Solomon Freehof. Endorsement of a Jewish commonwealth, Eisendrath argued, would never pass the board as presently constituted. Moreover, silence would strengthen the ACJ. He promised, for the future, to work at shuffling the composition of the Union's board to make it more reflective of pro-Zionist sentiment among Reform congregants. Silver, however, was deaf to Eisendrath's plea. In a strongly worded reply he argued that a resolution of non-concurrence would be interpreted as repudiation so that Reform Judaism would "again remain an isolated sect within the stream of American Jewish life."[69] He threatened to resign from the executive board, of which he was an ex-officio member by virtue of his vice-presidency of the CCAR. But Silver, too, realized that the votes for an endorsement were not there and he too did not want to provoke public controversy. His own compromise was that the executive board would defer decision to the next biennial meeting of the full Council. Silence, at least for the present, was preferable to taking a chance on defeat. When the executive board met a few days later and found itself divided almost equally between ratification and repudiation, it voted, as Silver had earlier suggested and as he urged at the meeting, in favor of postponement until the next meeting of the Council.[70]

That should have put the matter to rest for a while. However, when pressure continued and Eisendrath began to fear a schism within the Union, he decided to call an informal meeting of rabbis to recommend a program of action to the smaller Administrative Committee of the Union, which was to meet on November 30. Some statement of neutrality, Eisendrath thought, was necessary if the Union were both to remain within the American Jewish Conference and hold itself together. Silver was not persuaded, and he did not attend the meeting. Eighteen out of the twenty-six invitees, however, did. Freehof presided over a group with widely differing views on Zionism[71] that adopted a resolution which left controversial Zionist issues up to the individual Reform Jew and declared that the Union, although remaining in the Conference, was unable to associate itself with those parts of the Palestine Resolution that called for exclusive Jewish control of immigration into Palestine and the establishment of a Jewish Commonwealth. With the endorsement of the administrative committee, this resolution went to the executive board. Here Silver was present. Considering that he had wanted the UAHC to endorse the Palestine resolution, his principal statement to the group was a bit disingenuous, but factually it was truthful:

> I have never, in all my ministry, come to a Union meeting and urged that we adopt a Zionist platform. I have never come to the CCAR and urged them to adopt a Zionist platform. I never urged my own congregation to adopt a Zionist platform. . . . The attempt that has been made in the last year and a half, with all the best intentions in the world, to bring Zionists and non-Zionists together on a common

platform was doomed to failure, because it is clear that Zionists and non-Zionists, if they are to agree at all, must agree on a non-Zionist platform, and the Zionists will never agree to a non-Zionist platform.[72]

Following a brief discussion, Silver was selected to participate in a broadly representative drafting committee, which came up with a new resolution. This one, unlike that passed by the administrative committee, did not make reference to immigration and sovereignty and it did not use the language "unable to associate itself with," substituting instead "refrains from taking any action on the Palestine Resolution." The new resolution passed 22 to 2, only Julian Morgenstern and the vigorously anti-Zionist layman Gustave Efroymson voting in the negative. For Silver it was a minor victory. The new wording was less subject to misinterpretation. Even if the Union was not ready to adopt the two controversial points of the Palestine resolution, neither was its stand embarrassing to Silver in his position of Zionist leadership. Although Reform Judaism and Zionism were fused in Silver's own ideology, organizationally it was still best to keep them apart.

Reform Judaism and the State of Israel

With the establishment of the Jewish state, Silver might have been expected to settle there. For a variety of political and personal reasons he did not. But even as he remained in Cleveland, he repeatedly explained the significance of Israel for diaspora Jews. His answer was always more or less the same: the establishment of the Jewish state meant an end to *galut* (exile) even for the Jews outside its borders and therefore it was an "epochal event" for all Jews. Henceforth they would everywhere possess self-respect, security, and normality.

After 1948 Silver returned once more from Herzl to Ahad Ha'am, even admitting that "the East rather than the West will again become the decisive cultural milieu of the creative Jewish life of tomorrow."[73] Israel would be, as it was in ancient times, "the non-political center of world Jewry." But even the establishment of the state did not invalidate the mission of Israel in the diaspora. On the contrary, its existence made possible the redirection of diaspora Jewish energies from life saving and state building to synagogues, schools, and academies in the diaspora. And, although Israel might now be the focus of world Jewry, America could become "a great creative center of Jewish spiritual life" and the Jews there "a light unto the nations." Employing a term that would become common usage to describe the relationship between Israel and American Jewry, he spoke of their "interdependence."

As long as he was in a position of Zionist leadership, Silver had said little about the religious future of the state of Israel, perhaps because he did not want to lose the support of the Mizrachi party.[74] But after 1948 he spoke freely of the need for "a vital Liberal Judaism" in the new state in order to sustain its spiritual morale. He looked for a native Israeli expression of Reform Judaism, declaring: "We cannot import our special brand of reform Judaism into Israel. Our spiritual apparel may not be suitable raiment for them."[75] Nonetheless, in essence it would closely resemble his own Classical Reform outlook in that its chief characteristics would be prophetic idealism rather than attention to ritual and tradition.[76]

Although he did not settle in Israel himself, Silver hoped that younger Jewish diaspora idealists would make aliyah. He visited often himself, now unabashedly as a rabbi. At the dedication of Kfar Silver in 1956 he called himself *rav umoreh beyisrael* (rabbi and teacher in Israel) and offered a prayer to God for the agricultural school's welfare.[77] Theologically, Silver remained uncertain as to whether the restoration of the state possessed religious significance. In the early 1950s he thought that it had not altered the religious destiny of the Jewish people. It was national restoration, not religious redemption; freedom from *shibud malkhuyot* (political subjection), not *aharit ha-yamim* (the End of Days). As the culmination of the particularist thrust in Judaism, it made possible a renewed turning toward the universal messianic goal.[78] But by the time Israel was a decade old, Silver was ready to tell his rabbinical colleagues that the establishment of the state was an act in the continuing drama of universal salvation, a link between God's covenant with Abraham and the final messianic *ge'ulah shelemah* (complete redemption).[79]

Still, the 1950s in Silver's life most closely resembled the 1920s. Once again he focused on America with the same optimism about its future and the future of its Jewish community that he had expressed thirty years earlier. He had not lost Isaac Mayer Wise's ebullient hopes for American Judaism. Israel might be the principal spiritual center, but he did not see American Jewry as on the periphery.[80] Within Reform circles he was now, more than ever, a source of pride. He was the only strongly identified Reform rabbi who had played a major role in Jewish political history.

In Sum

Abba Hillel Silver did not conquer Reform Judaism for Zionism. Its gradual adoption of Zionist principles was under way before his time and was influenced by other factors, including the influx of East European Jews into the rabbinate and laity of the movement, the maturing of the settlement in Palestine, and the rise of Nazism. But surely Silver, a Jew deeply and fully committed to the principles of Reform Judaism, played a role in that development by demonstrating through his writings, speeches, and activities that Reform Judaism was compatible with Zionism.

It is somewhat ironic that this role should have been played by a Reform Jew who remained attached to the Classical Reform tradition and spurned its revision in other areas than Zionism. Silver was not enamored of Reform Judaism's return to ritualism;[81] he thought that the postwar emphasis on social justice was exaggerated; he did not adopt the increasing role of the rabbi as pastor; and—always the individualist—he rejected progressive egalitarianism in the administration of the CCAR.[82] In his ever rebounding optimism about American Jewry he resembled no one more than Isaac Mayer Wise. His theism, firmly rooted in the Prophets and the Pharisees, ran counter to more recent trends in the movement that looked to humanist thinkers or religious existentialists.[83] His emphasis on understanding Judaism historically, which he believed was the most secure foundation for Zionism, had its origins in the Wissenschaft des Judentums that he first encountered as a student at Hebrew Union College.

Yet Silver well recognized that Reform was only one interpretation of Judaism, that it served only one group of Jews. Zionism enabled him to transcend its confines even as he remained within its organizational framework. Although he did not force Zionist commitments upon fellow Reformers, he preached Zionism in their midst; although he did not appear as a Reform rabbi in Zionist parleys, he lent religious fervor to the movement. These two spheres of his activity were not compartmentalized in his Jewish worldview. In philosophy, if not in program, he was a religious Zionist not less than any member of Mizrahi, except that in his case the religion was Reform Judaism.

Notes

1. Isaiah Vinograd, *Abba Hillel Silver: Life, Vision, Achievement* (Hebrew), Tel Aviv, 1957, 61.
2. Marc Lee Raphael, *Abba Hillel Silver: A Profile in American Judaism* (New York and London, 1989), 215.

3. Herbert Weiner, ed., *Therefore Choose Life: Selected Sermons, Addresses, and Writings of Abba Hillel Silver*, vol. 1. (Cleveland and New York), 1967, vii.
4. David Polish, *Renew Our Days: The Zionist Issue in Reform Judaism* (Jerusalem, 1976), 117.
5. Solomon Freehof, "Abba Hillel Silver," *Central Conference of American Rabbis Yearbook* (hereafter *CCARY*) 74 (1964), 159.
6. Abba Hillel Silver to James G. Heller, December 23, 1930, The Papers of Abba Hillel Silver (Papers), Western Reserve Historical Society, Cleveland, Ohio, Roll 18, Folder 387. Cf. Leon I. Feuer, "The Influence of Abba Hillel Silver on the Evolution of Reform Judaism," in Jack Bemporad, ed., *A Rational Faith: Essays in Honor of Levi A. Olan* (New York, 1977), 81.
7. *CCARY* 73 (1963), 163.
8. Autobiography/memoirs, Papers, 211/1, p. 5A.
9. His boyhood friend and lifelong associate in Zionist affairs, Emanuel Neumann, saw the transformation as entirely external: "The years passed and a new Silver emerged, whom we did not easily identify with the boy we had known. Elegant in dress, polished in manner, faultless in speech, he appeared to have undergone a transformation. He had shed the habits and manners, the accents of his earlier environment. He seemed 'goyish.' It all smacked of 'assimilation.' " Neumann did not recognize that a deeper transformation had taken place. Emanual Neumann, *Abba Hillel Silver: Militant Zionist* (New York, 1967), 6.
10. George Lieberman to Silver, November 17, 1935, Papers, 193/99.
11. Silver to Edgar F. Magnin, February 12, 1947, Papers, 29/678.
12. Henry Englander to Silver, September 11, 1924, Papers, 28/665.
13. Julian Morgenstern to Silver, January 23, 1941, Papers, 29/675.
14. Morgenstern to Silver, January 29, 1937, Papers, 29/674.
15. Michael A. Meyer, *Hebrew Union College-Jewish Institute of Religion: A Centennial History, 1875–1975*, rev. ed. (Cincinnati, 1992), 131–32; Howard R. Greenstein, *Turning Point: Zionism and Reform Judaism* (Chico, Calif., 1981), 88–89.
16. A few months earlier Silver had suggested that Morgenstern (or Emil Leipziger or Jacob Marcus) might be appointed as one of the CCAR delegates to the American Jewish Conference in place of Rabbi Samuel Goldenson of Temple Emanu-El in New York, a leader of the American Council for Judaism. Silver to Solomon E. Freehof, July 29, 1943, Papers, 61/1446.
17. Silver to Joshua Liebman, November 3, 1943, Papers, 29/674.
18. He also implied that it would make contributions, not only to the college, but also to the Union of American Hebrew Congregations more difficult to obtain from Reform Zionists. Silver to Maurice N. Eisendrath, October 22, 1943, Papers, 61/446.
19. Silver to Moses J. Gries, April 26, 1917, Stephen S. Wise Papers, American Jewish Historical Society, Waltham, Mass. I am grateful to Prof. Michael Brenner, now of Munich University, for obtaining a copy of the letter.

20. Wise to Silver, April 28, 1917, Wise papers.
21. Wise to Silver, May 7, 1917, in Carl Hermann Voss, ed., *Stephen S. Wise: Servant of the People, Selected Letters* (Philadelphia, 1969), 78–80.
22. Silver to Wise, May 11, 1917, Wise Papers.
23. Morton Mayer Berman, *For Zion's Sake: A Personal and Family Chronicle* (Chicago, 1980), 81–82.
24. Vinograd, *Abba Hillel Silver*, 82–83.
25. Raphael, who examined the minutes of the congregation, makes no reference to it.
26. Silver used the 1916 occasion, when he was asked to address "Religion and the Jewish Child," to argue that Jewish religious education should, in part, be concerned with making the child conscious of "an allegiance which he owes to a whole people." *CCARY* 26 (1916), 236.
27. Silver to Max Heller, March 26, 1919, Papers, 17/375.
28. Silver to Wise, May 18, 1920, Papers, 17/376.
29. Silver to Edward N. Calisch, October 18, 1921; Polish, *Renew Our Days*, 157–61.
30. David Philipson to Silver, October 10, 1927, papers, 193/98; Lester Jaffe to Silver, October 31, 1938, Papers, 193/99. The second occasion (and there may well have been others in-between) was to help celebrate Philipson's jubilee.
31. Meyer, *Hebrew Union College*, 85–86.
32. Silver, "Isaac Mayer Wise: A Century of Reform Judaism," sermon delivered March 30, 1919, Papers, 145/45.
33. Silver, "What Has Become of the Melting Pot?" *The Temple* 4, no. 1 (n.d. but apparently 1922), 7.
34. Silver, "Our New Task," sermon delivered January 22, 1923, *The Temple* 4, no. 2, p. 8; the sermon was also printed in "Proceedings of the Twenty-Eighth Council of the Union of American Hebrew Congregations," *Proceedings of the Union of American Hebrew Congregations* (*PUAHC*), 9227–31.
35. On the earliest period see Michael A. Meyer, "American Reform Judaism and Zionism: Early Efforts at Ideological Rapprochement," chapter 21 in this volume.
36. Weiner, *Therefore Choose Life*, 216.
37. Silver, "The Democratic Impulse in Jewish History," *CCARY* 38 (1928), 199–216. This lecture was even reprinted almost in full and with approbation in the February 1930 issue of the *Liberal Jewish Monthly*, the distinctly anti-Zionist organ of British Liberal Judaism. In introducing the piece, its editor noted that "When the Zionist insists that a Jew must be a Jew by religion, then he is at one with Liberal Judaism in the most fundamental issue."
38. Silver, "Why Do the Heathen Rage," originally printed in installments in *Jewish Tribune*, July 23, July 30, August 6, and August 13, 1926, and then as a pamphlet, where the citation occurs on p. 22.
39. Ibid., 24.

40. Herbert Weiner, ed., *A Word in Its Season: Selected Sermons, Addresses, and Writings of Abba Hillel Silver*, vol. 2 (New York and Cleveland, 1972), 316.

41. Cf. Mordecai M. Kaplan, *Judaism as a Civilization: Toward a Reconstruction of American-Jewish Life* (1934) (New York, 1967), 113; but Silver cites from an earlier writing.

42. Silver, "Democratic Impulse," 215–16.

43. Silver, "My Dream of Palestine," *Jewish Tribune*, June 13, 1924, vol. 2. Cf. Daniel Jeremy Silver, ed., *In the Time of Harvest: Essays in Honor of Abba Hillel Silver on the Occasion of His 70th Birthday* (New York and London, 1963), 33–36.

44. *CCARY* 40 (1930), 89–108.

45. Solomon Freehof to Abba Hillel Silver, October 27, 1930, Papers, 18/387.

46. "Wolsey has a very definite persecution mania in regard to Zionism," James Heller to Silver, October 30, 1930, Papers, 18/387.

47. Louis Wolsey to Members of the Central Conference of American Rabbis, September 30, 1930, Papers, 18/387.

48. Silver to David Lefkowiz, October 24, 1930, Papers, 18/387. When Wolsey threatened to resign as chairman of the committee, Lefkowitz dissociated himself from Silver's language, declaring the circular letter simply "unwise" and Wolsey decided to stay on. Silver upbraided Lefkowitz for backing down and sought to exercise pressure by threatening to bring the matter up at the next convention unless the Executive Board of the Conference took action against the chairman. But this was not a serious threat. As indicated below, Silver did not want to divide the Conference. Silver to Lefkowitz, November 28, 1930, Lefkowitz to Silver, December 2, 1930, papers, 18/387.

49. Silver to Morris S. Lazaron, October 31, 1930, Papers 18/387.

50. *CCARY* 41 (1931), 98, 102–4, 114–17.

51. *The Rabbis of America to Labor Palestine* (New York, 1935), 5. See also Wise's editorial on the Jabotinsky visit in *Opinion*, January 1935, 5–6.

52. Edward L. Israel to Silver, October 18, 1934; Israel and endorsing committee to colleagues, December 8, 1934; Israel to Silver, February 8, 1935, Papers, 18/391.

53. Joseph L. Blau in the volume he edited, *Reform Judaism: A Historical Perspective. Essays from the Yearbook of the Central Conference of American Rabbis* (New York, 1973), 369–70. See also the more nuanced interpretation by Alexander Schindler in Raphael, *Abba Hilel Silver*, xxvi–xxviii.

54. Autobiography/memoirs, Papers 211/1, p. 9K.

55. Felix Levy to Silver, November 1, 1934, Papers 18/391.

56. Samuel Schulman to Lina Straus, September 10, 1918, Schulman Papers, American Jewish Archives (hereafter AJA). I am grateful to Mark Strauss-Cohn for this reference.

57. In Blau, *Reform Judaism*, 412.

58. Ibid., 413–14.

59. In a sermon three years earlier he had declared that cultural pluralism in America was "a vain and hopeless dream." Cultural Jews would

inevitably assimilate; only religious Jews would remain. Weiner, *Therefore Choose Life*, 391.

60. In Blau, *Reform Judaism*, 435–36.
61. Samuel S. Cohon to Silver, May 14, 1937, Cohon Papers, AJA, MSS Col. 276, 2/6. Silver apparently ignores Cohon's plea in his reply to him four days later although he comments on other portions of the platform draft that Cohon had enclosed.
62. "The Ancient Paths," in Weiner, *Therefore Choose Life*, 423, 426.
63. "Religion in Present-Day Jewish Life," *PUAHC*, Thirty-Sixth Biennial Council, Cincinnati, 1939, 249.
64. Transcript: "Transactions of the CCAR, 54th Annual Convention, New York City, June 22–27, 1943," AJA, MSS Col. 34, Box 37, 296.
65. In 1945 there were no counternominations to Silver for president either by mail or from the floor. But two non-Zionist rabbis, Louis Mann and Jonah B. Wise, were nominated by mail and Jacob Marcus from the floor for the vice-presidency. In a secret ballot Feldman won handily, receiving more votes than the combined total of his opponents. Transcript: "Proceedings of the 56th Annual Convention of the CCAR," Atlantic City, June 25–27, 1945, AJA, MSS Col. 34, Box 37, 231, 257–68. Cf. *CCARY* 55 (1945), 172–74, where the controversy is only hinted at.
66. Greenstein, *Turning Point*, 95, 156.
67. Wise to Freehof, November 24, 1944, Papers 29/674.
68. *CCARY*, vol. 56, 1946, 226–27.
69. Silver to Eisendrath, September 29, 1943, Papers 61/1446. When Stern turned to Silver, he replied similarly and added: "It is a fatal blunder to shackle Reform Judaism forever with a complex of ideas, which were always foreign to historic Judaism and to the historical aspirations of the Jewish people, and which having had their brief day among sections of Jews in Western Europe, finally suffered defeat with the destruction of that Jewry itself." Silver to The Honorable Judge Horace Stern, October 1, 1943, Papers 61/1446.
70. Proceedings of the Executive Board, October 3, 1943, *PUAHC*, Cincinnati, 1943, 110–11.
71. Among the Zionists present was Felix Levy who, like Eisendrath, was determined to preserve the UAHC from division by avoiding pro-Zionist or anti-Zionist endorsements. Silver, however, was shocked that Levy could support the sense of the meeting. He wrote to him afterwards that he was sure a resolution dissociating the Union from the Palestine resolution would be interpreted as nothing less than repudiation of free immigration and political sovereignty, which he now declared "two basic Zionist principles." Levy to Eisendrath, December 3, 1943; Silver to Levy, December 17, 1943, Papers, 61/1146.
72. Proceedings of the Executive Board, January 18, 1944, *PUAHC*, Cincinnati, 1947, 29. Cf. Samuel Halperin, *The Political World of American Zionism* (Detroit, 1961), 243–44, and Greenstein, *Turning Point*, 96–97, 107–8, which, however, are not accurate on all points.

73. "Liberal Judaism and Israel" (Address Delivered at the Fortieth Biennial Assembly of the Union of American Hebrew Congregations in Boston, November 1948), in Abba Hillel Silver, *Vision and Victory: A Collection of Addresses* (New York, 1949), 222.

74. Polish, *Renew Our Days*, 122.

75. "The Problems Which Lie Ahead," *CCARY* 68 (1958), 302.

76. Silver, *Vision and Victory*, 230.

77. Vinograd, *Abba Hillel Silver*, 450–52.

78. Silver, "Problems and Prospects of American Judaism" (Founders' Day Address at the Hebrew Union College, March 12, 1950); Silver, "There is Yet Room for Vision" (Commencement Address at the Hebrew Union College-Jewish Institute for Religion, June 7, 1952) in Weiner, *Therefore Choose Life*, 411, 434–35.

79. "The Problems Which Lie Ahead," *CCARY* 68 (1958), 295.

80. *CCARY* 60 (1950), 368; "On the Threshold of the Fourth Century" (Address Delivered at the Biennial Convention of the Union of American Hebrew Congregations in New York, April 1953), in the *Temple Bulletin*, Cleveland, May 17, 1953, 5–8.

81. In his congregation he did reintroduce the Friday evening and Saturday morning services and the teaching of Hebrew, but he kept the Sunday morning service as the principal religious activity of the week and saw little value in the reintroduction of "discarded rituals."

82. See Silver's notes for the 1963 dialogue with Freehof in Papers, 187/1044.

83. *CCARY* 57 (1947), 391; Feuer, "Influence of Abba Hillel Silver," 96.

Index